The Official Guide

Corel Linux OS Starter Kit

The Official Guide

Corel Linux OS Starter Kit

Joe Merlino &
Kate Wrightson

Osborne **McGraw-Hill**

Berkeley   New York   St. Louis   San Francisco
Auckland   Bogotá   Hamburg   London
Madrid   Mexico City   Milan   Montreal   New Delhi
Panama City   Paris   São Paulo
Singapore   Sydney   Tokyo   Toronto

Osborne/McGraw-Hill
2600 Tenth Street
Berkeley, California 94710
U.S.A.

For information on translations or book distributors outside the U.S.A., or to arrange bulk purchase discounts for sales promotions, premiums, or fund-raisers, please contact Osborne/**McGraw-Hill** at the above address.

Corel Linux OS Starter Kit: The Official Guide

1234567890 AGM AGM 019876543210

Book P/N 0-07-212457-1   and   CD P/N 0-07-212458-X
parts of
ISBN 0-07-212459-8

Publisher: Brandon A. Nordin
Associate Publisher and Editor-in-Chief: Scott Rogers
Acquisitions Editor: Megg Bonar
Acquisitions Coordinator: Stephane Thomas
Project Editor: Lisa Theobald
Technical Editor: Michael Clarke
Copy Editor: Nancy Crumpton
Proofreader: Linda Medoff
Indexer: Karin Arrigoni
Computer Designers: Liz Pauw, Dick Schwartz, and Elizabeth Jang
Illustrator: Robert Hansen, Beth Young, and Michael Mueller
Cover Designer: Will Voss

This book was composed with Corel VENTURA™ Publisher.

About the Authors...

Joe Merlino is a technical writer and avid Linux hobbyist. He is also a library worker and contributor to the Open Source Digital Library System project. He dabbles in Perl and UNIX shell scripting and has been a contributor to the *Linux Gazette*. He has also contributed several chapters to *StarOffice 5.0 for Linux Bible* (IDG Books), as well as *StarOffice 5.0 for Linux for Dummies* (IDG Books).

Kate Wrightson is a technical writer with several years of Linux experience and more than ten years of experience using UNIX. She works with university and college faculty to help them improve their teaching, especially through use of technology in their classrooms and in course preparation. She also spends time working with the USENET newsgroup creation process. Kate has published articles on topics ranging from the history of American higher education to clear business writing. Kate also contributed to the *StarOffice 5.0 for Linux Bible* (IDG Books) as well as *StarOffice 5.0 for Linux for Dummies* (IDG Books).

Contents At A Glance

Contents

Foreword

With the availability of the Corel® Linux® OS, Corel is furthering its dedication to innovation, high quality products, and services, and its commitment to providing solutions for the Linux environment. Corel Linux OS provides Linux power designed specifically for the desktop and offers renowned Linux performance and stability with incredible ease of use.

Corel's enhancements to Debian GNU/Linux and KDE deliver a graphical desktop environment that lets you get up and running fast. Featuring a simple four-step installation program, a full-featured file manager, centralized configuration and system updates, and an e-mail client and Web browser, Core Linux OS combines powerful performance with intelligent simplicity and is an exciting development in the operating system evolution.

Corel Linux OS is easy to install and configure and allows easy access to local and network drives *and* to the Internet with an innovative browser-style file manager. Plus, users can access system updates over the Web. With its outstanding file compatibility and network integration, I believe we now offer in Corel Linux OS a single source for end-to-end solutions for a wide range of productivity applications, development tools, and professional services for all major platforms.

Just as Corel software products bring powerful and advanced technology to your computing life, CorelPRESS™ titles bring you professional solutions to using Corel's products. Written by experts, and reviewed by Corel's product teams, CorelPRESS books offer everything you need to become familiar and proficient with our wide range of computing solutions.

Corel is excited about the new technologies available with Corel Linux OS, and we invite you to follow along in this CorelPRESS Official Guide. Authors Joe Merlino and Kate Wrightson, along with the product teams at Corel, have spent many hours working on the accuracy and features of this book, and we think you'll appreciate our efforts.

Congratulations to the team at Osborne who have created this excellent book, and to the team at Corel who supported the creation of this book!

Michael C. J. Cowpland
President and CEO
Corel Corporation

Acknowledgments

If you read a lot of computer books, you've probably read dozens of acknowledgment pages that start with "Even though nobody ever reads these pages, I'd like to thank…." (These are the same pages that always say "Writing a book is a group activity," but that part's true.) Well, we think people do read the acknowledgment sections—even people who don't know the authors, oddly enough!

So, let's start with "Writing a book is a group activity." Those who have the mental image of writers working quietly in candle-lit garrets, or in small clean rooms with a manual typewriter, have never watched someone write a computer book. The truth is, writing is a noisy, messy activity. It involves a lot of yelling down the hall at your co-author; e-mail back and forth with the software company and the technical editor; the phone ringing with "Did you guys really mean to do a search & replace that changed 'keyboard' to 'penguin' throughout the WHOLE BOOK?"; and endless runs to OfficeMax for more reams of paper, ink cartridges, and neon Post-It flags. (It's also a heck of a lot of fun.)

Thus, we offer our gratitude, thanks, and friendly slaps on the back to the other members of the *Corel Linux OS Starter Kit: The Official Guide* team:

- Megg Bonar, our intrepid acquisitions editor, set up the deal and watched out for us the whole way through. (Even though we know where her mom lives.)

- T. Michael Clarke provided an accurate and exhaustive technical edit. This book's accuracy is due, in large part, to Mike's work; we can't wait to work with him again.

- Stephane Thomas has an organizational mind like a steel trap; she kept track of everything we sent in, got us what we needed, and did it all with an unbelievably cheery attitude.

- Lisa Theobald rode herd on the overall project, despite some unforeseen delays. We knew that, with Lisa, any questions we had would be dealt with quickly and efficiently; we'd like to clone her.

- Nancy Crumpton is, without a doubt, the best copy editor we've ever seen. We marveled every time a copy edited chapter came in; Nancy's keen eye caught all errors and misphrasings.

- Linda Medoff contributed another set of eagle eyes to the project, doing the final proofreading and catching things that slipped past the rest of us.

- The entire production department at Osborne lent a hand to this book, especially with the annoying and unfixable problems caused by transferring Linux screenshots to Windows graphics programs.

We had some help from Corel, as well:

- Chip Maxwell was our liaison in Ottawa (cue Secret Agent music). Chip got us the software we needed, got us in touch with the folks who knew the answers to our odd questions, and fought the random dragon that wandered past.

- Erich Forler, the project manager for Corel Linux, put us on the right path for Corel-specific terminology and code behavior.

- Jason Grenier answered some tricky questions that had us stalled; without him, we'd still be wondering about our serial mouse.

There's no way to express the appreciation we have for David Fugate, our agent, and for Waterside Productions, with whom David works. Everyone at Waterside works hard and rapidly for their authors, and we are grateful for all they do for us.

We also want to thank our friends, who helped out both with technical questions and with keeping us sane. In particular, Joe would like to thank Jess Close, Cameron Perkins, and the rest of the gang on lbbs and the git.unix.linux newsgroup for answering all sorts of odd questions. Kate sends her love to the 'plexfolk, especially Russ Allbery, Eric Burns, Matt Gerber, Jon Lennox, and Jon Robertson, who happily debated and patiently explained until she got it, whether about Linux or Macintoshes.

Finally, this book proves that it's not impossible to work with your spouse. We managed to get through the book without any major upheavals, to either our home or our psyches. It's always a pleasure to work with someone else whose habits complement yours, and with whom the transition between "work" and "not work" is seamless and pleasant. Since we don't have kids, we'd like to thank our dogs, Tasha and Miso, for not complaining *too* much about the amount of time we spend staring at the big beige boxes.

Introduction

Corel Linux: that's an interesting combination of words. Many people who pick up this book will do so because of the first word, while others will grab it because of the second. We think there's good reason to respond to both.

Corel is one of those software companies that's been around forever; if you've used a vector-based graphics program in the last ten years, you have probably used (or at least wished you had) CorelDRAW. Corel also provides WordPerfect and WordPerfect Suite 2000 (which contains QuattroPro, Presentations, Trellix, and CorelCENTRAL), giving people who write an alternative to Microsoft Word. Linux, in contrast, is a relative newcomer to the computing scene. It's an operating system, like Windows or MacOS, but it's based on UNIX. The Linux revolution is picking up speed, with coverage from a multitude of major news outlets and an ever-increasing number of companies that are switching their allegiance to the plucky penguin.

When Corel decided to develop a Linux release of its own, some wondered. In a world with more than 100 Linux distributions already, why another one? What did Corel have to offer that the user couldn't find elsewhere? The answer is Corel Linux, a distribution targeted at the average computer user. It's a distribution with a single-user focus, tightly integrating the popular KDE desktop environment and providing a plethora of simple graphical administration tools. Corel Linux is a super way to get your feet wet in the Linux world.

However, don't think that we (or Corel) believe that only utter newbies should use this distribution! Yes, Corel Linux is friendly and easy to use. It's still got the power of Linux, though, and you can do all the advanced things that you'd do with another distribution. You can run servers, host multiple users, program, and work exclusively from the command line if you so desire. Since it's based on the Debian distribution, you'll find many of the same programs and commands in Corel Linux, and your regular Debian habits should work just fine.

Why We Wrote This Book

When you write computer books, you get used to hearing the question "So why did you decide to do a book about *<insert subject here>*?" We could be smart-alecky and answer "Because someone asked us to do it," but that's usually not the whole story. So, why *did* we write a book about Corel Linux?

We've been around Linux for a long time, and around UNIX systems even longer. We have become used to arcane commands, typing instead of mousing, and the gung-ho attitude of computer science experts: "it doesn't have to be easy, it just has to work." While this works for us, and for quite a few folks we know, it doesn't work for everyone. It certainly doesn't work this way for most of our co-workers, friends, and family. When we talked about Linux, people wondered what we meant. Frankly, we sounded like the ultimate geeks, talking about something that wasn't intended for the kind of person who uses a computer, but doesn't count "computer use" as a hobby.

That gulf of understanding is a problem. No matter how hard we tried to explain Linux, people were put off by the seeming complexity and sheer unfriendliness of the operating system. Windows and MacOS are popular for good reason: they're friendly, they're simple to use, and they don't require much attention. Linux didn't really have anything like that. Then we heard about Corel Linux and got the opportunity to write this book.

We believe that anyone can learn to use Linux at whatever level they want to. If you just want a single-user computer and a copy of WordPerfect to do your work at home, you can do that. If you want to run a powerful Web server and offer e-mail hosting to all your friends, you can do that, too. We show you how in this book. Linux doesn't have to be a mystery.

What We Used to Write the Book

Despite our firm belief that Linux is the better alternative in 99 percent of operating system choices, we aren't Linux purists. (Okay, Joe is.) We have a mixed-OS network, and Kate uses both Linux and Windows 98 regularly; there just isn't a Linux alternative (yet...) for a lot of the programs she needs to use. In this book, we've tried to give you information about how Linux differs from Windows or MacOS, and we've shown you how to get all three operating systems working together at a reasonable level of success.

For those who are curious, or who (for some odd reason) are trying to duplicate our exact setup, here's the technical information about the network we used to write the book:

- chinook: A 1994-vintage Gateway2000 486 bought used for $100. Also known as "Frankenputer" for the various items of hardware that have been grafted onto it. Currently running Red Hat Linux 6.1, it serves as our file server and gateway to the Internet.

- maguro: A generic PentiumII 233mHz machine that we found on eBay. Currently under Joe's desk in pieces waiting to be rehabbed as a Sun Solaris machine, it has run several Linux distributions including Corel Linux. We wrote much of the book using maguro.

- fugu: A custom-built hot rod. fugu uses two Intel Celeron 366 processors, overclocked to 550 MHz on an Abit BP-6 motherboard; it has 128MB of RAM and a 13GB hard drive. We've installed a program called VMWare on fugu. This hardware emulator package lets you create a "virtual machine" within the physical computer. fugu runs Red Hat 6.1 on the physical machine and Corel Linux on the virtual machine. We can compile a kernel on this machine in less than three minutes. (If you're wondering whether you should learn about working with hardware, you might be interested to know that the total cost of the components for this machine—not including the monitor—was under $900.)

- hamachi: A Packard-Bell 820 bought off the shelf at Circuit City for $500. It has a Cyrix M-II processor, a 2GB hard disk, and 32MB of RAM. It's currently running Windows 98.

All the computers are networked, with chinook serving as the gateway machine. Everything runs Linux except for hamachi, and we run Samba to include that machine. The network uses 3Com network cards and 10BaseT ethernet cabling.

What's in the Book?

In this book, we've tried to address all sides of the coin. (Okay, that assumes a three-sided coin, which you just can't find very often these days.)

We open the book with a discussion of UNIX and Linux history, explain how to install Corel Linux, and give you a bit of background on the X Window System. (We also sneak some troubleshooting tips in there as well.)

The next part of the book is devoted to KDE, the graphical user interface that's integrated into Corel Linux. We show you how to configure KDE, how to set up and use its Internet applications, and how to use some of the advanced features of the desktop.

The third part of the book is a basic introduction to Linux system administration: directories, users, files, and graphical tools.

The fourth part is a more advanced section dealing with scripting, runlevels, shells, networking, and various servers.

Part V deals with Corel WordPerfect 8, the basics of how to create complex documents, and how to construct Web pages with the Internet Publisher Web Editor.

Finally, we included four appendices that will help you with the kernel, common shell commands, Internet Linux resources, and `init` scripts.

Using the Book

We use some conventions in this book that you should know about before you dive in. Names of programs, URLs, and commands that you can type at the command line are all printed in the Courier font. Directory and file names, as well as the proper names of programs (such as Apache or Telnet) are printed in the font that's used for regular text. The Courier-ized terms are generally used for shell environment work.

You can do an immense amount with your Corel Linux system through graphical tools, though, so we've also used a particular way to describe a menu sequence. If, for example, we want you to open the IRC chat client, we write "Click the Application Starter icon in the KDE Panel and select Applications | Network | Chat Client from the Start menu." This means that you select Applications, then select Network from the small submenu that appears, and then select Chat Client from the sub-submenu. See how much easier it is to write (and read) Applications | Network | Chat Client?

Throughout the book, you'll see various boxes that are shadowed. These are *sidebars*, where we offer a bit of information that didn't quite fit into the regular text of the chapter. Sometimes sidebars contain advanced technical information; other times they showcase a particular procedure. Don't forget to scan through them as you read.

You'll also see Notes and Tips and the like—our way of indicating certain kinds of information to you. There are four kinds, and each has a specific purpose:

 A Note is a bit of information that's especially important to know. We also use Notes to point out other resources, whether books or online sources.

 A Tip may be a shortcut, a technical term explained, or a sneaky way to do something. Between us, Corel, and our technical editor, we've come up with some nice tips that will enhance your Corel Linux experience.

 A caution message is exactly that; it's an explanation of something that might harm your data or your computer. We plead with you to read all the Cautions.

 We don't use Remembers very often. When we do, we're refreshing your memory about something you've read elsewhere in the book, or reminding you of a definition.

PART I

Introduction to Corel Linux

CHAPTER 1

Why Linux, and Why Corel Linux?

In choosing to install Corel Linux, you have opted for an operating system that is quite different from other operating systems you may have used in the past. Linux is a new form of an old workhorse—the UNIX operating system—and it has become quite popular in the past few years. You may have already read several articles in major publications about the Linux phenomenon; it's news because Linux has the same capabilities as the dominant operating systems—in many ways, it has far more capabilities—and because it's maintained and developed by a volunteer community.

What is an operating system, anyway, and why do you care which one you use? At the most fundamental level, an *operating system* is the software that gives users access to the computer's hardware to run programs. Without some kind of operating system—no matter how rudimentary—the computer would be the high-tech equivalent of a car engine in neutral gear: running, but not doing anything constructive. An operating system gives you the things you need to make the car go, such as a clutch and gearshift, a steering wheel, or gas and brake pedals. The computer's operating system controls the microprocessor chip, the system's RAM, storage disks, monitor, keyboard, and other hardware devices used by the computer. It also keeps the time, and it schedules various tasks to be performed according to priority.

UNIX-Derived Systems Versus Windows and MacOS

The UNIX operating system has existed in one form or another since the early 1970s. Although many of today's computer users have probably never seen a UNIX computer in action, they have probably used a machine running UNIX without even knowing it. Many sites on the World Wide Web run UNIX or a UNIX-derived operating system, and almost all Internet e-mail is handled by a UNIX or UNIX-derived mail server at some point on its journey. UNIX or one of its derivatives—such as Linux or FreeBSD—is used by many businesses and almost all universities and research institutions to serve core computing needs.

Today, most personal computer users use Microsoft's Windows 95 and Windows 98 operating systems, with a significant minority using the Apple MacOS. These operating systems have something in common: they were designed from the very start to be used only on personal computers.

1

UNIX or UNIX-Derived?

You may be wondering, as you read further in this book, why we keep saying "UNIX or UNIX-derived operating systems." Aren't they all UNIX? Actually, no. Various operating systems, including Linux, share a great deal of structure with the original UNIX operating system, but they are not UNIX. UNIX is a trademarked proprietary operating system, while many of its derivatives are nonproprietary and share their code freely. Many of the tips and commands we describe throughout this book were initially found in UNIX but have been maintained in the derivative systems. So, we use "UNIX or UNIX-derived" to mean that although something is a traditional UNIX action or feature, it's applicable to both proprietary and free operating systems derived from the original UNIX system.

> **NOTE** *We use the term* personal computer *to refer to computers intended for use by individuals. Initially, the term and its acronym* PC *were used as trademarks for computers built by IBM; many other companies now make computers intended for the single-user market, and PC has become a generally used term.*

In a very real sense, both Windows and MacOS are *single-user operating systems*. Although Windows 95/98 has support for multiple user profiles, the various profiles are used only for personal configuration of visual appeal and not as a security measure. More important, machines running Windows or MacOS can be used by only one user at a time.

UNIX and its derivatives, however, were originally designed to be run on large mainframe computers with multiple users, who connected to the mainframe from individual terminals. Appropriate to that beginning, UNIX is a true *multiple-user operating system*. Many users can be connected to the same computer simultaneously and can perform individual tasks without the knowledge or annoyance of other users also connected. This mainframe heritage shows through in other areas, as well. Tasks can be automated through small programs called *scripts*, and those scripts can be run at preset times. Most crucial system actions keep logs of their activity, and problems with the system can often be solved simply by reading the logs and, if necessary, taking action based on the information recorded in them.

Best of all, because it was designed for computer professionals, UNIX and its derivatives give you fine control over your system's hardware. Other personal operating systems, such as Windows 95/98, remove some of this control as an "ease of use" feature; we hope that with Corel Linux and this book, we can demonstrate how you can have UNIX's control without sacrificing ease of use. With the development of UNIX-based operating systems for consumer-level computer hardware, the power of the mainframe has arrived on the desktop.

The History of Linux

When computers first arrived on the research scene, back in the days of room-sized mainframes, all software was free software. Each computer manufacturer designed its machines differently from the others, and thus had to supply a unique operating system so that the computer could be used. It was common for manufacturers to share the *source code* of those operating systems with users, so that improvements or customizations could be made for more efficient use of the computer. (Source code is the program that a developer writes to make a given program operate.) Most customers were computer scientists in research laboratories, and software was a fun item to be amended, traded, shared, and generally treated as a recipe.

In the late 1970s, this unfettered practice of sharing software began to change. The first indication of what was to come was in 1976, when a young entrepreneur published an "Open Letter to Hobbyists" in the *Homebrew Computer Club Newsletter*. That entrepreneur was named William Henry Gates III. Gates was then a partner in a fledgling software company called Micro-Soft, and he had a complaint:

> Almost a year ago, Paul Allen and myself, expecting the hobby market to expand, hired Monte Davidoff and developed Altair BASIC. Though the initial work took only two months, the three of us have spent most of the last year documenting, improving, and adding features to BASIC. Now we have 4K, 8K, EXTENDED, ROM, and DISK BASIC. The value of the computer time we have used exceeds $40,000.

> The feedback we have gotten from the hundreds of people who say they are using BASIC has all been positive. Two surprising things are apparent, however 1) Most of these "users" never bought BASIC (less than 10% of all Altair owners have bought BASIC) and 2) The amount of royalties we have received from sales to hobbyists makes the time spent on Altair BASIC worth less than $2 an hour.

Why is this? As the majority of hobbyists must be aware, most of you steal your software. Hardware must be paid for, but software is something to share. Who cares if the people who worked on it get paid?

— *Homebrew Computer Club Newsletter*, vol. 2, no. 1, January 1976

Whether this letter was the primary cause, or merely a harbinger of things to come, it heralded a change in the way software was treated. As computers became more complex, and the sale of computers to individuals grew, computer manufacturers did less of their software writing in-house and began to contract it out to software specialists such as Micro-Soft. Following Gates's logic, these specialists were reluctant to divulge the secrets of their trade. They began to release their software in the form of executable binaries and kept their source code a secret.

Within a few years, most of the software in common use was *proprietary*: released as executable binary files instead of source code, often trademarked, and with copyrights aggressively enforced. Most computer users accepted this, having no knowledge of the free exchanges that had happened between research scientists a decade before. The personal computer was sweeping the world, and most purchasers had never had access to a large mainframe. However, some of those research scientists were offended by the new "rules" about software and began to complain. The most prominent of these was a computer scientist at the Massachusetts Institute of Technology named Richard Stallman.

Stallman's objections to proprietary software were both practical and philosophical. On the practical side, he was frustrated that any problems found by a user could not be fixed unless the software company chose to fix them. A user's modifications or improvements stood little chance of actually being implemented. On the philosophical side, he believed that it was wrong for corporations to tell individuals that they were not allowed to help or share with their neighbors and fellow users.

Stallman considered his options and decided that he needed to do something to protect and strengthen the community of which he had been a part. He decided that the best thing he could do would be to create *free software*.

NOTE *Stallman uses the word* free *in a very specific way. In this context,* free *means "free to copy, modify, and distribute," not necessarily "zero-cost." A common slogan in the free software community is "Free speech, not free beer."*

Source Code Versus Binaries

When a programmer writes a program, she does so by using a *programming language*. These languages contain commands that describe actions to be performed and various conditions to be met. A listing of these commands, which constitute a given program, is called *source code*. A fragment of source code in the C programming language might look like this:

```
/* Drop the "current user" thing */
free_uid(current);

/* Give kmod all privileges.. */
current->uid = current->euid = current->fsuid = 0;
cap_set_full(current->cap_inheritable);
cap_set_full(current->cap_effective);
```

As cryptic as this may seem, the language exists for human purposes. To a programmer, this is meaningful stuff; to a computer, it means nothing. Computers don't speak English; they don't even speak C. Computers speak *binary*. When you get to the very basics, computers are electrical devices, and binary is an electrical language.

The binary language is made up of two elements: the number 0 and the number 1. Electrical current is either present (1) or not (0). These 1's and 0's are combined to form larger pieces of information, whether instructions or data. Clearly, something needs to happen to translate the source code into binary; this is a process called *compilation*. Source code is fed into a program called a *compiler*, which translates it into binary, which can then be run on a computer.

Stallman reasoned that the most important thing he could write would be an operating system, since without that, no other programs could be run. He decided to pattern his operating system after the popular and powerful UNIX operating system, which was owned by AT&T at that time (and was a proprietary system). He named his system GNU, an acronym for "GNU's Not UNIX." This type of acronym, common in the free software world, is called a *recursive acronym* since it refers to itself. It's also a pun on the recursive function frequently used in programming. In 1984, Stallman began to work on the first piece of GNU: the text editor `emacs`.

Soon after, he began to work on GCC, the GNU C Compiler. With these two tools, he was able to write and compile the rest of the necessary software; he also made these tools freely available for others to use. In keeping with his belief in free software, Stallman created a license under which he distributed his creations, called the GNU General Public License, or GPL. The GPL states that the user of a program released under GPL has the right to copy, modify, and distribute the program so long as he, in turn, grants those same rights to others. Because it is impossible to modify a program without having access to the source code, anyone distributing software under the GPL must make the source code available as well.

With `emacs` and GCC in distribution, other programmers began contacting Stallman wanting to get involved with the GNU project. To facilitate this, the Free Software Foundation was established. A nonprofit charitable organization, the FSF coordinates development activities, produces documentation, and distributes software. It has developed, and maintains, a large collection of free software including `emacs`, GCC, `glibc` (the GNU C Library), `bash` (a command shell provided with Corel Linux), and other useful programs. The FSF's work continues, but its goal of creating a complete GNU operating system has not yet been realized. As things turned out, however, a GNU operating system was not necessary for the existence of a complete free operating system.

In 1991, Linus Torvalds was a computer science student at the University of Helsinki. He enjoyed programming on the university's UNIX system but was frustrated that he couldn't use a version of UNIX on his—then state-of-the-art—386 personal computer. He had been introduced to Minix, a stripped-down version of UNIX for the 386, but found many of its features lacking. Besides, he wanted to tackle a large project. So, in a moment of either brilliance or foolhardiness (depending on whom you ask), he decided to create, wholly from scratch, a version of UNIX for the PC.

By October of 1991, Torvalds had the beginning of his system. He decided that it had enough potential to warrant further development, so he put the source code on the university's file server and posted a message to the USENET newsgroup `comp.os.minix`:

```
Do you pine for the nice days of minix-1.1, when men were men and wrote
their own device drivers? Are you without a nice project and just dying to
cut your teeth on a OS you can try to modify for your needs? Are you finding
it frustrating when everything works on minix? No more all-nighters to get a
nifty program working? Then this post might be just for you :-)

As I mentioned a month(?) ago, I'm working on a free version of a
minix-lookalike for AT-386 computers. It has finally reached the stage where
```

```
it's even usable (though may not be depending on what you want), and I am
willing to put out the sources for wider distribution. It is just version
0.02 (+1 (very small) patch already), but I've successfully run
bash/gcc/gnu-make/gnu-sed/compress etc under it.

Sources for this pet project of mine can be found at nic.funet.fi
(128.214.6.100) in the directory /pub/OS/Linux.
```

[Message ID <1991Oct5.054106.4647@klaava.Helsinki.fi>, archived at
http://www.li.org/linuxhistory.shtml]

Readers of `comp.os.minix` jumped at the opportunity to help the project, and things began to move along. Version 0.11 was released in December 1991 and was considered "fairly usable"; version 1.0.0, the first official release version, was released on March 13, 1994. Torvalds released his system under the GPL because he wanted anyone interested to be able to participate in Linux's development. Since GNU software was also free and GPL'd, people using Linux used many GNU programs to extend Linux's functionality.

Neither GNU software nor the Linux kernel is usable by itself. Each requires the other, or its equivalent, to work. This has led to the current practice of creating *distributions*. A distribution is a bundled collection of software that constitutes an operating system and a suite of applications. At the time we wrote this book, 101 separate distributions of Linux were available, including the Corel Linux distribution you have chosen to use. Each of these distributions is slightly—sometimes greatly—different from the others, and each has its own focus. For example, the minimal Tomsrtbt distribution is designed to fit on only two floppy disks, the popular Slackware distribution is designed for hard-core UNIX users, and the Debian GNU/Linux distribution is designed to be as close as possible to the FSF's goal of an entire operating system comprising nothing but free software, using the foundation's definition of *free*.

In 1998 and 1999, Linux experienced an explosion in popularity. While it is still very much in the minority of operating systems in use, it's estimated that in 1998 alone, the Linux user base grew 212 percent. In 1999, two Linux companies held Initial Public Offerings (IPOs) of their stock and saw their values increase five- and tenfold. Linux exhibits are now the hottest attractions at computer industry trade shows, such as Comdex, and trade shows devoted solely to Linux have become commonplace. Linux is on the march, aiming toward Torvalds's joking goal of "world domination."

Understanding the Linux Community

The advent of Linux and other free software has created more than just a technological niche; it has also created an interesting and vibrant culture, usually referred to as "the Linux community." To a newcomer, this community can be bewildering and somewhat off-putting until one begins to understand the history, mythology, and shared jokes, as well as the personalities of its leading figures. (To be honest, even those who have been in the community for a long time still find it baffling at times.) While it's not necessary to become a member of the Linux community—or even to have much contact with it at all—to run Linux, we feel that knowing a few key things about it will make the sailing smoother if you happen to find yourself among the faithful.

Many Linux users are extremely passionate about Linux and free software. There are probably nearly as many reasons for this passion as there are people experiencing it, but one major factor is that no single person or entity owns or controls Linux.

For people who spend a good part of their lives working on their computers, that fact means that no person or corporation controls the tools with which they work. Many Linux users contrast this with the practices of Microsoft or Apple; users of those operating systems are at the mercy of the corporations that provide them for changes or improvements to the software they use. If the corporate business plans are at odds with the consumer's needs, the consumer has little to say about it.

TIP	*Even Torvalds does not own Linux, though he does hold the trademark on the word* Linux. *In fact, the only authority that he has is to declare an official kernel release, or upgrade, and he has this authority only because people have agreed to listen to him on this single topic.*

Others are passionate about Linux because the technology is simply superior to other common operating systems. Linux is more stable, flexible, and powerful than Windows or MacOS, as proven by multiple independent benchmarking tests. Windows NT and commercial UNIX distributions are Linux's main technological rivals, and they are far more expensive than Linux.

Whatever the reason for an individual user's passion about Linux, it's a good idea to develop some understanding of the passion itself. These passions are a main identifier of the Linux community and are the driving force behind the rapid pace of Linux's evolution. People work devotedly for the Linux cause because it is a community with shared goals, not just a set of software commands purchased from a computer store shelf.

Like any community, the Linux community is, unfortunately, also awash in politics and personality. Some members of the community are what might be called "free software absolutists." These are people who believe that the only good software is free software, and they tend to be suspicious of any corporate involvement with Linux. Like Stallman, with whom they tend to identify, their interest in free software is as philosophical as it is technical.

In contrast, there are those whose outlook is most personified by Eric S. Raymond. Raymond, sometimes called an "open source evangelist," takes a more practical approach to free software advocacy. He believes that the best software is that which is the best at what it does, and that free software happens to be better because it is technologically superior. He believes that the Linux community's priority should be to encourage the use of free software, rather than to maintain philosophical purity. Therefore, he uses the term *open source* instead of *free software*, because corporations may be reluctant to embrace something that sounds unbusinesslike.

TIP	*Eric Raymond is the author of a highly influential monograph called "The Cathedral and the Bazaar," which is credited with playing a major role in Netscape's decision to release the code for its popular Web browser. The monograph explains the difference between the proprietary and open source development models and is available at* `http://www.tuxedo.org/~esr/writings`.

Of course, this binary division is a gross oversimplification of the community's diversity of opinion, but it's as close as we can get in a few paragraphs. You'll find many shades of opinion, as well as people who seem to hold both views at once. Debates between factions can seem loud and rancorous, but remember how close the two camps really are. Both agree that free software is good and should be widely used; the disagreement is about the extent to which the social benefits of free software should be emphasized over the commercial benefits.

In contrast to both of these viewpoints, Torvalds rarely talks about anything other than the technology itself. It was a technological curiosity that inspired his work in the first place, and it's clear that technology is where his interests lie. He doesn't talk about the politics of Linux at all, and there is a certain wisdom in that decision; Torvalds is one of the few people in the Linux world whom nearly everyone likes and respects.

Why have we gone into this detail about a community you may not be interested in? For a couple of reasons: first, we encourage you to use community resources when you're having trouble or have questions about running Linux; second, we hope that you'll find Corel Linux an interesting and useful operating system, and that you'll become involved in the Linux movement. In both cases, you'll find yourself interacting with members of the Linux community; their responses to you may very well be colored by their philosophical stance.

Corel Linux

The Corel Corporation has decided to join the Linux community by releasing its own Linux distribution. We assume that you've purchased the distribution already, or that you've bought this book because the distribution is included on the CD. Corel Linux is designed to be easy to install and use, especially for people who are familiar with the Microsoft Windows operating system. Based on the Debian GNU/Linux distribution, Corel has added a few unique items: an improved File Manager, an easy-to-use software upgrade agent, and improved communication with the Microsoft Windows platform, among others. Corel has also worked with the developers of the KDE desktop, a user interface that is tightly interwoven with the operating system and is a straightforward and graphical way to use your computer.

Corel's Linux distribution is a good introduction for those new to Linux as well as a strong new distribution for those experienced with the operating system. In this book, you'll find tips and useful tricks that help you use Corel Linux to the edges of its ability, whether you're using Linux for the first time or you're an old hand. We think you'll enjoy running Corel Linux and hope that you'll become part of the Linux community.

CHAPTER 2

Installing Corel Linux

Obviously, before you can do anything with Corel Linux, you must install it first. In this chapter, we provide installation paths for both the basic and advanced installation options. Corel Linux has a simple installation procedure that is clear and easy to follow, so you won't have problems getting it in place and ready to run. Once you have the operating system installed, you can go ahead and use the rest of the book freely.

At the end of this chapter, we also provide instruction on creating disk partitions. You may want to use partitions to organize the various file systems that are part of Corel Linux, or you may want to install two separate operating systems on your computer. You can do both with the Corel Linux disk-partitioning tools.

Basic Installation of Corel Linux

To get Corel Linux running on your system, all you need to do is to follow this simple procedure. Most of the work is done by Corel Linux itself; you have to answer a few questions and select a username, but the bulk of the installation is simply waiting for Corel Linux to install itself. Use the following steps to install the Corel Linux distribution, and then use the rest of the book to learn more about your new operating system.

1. Configure your computer's BIOS to boot from a CD-ROM.

   Before you begin, you need to ensure that your computer will search the CD-ROM drive first. This makes it possible for the computer to start up using Linux, and not whatever other operating system you have installed; you won't be able to install Linux from within another operating system. This change is made within the computer chip's BIOS, or basic operating system. The BIOS controls the order in which the computer components activate during startup. To change your computer's BIOS, see the sidebar "Altering BIOS Settings," later in the chapter.

TIP *We discuss the startup procedure, including BIOS, in more detail in Chapter 10, "Start Up and Shut Down."*

CAUTION *If you cannot change the BIOS to boot from CD-ROM, you will need to use the boot disk included with your Corel Linux distribution.*

2. Insert the Corel Linux CD-ROM into the CD-ROM drive. If you need to use the boot disk because you cannot configure the BIOS, insert it into your floppy drive now.

3. Shut down your computer, using whatever method is required by the current operating system.

4. After a few moments, restart the computer.

    The computer boots from the CD-ROM (or floppy drive). The Corel Linux installation splash screen appears, as in Figure 2-1, and displays the message "Detecting hardware...."

5. After your hardware configuration has been determined, the Corel Linux License Agreement screen appears, as shown in Figure 2-2. Read the license; it contains the terms by which you agree to abide when using this software. Click OK when you have finished reading the license agreement.

    The Corel Linux username screen appears, as in Figure 2-3, asking you to enter a username. This will be the name of your regular *user account*—the account you use for everyday activities.

FIGURE 2-1   Corel Linux displays this screen while it determines your hardware configuration

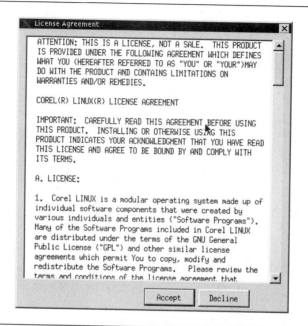

FIGURE 2-2 You must accept the terms of the Corel Linux License Agreement before you install the operating system

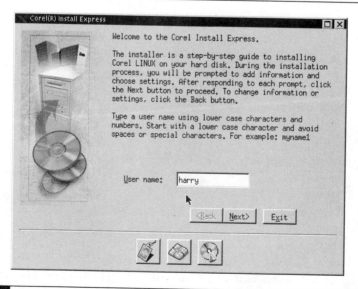

FIGURE 2-3 Select a username that is simple and easy to remember

6. Enter a username in the box, and click Next.

The installation type screen appears (Figure 2-4).

7. Select Install Standard Desktop, and then click Next.

The disk partition options screen appears, as shown in Figure 2-5. Disk *partitions* are used to keep certain information separate from other. For this installation, we assume that you want to install Corel Linux as the sole operating system on your computer. If you want more information about partitioning, see the final section of this chapter.

8. Select Take Over Disk, and then click Next.

9. When a confirmation screen appears, as in Figure 2-6, check to be sure that your username is spelled properly and that the installation options you have selected are correct.

10. (Optional) Select the Scan For Bad Blocks While Formatting check box.

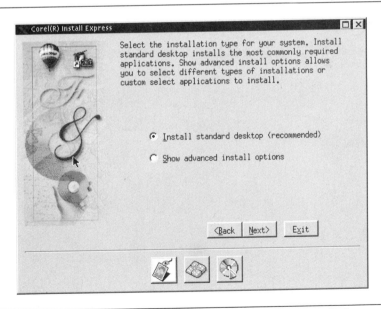

FIGURE 2-4   You can choose from several types of Corel Linux installations

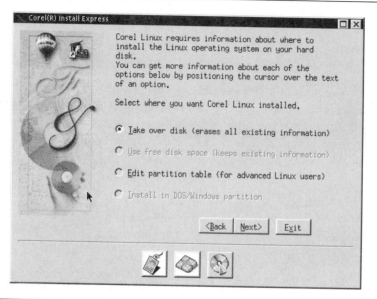

FIGURE 2-5 Use the disk partition options screen if you need to segment your hard drive

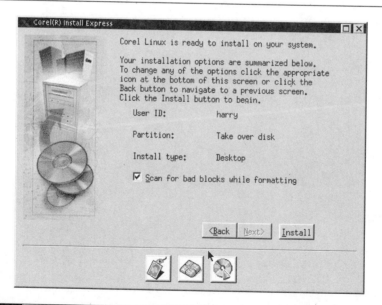

FIGURE 2-6 The confirmation screen is your last chance to correct errors in your username or installation options

2

This option verifies the integrity of the disk surface during installation, looking for bad sectors and avoiding them. This can be helpful to ensure that your disk's physical structure is okay, but it does slow down the process. If you have a slow computer (a 386 or 486), you may want to save this check for later.

11. Click Install.

A progress bar appears across the screen, as in Figure 2-7. This bar shows the percentile completion of disk formatting and package installation.

NOTE *How long the installation takes depends on a number of factors: processor speed, the speed of the CD-ROM drive, the speed of the hard drive, how the CD-ROM and hard drive are connected to the motherboard, how much memory you have, what type of installation you've selected, and so on. As an estimate, installation can range anywhere from 30–40 minutes on a very fast machine, to more than an hour on a slower machine. Plan to do something else while Corel Linux is installing; rest assured that the process is working, even if the progress bar appears to be standing still.*

FIGURE 2-7   Keep an eye on the progress bar to track your Corel Linux installation

12. When installation is complete, a dialog box appears, asking if you want to reboot so that Corel Linux can take effect. Click OK.

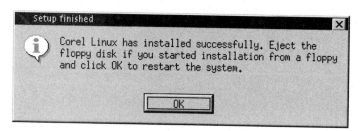

13. Remove the CD-ROM from the CD-ROM drive and reconfigure the BIOS to boot from the Master Boot Record if you changed it at the beginning of the process.

The system reboots, and the main Corel Linux splash screen appears, as you can see in Figure 2-8.

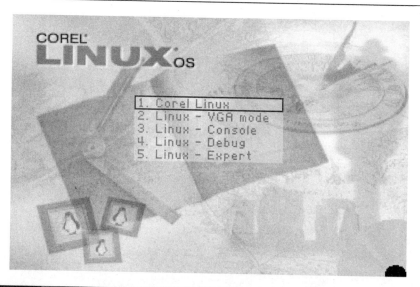

FIGURE 2-8   The Corel Linux splash screen greets you each time you log in

2

14. Use the arrow keys to select Corel Linux in the drop-down box, and then press ENTER.

The system takes a few minutes to configure; subsequent boot-ups will go much faster. Once Corel Linux has configured itself, the login screen appears, as shown in Figure 2-9.

15. Select your username from the drop-down box, and then click Login.

Now you are logged into your Corel Linux computer! We recommend that you skim through the other chapters in this book to get an idea of the capabilities of your computer before you get down to serious work.

If you are newly arrived to Linux from Windows or MacOS (or another UNIX-derived operating system), you'll need to unlearn some old habits and learn some new ones. You'll find the KDE chapters (Chapters 5–9) helpful in understanding the user environment of the KDE desktop; you should also read the basic system administration chapters (Chapters 10–14) to learn more about the operating system that underlies that desktop. Welcome to the Linux community!

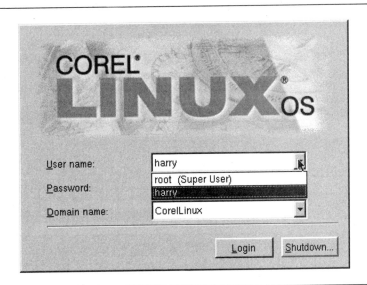

FIGURE 2-9   Select the proper username from the login screen

Altering BIOS Settings

The procedure required to change BIOS settings varies from computer to computer. Generally, you will need to reboot your computer first; when the computer restarts, watch the screen carefully. You should see a message that says something like "Press <x> to enter setup." <x> is a particular key, often the ESC key or one of the F (function) keys along the top of the keyboard. Press this key to open the BIOS setup menu.

What you do next depends on the particular BIOS used by your computer. Look for an option called "Boot Devices," "Boot Order," or something similar. If you don't have an option labeled that clearly, check each submenu for options called "Primary boot device," "Secondary boot device," and so on. Some computers simply do not permit you to edit boot devices; in that case, you'll need to use the boot disk that came with your Corel Linux distribution.

Assuming that you have found your BIOS's method of assigning the boot device, set the primary boot device to CD-ROM. Most modern BIOSes should be able to do this. If yours won't, set it to Floppy (or however your BIOS refers to the disk drive). Save your changes and exit BIOS setup.

Although the various BIOSes differ in their organization, most are set up in a logical fashion. A little careful thought often goes a long way toward finding your way around the BIOS menu. Of course, if you have your motherboard manual—which you should have handy if you purchased your computer new—consult that. The BIOS setup should be explained in detail there.

Advanced Installation of Corel Linux

You may want to perform a more precise installation of Corel Linux than the basic installation provided through the process described previously. If you take advantage of the various installation options available to you, you can choose what parts of the Corel Linux distribution that you want to install; this ranges from a bare-bones minimal installation to a complex development installation with extra libraries and programs to a set of servers that you can use to perform various functions.

Making a Boot Disk

If you purchased Corel Linux as a boxed set, you probably found a boot disk in the box. If the version you purchased did not include a boot disk, or you downloaded Corel Linux from the Internet or acquired it in some other way, you can make your own boot disk, and we recommend that you do so. It is an excellent precaution to take and will make you quite happy if you have a massive system crash that causes Corel Linux to become corrupted.

To make a boot disk on a machine with Corel Linux already installed, use this process:

1. Insert a blank disk into the Linux machine's disk drive.

2. Log into the machine as root and open a terminal window.

3. Insert the Corel Linux CD-ROM into the CD-ROM drive.

4. Mount the CD-ROM by typing **`mount -t iso9660 /dev/cdrom /mnt/cdrom`** at the shell prompt.

5. Now, type the command **`dd if=/mnt/cdrom/boot/boot1440.img of=/dev/fd0`** at the shell prompt.

6. When the file has finished transferring, remove the disk.

7. Label the disk "Corel Linux Boot Disk" and keep it in a safe place.

If you have already had a system failure and do not have a boot disk, you can make one with a Windows 95/98 computer in the following way:

1. Insert a blank disk into the Windows computer's floppy drive.

2. Insert the Corel Linux CD-ROM into the CD-ROM drive.

3. Double-click the My Computer icon.

4. Right-click the CD-ROM drive icon and select the Open option from the pop-up menu.

5. Double-click the Tools folder icon.

6. Double-click the BOOTFLOP.BAT file and follow the instructions.

7. Remove the disk and label it "Corel Linux Boot Disk."

8. Keep the boot disk in a safe place.

You can even make a purely custom installation and install only the packages you want, though this can be tricky to do properly. To install Corel Linux with the advanced options, use the following process:

1. Configure your computer's BIOS to boot from a CD-ROM.

   Before you begin, you need to ensure that your computer will search the CD-ROM drive first. This makes it possible for the computer to start up using Linux, and not whatever other operating system you have installed; you won't be able to install Linux from within another operating system. This change is made within the computer chip's BIOS, or basic operating system. The BIOS controls the order in which the computer components activate during startup. For more information on changing your computer's BIOS settings, see the sidebar "Altering BIOS Settings," earlier in the chapter.

> **TIP** *We discuss the start-up procedure, including BIOS, in more detail in Chapter 10.*

> **CAUTION** *If you cannot change the BIOS to boot from CD-ROM, you will need to use the boot disk included with your Corel Linux distribution.*

2. Insert the Corel Linux CD-ROM into the CD-ROM drive. If you need to use the boot disk because you cannot configure the BIOS, insert it into your floppy drive now.

LILO: What It Is and Why It's Necessary

A crucial piece of the operating system puzzle, LILO (LInux LOader), is installed automatically with Corel Linux. LILO is the program that extracts the operating system kernel from the hard disk drive and loads it into memory. By default, LILO is installed on a special sector of the hard disk called the Master Boot Record. The Master Boot Record is the first thing that is read when your computer starts. See Chapter 10 for more details on the Linux startup process.

Every operating system has some type of boot loader, but unlike the boot loader for other proprietary operating systems, LILO allows you to define exactly what should be booted and to specify a number of options for booting. Not only that, but LILO can also let you define more than one option for booting. For example, you could install both Windows 95 and Corel Linux on your computer, and use LILO to control which operating system to run. If you are interested in building such a system, some helpful documents are available at `http://www.linuxdoc.org/HOWTO/HOWTO-INDEX-3.html#ss.` `3.1`. Look through Appendix A, "How to Compile a Kernel," for more information about how LILO is configured and run.

3. Shut down your computer, using whatever method is required by the current operating system.

4. Restart the computer.

   The computer boots from the CD-ROM (or floppy drive). The Corel Linux installation splash screen appears, as in Figure 2-1, and displays the message "Detecting hardware." After your hardware configuration has been determined, the Corel Linux license screen appears, as shown in Figure 2-2. Read the license; it contains the terms by which you agree to abide when using this software.

5. Click OK when you have finished reading the license.

   The Corel Linux username screen appears, as in Figure 2-3, asking you for a username. The name you select will be the name of your regular *user account*, the account you will use for your everyday activities.

6. Enter a username in the box.

7. Click OK when you have finished entering your username.

The installation type screen appears (Figure 2-4).

8. Select Show Advanced Install Options.

9. Click OK.

The advanced install options screen appears, as shown in Figure 2-10.

10. Select one of the four options:

- ■ **Desktop Minimum**   Select this option to install only the base Linux system, the KDE desktop, and the most commonly used applications. Installation proceeds as normal from step 11.

- ■ **Desktop Plus**   Select this option to install all items from the Desktop Minimum option as well as software development tools including development libraries and extra types of editors. You probably don't need to install Desktop Plus unless you plan to program. Installation proceeds as normal from step 11.

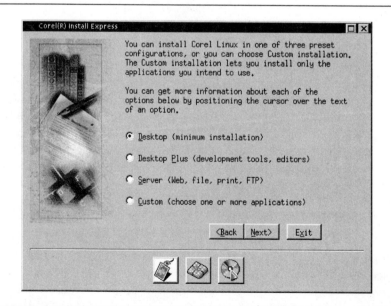

FIGURE 2-10   Select specific installation options on the advanced install options screen

- **Server**   If you select this option, you will be shown a screen (as seen
  in Figure 2-11) in which you can choose to install Web Server, Mail
  Server, or File/Print Server. Choose the options you want; the default
  choice is to install all three. Installation proceeds as normal, with one
  exception in step 11 (noted at that step).

NOTE   *Learn more about these servers in Part IV. The Web server, Apache,
is covered in Chapter 26, "Web Services"; the mail servers,* exim *and*
qmail, *are covered in Chapter 23, "Mail Services"; file and print servers
are covered in Chapter 24, "File and Print Sharing." If you realize later
that you wanted to install a particular program but didn't do so, you can
always use the Corel Update tool to install the new package.*

- **Custom**   If you select this option, you'll see a package manager screen
  (Figure 2-12). A number of categories are available for selection; you
  can expand the category by clicking the +. Many categories have
  subcategories; if you select the check box next to a category, you select
  that category and all its subcategories. Installation proceeds as normal,
  with one exception in step 11 (noted at that step).

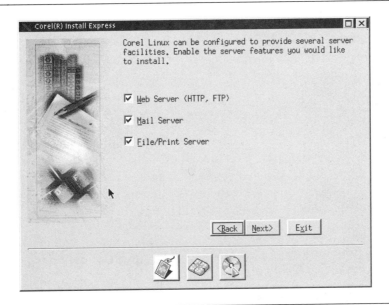

FIGURE 2-11   Select the servers you wish to install on the Server option screen

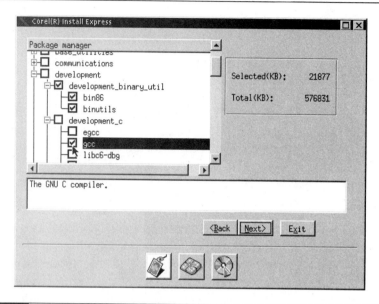

FIGURE 2-12   Use the Custom installation option to install only specific items

CAUTION   *We recommend that you use the Custom installation option only after you have familiarized yourself with Corel Linux and Linux in general. It's easy to forget to select something that is critical to the smooth operation of your computer.*

11. After you have made your selection, click Next.

    The Disk Partition Options screen, shown in Figure 2-5, appears. Disk *partitions* are used to keep certain information separate from other. For this installation, we assume that you want to install Corel Linux as the sole operating system on your computer. If you want more information about partitioning, see the final section of this chapter.

NOTE   *If you selected either the Server or the Custom installation option in step 10, your only options on the Disk Partition Options screen will be Take Over Disk and Edit Partition Table.*

12. Select Take Over Disk.

2

13. Click Finish. A confirmation screen appears, as shown in Figure 2-6. Check to be sure that your username is spelled properly and that the installation options you have selected are correct.

14. (Optional) Select the Scan For Bad Blocks While Formatting check box (see Figure 2-6).

This option verifies the integrity of the disk surface during installation, looking for bad sectors and avoiding them. Scanning can be helpful to ensure that your disk's physical structure is okay, but it does slow down the process. If you have a slow computer (a 386 or 486), you may want to save this check for later.

15. Click Install.

A progress bar appears across the screen, as shown in Figure 2-7. This bar shows the percentile completion of disk formatting and package installation.

> **NOTE** *How long the installation takes depends on a number of factors, such as processor speed, the speed of the CD-ROM drive, the speed of the hard drive, how the CD-ROM and hard drive are connected to the motherboard, how much memory you have, and what installation options you've selected. As an estimate, installation can range anywhere from 30–40 minutes on a very fast machine to more than an hour on a slow machine. Plan to do something else while Corel Linux is installing; rest assured that the process is working, even if the progress bar appears to be standing still.*

16. When installation is complete, a dialog box appears asking if you want to reboot so that Corel Linux can take effect. Click OK. Remove the CD-ROM from the CD-ROM drive and reconfigure the BIOS to boot from the Master Boot Record if you changed it at the beginning of the process.

The system reboots, and the main Corel Linux splash screen appears, as shown in Figure 2-8.

17. Use the arrow keys to select Corel Linux in the drop-down box, and then press ENTER.

The system takes a few minutes to configure itself for use; subsequent boot-ups will go much faster. Once Corel Linux has configured itself, the login screen appears, as shown in Figure 2-9.

18. Select your username from the drop-down box, and then click Login.

Now you are logged into your Corel Linux computer! We recommend that you skim through the other chapters in this book to get an idea of the capabilities of your computer before you get down to work.

Disk Partitions

Many people like to keep multiple *disk partitions* on their hard disks. A partition is a section of the physical hard disk that is reserved for use by a particular file system. A partition may contain various parts of the Linux file system; for example, you could make one partition that contains the base system, one for the /usr directory, one for the /home directory, and so on. Partitions may also be used to house other operating systems, such as DOS, Windows, Solaris, OS/2, and so on. Computers with two operating systems installed are referred to as *dual-boot machines*, since you can choose what operating system you want to run at startup.

CAUTION | *Before you decide to partition, you should read the documents at* `http://www.linuxdoc.org/HOWTO/HOWTO-INDEX-3.html#ss.3.1`*. It's not something that you should do lightly; you may lose data or need to reinstall other operating systems. Be aware of what you're doing before you partition a disk that already has data on it.*

If you want to partition your disk, you must do so during installation of Corel Linux. Partitions are controlled on the Disk Partition Options screen, where you see the message "Corel Linux requires information about where to install the Linux operating system." To set up partitions, use the following procedure.

CAUTION | *Editing your partition table carries with it the risk of data destruction. Before you decide to partition your disk, make sure you have backup copies of any important files already on your disk. (This is a good idea anyway.) During the partition procedure, remain alert; do not commit to any changes in the partition table unless you are absolutely sure that you have things the way you want them. The only way to fix a partitioning error is to wipe the hard drive, reinstall Corel Linux, and repartition the drive. You will lose all data in the partitions if you do so. However, if you change your mind about partitioning during install, and you haven't clicked the Install button yet, you can back out of your decision.*

2

1. On the Disk Partition Options screen, click the Edit Partition Table (For Advanced Linux Users) button.

   A new screen appears, showing your disk and any existing partitions in tree format (Figure 2-13).

   If you are installing Corel Linux on your primary hard drive, you should see that disk labeled as /dev/hda. Under it, you will see two partitions: /dev/hda1, of the type "Linux," and /dev/hda2, of the type "Swap."

2. If you click one of the partitions to select it, and then click the Properties button, you will see a detailed description of that partition along with a pie graph showing how much of the disk that partition occupies. A sample Properties description is shown in Figure 2-14. Click OK to close this screen and return to the tree diagram.

NOTE *You must have at least one swap partition, where Linux "swaps out" data from memory when the system's RAM is full. How much swap space you need is debatable; some say that your swap partition should be equal to the amount of system memory you have, while others say it should be as much as four times your physical system memory. We think the answer depends on how much memory you have and what kinds of programs you run. A machine with relatively little RAM (32MB or so) will need more swap space, since physical memory will fill faster than on a machine with 128MB or more of memory. We recommend creating a swap partition at least twice the amount of your RAM if you have more than 32MB of system memory, and at least four times your RAM if you have 32MB or less.*

   In the default configuration, /dev/hda1 takes up all disk space that is not explicitly allocated to the swap partition. You can't create another partition until you reduce the size of /dev/hda1. Unfortunately, the only way to do this is to delete /dev/hda1 and re-create it.

3. In the tree diagram, click /dev/hda1 to select it, and then click Delete.

4. Click Yes to confirm the deletion.

5. Click /dev/hda to select it, and then click Add.

   The Add New Partition dialog box opens, as shown in Figure 2-15, with details of your new partition (this resembles the Properties window shown in Figure 2-14).

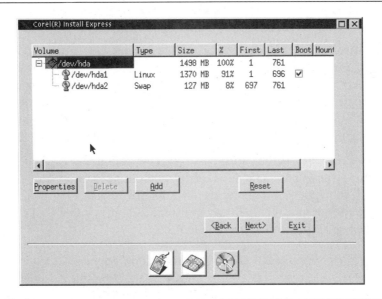

FIGURE 2-13   Use this diagram to guide your disk partition selections

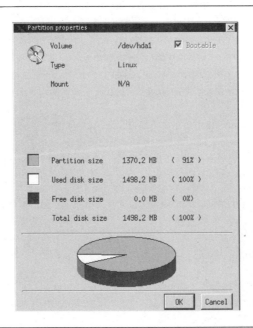

FIGURE 2-14   Use the Partition Properties screen to learn more about each disk partition

> **NOTE** *The numbers in the bottom four fields may be different, depending on the size of your hard disk and how much swap space you have allocated.*

The information on this screen explains that the partition (or *volume*) being created is a Linux partition; moreover, it will be the *root partition*, the most basic partition on the machine. The partition is also bootable, meaning that the partition is read at startup. The data in the Region(cyl) field explains the physical location of the partition on the hard disk.

Finally, the partition will occupy 2MB of space on the hard drive, which is insufficient space for a root partition, so you need to make this partition larger.

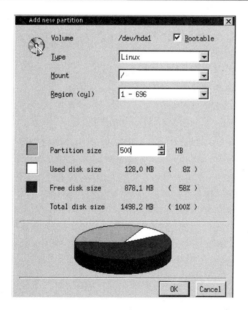

FIGURE 2-15 Your new partition's settings are shown in this dialog box

NOTE *At the minimum, the root partition needs to contain the directories /bin, /boot, /etc, and /. If you are putting all other file systems in their own partitions, you can keep the root partition at about 300MB or so. If you plan to keep other file systems in the root partition, it will have to be large enough to contain them. We discuss file systems in detail in Chapter 11, "Corel Linux Directory Structures."*

6. Change the partition size in one of two ways: use the arrow buttons to the right of the partition size field to set the partition size, or click in the partition size field and edit the number, using the keyboard.

   After a couple of seconds, the pie graph changes to show the size of the new partition.

7. Click OK.

   The partition properties window closes, and you return to the main Partition Editor screen (see Figure 2-13). Your new /dev/hda1 partition should be visible in the disk tree. Now you can add a new partition.

8. Click the /dev/hda entry to select it, and then click Add.

   The Add New Partition window opens again (see Figure 2-15); you are now editing /dev/hda3.

REMEMBER *//dev/hda2 is the swap partition by default. You probably should leave it there unless you have a good reason to move it.*

9. Uncheck the Bootable check box.

   Generally, you want only one bootable partition if you are running a single operating system. If you have a dual-boot system, both operating system partitions will need to be bootable.

10. Click the down arrow button to the right of the Mounted On field, and then select the file system you want to create on this partition from the drop-down box. For this example, select /home.

2

11. Edit the size of the partition using the arrow buttons next to the partition size field. Then click OK.

    The window closes, and the main partition screen (shown in Figure 2-13) reappears. Your new partition, /dev/hda3, should appear in the disk tree.

12. Repeat this process for each partition you want to create. As a rule, you should not need to create any other bootable partitions unless you plan to install a second operating system on the same computer.

13. Click Next when you have created all the partitions you want.

    You will return to the main installation sequence at step 11, as described previously.

CHAPTER 3

The X Window System

Many people who have had little or no exposure to Linux or other UNIX-derived operating systems think that Linux can be used only with a *command-line interface*, in which the user types (often arcane) commands at a prompt to get things done. It's the same interface that computers running the DOS operating system used. While this interface is still available with Linux—and many users prefer command-line interfaces—almost all current Linux distributions include a UNIX-based *graphical user interface*, or GUI, called the *X Window System*.

The X Window System is as old as the Microsoft Windows or Apple Macintosh operating systems, which also use GUIs. The X Window System was developed at MIT in 1984, the same year that saw the debut of the Macintosh computer and long before the first release of Windows.

| NOTE | *All three of these systems owe an immense debt to the research done at Xerox's Palo Alto Research Center (PARC) in the 1970s.* |

What Makes the X Window System Different?

What sets the X Window System apart from the Macintosh and Windows GUIs? There are a few major differences:

- *X is not part of the core operating system.* Linux can work perfectly well without it; in fact, to conserve system resources, several kinds of machines shouldn't run X, such as machines operating only as *servers* instead of as *workstations*. (A server provides services to other computers; a workstation is used for individual work.) Like any GUI, X consumes a healthy portion of system resources. Because X is run separately from the main operating system, the likelihood of a problem with X crashing the system is reduced. Should X crash, it can be taken care of separately without having to restart the computer. This is not true of Windows or MacOS, in which the tight integration between GUI and operating system can result in unrecoverable system crashes.

- *From the very beginning, the X Window System was designed with networks in mind.* The base of the X Window System is a server to which various applications can connect, as clients. This allows, for example, a graphics application running on Machine A to be displayed on the monitor of Machine B. This level of network functionality is beginning to be included in other operating systems, such as Windows NT, but has been part of the X Window System from the beginning.

■ X provides only the basic graphical functions. The details of a given user interface are provided by a *window manager,* which handles individual configurations and provides the "look and feel" of the user interface. (Window managers—and their successors, called *desktops*—are covered in Chapter 5, "Desktops Versus Window Managers.") It is possible to run any one of a number of window managers or desktops on top of the basic X Window System; this allows a great range of customization in the appearance and use of the Linux operating system.

Corel Linux uses the X Window System; Corel has chosen to use a specialized version of the popular KDE desktop as its user interface. We cover KDE in detail in Part II of this book. KDE is a system that includes a window manager and a variety of advanced features; these features provide a graphical user interface that has proved quite friendly and familiar to users of Windows or MacOS who are making the transition to Linux.

Most of the X Window System's features will be properly configured automatically when you install Corel Linux. In this chapter, we show you the basics of X configuration, so you'll know what it looks like and how to use some of the unique features found in X if you want to configure your own installation further.

> **CAUTION** *If you make a mistake while configuring X, you can actually harm your computer's hardware. It's one of the few places where you can really cause trouble with Linux. X is immensely complicated, so you won't want—or need—to do much with it directly. Still, it's critical to have a basic understanding of X and how it works with Linux to understand various things that your computer does automatically.*

The Basic Structure of the X Window System

The X Window System is not actually a program; it doesn't produce output or perform a certain set of tasks whenever you request them. Rather, it is a *standard,* maintained by an organization called the X Consortium (find its Web site at `http://www.x.org`). This standard is a set of rules by which all graphical display functions must abide. The current specification for X is called X11R6, and it is the sixth revision of the eleventh version of X.

Corel Linux, and most other Linux distributions, use a particular implementation of the X Window System called XFree86. As the name implies, XFree86 is a free implementation of the X standard and is designed to run on Intel *x*86-series hardware: the 386, 486, and Pentium chip series. There are many other implementations of X, some free and some commercial. These versions run on almost every kind of computer and under many different operating systems, including Microsoft Windows, Macintosh, IBM's OS/2, and Amiga.

> **TIP**   *Learn more than you ever thought you could know about XFree86 at its Web site, located at* `http://www.xfree86.org`.

The X Window System is based on a *client-server architecture*. Such architectures are common in today's networked computer environments. For example, when you get your e-mail, you will usually connect your computer to a remote *mail server*, a central computer that handles electronic mail for a number of *clients*. A diagram of this architecture is shown in Figure 3-1.

X operates in this way. Even though it seems that the situation is reversed, it isn't, really—it just appears to be backward. When you use X on your workstation, you are actually running an X server on that machine. The service that your machine provides is the basic display function: drawing windows on the screen, interpreting mouse and keyboard actions, and so forth. The various programs that you use—word processors, Web browsers, solitaire games, and others—whether they're on your computer or across a network such as the Internet, act as clients that connect to the X server and use its display services, and thus appear on your screen. It may seem odd that a client program would need to connect to a server on the same machine, but there is really no logical reason to treat the local machine differently than any other machine on the same network. This client-server

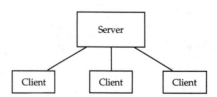

FIGURE 3-1   The client-server architecture uses a central computer to serve several clients

3

architecture allows the process of drawing the display to be separated from the application and from the operating system.

There are a number of different X server programs, each suited to a particular type of video hardware. When you installed Corel Linux, the installation program attempted to determine the video hardware used by your computer so it could install the appropriate X server onto your computer. The information about that particular X server, along with certain information about your video hardware, monitor, keyboard, and mouse, are all recorded in the file /etc/X11/Xf86config. When the X Window System is started, it reads this file to get the information necessary for the system to operate correctly.

The X Window System on Corel Linux

Historically, installing and configuring the X Window System has been one of the hardest parts of running a Linux system. However, thanks to a great deal of development effort over the past year or two, it is now possible for video hardware to be autodetected and X to be appropriately configured for that hardware, as part of the regular installation process. In fact, Corel Linux actually uses X during the installation process! When you start your Corel Linux computer, X starts automatically; you don't have to start it by hand. You'll see a graphical login window after the initial startup screen fades.

The heart of Corel Linux, and the program responsible for putting that login window on the screen, is a program called `kdm`, the K Display Manager. `kdm` is a replacement for `xdm`, the X Display Manager, a manager that is the default display manager for XFree86. `kdm`, however, works more closely with KDE and provides a better bond between the X Window System and the GUI.

> **NOTE**
>
> *If X does not start when you start your computer, the odds are good that you have a video card that's not supported by XFree86. This is highly unlikely, since XFree86 provides servers for the vast majority of popular video cards in use today, but it is possible. If this is the case, there's not much you can do without replacing your video card. You might be able to get the current card to work with a commercial X server, but it's likely to be a lot cheaper to simply buy a supported video card. To find out whether or not your card is compatible, consult the Linux Hardware Compatibility FAQ at* `http://www.linuxdoc.org/HOWTO/Hardware-HOWTO-6.html,` *and the XFree86 FAQ at* `http://www.xfree86.org/FAQ/.`

Dealing with Basic Configuration Problems

If your Corel Linux installation process went smoothly, XFree86 should be configured properly for your system. Test the installation by powering on the machine, making sure X starts (do you get the graphical login screen?), and checking that the keyboard and mouse work as expected. If everything seems 9to be working properly, the installation was successful.

One thing you may need to do is to adjust the settings on your monitor. If the display seems to be cut off at the edges, or if black space is around the edges of the display, use the sizing and positioning controls on your monitor to adjust the display so that the entire screen is filled but no part of the display is hanging off the edge of the screen. A lot of people leave a thick black margin around the display (probably the same margin that appeared when the monitor was first used), and we don't understand why; monitors are designed to give clear displays all the way to the edge of the glass. If you leave a margin, you might as well have saved a few bucks and bought a smaller monitor.

You may have a sporadic problem with X "hanging" or "freezing." This can happen for a number of reasons and is usually not indicative of a serious problem. If this happens to you, press the CTRL, ALT, and BACKSPACE keys all at the same time. This should kill and restart X.

Troubleshooting for the X Window System is covered more fully in Chapter 4, "Troubleshooting Your Installation."

CHAPTER 4

Troubleshooting Your Installation

The installation procedure for Corel Linux, as we described it in Chapter 2, "Installing Corel Linux," is fairly foolproof. Provided that your hardware is supported under Linux (see Chapter 19, "Dealing with Hardware"), there isn't much that should go wrong when you install the operating system.

In this chapter, however, we have attempted to identify those things that might potentially cause problems or confusion during installation. We also offer some clues that might help you avoid or solve your problems. In general, reading every screen carefully during installation, and keeping track of things you've selected or chosen not to select, will keep your installation running smoothly. It's also handy to keep a notepad and pen close by, so you can take notes if necessary.

Problems with Initial Installation of Corel Linux

When installing Corel Linux for the first time, you'll probably have no trouble at all. Before you begin, read Chapter 2 carefully and make sure that you have both the Corel Linux CD and boot disk handy. If you downloaded Corel Linux, rather than purchasing it on CD, you'll need to pay attention; you may need to redownload if something happens and you can't get the installation to work.

If you downloaded the operating system, you will need to burn the OS onto a CD before you can install it.

"How do I change the boot device in my computer's BIOS setup?"

In this case, you should first find the motherboard manual that came with your computer. Look for a section called "BIOS Setup," "Setup Menus," or something similar. Your motherboard manual is the authoritative source for information about your specific computer. If you don't have one, see if you can find the manufacturer's Web site; many hardware manufacturers now make their manuals available online.

The motherboard manufacturer is probably not the same as the company that built your computer. That is, looking on the Gateway Web site may not tell you anything about the motherboards used in Gateway PCs. Sometimes a call to tech support at the computer's manufacturer can get you the right info, or it will be in the manual that came with your PC.

However, you may have to take the cover off the PC and look directly at the motherboard if you can't find a manufacturer name in any other way.

If you've exhausted all avenues of possibility and you simply can't get a copy of the motherboard documentation, you'll have to hunt through the various menus of the BIOS program until you find the appropriate setting. There is, unfortunately, no standard for the way in which BIOS setup menus are organized. In the two motherboard manuals we had handy while writing this chapter, one defines the boot sequence in the Advanced CMOS Setup menu, and the other uses the BIOS Features Setup menu. The bottom line is that you'll have to look through each menu until you find something that looks promising. The boot sequence is a basic parameter, though, and should not be hidden in an exotic location among the menus.

As a last resort, try making a boot disk as described in Chapter 2. Insert it into the floppy drive and reboot the machine. Most motherboards are set up so that the floppy drive is the first boot device; if nothing is in the floppy drive, the motherboard moves to the boot sector of the hard drive as the second device. If you have a boot disk in the drive when the machine is started, it will probably boot from the disk without you having to change anything.

"Halfway through the installation program, I realized that I made a mistake in a previous step."

During the Corel Linux installation process, each screen has a Back button. You can use that button to return to the previous step and edit it, if necessary. If you need to, you can step all the way back to the initial screen using the Back buttons. When you realize you've made a mistake, or you have changed your mind about some aspect of the installation, simply go back and fix it, and then continue the installation from that point. You can do this at any point during installation until you click the Install button on the final screen.

> **NOTE** *Nothing is done to the system until you click Install. This includes any modifications you make to the partition table, so even though Install Express doesn't show the partitions you've created or deleted, the changes are not physically made on the hard disk until you click Install.*

After you click that button and the installation has begun, there isn't much you can do if you realize you've made an error or you've changed your mind.

It's never a good idea to stop an installation while it's in process, so let it finish. Then, simply reinstall Corel Linux. As long as you haven't put any new data on the computer, you won't lose anything but the time a second installation takes.

"Installation seems to be taking an awfully long time."

You probably have a slow computer. The only cure is being patient (and adding some more system memory when you get a chance). If you think that the installation has stopped—you went out for lunch when the progress bar was at 24 percent, and it was at 28 percent when you got home—take a look at the drive lights on the front of your computer. Both the hard drive light and the CD-ROM light should be flickering. If both of them stop blinking for a long period of time, something may have gone wrong.

However, what constitutes "a long period of time" is largely dependent on the speed of the slowest component of your computer. If you have a very slow CD-ROM drive, for example, it may take a long time for the various bits of data to be read from it, and thus the installation is slow.

If you're convinced that the installation has failed, there is not much you can do but shut off the machine and try again. Be aware, though, that if you selected the Scan For Bad Blocks During Install option on the final installation screen, the installation process will take far longer and will appear to stop at times. This is because the setup program is examining every sector of the physical hard drive for errors or damage. Despite the time it takes, though, we still recommend selecting this option; it alerts you if any part of your hard disk is unusable.

Problems After Installation

Once you have gotten Corel Linux installed properly, you may still find some lingering trouble as you use the operating system. The most common problems are those that happen at startup; in some cases, they're not anything that can be fixed. In other cases, the problem is simply a lack of available resources; and in still other cases, it's the result of the previous Corel Linux session. Following are the two most common complaints after a successful installation.

"The first time I boot my machine after installing Corel Linux, it takes forever to start."

When you boot up the computer for the first time after installing, Corel Linux must configure a number of items before it can work properly. This can take some time, and it is normal for the LILO splash screen to display the "Configuring System" message for what seems like forever. We do not recommend that you try to reboot the computer during this process; some configurations may not yet be complete, and if they are corrupted, it may cause trouble in subsequent boots.

If the machine has been idle for much longer than you think it should be (hours, not minutes), you may have no choice but to reboot. If you do this, select the Expert option the next time the LILO splash screen appears. This turns off the installation splash screen and permits you to see exactly which step in the boot process is causing the system to hang up.

"Even though Corel Linux is installed correctly, it still seems to take a long time to boot."

If you're not using DHCP to obtain a dynamic IP number from your Internet Service Provider (as explained in Chapter 20, "Networking"), you may experience a delay as the DHCP client attempts to connect to a nonexistent server. To correct this, log in as root and delete the file /etc/rc2.d/S13dhcpd; or open the Control Center by selecting Network | TCP/IP, and then select Static IP.

If you are using DHCP, the machine may be attempting to access your DHCP server before the network has come up. To fix this, rename the /etc/rc2.d/S13dhcpcd file to /etc/rc2.d/S19dhcpcd. If that does not correct the problem, remove the file altogether and run `dhcpcd` by hand after you have logged in.

> **NOTE** *After you've read through the rest of this book, especially Part IV, it is a good idea to go through /etc/rc2.d and remove all of the links you don't need. This will conserve system resources by not starting processes that you don't use and will help the boot process to move more quickly.*

You may also experience delays after a reboot if you did not shut down Corel Linux properly. When Linux is booted after a sudden shutdown, it must verify the integrity of the entire file system. This involves taking an inventory of every file on the disk, and this takes time. However, if you shut down Linux properly every time you need to do so, you won't have to worry about it. We explain the shutdown process in Chapter 10, "Start Up and Shut Down."

Problems with the X Window System

Unfortunately, if you experience trouble with the X Window System, there's not much likelihood of the answer being brief or easy. X is immensely complicated;

O'Reilly publishes a major series on X, and it consists of more than ten volumes. Luckily, the chances that you'll have a problem with X are very slender—unless, of course, you do something to the X configuration files yourself.

Problems you've caused may be recoverable if you quickly consult the XFree86 FAQ at `http://www.xfree86.org/FAQ/`, or by reading the Configuration FAQ at `http://www.xfree86.org/3.3.5/Config.html` before you start messing with the configuration files. In the case of X, we strongly recommend that you listen to more "official" solutions, rather than soliciting advice from those whose experience with X is only fractionally greater than yours.

> **CAUTION**   *You should be especially careful of X configuration files that helpful persons send to you. One person's configuration file is not going to work on someone else's system, 999 times out of 1000. In fact, you could cause more problems than you started with if you use other people's files without knowing what's in them.*

Other Problems

Any other problems you experience are likely to be problems with specific processes or programs. If you attempt to launch a program from an icon or a menu and it won't start, try opening a terminal window and launching the program from the command line. You can usually get some idea of what's happening from the error messages that print to the screen. We also recommend that you read the chapters in this book that pertain to that program, should it be a part of the operating system.

If you don't find the help you need, consult Appendix C, "Linux Resources on the Internet," for pointers to the wide variety of Internet resources. The Internet is the single best source of up-to-date support for Linux problems. Web pages, newsgroups, and mailing lists devoted to Linux and its various components are plentiful, and chances are that someone else has had the same problem that you are experiencing.

PART II

The K Desktop Environment

CHAPTER 5

Desktops Versus Window Managers

Part of what makes Corel's Linux distribution so unique is its close integration with the *K Desktop Environment,* or KDE. KDE will run on almost any kind of UNIX system, but it has found its most comfortable niche as a desktop for Linux systems. KDE works together with the X Window System to provide the sort of computing experience that Windows and Macintosh users are accustomed to. So, if you're coming from a Windows or Mac world, KDE will make your transition to Linux a little less intimidating.

> **NOTE**
> *KDE is one of the two dominant desktop environments available to Linux users. The other is called Gnome. It's unlikely that you'll run Gnome with the Corel Linux distribution, since KDE is so tightly integrated into the Corel packages. Still, it's useful to know that Gnome exists, especially if you become interested in the Linux movement and want to participate in online discussions or join a local user group.*

KDE, like Linux itself, is the product of a great deal of volunteer labor. The Open Source movement, as described in Chapter 1, "Why Linux, and Why Corel Linux?," allows software to be tested by thousands of users, many of whom are motivated by finding flaws and bugs. This makes Open Source software more robust and gets it improved more frequently than that with closed code. If you find that you enjoy KDE and want to help with the project, check out the KDE Web pages.

> **TIP**
> *Interested in learning more about KDE? We strongly suggest that you spend some time looking at the KDE Web site, located at* `http://www.kde.org`*. You can also access site mirrors around the world if you're having trouble accessing the main site located in Germany. The KDE site contains FAQs (Frequently Asked Questions), archives of downloadable programs, frequent updates on new applications, and other KDE news.*

There's always room for new volunteers, whether in the technical programming aspects or in more user-oriented ways, such as translation or documentation. If you're not interested in volunteering, the KDE Web pages are still a great resource; they contain a file archive of the latest programs and applications, frequently updated news items about KDE, and an extensive FAQ. However, Corel Linux includes enhancements that are not part of the standard KDE distribution, so you may need to consult Corel-specific documentation for some questions.

The Basic Functions of KDE

To understand why the KDE desktop is different from what has come before, we first need to talk a bit about how you and your computer work together. In Chapter 3, "The X Window System," we describe how the X Window System provides the basic graphics capabilities for creating displays on your monitor. It provides software drivers for various pieces of video hardware, and it has a programming interface that allows you to create graphical applications. If you don't run X, you cannot have a graphical interface for any software on the computer.

The X Window System is not, however, what you see when you boot up your Corel Linux computer. X is a mechanism that permits the graphical user interface, or GUI, to work. X itself does not control the "look and feel" of the user interface; that's the job of the window manager. X is the middle part of the GUI sandwich: the bottom layer is Linux, which operates the computer; the middle layer is X, which controls the graphics capabilities; and the final layer is the GUI, in this case KDE.

A *window manager* is a set of software functions that control how windows are drawn on the screens, how decorations such as title bars and icons are displayed, and how the mouse interacts with the various images on the screen. If you've worked with Linux before, you may have tried out some of the many window managers available: fvwm, AfterStep, BlackBox, WindowMaker, Enlightenment, and others. Each window manager has its own unique look, its own level of user configurability, its own menu system, and its own style of behavior. Some are far more complicated than others; Enlightenment, for example, lets the user configure just about every aspect of the window manager, whereas BlackBox permits configuration of only the most basic functions.

KDE has its own window manager as well, called KWM (for K Window Manager). KWM is highly configurable, and it's designed for easy use, like most of the KDE components. In Part II, "The K Desktop Environment," we'll describe KWM and its uses. We cover KWM especially in Chapter 8, "Advanced KDE Techniques."

> **NOTE** *Just as KDE stands for the K Desktop Environment, many of its components' names are prefixed with K. The K doesn't stand for anything; it's a remnant of the years when programmers named their projects with single letters.*

What's a Desktop Environment?

Welcome to the wonderfully confusing world of user environments. At the start of this chapter, we called KDE a desktop environment, but then we described a window manager and noted that KDE has a window manager as well. It is extremely easy to get mixed up with all these different terms to describe the graphical user interface, and it doesn't help that people often use them imprecisely in ordinary conversation. So what exactly do we mean when we say that KDE is a desktop environment?

What Does a Desktop Comprise?

A desktop environment is a couple of things, actually. The first aspect of a desktop environment (which we're just going to call a *desktop* from here on out) is that it provides certain kinds of functions: the ability to click and drag files from one folder window to another or from one application to another, for example. The X Window System doesn't provide these functions, so it is up to the desktop to provide them.

The second aspect of a desktop is that it provides a complete suite of programs designed to make it easier for the user to access various kinds of data and applications. For example, one of the main features of KDE is the *Panel*, shown in the following illustration. The KDE Panel runs along the bottom of the screen (or along the left side, if you prefer). It contains icons that represent programs, currently open applications, links to menus, and various other handy items. All you have to do is click.

If you've used Windows 95 or Windows 98, you're already familiar with a similar taskbar. Strictly speaking, the KDE Panel is not a necessary part of running Linux or even KDE; you can launch programs in several other ways, including from the command line or File Manager. The designers of KDE, however, felt that the Panel was an important part of the entire desktop.

| NOTE | *You might choose between File Manager and the command line to run a given application for a number of reasons. Many UNIX-derived programs have optional features that can be accessed only with command-line options. As we explain in Chapter 16, "The Administrator's Tools: Shells and Text Editors," it is possible to combine UNIX commands into compound instructions to the operating system. Using File Manager is also an option; it's especially useful when you didn't choose to place a program in the Start menu.* |

These two aspects of a desktop combine to create much of what we now think of as the "computing experience." How the screen looks, how the mouse behaves, how we access applications and other data, how we navigate the computer's file system, along with a host of other details, give our interactions with computers a certain texture. Most users don't think a lot about these background issues, but when someone expresses a strong allegiance to a particular operating system, desktop environment, or window manager, it is often this texture that provides the basis for those strong feelings.

5

What's Different About Corel's Version of KDE?

Corel Linux uses a modified version of KDE. What's modified about it? Well, for one thing, Corel Linux installs and runs KDE by default. This means you don't have to select and install a desktop or window manager before you start working with Corel Linux; KDE is there from the very start.

Another modification is that Corel added some "Corel-flavored" twists to the standard KDE distribution. You see the most obvious of these Corel adaptations on the graphical login screen, where the Corel Linux logo runs across the top of the login panel itself. Corel WordPerfect is part of the Corel Linux distribution, as is Netscape, and both are in the default desktop configuration; but this is not the case with regular distributions of KDE.

NOTE *If you downloaded Corel Linux from the Corel Web site, WordPerfect is not included with the distribution.*

Corel has also redesigned several of the standard KDE applications. For example, the Corel File Manager will look especially familiar to those who have worked with Windows 95's Explorer.

NOTE *Throughout this section, we will use the Corel Linux terms to refer to KDE elements of Corel Linux. See the sidebar "KDE Naming Conventions" for more information on program and applications names.*

KDE Naming Conventions

In its work with the KDE development team, Corel has adapted some elements of KDE so much that they deserve new names. For example, the KDE File Manager has been replaced with the Corel File Manager. In this book, we use the Corel Linux names for KDE elements, since this is a book about Corel Linux. However, we also encourage you to consult Internet resources and other books about KDE, where you may not find the Corel term for the item you're working with. If the general KDE term for a particular element is significantly different from the Corel term, we let you know with a paragraph labeled "Reminder."

Just remember, if the name is different in the Corel Linux distribution, chances are that the element itself has changed slightly from the standard KDE element. Don't be surprised if you get answers that don't quite work for Corel-specific KDE material when you query in a general KDE forum; you'll still be able to use the answers, although perhaps your screen will look different from that described in the response.

Finally, Corel has added some unique goodies to the basic Linux and KDE distributions. You'll find useful packages like Corel Update, which makes installing and upgrading software a breeze, and Event Viewer, which allows easy and intuitive access to system logs. Neither of these programs is available with the regular KDE distribution. With this tight integration of standard KDE features and the additional features selected and developed for the Corel Linux distribution, the Corel Linux desktop provides easy access to the power of Linux while maintaining the ease of use to which Macintosh and Windows users are accustomed.

Components of the Desktop

The first few pages of this chapter have been somewhat abstract, and we apologize. It's important, though, to understand what you're dealing with when you work in a desktop environment. KDE is a robust and integrated way to work, but it's still an overlay that covers the basic Linux operating system. You don't *need* KDE; it just makes things easier. If you haven't already read Chapter 3, please do so; if you have a grasp of X, you'll have a better understanding of how KDE works and how to fix problems.

In this section, we'll leave the abstract behind and spend some time looking at the KDE desktop. What we describe here is the default installation of KDE, the one you get when you install Corel Linux directly from the CD. In later chapters of Part II, you'll learn how to configure the desktop with various themes, change icons, and move basic KDE elements to convenient spaces. We recommend that you read through this chapter before beginning to tinker, though, just to get a good feel for the basics.

When you first log into your Corel Linux machine, you will see a desktop that looks like the one shown in Figure 5-1. The desktop is everything you see on the monitor: the KDE Panel, backgrounds, icons, and so on. However, the desktop is also the colored expanse that underlies all the other elements.

The desktop in KDE is usually static; it doesn't do much. However, if you put the mouse cursor over an empty part of the desktop and right-click, you'll see a

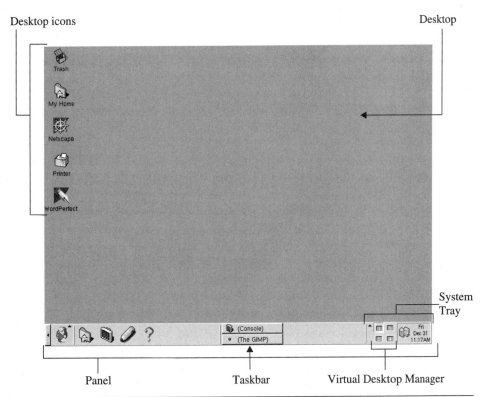

FIGURE 5-1   The KDE desktop's default appearance is neutral and straightforward

context menu with various options, including Logout, Help, Lock Screen, and a number of ways to arrange your open windows.

Desktop Icons

Running along the left side of your desktop are icons you'll use to launch programs or manage files more quickly than is possible with the menu system. You can create other icons for frequently used programs. The default icons are discussed in the sections that follow.

TRASH   Like the Recycle Bin in Windows or the Trash icon on a Macintosh, the Trash icon in KDE links to a folder in which you can store files you wish to delete later.

CAUTION   *When you are ready to empty the Trash folder, make sure you really want to delete the files contained in it. Unlike MacOS or Windows, Linux cannot recover deleted files after they've been trashed.*

MY HOME   This provides a quick way to open File Manager. If you use the My Home icon to launch File Manager, it will open to your home directory (assuming you're logged in as a user, and not as root). There is no clear advantage to doing it this way, other than it saves you a couple of mouse clicks over using the menus to open File Manager.

NETSCAPE   This icon launches Netscape. Corel Linux installs Netscape as part of the basic installation process, so you don't need to do anything special to set up a Web browser.

NOTE   *Netscape is your only option for a graphical Web browser under Linux since Microsoft Explorer is not available for the Linux OS, nor are the browsers unique to Macintosh. You do have the UNIX text-based browser* lynx *available as part of the default installation, but if you wish to view any graphic elements, you'll need to use Netscape. The File Manager also has limited Web browser capabilities. Remember that you can use various Linux tools for e-mail or newsgroup reading. Linux tools, and KDE-specific tools, are much more powerful and precise. We cover Internet applications thoroughly in Chapter 9, "Using the Internet with Corel Linux."*

PRINTER   This icon launches the printer utility, which gives you the opportunity to configure a particular printer attached to your computer (or to your network, if you're running Corel Linux on a networked system). You can't print a document or file directly by using the Printer icon; you'll have to issue a print command from within an application or at a terminal prompt.

WORDPERFECT   This icon launches the WordPerfect word processor. WordPerfect installs automatically when you install Corel Linux, if you purchased a retail version of the distribution. WordPerfect is not included in the download version.

The KDE Panel

Along the bottom of your screen, as you saw in the first illustration in this chapter, is the KDE Panel. The Panel is really the core of KDE's user experience. By default, it contains icons that represent frequently used programs or commands; if it doesn't contain the items you use often, you can add the things you use and remove things you don't use. Some people prefer to use Panel icons instead of desktop icons for frequently used applications, and that's certainly possible. You can also move the location of the KDE Panel or collapse it and reopen it only when you need to use it.

As you read through this section, you may wonder why you see some of these buttons and not others. If this is the case, check to see that the KDE Panel is at its full size; if your monitor is too small for the screen resolution you're using, the Panel automatically layers icons in order to fit. It may be a good idea to remove icons you don't use much to get the KDE Panel neatly located on your desktop.

PANEL COLLAPSE BAR   Located at the left end of the KDE Panel, this slim textured bar allows you to collapse the Panel or reopen it to its full length. Just click it; the Panel slides behind the bar you've clicked and will remain there until you click it again. If you like to work in full-screen mode when you're using an application, you will probably want to collapse the Panel so that it doesn't obscure what you're working on.

APPLICATION STARTER   The Application Starter icon launches the Start menu, which works like the Windows 95 and Windows 98 Start menu. You can launch programs, navigate files, or execute commands via the Start menu. In many of the processes we describe in this book, we begin with

"Open the Start menu." Just click the Application Starter icon to open the menu, and then continue with your selections from that point.

FILE MANAGER   In the previous section of this chapter, we described the My Home desktop icon, which launches File Manager opened to your home directory. If you prefer, you can use this KDE Panel button to launch File Manager instead. When you're logged in as a user, the File Manager will show you the contents of your home directory. When you're logged in as root, the File Manager displays the entire directory structure of the computer.

TERMINAL EMULATOR   Use this icon to launch a *terminal window* on top of your desktop. A terminal window is a simple window containing only a command-line prompt. You can use this prompt to issue any text commands that you'd issue in a text-only environment or to run nongraphical Linux programs. The terminal window is a handy shortcut; use it, and you don't have to log out of KDE to a shell prompt to do text-based work. In fact, because Corel Linux uses a graphical login screen, you need to use the terminal emulator to do any work at all from a command prompt.

TEXT EDITOR   Click this button to launch KDE's Text Editor, a basic text editor that works like a minimal word processor. You won't be able to do much formatting in Text Editor, but you can get the basics down. For full-fledged word processing, use WordPerfect; for quick notes or plain-text files, Text Editor is just fine. We'll cover other UNIX text editors in Chapter 16.

HELP   The Help button opens KDE's extensive online help system. Like most other operating systems, KDE provides a series of pages that offer tips and solutions to problems. The help pages contain hyperlinks that move you quickly through the help system to an answer. You'll also find that the help pages in individual applications use the standard KDE help format, so help will always look the same. KDE help does not have a comprehensive index function though, so you'll have to click around until you find the page you want.

VIRTUAL DESKTOP MANAGER   The Virtual Desktop Manager icon is actually a set of several very small icons stacked together in the space of a regular KDE Panel icon. Virtual Desktop Manager controls KDE's virtual desktops, a concept we discuss later in this chapter. The 1 button is likely depressed on your screen, since 1 is the default desktop. You can also right-click this icon for a quick look at what each desktop contains.

TASKBAR AND SYSTEM TRAY   These two items are described in the next sections of this chapter. They're actually applets, or small running programs, that are *docked* (anchored) to the Panel without actually being part of the Panel itself.

 CLOCK/DATE   The final item on the Panel is the date and time. This is handy, especially if you don't wear a watch while you're on the computer. KDE gets the date and time from your system settings, so if it's incorrect, you need to configure your basic Linux settings to show the correct date and time. (You should do this anyway, as it's important to have accurate timestamps on files and in logs.)

Components of the Taskbar

Within the KDE Panel, you'll see the rectangular buttons of the Taskbar; two Taskbar buttons, labeled Console and the GIMP, are shown in Figure 5-1. The Taskbar contains an icon for each window that is currently open, whether or not it is active. (The *active window* is the window in which you're currently working; you'll also hear this window referred to as *having the focus*.) The icons are labeled with the window's name—usually the name of the application running in the window. You can configure the Taskbar's appearance as you can the rest of the Panel; see Chapter 7, "Configuring Your Desktop with the Control Center," for more information on KDE configuration.

Left-click on a Taskbar icon to bring that window to the foreground and make it active. Right-click on a Taskbar icon to open a context menu containing various options that can be applied to that window. The Taskbar makes it possible to run several applications at the same time and still maintain a clean desktop. You can accomplish much the same goal by using virtual desktops, described a bit later in this chapter, but the Taskbar allows you to keep all your windows on the same desktop.

The System Tray Applet

As noted earlier, the KDE Panel contains icons that represent various applications and programs. It also contains various applets that have been attached, or *docked into*, the Panel. The most obvious of these is the System Tray, which shows icons for programs that are running in the background—that is, programs that you don't work with directly but that you should know are active. The System Tray also contains the date and time icon; when no background programs are active, you'll see only the date and time information in the System Tray.

Virtual Desktop Manager and Virtual Desktops

When we described the KDE Panel, we showed the Desktop Manager icon and mentioned that the Manager represents the *virtual desktops* available to you. Four virtual desktops are shown in the illustration here.

 A virtual desktop can be difficult to visualize; in a very real sense, using the desktop metaphor to describe the computer workspace is already a "virtual desktop" concept. In KDE, however, the term *virtual desktop* is used to describe a set of identical desktops that you can switch among by clicking the appropriate desktop icon in Virtual Desktop Manager. You can run different programs on each desktop, but your personal configuration of KDE looks the same on all of them. You don't have to use virtual desktops to use either Corel Linux or KDE; they're useful tools, but they're not critical. Certainly, people using MacOS or Windows get by with one desktop. Virtual desktops are simply an option.

The logical question at this point is "Why?" It's a question of organization, mostly. We find it helpful to use virtual desktops to manage different kinds of programs. For example, when we're writing about Corel Linux in WordPerfect on Desktop 1, we may want to have Netscape open to the Corel home page. It's annoying to keep minimizing Netscape and reopening it, or to layer the windows, so we open Netscape on Desktop 2 and use Virtual Desktop Manager buttons to switch between desktops.

> **TIP**   *Virtual desktops are also incredibly useful if you have a bad procrastination habit and like to waste time playing on the Internet. Open your fun applications on separate desktops from your work applications; they'll still run, but you won't be constantly distracted.*

Use the four buttons of Virtual Desktop Manager to move among your desktops. You can also click the small arrow to the left of the Desktop Manager buttons to open a miniature graphical pane that shows all four desktops at once. Click the appropriate pane to open that desktop.

 This graphic representation makes the concept a little easier to understand. If you're having trouble with it, you can either ignore the concept altogether and use Desktop 1 exclusively, or you can open a different program on each desktop and view it in the graphical pane as a conceptual aid.

> **TIP**   *If you decide that you really hate virtual desktops, you can configure KDE to show you only two desktops. KDE's minimum is two; you can always choose to ignore the second one. We cover that option in Chapter 8.*

CHAPTER 6

Corel File Manager

B ecause Linux is based on UNIX, and UNIX was originally a text-based
system, it is entirely possible to navigate through your directories, and
manage your files, without a file manager of any sort. Basic command-line tools
allow you to create, move, copy, concatenate, edit, and delete files with simple
text commands. Most people who have worked with UNIX or Linux for any
reasonable length of time, and even many people new to UNIX-based operating
systems, find that the standard text commands offer a quick and simple way to
manage files and data.

Still, graphical tools give the file management process a more intuitive feel.
It is simply easier to understand the structure of directories if they're laid out in
an intelligible visual format rather than a long string of filenames that run off the
screen before you can see them. Most people understand abstract data better when
it is presented visually, and file management is no different. If we conceive of our
file systems in spatial terms, then it seems "more real" to drag a file from one
directory to another. Most modern graphical user interfaces use a visual file
manager, and Corel Linux is no exception.

Corel File Manager Basics

Corel Linux uses Corel File Manager, or CFM, which resembles Windows 95/98's
Explorer. If you're new to Linux, coming from a Windows environment, much of
the material explained in this chapter will be familiar to you.

You can use File Manager to do just about anything with your system files,
whether they are applications, configuration files, or data files. In fact, you may
find it takes longer to read this chapter than it takes you to figure out how File
Manager works since its design is so straightforward.

There are three ways to access File Manager. In fact, you can quickly open File
Manager in more ways than any other component of Corel Linux. This should give
you some idea of the importance of a graphical file manager! Use one of the
following methods to open File Manager before continuing with the chapter:

■ Click the File Manager icon in the KDE Panel.

Windows 95/98 Users

If you have chosen Corel Linux as your first Linux distribution, and your previous computer experience is with Windows 95 or Windows 98, you probably skimmed much of this chapter thinking "Hey, I know that already." Good for you! We suggest that you look over the display configuration options, as well as File Manager's Internet capabilities, but you're probably already set to use basic File Manager if you used the Windows Explorer regularly. If you preferred to use the My Computer desktop icon and open separate folder windows for each directory, you would probably benefit from thoroughly reading this chapter.

If you skipped straight from Windows 3.1 to Corel Linux, you will probably find File Manager somewhat familiar. If you came straight from DOS, you may actually find yourself popping open terminal windows for that comforting command-line interface—but then, if you came straight from DOS, this is probably not your first UNIX-based box.

6

Macintosh Users

Mac users have a bit more to learn since you are migrating not only to a new operating system but to a new kind of computer. It may be to your best benefit to jump straight in and treat everything as a wholly new experience, rather than to look for the few similarities between MacOS and KDE/Corel Linux.

That said, here's a bit of tinkering to get File Manager looking a bit more like the Macintosh Finder. While you should play with all the options in the View menu, we especially recommend making these two changes:

■ Deselect the Tree option, making the File Manager window one big pane.

■ Select the Large Icons option, making the files appear in a horizontal format instead of a vertical one.

Think of File Manager as the equivalent of the hard drive icon at the upper right of the Mac desktop. You certainly won't mistake KDE for the MacOS, but these changes may make File Manager a little friendlier.

■ Click the My Home desktop icon.

■ Click the Application Starter icon and select File Manager from the Start menu.

Getting Around in File Manager

Now that you have File Manager open, as shown in Figure 6-1, you'll notice that the File Manager window is separated into two panes. On the left side, your

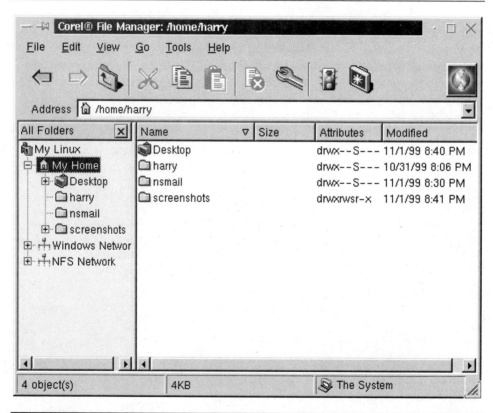

FIGURE 6-1 File Manager's tree structure shows your computer's contents in a simple visual display

computer's entire directory structure is shown. This type of display is commonly called a *tree* or *file tree* since directories branch from each other as they become more specific. On the right side, the selected directory's contents are shown.

> **NOTE** *If you come to Linux from Windows 95 or Windows 98, this is all familiar. Feel free to skip to the next section of this chapter if you have used Explorer confidently in the past.*

When you open File Manager, one directory in the left pane will be highlighted. By default, this is your home directory, labeled in File Manager as "My Home." Therefore, the right pane shows the files and subdirectories contained in the My Home directory. Were you to select another directory in the left pane, that directory's contents would show in the right pane. In other words, the right pane contains all the data collected in the directory selected in the left pane. If you want to change directories, locate the directory you wish to switch to and click its entry in the left pane. The highlighting will move to the new selection, and that directory's contents appear in the right pane.

Notice that some directories have small plus signs (+) to the immediate left of the directory name, while other directories have none. The plus sign indicates that the directory contains subdirectories; in File Manager terms, the folder with the plus sign contains other folders nested inside. If you click the plus sign (carefully because it's tiny), the directory tree expands to show those subdirectories in the left pane. Just as with the main directories, you can click a subdirectory and display its contents in the right pane. When you've expanded a directory tree in this manner, the plus sign changes to a minus sign (–). Click the minus sign to collapse the branch back to the parent directory.

> **TIP** *While it's faster to leave all directories fully expanded so that you can see all the subdirectories as well, it means that you'll have to scroll up and down the left pane, as in Figure 6-2. Once you get a handle on your directory structure, select a few directories—or perhaps only your home directory—to leave expanded and open the remainder only when you need them.*

Take another look at the File Manager window. Above the left and right panes that display the file trees, a field is labeled "Address." This field contains the full *path name* of the selected directory. *Path name* means the specific location of this directory on your hard drive, and it contains the current directory and all directories above it. In other words, the path name /home/barney means that the directory barney is a

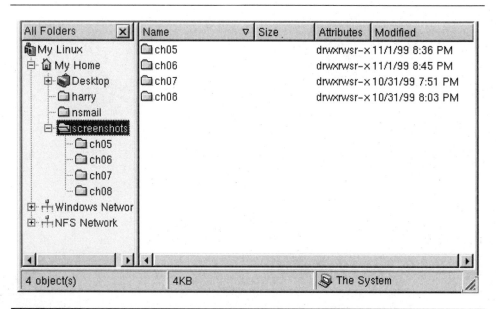

FIGURE 6-2   Expand and contract the file tree by clicking the small + and – boxes

subdirectory of the home directory, which in turn is a subdirectory of the / directory
(also known as the root directory).

TIP   *If you already know the full path name of the directory you want to view
in File Manager, just type the path name into the Address field. In some
cases, this is faster than clicking through several levels of folders in the
graphical tree.*

There are still other ways to navigate through File Manager. Above the
Address field is a comprehensive toolbar.

The arrow pointing to the left returns you to the previous directory, while the arrow pointing to the right moves you to the next level of subdirectories. (This assumes that you have both higher and lower levels of directories available; if you don't, clicking the arrows does nothing.) The folder with the arrow pointing upward takes you to the parent directory of the currently selected directory; for example, if you're currently in /home/barney, clicking this icon will take you to the /home directory.

No matter the method in which you choose to navigate File Manager, Corel Linux provides a highly intuitive way of getting around your file system. You can access any directory, file, program, or device on your computer, assuming you have the permission privileges to do so. (Some critical data is reserved only for the root user, while other material can be granted to certain regular users.) For more information on file permissions, see Chapter 12, "User Space and User Accounts."

Using File Manager for Basic Tasks

In addition to simply moving around the file system in an efficient manner, File Manager provides a single location where you can perform a number of basic operations on various files. In particular, you can use File Manager to copy files from one directory to another, delete files, rename files, and set file permissions. This section offers brief descriptions of each function, along with some tips on using File Manager more efficiently.

Copying a File

You may wish to make a copy of an important file so that you can edit the copy without compromising the original data. You may also want to copy a file from your hard drive to a floppy disk so that you have a copy on both the main computer and on the disk. Whatever your reason, copying is one of the most common file management tasks.

To copy a file within File Manager, use this process:

1. Select the directory containing the file in the left pane.

   The contents of that directory, including the file to be copied, appear in the right pane.

2. Use the mouse to click and drag the file from its position in the right pane to its new location in the left pane.

   You'll see the directories in the left pane highlight as the clicked mouse moves over them.

3. When you have reached the new destination directory, release the mouse button.

4. The file automatically copies to the new location.

You can also copy a file by using the right-click context menus. Locate the file to be copied in File Manager. Right-click the filename and select Copy from the context menu that pops open. Navigate to the new destination directory using the File Manager navigation tools and right-click an empty area of the right pane. (It doesn't matter where you right-click; File Manager will automatically place the file in the correct position.) Select Paste from the pop-up context menu. File Manager pastes a copy of the file into the new destination directory.

Deleting a File

Corel Linux and KDE have both modified traditional Linux behavior to make file deletion more like the method used in Windows and MacOS. In traditional text-based UNIX and Linux systems, you type a specific command to delete a file; in those systems, deleting a file means that it's instantly gone and irretrievable. It can be a shocking experience to realize that you inadvertently deleted an important file. Desktop environments, including KDE, Windows, and MacOS, insert an intermediate step into the delete process. When you delete a file using File Manager in Corel Linux, the file moves to the Trash folder instead of deleting automatically.

> **CAUTION** *If you delete a file using any other method than the one described next or by actually dragging the file icon to the Trash icon, you may not be able to retrieve the file should you want to get it back. If you delete a file at a command prompt, you will definitely lose it permanently. Make sure you mean to delete files before you throw them away; it can be an expensive mistake.*

To delete a file in File Manager, use the navigation tools to locate the intended file so that it appears in the right pane of the File Manager window. Right-click the file you want to delete and select Move To Trash from the context menu that pops up. A dialog box appears, asking you to confirm that you really do want to delete this file. Click the Yes button if you do and the No button if you made a mistake. When you click Yes, File Manager deletes the file *from File Manager.*

When you delete a file using this method, File Manager actually moves the file to the Trash folder instead of removing it from the hard drive. So, you won't see the file in File Manager, but it's still resident in the Trash folder. The file can be "undeleted" as long as you don't empty the Trash folder; just click and drag it into the proper folder or use File Manager to move it back. Files in the Trash can also be found in your home directory, in the $HOME/Desktop/trash folder. As soon as you empty the Trash folder, however, the file is gone for good.

| **NOTE** | *People with significant experience in other text-based operating systems may find this confusing, especially if you check your disk after moving an item to Trash and see that there is no new open space. (There won't be open space because the file has simply changed directories; it has not been deleted.) You can continue to delete files with* rm *(the UNIX remove command) inside a terminal window, but you will miss out on the ability to recover files from the Trash.* |

Renaming a File

At times, you may need to change a file's name. Perhaps you started out with a basic naming structure, and you now need to use a specific kind of name. For example, perhaps you save all your word-processed letters as Letter1, Letter2, Letter3, and so on. When you realize that you can't tell anything about them except the order in which they were written, you may want to rename the files to something more distinct: Hennig1 and Hart1, or oct1945-1 and oct1945-2, or anything else that makes sense to you.

To rename a file using File Manager, navigate through File Manager until the contents of the appropriate directory are in the right pane. Right-click the file that you want to rename and select Rename from the context menu that pops up. In the right pane, you'll see a blinking cursor appear in the filename. Type the file's new name and press ENTER. If you gave the file a new initial letter that changes its alphabetical listing, the file will move once you've pressed the ENTER key.

| **NOTE** | *Filenames must be one continuous string of characters. Multiple words, as in Windows and Macintosh, are not permitted in UNIX/Linux. If you want to use multiple words in a filename, link them with an underscore, as in my_file, or a dot, as in cheese.sandwich.recipe. Although a filename can be any length, it is generally recommended that you keep your filenames to 14 characters or less to make them easier to handle. Certain characters cannot be used in filenames because they are special characters in the UNIX command language: the most common of these characters are ! @ # $ % ^ & * ( ) ' " ? \ | ; < > ` + -. Form the habit of using only letters, numbers, underscores, and dots, and you won't have problems with filenames.* |

If you want to move the file to a different directory at the same time as you rename it, it's easier to do that by copying the file to its new location first and then using this process to rename it.

If you're comfortable with renaming and moving files at a command prompt, it's often quicker to do it that way. See Chapter 16, "The Administrator's Tools: Shells and Text Editors," for more information about managing files from the command line.

Changing a File's Permissions

File permissions are an important concept in the Linux environment. Basically, permissions are codes that tell the operating system who has access to a given file, and what kind of access they may have. There are three levels of access: user (you alone), group (defined by the system administrator), and global (everyone who has access to your machine via the Internet, a local network, or any other connection mechanism). In addition, there are three types of access: read (view only), write (make changes to a text file), and execute (run a program). Each level can have one of the three types of permissions. It is a bit confusing, so we've devoted a major part of Chapter 12 to explaining permissions.

In this chapter, we'll just tell you how to use File Manager to change the permissions on a given file. To figure out what permissions to grant, see Chapter 12 before you change anything.

CAUTION	*Pay attention to file permissions. You can inadvertently create major security headaches for yourself if you leave files more open than they need to be. Cultivate a conservative attitude when it comes to setting permissions and allocate permissions on a need-only basis.*

To change file permissions using File Manager, use the navigation tools to get the desired file to appear in the right pane. Right-click the filename and select Properties from the context menu that pops up. The Properties screen appears, as shown in Figure 6-3.

Click the Permissions tab in the Properties screen and use the check boxes on the Permissions tab to set the appropriate permissions for the selected file or directory. When you've finished, click OK. The Properties screen will close, and the new file permissions take effect.

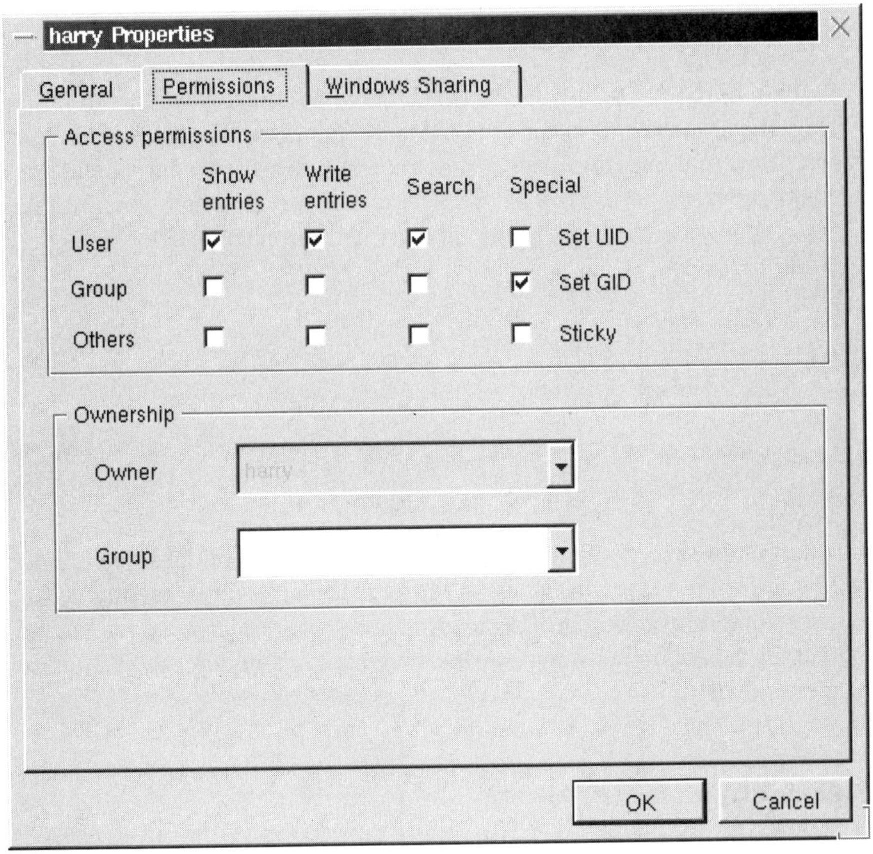

FIGURE 6-3   Use File Manager to configure file permissions with the Properties tool

Remember that Chapter 12 has a more in-depth explanation of permissions and why you'd select certain kinds for certain files and directories.

Customizing File Manager

One of the most basic philosophical concepts of Linux is that just about everything should support some degree of configurability, either by the root account or by the individual user. While something as basic and clear as a file manager presents a rather limited set of possibilities for configuration, there's still a lot of room for changing things about the style in which the information is presented to you.

These configuration settings are located in the View drop-down menu of the File Manager window. The menu contains a list of features, which are described here, and you can choose whether or not they're displayed when you open File Manager. Some of them are merely cosmetic, and it doesn't matter whether or not they're active. Others have more of an effect on the way in which you use File Manager, so you may want to leave them activated (or inactive), depending on the way you prefer to work.

Tool Bar

The tool bar is the set of large iconic buttons across the top of the screen. Since all of the button functions are also available through the drop-down menus, it is not necessary to display the toolbar. However, it saves a few microseconds to click a button, rather than search through a drop-down menu. You don't need it unless you prefer to click just once.

Address Bar

The Address bar contains the Address field that shows the full path name of the currently selected directory. In general, we advise that you keep the Address bar visible. When working with Linux, it's always a good idea to know the absolute path name of the file you're working with. When you need to use the command line for some task and don't have the point-and-click interface of File Manager available, you'll already be familiar with conventional UNIX filename strategies if you keep an eye on the Address bar.

Status Bar

Another item that's useful, if not critical, is the Status bar. This bar runs along the bottom of the File Manager window and shows statistical information about the selected directory. From the Status bar, you can learn the number of objects in a selected directory, the total size of the directory, and whether the directory is located on the local computer or on a remote computer (either on your local network or via the Internet). If you select a single file in the right pane, the Status bar gives you the same information about the individual file.

Tree

We do not recommend that you disable the Tree option. This option controls whether or not you see the left pane of the File Manager window. If it is not active, you will only see the file tree in the right pane. It's not a huge problem if you prefer a single-paned File Manager, but it will take you a bit longer to search through your directories for a given file. We have written this chapter (and other references to File Manager throughout this book) assuming that you have the Tree option active and that you see both the left and right panes of the File Manager window.

Large Icons

boot.catalog   boot1440.img

If you prefer pictorial representations to text labels, select the Large Icons option in the View menu. When this option is active, the right pane's display changes from a vertical listing of files in alphabetical order to a horizontal display. The icons that indicate the file type also become larger. This is useful if you tend to keep several file types in one directory, especially if they have similar names. For example, one of our dogs is named Miso. If we had a directory called /home/dogs that contained a photo called miso.jpg, a story called miso.txt, and a music file called miso.mp3, each file type would have a different icon when the Large Icons options is active.

Show Hidden Files

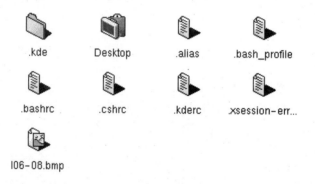

Show Hidden Files is an option that helps you work with a traditional UNIX filenaming method that can be quite confusing to new users. In UNIX-based operating systems, like Linux, configuration files are usually named with a leading dot and the final characters *rc*. That is, the configuration file for the newsreader `trn` is called .trnrc, the configuration file for the mail program `pine` is called .pinerc, and so on. By default, File Manager doesn't show you these leading-dot files when you open the File Manager window. It assumes you want to see only files that you have created or that belong to applications you've installed. If you turn on Show Hidden Files, you'll be able to see these "dot files" in the directories in which they reside. This is helpful, and we recommend that you activate this option.

Using these six display options should allow you to configure File Manager so that it displays file system information in a way that makes you as happy as a file manager possibly can. (Granted, that's probably not very happy, but it's worth a shot.)

Using File Manager as an Internet Tool

We've spent quite a few pages describing the convenience that File Manager brings to your daily file maintenance tasks. However, File Manager also has a hidden capability: it's an excellent way to grab files from other computers! Whether you use File Manager on a local network or across the world via the Internet, you can use it as a Web browser or as an FTP client.

Obviously, you can't use File Manager as an Internet client if you don't have an active connection to the Internet. You'll need to configure your machine to work with your local Internet Service Provider, cable modem or DSL company, or workplace Ethernet connection before you can use File Manager or any other Internet program. See Chapter 9, "Using the Internet with Corel Linux," for information on getting hooked up with your new Linux machine.

Web Browsing with File Manager

Yes, File Manager is also a Web browser. It is not, however, an advanced Web browser; most importantly, File Manager does not support Java or JavaScript if included in the Web page being viewed. Since Netscape is part of the Corel Linux installation, use that for most Web browsing and use File Manager only when you need a quick alternative.

To use File Manager as a Web browser, open the drop-down File menu and select Open Location. The Open Location dialog box appears on the screen; just type the URL you want to view into the entry field and click OK. When the page finishes loading, it will display in the right pane of the File Manager window, as shown in Figure 6-4. Your local machine's directory structure remains visible in the left pane.

 If you don't like having Web pages squished into the right pane of the File Manager window, you can change the display by deselecting Tree in the View drop-down menu. This will allow the right pane to fill the entire File Manager window and will hide the left pane until you reselect Tree.

Since File Manager is not designed as a Web browser, you won't want to rely on it for most recreational webbing. However, it's fast, and it's a good way to

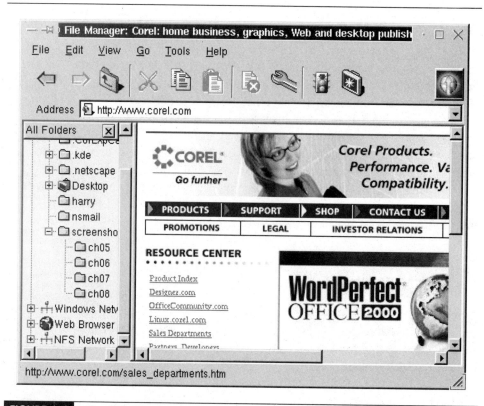

FIGURE 6-4   Use File Manager as a quick alternative to Netscape for Web browsing

check something you need to see right away. Be aware that using File Manager as a Web browser does put quite a bit of load on your system memory, so you may want to use Netscape to check the Web if you're running several critical programs at the same time. The larger your swap partition or the more RAM you have, the less of a problem File Manager's memory hog-ness will be.

Transfer Files from the Internet with File Manager

We do recommend that you use File Manager instead of Netscape for one particular kind of use: File Transfer Protocol, or FTP, sessions. (This is, of course, if you choose not to run a separate FTP program.) File Manager makes it easy and logical to get files from the Internet's many file archives; because File Manager is graphical and you use it frequently, it's easy to put those downloaded files in the correct location in your directory structure. Unlike Netscape, using File Manager allows you to view both the remote location and your local computer at the same time. This can be quite handy. If you're interested in FTP clients that run independently, see Chapter 9. To use File Manager as an FTP client, use the following method:

1. Open File Manager using one of the following methods:

   ■ Click the File Manager icon in the Panel.

   ■ Click the My Home desktop icon.

   ■ Click the Application Starter icon and select File Manager from the Start menu.

2. From the File Manager drop-down menu, select File | Open Location.

3. In the Open Location dialog box, type the URL of the FTP archive to which you want to connect.

   URLs for FTP sites usually start with `ftp://` instead of `http://`. Figure 6-5 shows File Manager in an active FTP session with `ftp://ftp.kde.org`, which contains the latest releases of software written explicitly for the KDE desktop environment.

   Once you have connected to the remote site, the site's directory structure will appear in the right pane of the File Manager window, while your local directory structure remains visible in the left pane.

4. Navigate through the remote site's files using the same navigation tools you use regularly in File Manager.

5. Locate the file you want to download and click and drag it to the folder on your local machine in which you want to place the file.

File Manager copies the file from the remote location to the folder you've selected on your own computer. You'll see a progress bar that measures the amount of the download that's been completed; depending on the size of the file and the speed of your Internet connection, this may flicker past rapidly, or it may be an all-night job.

Corel Linux File Manager makes an unusually good FTP client. Many good graphical FTP clients are now available for Linux, but it may not be necessary for you to download and compile one if you're comfortable getting files with File Manager from remote locations. As a Linux user, you are likely to become quite

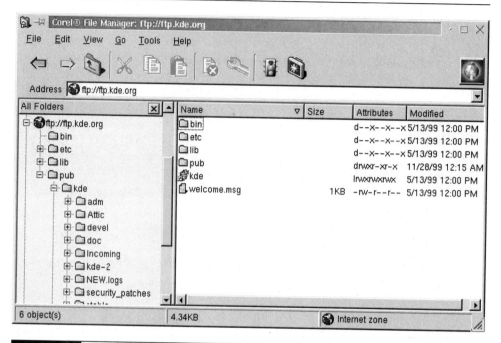

FIGURE 6-5 Use File Manager to download files from various Internet file archives

familiar with FTP as you download new releases of your favorite programs or try out new offerings. It makes sense to find a file transfer method that you like and that works without much fuss. File Manager may very well solve that need for you and remove the bother of running a separate program.

CHAPTER 7

Configuring Your Desktop with the Control Center

One of the best features of KDE is its high configurability. In Chapters 5 and 6, we described the basic KDE installation: its features and its layout. However, you may find the default KDE installation to be unattractive or unsuited to the way you work on your computer. That's where the configuration options enter the picture; almost everything you see on your screen can be changed, moved, deleted, or otherwise altered to make your computing experience as comfortable as possible.

Corel Linux handles many of these configuration choices through a utility called the *Control Center*. In the Control Center, you'll find tools to control almost all the aspects of KDE's appearance:

- The desktop
- Individual windows
- Display options
- Fonts
- Desktop and Panel icons
- Language
- Screensavers
- Keyboard shortcuts
- Mouse behavior
- Network settings

In this chapter, we work through the Control Center and explain each option. We also provide some configuration tips that will speed up your work, or that simply make it easier to work with Corel Linux and KDE. Even if you like the default desktop that appeared when you installed Corel Linux, we suggest that you spend some time looking through the Control Center. You may find options that are useful to you even if you don't want to change the visual appearance of the KDE desktop; other important functions, such as mouse behavior and keyboard tricks, are also controlled through the Control Center. We also discuss two other major desktop configuration issues in this chapter: organizing the KDE Panel to your taste, and applying various desktop themes to KDE.

Using the Control Center

Before you continue, you should open the Control Center:

1. Click the Application Starter icon (the globe icon in the KDE Panel).

2. From the Start menu, select Control Center.

The Control Center opens (Figure 7-1), and you're ready to go.

As you can see in Figure 7-1, the Control Center is composed of two panes. The left pane contains a tree structure, similar to the structure used in File Manager (except this tree doesn't represent your directory system). The tree comprises expandable main headings; the small plus sign next to a heading indicates that there are levels below the one shown. Click the plus sign to expand that heading and select one of the suboptions. When an option is selected in the left pane, a set of controls for that option is displayed in the right pane. Using these controls, you can manipulate the look and behavior of your desktop.

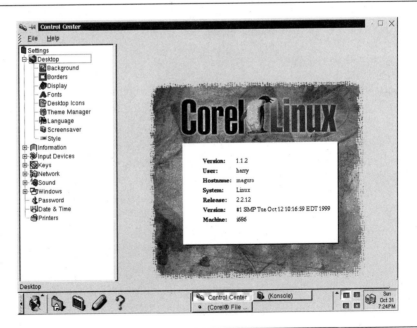

FIGURE 7-1   Configure KDE with the Control Center

The main section headings in the Control Center are Desktop, Information, Input Devices, Keys, Network, Sound, Windows, Password, Date & Time, and Printers. The last three options do not have suboptions, so the control sets will display in the right pane as soon as you select the section heading. The other sections do have a variety of suboptions, which we describe in following paragraphs.

NOTE	*You may never need to use some of these Control Center options. Consider this chapter a thorough reference should you need to change something obscure. It's a good idea to know what the Control Center can do, even if you don't plan to do much with it. In general, if you want to change something about KDE's appearance, you'll start at the Control Center.*

Desktop

The Desktop section in the Control Center allows you to control what you see on your monitor when you start Corel Linux. In this section are control sets for the desktop background, window borders, display options, fonts, desktop icons, language, screensavers, and other desktop styles. You may find that this section contains most of the controls for the work you want to do with the Control Center.

Background

The Background option (Figure 7-2) controls the appearance of the KDE desktop itself. Whatever you select in this option will appear as the backdrop for everything else on the desktop: icons, application windows, the KDE Panel, and so forth. (Windows users will recognize this as the "wallpaper" selection.)

Select a background color or choose an image to use as the backdrop; colors can either be solid or gradient.

- If you want all your virtual desktops (a concept described in Chapter 5, "Desktops Versus Window Managers") to have the same background, or you want each desktop to have a different background, define that in this window.

- Select Dock Into The Panel if you change backgrounds frequently. Selecting this option places a small icon into the System Tray; click the icon to open this window directly without having to navigate through the Control Center.

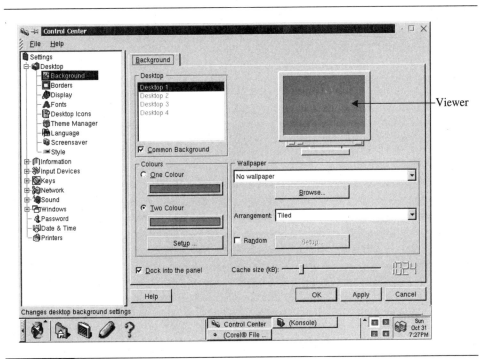

Viewer

FIGURE 7-2   The Background option of the Control Center

■ Use the Viewer at the upper-right of the Control Center window to see how changes will look on a miniature version of your desktop; click the Apply button if you want to see the changes on your actual desktop.

■ Click the OK button when you've finished and wish to save your changes and exit the Background window.

Borders

The Borders option contains controls that help you manage your desktop more effectively. There are two kinds of border controls in this option: Active and Magic. This tool does not control individual window borders, but rather the desktop's own borders. Some users find these options to be very helpful, while others find them immensely annoying. These tools, probably more than any other control set in the Control Center, are ones you should play with before you decide to use or ignore them.

Active Borders

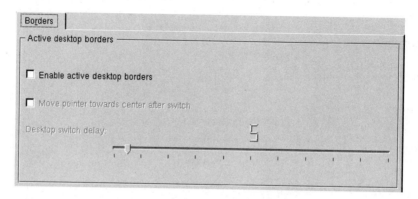

Active borders are used in conjunction with virtual desktops. When active borders are selected, you can switch among virtual desktops simply by moving your mouse. Move the mouse cursor to the edge of the screen that borders the desktop you want to switch to and hold it there for a specified time (the default is 5 milliseconds, hardly a blink). To enable this feature, click the Enable Active Desktop Borders check box.

If you've enabled active borders, you'll probably also want to select the next check box, Move Pointer Toward Center After Switch. This option makes your mouse cursor bounce to the center of the new desktop after you've moved into it. Using this feature gets rid of one of the more irritating side effects of active borders, a rapid switch between two desktops if you can't get your mouse cursor out of the way before the delay time ends.

Immediately below the check boxes is a slider that you can use to set the delay time, or how long your mouse cursor needs to remain on the active border before the desktop changes.

Click the Apply button to activate your changes.

NOTE   *If you have turned off virtual desktops, a process described in Chapter 8, "Advanced KDE Techniques," you won't be able to use this option.*

Magic Borders

Magic borders are an organizational tool, rather than a navigational tool like active borders. If you activate magic borders, you turn on the desktop's "snap zone," a region around the edge of the entire desktop. When the snap zone is activated and you drag an application or program window toward the edge of the screen, the window automatically snaps to the edge of the screen. You can increase or decrease the size of the snap zone by using the sliders in this window. Individual windows also have snap zones and can snap to each other.

Click the OK button to save your changes and exit this window.

> **NOTE** *Why would you use magic borders? They're useful for people who like to leave multiple windows open while they work but don't like the messiness of having windows stacked all over the screen. Magic borders align open windows perfectly with the edge of the screen and provide a more organized desktop appearance.*

Display

The Display option lets you set the color of the various *widgets*, or components, that collectively make up an application or program window. Use this tool to set the colors of active and inactive windows, borders, title text, text, and other parts of a window. The Control Center provides several preset color schemes; you can also build your own schemes if the ones offered are too tame or just not right. Figure 7-3 shows the Colors tab of the Display option.

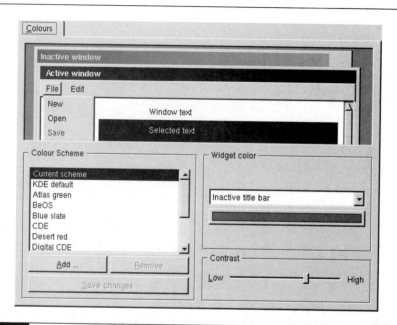

FIGURE 7-3   The Colors tab of the Control Center's Display option

 If you define your own color schemes, make sure that you don't have low contrast where high contrast is needed, such as between window text and window background. It's quite hard to see what you're doing if you're typing dark green text on a dark blue background!

See the effects of your selections in the preview window of the Display option. Once you've selected a scheme that works for you, click the Apply button to see the effect on your regular desktop. When you're satisfied, click the OK button to save changes and exit the window.

Fonts

Use the Fonts option, shown in Figure 7-4, to define the fonts used in various desktop elements. The choices you make here will not just affect the fonts used within a window, but also the fonts used for KDE Panel buttons, the KDE Panel clock, window titles, and so on. You can also set a systemwide preference for a proportional font and/or a *fixed-width font* with this tool.

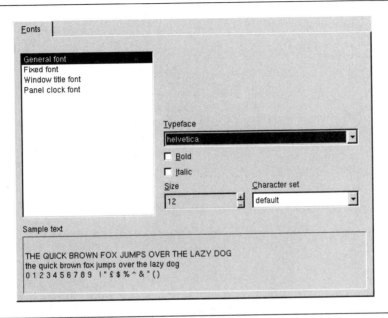

FIGURE 7-4 Use the Fonts option to define desktop fonts

  Fixed-width fonts (sometimes called monospace fonts) are those in which each letter takes up the same amount of space, regardless of what letter it is. An i in a fixed-width font is just as wide as an m. Courier is the classic fixed-width font; it looks like an old typewriter font. Proportional fonts are those in which each letter has a slightly different width. This book is written with a proportional font; we use a fixed-width font for examples of code and other things you need to type.

To change a font, select the category you want to change and the font you want to use, and click the Apply button to see the changes on your desktop. Click the OK button to save your changes and exit the Font window.

Desktop Icons

This option, shown in Figure 7-5, controls the way in which desktop icons are displayed. The KDE Panel isn't affected by choices you make in this window; rather, this window affects the desktop icons that line the left side of your screen, as described in Chapter 5.

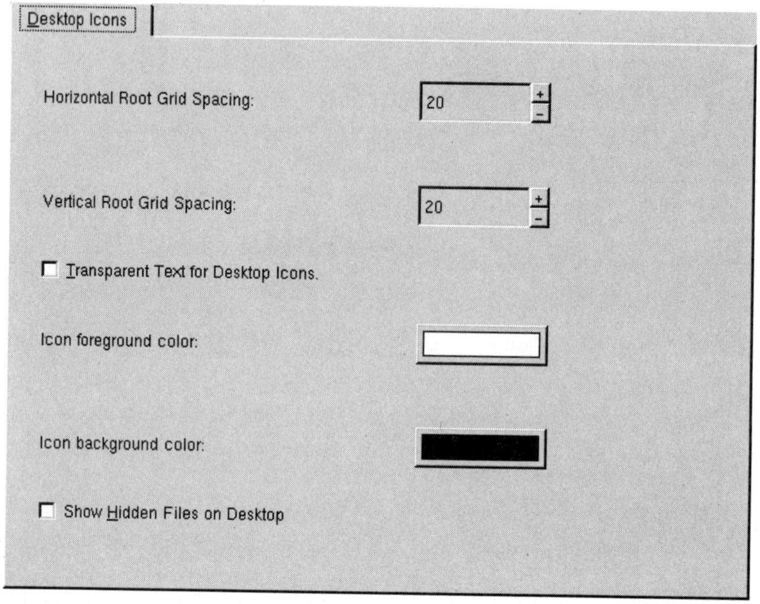

Desktop Icons

Horizontal Root Grid Spacing: 20   [+] [-]

Vertical Root Grid Spacing: 20   [+] [-]

☐ Transparent Text for Desktop Icons.

Icon foreground color:

Icon background color:

☐ Show Hidden Files on Desktop

FIGURE 7-5   The Desktop Icons option controls how desktop icons are displayed

- ■ Use the Horizontal and Vertical Grid Spacing elements to control the placement of icons: do you want your icons bunched close together, or do you prefer a more spacious arrangement?

- ■ Control the way in which an icon's text label appears. Normally, the label is displayed on an opaque background. You can change the text color and the background color, or you can click the Transparent Text For Desktop Icons check box and remove the background completely. (If you select Transparent Text, you will need to log out of Corel Linux and log back in again before the changes can be seen.)

Click the Apply button to see the effects of your selections on your desktop, and click the OK button to save your changes and exit this window.

Language

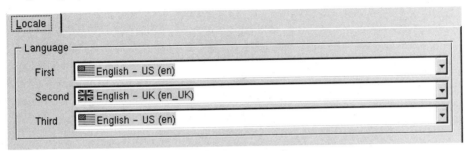

Use this option to change the language used by KDE. By default, KDE uses the English language (as do the Corel Linux distribution and this book). If you want KDE to operate in a different language, select the appropriate language from the drop-down menu and click the OK button to save your changes and exit the window.

 The new language will apply only to applications and programs you start after you click OK. If you want to see everything on your desktop in the newly chosen language, you'll have to log out and log back in again. This works only if the applications already have translated modules available, however. Currently, Corel Linux is English only; if you add other applications, they may include support for non-English languages.

Screensaver

With this option, you can set the screensaver you want to use (if you want to use a screensaver), as shown in Figure 7-6. See the various screensavers in the preview window and select from several options in the Settings area that affect the screensaver's operation:

- **Wait For __ Min.**   Set the time delay that the computer must remain idle before the screensaver is activated.

- **Require Password**   Choose whether you want to password-protect your screensaver. This is especially useful if you are away from your desk frequently and don't want people bumping your mouse just to see what you're up to, but you don't want to go to the hassle of logging out if you

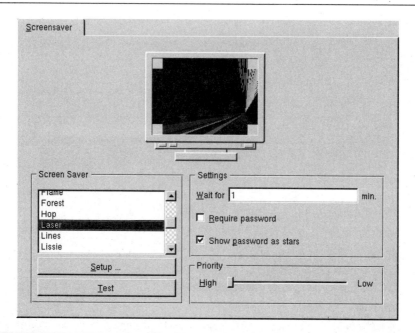

FIGURE 7-6 Set the screensaver here

just want a cup of coffee. The password for your screensaver is your
regular login password.

■ **Show Password As Stars**   This useful option improves the security of
your screensaver password function. If you select this option, every time
you type your password into the dialog box, the password will display as
asterisks instead of showing the actual password you use.

CAUTION   *There is a slight security risk in using your login password as your
screensaver password. Ideally, you should have separate passwords for each.
Just remember that someone who figures out your screensaver password will
also know your login password; don't use something really obvious like your
child's name or the name of the stuffed toy sitting on your monitor.*

Some of the screensavers have special configuration options, such as speed
or color, that you can alter by clicking the Setup button and making the changes
you want.

Style

Style

☑ Draw widgets in the style of Windows 95

☐ Menubar on top of the screen in the style of MacOS

☐ Apply fonts and colors to non-KDE apps

The Style option controls the manner in which various window elements are shown on the desktop. There are three choices:

- **Draw Widgets In The Style Of Windows 95**   Select this option to change KDE's display to one similar to Windows.

- **Menubar On Top Of The Screen In The Style Of MacOS**   Select this option to mimic the MacOS desktop appearance more closely.

- **Apply Fonts And Colors To Non-KDE Apps**   Select this option to apply your display choices to non-KDE applications such as Netscape, The GIMP, and other third-party programs that you've installed.

Information

Despite its location in the Control Center, you can't actually configure anything under the Information section. Rather, this section provides a great deal of useful machine-level information about your Corel Linux system. When you select an entry in the left pane of this window, Control Center shows an information screen in the right pane. This is extremely useful for diagnostic purposes; the information contained in this heading is described in Table 7-1.

Input Devices

This section contains control sets for your computer's input devices: keyboard and mouse. While it may seem that these devices don't need much configuration, small

7

Option	Information Provided
Devices	Information about the devices installed on your computer. Refers primarily to any input/output devices that are upgradable or removable.
DMA Channels	Direct Memory Access channel data. DMA is data that is sent directly to memory from a given device without passing through the microprocessor.
Interrupts	Interrupt Request Value data. Each device in the computer has a unique IRQ value so that the processor can control the various signals in the data stream.
I/O Ports	Input/Output Port data. Each device that you plug into your computer is assigned an I/O port.
Memory	Information about your system RAM.
Partitions	Information about the manner in which your hard disk is divided.
PCI	Information about your computer's PCI slots. These are expansion slots that take a specific sort of board.
Processor	Basic information about your microprocessor chip.
SCSI	Information about any SCSI devices you have installed.
Samba Status	Information about your Samba network (see Chapter 20, "Networking," for more information about Samba).
Sound	Information about your sound card.
X Server	Information about the X Window System software running on your computer.

TABLE 7-1   System Information from the Control Center

changes in the way that your computer processes the data sent from input devices can really affect the way you interact with your computer.

NOTE   *We assume you're using a mouse. If you have a different kind of input device that you use instead of a mouse, such as a pen and tablet or a trackball, we assume you know how to use it. You will need to find a Linux driver for your input device to use it; if a Linux driver doesn't exist, you won't be able to use that device until a driver has been written and installed. Most existing drivers are included with the kernel source code; for the newest drivers or the newest input device hardware, you may need to contact the manufacturer for an appropriate driver.*

International Keyboard

If you've ever thought about typing in another language, you may wonder how computers handle various sorts of character sets. There are a wide variety of keyboards built for various languages: ideographic keyboards for Asian languages; Cyrillic keyboards for Russian and other Eastern European languages; and accented keyboards for Roman-alphabet languages that have letters different from English, such as French or German. KDE has drivers available for a number of these keyboards; if you use a keyboard different from the default English keyboard, select the appropriate driver in the drop-down box and click the OK button to save your changes.

Keyboard

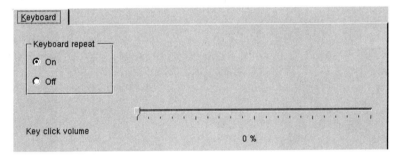

Use this option to set two keyboard-specific options: repeat and volume.

- **Keyboard Repeat**   Select this option if you want a letter to continue appearing on the screen as long as you have the corresponding key held down. For example, when keyboard repeat is turned off, pressing the R key will produce only one *R* on the screen no matter how long you hold down the key. If repeat is turned on, you'll see *RRRRRRRR* for as long as you hold down the key.
- **Keyclick Volume**   Select this option and set the appropriate volume level if you like to hear yourself type. This option toggles a small clicking sound in KDE itself that plays every time KDE senses a keystroke; it doesn't affect the actual physical sound made by your keyboard.

Click the OK button to save your changes and exit this window.

Mouse

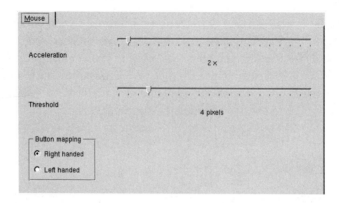

With this option, you can configure the mouse's behavior. Mouse behavior is a highly individual choice; you may love a very fast mouse or you may find fast mice to be unsettling. Tinker with these settings until you find levels that make you the most comfortable.

- **Acceleration**   This setting controls how fast the pointer onscreen moves when you move the mouse on its pad.

- **Threshold**   This setting controls how close the pointer needs to be to an item in order to select it when the mouse button is clicked.

- **Button Mapping**   This setting controls the mouse buttons and whether you want to use them with a right-handed configuration (left mouse button as the single-click button) or with a left-handed configuration (mirrored, so that the right mouse button is the single-click button).

Click the OK button to save your changes and exit the Mouse window.

Keys

In this section, you can set up various keyboard shortcuts to perform actions you use frequently. For example, the familiar keyboard shortcut CTRL-S executes the Save command just as if you'd used the menu system to navigate to the Save command. The Keys header contains two types of key patterns: Global Keys (system commands) and Standard Keys (application commands).

> TIP
>
> *Before you set up your own keyboard shortcuts, review the default shortcuts that KDE has already defined. You may find that you're duplicating effort by creating your own shortcuts. Of course, if you find your own key sequences to be more memorable than the default ones, substitute your own.*

Global Keys

Global Keys shortcuts are those that perform system functions, such as changing desktops or selecting desktop icons. The various Global Keys combinations already defined by default are shown in the scrolling box in the right pane. If you want to define a new Global Key action, use this procedure:

1. In the Global Shortcuts tab, shown in Figure 7-7, select the action you want to perform in the Action window of the left pane.

2. Select a *metakey* in the Choose A Key For The Selected Action window at the bottom of the right pane.

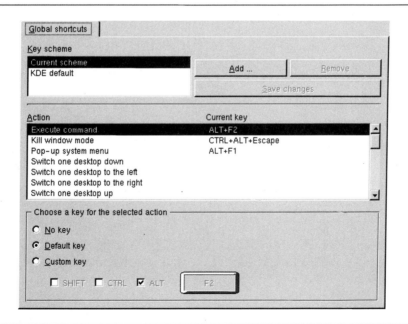

FIGURE 7-7   Set shortcut keys in the Global Shortcuts tab

A metakey is a key that needs to be pressed as part of the keystroke combination: metakeys are SHIFT, CTRL, and ALT.

3. Press the key (on your keyboard) that you want to use in the combination. The key combination appears in the Action window.

4. Click OK to save your new keystroke combination.

Standard Keys

The Standard Keys shortcuts control the basic functions used when working with text. Save, Open, Cut, Paste, and other familiar functions all have Standard Keys shortcuts. The various Standard Keys combinations already defined are listed in the scrolling box in the right pane (Figure 7-8).

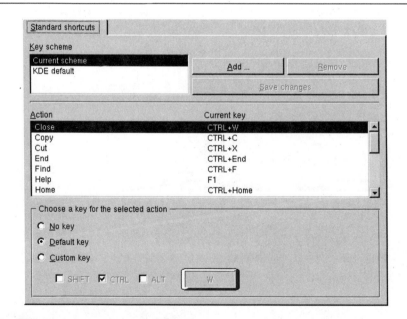

FIGURE 7-8   Set standard shortcuts from here

If you want to define a new Standard Key action, use this procedure:

1. Select the action you want to perform in the Action window of the right pane, shown in Figure 7-8.

   Select a metakey in the Choose A Key For The Selected Action window at the bottom of the right pane.

2. Press the key (on your keyboard) that you want to use in the combination. The key combination appears in the Action window.

3. Click OK to save your new keystroke combination.

Network

Use this section to configure your system for Ethernet and Samba networking. We cover networking thoroughly in Chapter 20.

Windows

The Windows section allows you to configure various elements of desktop windows, such as how the title bar buttons display and what each mouse button does when clicked within a particular kind of window.

Advanced

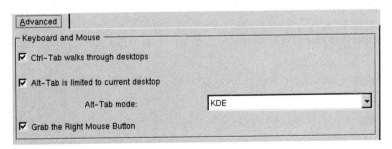

The Advanced option displays a control set that affects the behavior of the ALT-TAB key combination. You can also use this window to define a particular style of window based on its title or its class (window "class" is an X Window function that tells the computer the window type and how to display it).

Buttons

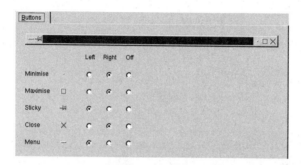

With the Buttons option, shown on Figure 7-9, you can control the placement of various small buttons that appear in the title bar of each open window. These buttons control whether the window is minimized, maximized, closed, and so on. Select whether you want these buttons to be displayed at the left of the title bar, at the right, or not at all.

Mouse

With this option, you can define the behavior of up to three mouse buttons for four kinds of window attributes. You can assign any of the window attributes to any of the three mouse buttons:

- **Window Raise**   "Rolls up" the window, leaving just the title bar on the desktop.

- **Window Lower**   "Rolls down" a window that had been rolled up, returning the window to full size underneath the title bar.

- **Window Activation**   Makes the selected window the active window.

- **Window Operations Menu**   Displays a menu from which you can perform standard window management tasks, such as moving, resizing, closing, and so on.

Click the OK button to save your changes and exit the Mouse configuration tool.

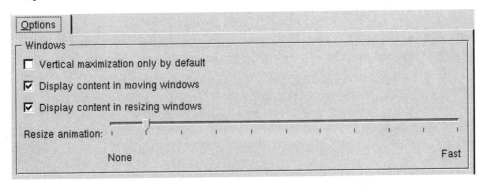

Mouse		
Titlebar and frame:	Active	Inactive
Left Button	Raise	Activate and raise
Middle Button	Lower	Activate and lower
Right Button	Operations menu	Activate

Inactive inner window:

Left Button	Activate, raise and pass click
Middle Button	Activate and pass click
Right Button	Activate and pass click

Inner window, titlebar and frame:

ALT + Left Button	Move
ALT + Middle Button	Toggle raise and lower
ALT + Right Button	Resize

FIGURE 7-9   Define behavior of up to three buttons for four kinds of window attributes

Properties

Options	

Windows

☐ Vertical maximization only by default

☑ Display content in moving windows

☑ Display content in resizing windows

Resize animation:

None   Fast

7

Use the Properties option to define several miscellaneous window behaviors:

- **Vertical Maximization Only By Default**   When opened, each window stretches from the top of the screen to the bottom. You must manually resize each window if you don't want it to display at full height.

- **Display Content In Moving Windows**   When selected, a moving window will show the window's content as it moves. This slows system speed a bit, as the computer must redraw the window content both as the window moves and when it comes to rest.

- **Display Content In Resizing Windows**   When selected, window content will show as a window resizes in response to your mouse operation. As with the previous option, this will slow system speed while the window is resizing.

- **Placement Policy**   Allows you to configure the manner in which new windows are placed on the screen when they first appear. You have five options:

  - **Smart**, which places the new window in the position where it will overlap other windows the least.

  - **Cascade**, which lines windows so that their upper-left corners cascade diagonally down and to the right.

  - **Interactive**, which allows windows to overlap only up to a certain percentage.

  - **Random**, which places new windows randomly.

  - **Manual**, which places a new window under the mouse cursor—you must click the cursor to set the window position.

- **Focus Policy**   Determines the manner in which a window receives the focus, or becomes the active window. You have four options:

  - **Click To Focus**, under which you must click the window to give it the focus

  - **Focus Follows Mouse**, under which the active window is whatever window has the mouse cursor

  - **Classic Focus Follows Mouse**, which is much the same except that the window loses focus when the mouse cursor leaves it

- **Classic Sloppy Focus**, in which the ALT-TAB key combination switches focus between open windows.

Titlebar

The Titlebar option, shown in Figure 7-10, gives you a control set that determines the appearance and behavior of an individual window's title bar. The control set affects four elements:

- **Title Alignment**   Choose whether the window title is aligned to the left, center, or right.

- **Appearance**   Affects the title bar color, whether the color is solid or gradient, or applies an image to the title bar in place of a color.

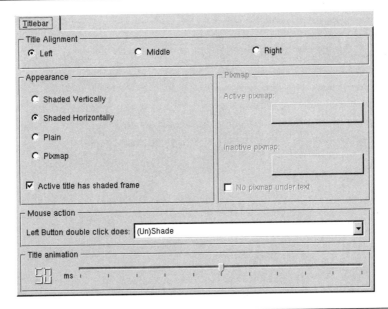

FIGURE 7-10   Control the title bar with this tab

CAUTION   *Using an image in a window title bar may make the title difficult to read.*

- **Mouse Action**   Configure mouse buttons to roll up or roll down the window when clicked in the title bar. You can also assign one of four other actions to a given mouse button: maximize, iconify, sticky, or close.

- **Title Animation**   When a window title is too long for the title bar, KDE scrolls the title from left to right. The slider under this option controls that scroll speed.

Password

Change Password	

Password Settings

User name: harry
Domain: maguro

Old password:
New password:
Re–type password:

☐ Synchronization

Use the Password section to change your login password. The Change Password screen prompts you to type both your old password and your new password to verify that the person changing the password is actually you.

Date & Time

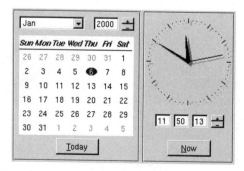

This section shows an interactive clock and calendar that you can use to set the correct time and date on your computer. This sets the actual system time, which displays in the KDE Panel and is used for any timestamps made on internal logs or documents. It's a good idea to keep this current and correct, especially if you live in a region where the clock time changes seasonally.

Printers

Print	

Installed Printers:

Printer Name	Hostname

Use the Printer section to select and configure printers that are attached to your computer. You cannot print documents directly from the Printer section of the Control Center, but you can make sure that your printer is working correctly before you issue print commands from individual applications. Printing is discussed in more detail in Part IV, "Essential Linux System Administration."

To use the Control Center's Printer options to connect to a local or network printer, you must have the root password. On this screen, click Modify and enter the root password when prompted. You can now click the Add button to start the Add Printer Wizard; see Chapter 19, "Dealing with Hardware," for more information on configuring printers.

Applying Desktop Themes

One of the more enjoyable aspects of KDE is the ability to apply themes to the desktop. A *theme* is a group of stylistic elements that work together to give your desktop and windows a certain thematic "look." For example, you might apply a wildlife theme that contains a meadow photograph for the background and icons that represent various insects. Corel Linux's version of KDE supports themes and provides a built-in Theme Manager, shown in Figure 7-11, to make theme installation easy and quick.

To install or change a desktop theme, use this procedure:

1. Click the Application Manager icon in the Panel.

2. From the Start menu, choose Control Center | Desktop | Theme Manager.

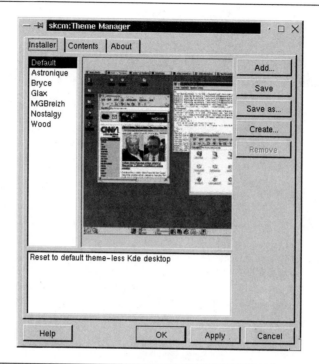

FIGURE 7-11   Apply desktop themes with the intuitive Theme Manager

The Theme Manager window appears.

3. Select a theme from the list at the left. The selected theme is displayed in the small preview window.

4. Click the Apply button. The theme is applied to your desktop.

5. Click the OK button to save your changes and exit Theme Manager.

If you want to use only certain parts of a particular theme, you can select those parts through Theme Manager.

1. Open Theme Manager using the process described previously and click the Contents tab. On this tab, you'll see all the elements that compose the currently selected theme.

2. Check the boxes next to the elements you want to use and uncheck the boxes next to elements you don't want to apply to your desktop.

3. When you've made your selections, click the OK button to save your changes and exit.

You can download a large number of themes from the KDE theme archive at `http://kde.themes.org`. It is possible to create your own themes, but it requires some knowledge of graphic design programs to create the individual elements. If you want to build your own themes, consult the online KDE documentation for a full explanation of the process. You can find the correct pages at `http://kde.themes.org/php/docs.phtml?docid=21`.

Organizing the KDE Panel

7

While the Control Center gives you many options for customizing your desktop, you should also consider configuring the KDE Panel to your liking. The Panel is a major part of the KDE user experience, and it is just as configurable as the rest of the desktop. You can change every aspect of the Panel on this tab; Panel configurations are grouped into three general categories: the general appearance of the Panel itself, the appearance of the Panel icons, and the addition or removal of icons from the Panel.

KDE Panel Appearance

Many KDE Panel behaviors can be controlled by right-clicking the Panel and selecting Configure from the context menu that appears. The Panel configuration window is shown in Figure 7-12. (Note that this window has five different tabs; we are concerned only with the Panel tab in this section.)

Select the Panel tab of the Configuration window if it isn't already selected.

- **Location** Display the KDE Panel at the top, bottom, left, or right of the KDE desktop.

- **Size** Choose whether the Panel and its icons display as tiny, normal, or large.

- **Taskbar Location** Display the Taskbar at the top, bottom, or top left of the KDE desktop, dock the Taskbar into the Panel itself, or hide the Taskbar altogether.

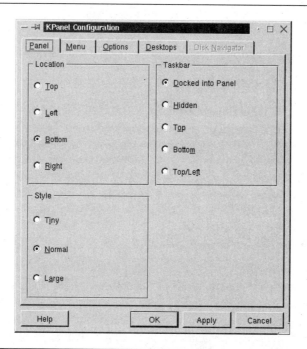

FIGURE 7-12   Use the Panel Configuration window to make the Panel work for you

KDE Panel Icons

Since the KDE Panel is composed primarily of iconic representations of your programs and applications, it's logical that you can configure these icons to appear in the way you like best. Right-click on any Panel icon to open a context menu containing the entries Move, Remove, and Properties.

- ■ **Move**   Select this option and then click and drag the icon to slide it left or right in the Panel. Click the desktop to set the new position. Use this option to rearrange your most frequently used icons to a convenient location on the Panel.

- ■ **Remove**   Select this option to remove a rarely used icon from the Panel.

> **TIP**   *You can always access any program or application from Application Manager and the Start menu. You don't need to have a KDE Panel icon for every program that's installed on your computer.*

■ **Properties** Opens the Properties window, which contains four tabs. The General tab shows the program's name and basic information about the icon. The Permissions tab lets you change file permissions on the associated file. The Execute tab allows you to change information about the program launched when the icon is clicked. The Application tab shows information about the associated application.

> **TIP** *If you want to change the picture shown on the icon, you can do so on the Execute tab of the Properties window.*

Adding an Icon to the KDE Panel

You'll probably want to add icons to the KDE Panel so that you can launch your favorite programs, not just the ones included in the Panel by default. To add an icon to the Panel, follow these steps:

1. Click the Application Manager icon in the KDE Panel and choose File Manager from the Start menu.

2. Navigate to the application that you want to link to the Panel.

3. Click the application and drag it to the desktop.

4. Release the mouse button.

5. Select Link from the context menu that appears. A link to the application appears on the desktop.

6. Drag the link over the Panel. The link appears in the Panel but also remains on the desktop.

7. Right-click the link on the desktop and select Move to Trash from the context menu.

8. Right-click the new link in the Panel and select Properties from the context menu.

9. In the Properties window, select the Execute tab of the Properties window.

10. Replace the path shown in the Execute field with the complete path name of the application you want to launch with this icon.

7

TIP   *You can find the full path name in the Address field of File Manager. If the file you want to launch is not currently selected in File Manager, browse through the directory structure until you find it.*

11. If you want to change the icon's image, click the icon shown in the Properties window.

12. Select a new icon from the options that appear.

13. Click OK to close the Properties window.

14. Right-click in the Panel background and select Restart from the context menu.

   The Panel restarts and now contains your new icon. You can now launch the linked application simply by clicking the new Panel icon.

CHAPTER 8

Advanced KDE Techniques

W hile you can use Corel Linux happily and fully without ever going beyond the KDE techniques explained in Chapters 5, 6, and 7, you might want to use more advanced KDE techniques to accomplish specific tasks or configure certain sections of your system. In this chapter, we discuss the KDE Window Manager, a tool you can use in certain circumstances instead of regular KDE. We also discuss the Pager and virtual desktops in more detail than we provided in Chapter 5 "Desktops Versus Window Managers," and offer some tips for using virtual desktops more effectively to streamline the way in which you work within Corel Linux. Finally, we address the question of terminal windows and why you might prefer to perform some Linux (and desktop) functions at a command prompt instead of via the KDE graphical administration tools.

The KDE Window Manager

All UNIX programs can eventually be reduced to a set of commands. Window Manager provides a specific set of commands that are useful in programming or that can be used to make specific tweaks to the desktop environment. Window Manager commands can be used in scripts that you write to automate given sets of procedures, or they can be used within actual programs that you may want to write for the KDE platform.

Window Manager, unlike File Manager, is not a graphical tool. That is, you cannot open a separate window that contains Window Manager. Instead, it is a mechanism that translates text commands into actions that affect the "behind the scenes" operation of KDE. Yes, this is slightly confusing; almost every other manager function in KDE opens a separate window that you can use to manage something about the desktop. Window Manager is the exception to that rule.

| NOTE | *You may never use the Window Manager function of KDE; you certainly don't need to use Window Manager to use KDE effectively. We include this section for those readers who want to write scripts that affect window performance, or who may want to write programs that take window behavior into consideration. We suggest using this information in conjunction with Chapter 17, "The Shell Expanded: Basic Scripting."* |

Command-Line Options

Window Manager provides two command-line options. We discuss command-line options more thoroughly in Chapter 17. For the purposes of this chapter, it's sufficient to know that you can use command-line options to control the behavior of Window Manager.

-version

Type **kwm -version** at a command prompt to learn the version of Window Manager that you're using. This becomes more important as future versions of Corel Linux are released, since the most current versions of Window Manager may have more functions or have a more streamlined method of performing certain tasks. You'll also need the version number if you're asking for help in an online forum, since answers may vary depending on the version of Window Manager that you're using.

 You can open a terminal window, which contains a command prompt, by clicking the Terminal Emulator button in the KDE Panel.

-nosession

Type **kwm -nosession** at a command prompt to start a new session of Window Manager without restoring the previous session. You might use this function if you were testing a new setup for your desktop or testing a script; restoring the previous session would not allow the new settings to take effect. This command is applicable only when used from text mode.

Keyboard Shortcuts

Certain Window Manager functions can be accessed through keyboard shortcuts, without having to use the mouse or other graphical tools. (If you looked through the Global Keys listings in the Control Center while reading Chapter 7, "Configuring Your Desktop with the Control Center," these shortcuts may look familiar.)

- ALT-ESC or CTRL-ESC opens the current session manager, which shows all desktops and their contents. You can also click the Logout button in this manager to log out of KDE.

- ALT-TAB (or ALT-SHIFT-TAB) cycles through all open windows on the current desktop.

- ALT-F3 opens the Window Operations menu, which allows you to perform basic window management tasks such as resizing, closing, maximizing, and so forth.

- ALT-F4 closes the active window.

- CTRL-F1 (and CTRL-F keys through F8) switches to the virtual desktop that uses the selected number. That is, pressing CTRL-F3 switches to Desktop 3. Desktops 5–8 need to be configured before they're available; see the upcoming section "Doubling the Number of Virtual Desktops" or instructions on increasing your number of virtual desktops.

- CTRL-ALT-ESC invokes Destroy Window mode. When you press this key combination, the cursor becomes a skull and crossbones. Click a window with the new cursor to close that window, killing any processes running within it. (*Kill* is the UNIX term for ending a process manually.) This is especially useful if the process inside that window is stalled or otherwise unresponsive.

Miniature Command-Line Window

Use the keyboard shortcut ALT-F2 to open a small command-line window, shown in Figure 8-1. (You can also invoke this window by right-clicking the desktop and selecting Execute Command from the context menu, or by clicking the Application Starter icon and selecting Start | Run.) Use this window to enter single UNIX shell commands or to execute the following commands:

- Enter a URL to open a File Manager window showing the specified Web location.

- Enter the phrase **man** followed by a UNIX command to open a File Manager window displaying the *man page* for that command.

> **NOTE**   *A man page is a text document written by the programmer who developed the given command. It is a help document of sorts; some man pages are extremely detailed and helpful, while others are quite confusing.*

- Use the SHELL environment variable to execute the command in a shell other than the default. (See Chapter 16, "The Administrator's Tools: Shells and Text Editors," for more information on shell usage.)

Within the miniature command-line window, you can use the up-arrow key to recall previously entered commands and the TAB key to complete partially entered

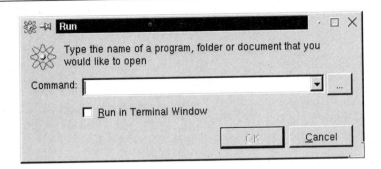

FIGURE 8-1   Use the miniature command-line window to issue a single command

filenames; the Run box auto-completes paths and executable names in full paths, but you may need to use TAB in some cases. Select the Run In Terminal Window check box if you want the output from your shell command to open in a new terminal window.

Window Manager Commands

Use the miniature command-line window or a regular terminal window to issue text commands directly to Window Manager. Issue these commands with the following syntax:

```
kwmcom [command]
```

Type this at a shell prompt and replace *[command]* with the command you want to issue. The commands that Window Manager recognizes are listed in Table 8-1.

You probably won't use these commands very often, because most of these operations are easier to perform with menus, mouse clicks, or graphical tools. However, if you need to use a shell command to control your desktop, you'll find Table 8-1 a useful reference. If you plan to write KDE programs that affect the desktop, you'll find this especially helpful.

ommand	Function
refreshScreen	Refreshes the screen. Use after making changes.
darkenScreen	Turns the screen dark. Warning: This command makes the desktop unresponsive to keyboard or mouse input.
logout	Displays the logout dialog box.
commandLine	Opens the miniature command-line window.
taskManager	Displays the Current Session manager window.
configure	Reloads the screen configuration from the .kwmrc file.
winMove	Moves the currently active window.
winResize	Resizes the currently active window.
winRestore	Restores the currently active window.
winIconify	Iconifies the currently active window.
winClose	Closes the currently active window.
winShade	"Rolls up" the window so that only the title bar is visible on the desktop.
winSticky	Makes the currently active window sticky (so that it appears on all virtual desktops).
winOperations	Displays the Window Operations menu.
deskUnclutter	Tiles all open windows on the desktop.
deskCascade	Overlaps all open windows on the desktop, with all title bars showing.
desktop[1-8]	Switches to the specified desktop (enter the number of the desktop you want to switch to).
desktop+1	Switch to the next desktop.
desktop-1	Switch to the previous desktop.
desktop+2	Move up the desktop list by two.
desktop-2	Move down the desktop list by two.
desktop%2	Toggles between an odd-numbered desktop and the next higher even-numbered desktop (e.g., between Desktop 1 and Desktop 2, or between 3 and 4).

TABLE 8-1   Window Manager Text Commands

Using Virtual Desktop Manager Effectively

In Chapter 5, we described Virtual Desktop Manager briefly as a tool that lets you shift among four virtual desktops. A virtual desktop is exactly what it sounds like—it's another desktop, like the one you see when you boot up your computer.

In KDE, you get four virtual desktops, and you can move among them by using the buttons of the Virtual Desktop Manager icon, docked at the right side of the KDE Panel.

NOTE   *While Corel Linux uses the term* Virtual Desktop Manager *to refer to the utility that controls virtual desktops, you probably won't see that term used outside of Corel-specific documentation. Those using a standard KDE distribution will probably call this utility the* Pager, *and you'll see that term in general KDE documentation.*

These desktops may seem like a developer's idle creation, without much sense or utility. However, you can use Virtual Desktop Manager and the desktops to coordinate and organize the work that you do on your computer, so that you've got certain kinds of tasks on one desktop and other kinds of tasks on other desktops. For example, if you have several kinds of job tasks that you need to keep open at the same time, assign a desktop to each kind of task. You may have system administration tools open on Desktop 1, programs from an office suite open on Desktop 2, Internet programs like Krn or Netscape open on Desktop 3, and stress-relief toys like Solitaire or Sokoban open on Desktop 4.

If you forget which applications are open in each window, click the small arrow to the left of the Desktop 1 button in the Virtual Desktop Manager icon. This arrow opens a graphical representation of your desktops so you can see what's running on each. If you use the Control Center to assign different backgrounds to each desktop, it will be even easier to keep track of what you have open on each.

> TIP
>
> *If you want to open a particular application on all four desktops, click the Sticky button in the application's title bar. (See Chapter 7 for more information on title bar buttons.) A sticky window appears on all desktops, regardless of the desktop in which it was originally opened.*

Virtual desktops can be especially helpful for system administration tasks. For example, if you keep one desktop devoted to system administration, you'll eventually develop a mental habit of shifting into "sysadmin mode" when you shift to that desktop. That's a good way to keep out of the bad habit of doing ordinary tasks when logged in as root. Train yourself to log in as root, as described in Chapter 12, "User Space and User Accounts," only when you see the desktop you've devoted to administration, and you'll cut down on the number of mistakes you make in operating your computer.

> NOTE
>
> *By default, when you log in as root, Corel Linux changes the title bars of open windows to the color red. When you're logged in as a user, they appear blue. If you changed title bar appearance when you configured KDE, you may not see a change.*

Doubling the Number of Virtual Desktops

For some people, four desktops are simply not enough. Corel Linux lets you add up to eight virtual desktops. To add additional desktops beyond the four initially provided, use this process:

1. Right-click the KDE Panel background.

2. Select Configure from the context menu.

3. Click the Desktops tab of the Configure window.

   Select the number of visible desktops you want to have. You can choose two, four, six, or eight.

4. Click the OK button to save your choices and exit the Configure window.

   After you exit the Configure window, you'll see the new number of desktops reflected in the Virtual Desktop Manager icon in the KDE Panel. If you selected eight visible desktops, you'll see eight buttons in the manager; all eight desktops will also be visible in the graphical desktop guide that appears when you click the small arrow next to the Virtual Desktop Manager buttons.

Turning Off Virtual Desktops

Unfortunately for those who don't like them, you cannot completely turn off virtual desktops in Corel Linux. However, you can minimize their impact on your daily habits by making the configuration changes described in the next two paragraphs.

First, use the process in the preceding section to set the number of virtual desktops to two, the lowest possible. You'll still have an extra desktop available, but you don't have to use it. It will merely remain idle.

Next, click the Application Manager icon in the KDE Panel and select Control Center from the Start menu. Select the Borders suboption of the Desktop heading and turn off Active Borders. (See Chapter 7 for more information on working with the Control Center.) With Active Borders deactivated, you won't run the risk of shifting to the other desktop if you slide your mouse cursor too close to the screen edge.

Once you've turned off Active Borders and reduced the number of desktops, you have configured your computer to be as close as possible to a single desktop system. You'll still have that second desktop available through the Virtual Desktop Manager, if you need it.

Terminal Windows Versus KDE's Graphical Tools

No matter your background before you installed Corel Linux, you might wonder whether it's better to use a terminal window or a graphical tool to perform any given administrative task in KDE. Those who come from a Linux background may ask why a graphical tool is needed when a text command works just fine, while those from a graphical interface background may wonder why anyone uses text commands if the graphical tool is just as easy. Neither of these positions is wrong, and neither is wholly correct. Rather, the question of text versus graphical tool is largely a question of preference. Like many other parts of the Linux design philosophy, there are usually at least two ways to do any given task.

That said, there are advantages and disadvantages to each method. Graphical tools allow you to do routine tasks quickly. They are quite intuitive, so you don't have to spend a lot of time studying syntax or other reasons why you must use a given command in a certain way. You can often just open the tool and get going while the program leads you through the process. However, graphical tools often incorporate only the most commonly used aspects of any given task, meaning that you lose some options if you choose to use only graphical administration tools on your system.

Command-line tools also have some advantages. The foremost advantage is that UNIX and its derivative operating systems, like Linux, have a rich and detailed history of command-line operation and a powerful command syntax that has evolved throughout the years of UNIX development. This syntax allows several different tasks to be performed at one time, with the output of one task affecting the performance of the next. For example, you could ask the computer to list the files in a given folder, put the output of the list into a text file, and sort the output by file size. If using a graphical tool, you'd probably have to perform separate actions for each of these tasks.

Probably the most useful aspect of command-line interactions with the computer is that an entire series of tasks can be directed by a single script. Linux systems support a scripting syntax at the command-line level that makes it easy to combine single commands into complex chains of actions. Of course, this requires a fairly significant investment of time into learning the scripting language and the correct syntax to get the script working properly, but the time investment usually pays off as you save time each time you run the script.

Using text-based commands has significant disadvantages, however. UNIX command syntax is so powerful and flexible, and the number of commands is so vast, that no single person knows every single command possible at the command line. Any five given UNIX-based system administrators will perform the same set of functions in a different manner; it can be difficult to understand command syntax when you're getting different suggestions from every expert you ask. Another disadvantage is that it's possible—especially if you're logged in as root—to do serious and nonreversible damage to your computer. Graphical tools usually prevent such catastrophes from happening, if only because you have a second image of what you're about to do before you click the button.

Most people who run Linux and use a graphical interface end up using a blend of graphical and command-line tools to administer their systems. We fall into that group; while we use a lot of terminal windows to maintain and run our computers, we also use graphical tools when they are more convenient or when we're just used to using them. There is no correct answer to the question of terminal windows versus graphical tools; it's completely up to your comfort level. While it's possible to run a machine using solely one or the other, it's unlikely that you will do that with your Corel Linux system because both methods are so easily available.

Like the other aspects of system administration that we discuss in other parts of this book, you have the choice to administer your system using the tools that you're comfortable with. If you find that you'd rather change passwords in a terminal window by using the `passwd` command, rather than using the Password heading in the Control Center, go ahead. If you find yourself at a terminal prompt with an utterly blank memory of the correct syntax, close the terminal window and use a graphical tool instead. The flexibility of Corel Linux means that you can accomplish the same tasks in several different ways.

CHAPTER 9

Using the Internet with Corel Linux

It's rare these days to find computers that aren't connected to the Internet in some way, whether via a modem or through a direct connection. Certainly, it would be quite difficult to be a Linux aficionado without having Internet access; so much discussion and software information is released on the Internet that it's hard to keep up to date without frequent access. In this section, we outline the procedure necessary to connect your Corel Linux machine to a Linux-friendly Internet Service Provider (ISP). We also describe the basic Internet software that was installed when you installed Corel Linux; its Internet suite includes a news reader, an e-mail program, and two types of chat clients. You can even use File Manager as an effective FTP client.

You may have already set up a PPP (Point to Point Protocol) connection for your existing ISP account. If this is the case, feel free to ignore this section and jump to the section of this chapter titled "Using KDE's Integrated Internet Tools."

Configuring an Internet Connection with Dial-Up

To access the Internet from your Corel Linux machine, you need to set up a connection to an Internet Service Provider. In this section, we assume that you already have an account with an ISP that supports Linux computers. If you don't, see the sidebar titled "Linux-Compatible ISPs" for some hints on finding and working with a provider that offers Internet access to Linux users. We also assume that you want to set up a PPP connection, which allows you to view Web pages and other nontext portions of material available on the Internet. Finally, we assume that you have installed a modem (or that one has been installed for you), that it works, and that it's connected to a working phone line. You may want to consult the material provided by the Linux Documentation Project on modem setup, which can be found at `http://www.linuxdoc.org/HOWTO/Modem-HOWTO.html`.

Setting Up Your Account Information

Configuring your PPP connection with Corel Linux is quite simple. Corel Linux provides a tool called Dial-Up that takes the basic information about your connection and sets up the appropriate files to establish the connection. The most important thing to remember in this process is to type everything exactly as it's

Linux-Compatible ISPs

To get Internet access on your Corel Linux machine, you'll need to have an account with a service provider that permits the use of Linux software to connect. Basically, this means a provider that does not require proprietary software to access the ISP's computers; most proprietary ISP software, such as that used by America Online, is available only for Windows and Macintosh computers. An ISP that offers a regular PPP (Point to Point Protocol) account is a good choice since you can use Corel Linux's Dial-Up utility to connect. The more important reason to select an ISP that is at least Linux-aware is that you may need to call the help desk on occasion. If the only help offered is that specific to Windows or Macintosh, it's not much help to you.

You may have local service providers who support Linux users, especially if you're in a large city or near a college or university campus. Or, you might want the convenience of a national ISP, especially if you travel and need to dial into a local service point in many different cities. Find a list of Linux-friendly ISPs at `http://howto.linuxberg.com/isp.html` and locate a few that are within your local calling distance, and then call and ask some questions. Here are a few basic queries to get you started:

- Do you require proprietary software be used to connect to a user account? If so, is this software available for Linux users?

- Are your technical assistance personnel familiar with Linux? Do you offer training so that they can answer questions from Linux users?

- Do any of your users use Linux? How many? Do you have support materials written for your Linux users?

You may not get favorable answers to all of these questions; in some cases, the cost of an account with a less-than-perfect ISP may be more crucial for you than the quality of the technical support at another provider. As long as the account you select is a regular PPP account, you should be able to do whatever you need to do; just be aware that you may have to solve your own problems instead of relying on the help desk for aid.

given to you, including capitalization and punctuation. This will save you the hassle of redoing everything when it becomes clear that you've mistyped all the IP numbers or your password.

> **NOTE** *If you are looking for help with your PPP connection in various Web documentation, you may not find the term "Dial-Up" for this utility. Try looking for the name "Kppp," which is the name for this utility in the standard KDE distribution.*

Before you begin working with Dial-Up, take a moment to gather all the information you'll need. If you have a new ISP account, you were probably given a sheet with connection information. If not, or if you're using an existing account, check the ISP's Web site to see if the data is posted there. Failing both of those options, call the help desk and ask for the data you need. To use Dial-Up successfully, you need the following information:

- Your login ID (username). Know your password or the password the ISP created for your first login. *free , free*
- The ISP's modem bank telephone number. *1890 9240 f2*
- The IP numbers of the Domain Name Server, or DNS, machines.
- Whether your ISP assigns IP numbers statically or dynamically; if statically, you'll need your IP number and the subnet mask number. *dynamically*
- Information about the ISP gateway computer.

DNS Addresses
194.145.128.1
194.145.128.2
Domain Name
iolfree.ie

You'll also need to know your modem's device name and whether the modem uses hardware or software flow control; *flow control* is the method by which your modem exchanges information with the modem at your ISP. The device name is set in the operating system; it's likely to be /dev/modem or /dev/cua1.

/dev/cua0   h/w

> **NOTE** *The designation cuaX, where X is a given number, is how Linux assigns ports used for communications devices. If you're coming from a Windows environment, the same concept is represented there as "com ports." What was on com1 in Windows will be /dev/cua0 in Linux; what was on com2 will be on /dev/cua1. (Remember that UNIX and its derivatives begin counting with zero.)*

e-Mail or SMTP Host
Mail. iolfree.ie
kilnageer@iolfree.ie

NNTP or news host
news.iol.ie

(handwritten margin note, top left)
proxy. 1olfree.in
port: 8080

Once you have all the information in front of you, it's time to configure Dial-Up.

1. Click the Application Manager icon in the KDE Panel and select Applications | Network | Dial-Up from the Start menu.

2. On the Dial-Up screen, click the Setup button.

3. The Dial-Up Configuration window appears, as shown in Figure 9-1.

4. Click the New button to open the New Account dialog box.

5. Click the Dial tab if it is not already on top.

6. Enter the ISP's dial-up phone number, the authentication type, and the connection name on this tab.

   The connection name is just for your use, so you can put anything you want here. The ISP's name is easiest.

> **NOTE**   *You do have to select an authentication type; if your ISP doesn't use authentication, just choose Script Based.*

9

7. Click the IP tab of the New Account screen.

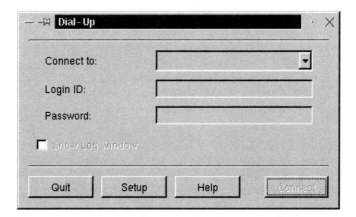

FIGURE 9-1   Use Dial-Up for a rapid and accurate configuration of your dial-up Internet connection

(handwritten note, bottom right)
1 800 923 111

8. Select the DHCP button.

 If your ISP provides static IP service—that is, if you have paid for a single IP number to be permanently assigned to your computer— select the Static IP Address button and enter your IP number and subnet mask information.

9. Click the DNS tab of the New Account screen.

10. Enter the IP numbers of your ISP's Domain Name Server computers.

Your ISP should have provided two DNS numbers. Enter the first (sometimes labeled "primary") into the DNS IP Address box and click the Add button. The number appears in the DNS Address List window. Enter the second (sometimes labeled "secondary") into the DNS IP Address box and click the Add button again. The second number also appears in the Address List window.

11. Click the Gateway tab of the New Account screen.

Most ISPs don't provide specific information about their gateway computer: the computer that handles all incoming and outgoing Internet traffic. This makes it easier for system maintenance. If, for some reason, your ISP has given you a specific gateway IP number, enter it on this tab; otherwise, skip to the next step.

12. Click the Login Script tab of the New Account screen.

On this tab, you create and edit the script used to send your login ID and password to the ISP during the login procedure. You may not need this; if your ISP doesn't use a text-based login process, it gets your ID and password during the connection process that it does use. If that's the case, leave this page blank.

If your ISP does use a text-based login process, and you want to automate that process so that you don't have to sit waiting for the login window to appear, you can write a login script, as shown in Figure 9-2, on this tab to make that process easier. See the following section for information on setting up a script.

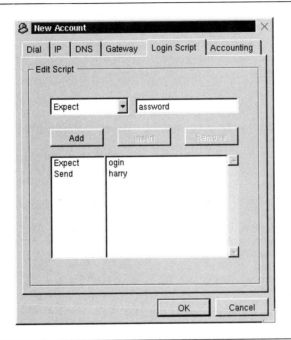

FIGURE 9-2   Write a brief script to automate the ISP login process

Login Speed Through Login Scripts

If your ISP uses a text-based login and you'd like to create a script to handle that task for you, follow these steps to create a basic login script. You may need to tinker with this a bit, since different ISPs use slightly different event sequences for their login procedures. The script developed here should work for most; if it doesn't work for you, ask your (Linux-friendly) ISP for help.

The login script is composed of two elements: words that the ISP sends to you (that your computer expects to see), and words that you send to the ISP. Begin building your login script on the Login Script tab of the Dial-Up Configuration screen.

1. Type **ogin:** in the text entry box next to the word Expect.

Omit the first letter of the terms you expect from the ISP; some ISPs use uppercase, and some use lower, so leaving out the first letter solves the problem.

2. Click the Add button.

The `ogin:` term appears in the script pane.

3. Click Expect and choose Send from the drop-down list.

Expect changes to Send, which formats the next entry in the script as something that your computer will send to the ISP.

4. Type your username in the text entry box next to Send.

5. Click the Add button.

6. Click Send and choose Expect from the drop-down list.

7. Type **assword:** in the text entry box next to Expect.

As with `ogin:`, delete the first letter to avoid case confusion.

8. Click Expect and choose Send from the drop-down list.

9. Type your password in the text entry box next to Send.

10. Click the Add button.

You've now completed a basic login script. Test it with your ISP; if it doesn't work, make sure you've typed your username and password correctly and that you have Send and Expect correctly applied to the script elements. If it still doesn't work, contact your ISP.

11. (Optional) Click the Accounting tab of the New Account screen.

KDE provides a feature that keeps track of how much data you have transferred through your ISP connection. Most users of U.S. ISPs will not use this feature, since American ISPs tend to control usage by time, rather than by bandwidth usage. Many users on other continents (especially Europe), however, must keep a close eye on their usage to keep the ISP bill under control.

12. Click the OK button.

When you have supplied all the information requested by Dial-Up and clicked the OK button, the New Account screen closes. Leave the Dial-Up Configuration window open, as you'll continue to use it in the next two sections of this chapter for modem configuration and testing.

Setting Up Your Modem

Here you'll use Dial-Up to confirm that your modem is working correctly. We assume that you've set up your modem at the operating system level already, as described in Chapter 19, "Dealing with Hardware." If not, or if you're installing a new modem as you work through this chapter, you'll need to return to that chapter and follow the directions to make sure that your modem and Corel Linux are talking to each other. This section covers modems only as part of setting up a working PPP connection.

The Dial-Up modem configuration process is quite similar to the New Account process you just finished. If you left Dial-Up open to the Configuration window, you can begin right away. If you closed Dial-Up, reopen it by clicking the Application Manager icon in the KDE Panel and selecting Applications | Network | Dial-Up from the Start menu.

9

1. Click the Device tab at the top of the Dial-Up Configuration window.

2. Click the Modem Device button.

3. Choose the device name of your modem from the drop-down list.

   The *device name* is the name by which Linux knows your modem. You learned the device name of your modem when you installed it or installed Corel Linux.

4. In the other boxes of the Modem Device tab, as shown in Figure 9-3, enter required information about your modem.

   ■ **Flow Control**   The method your modem uses to exchange information with another computer. It's preferable to use hardware control rather than software control. Select CRTSCTS to set hardware control. (If you want or need to use software control, which some modems require, select XON/XOFF.)

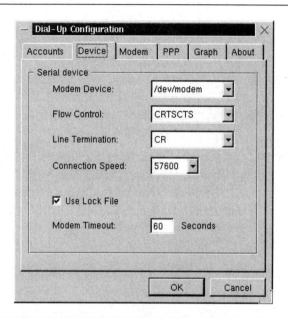

FIGURE 9-3   Configure your modem with Dial-Up's easy tools

- **Line Termination**   Ignore this for now. If you have consistent trouble with your modem connection, try switching this option on and off; however, line termination is usually not the first culprit.

- **Connection Speed**   Select the highest speed your modem can handle (the speed written on the box). While connections vary in actual speed, and your modem can handle speeds lower than the top speed, you can't get faster speed from a slow modem.

5. Click the Modem tab of the Dial-Up Configuration screen.

6. Enter a number in the Busy Waits text box.

   This number is the number of seconds your computer will wait before redialing when it gets a busy signal at the ISP. A number between five and ten is reasonable. If you find that you use this feature a lot—that is, your ISP has frequent busy signals—you may want to investigate a new ISP since your current provider does not have sufficient modems for its user base.

7. (Optional) Click the Modem Commands button and edit the default settings in the Edit Modem Commands box.

   You probably don't need to do this unless you have an unusual modem. Most modems sold in the United States and Canada are Hayes or Hayes-compatible devices, which use standard *init strings*. The init string is a list of codes that tell your modem how to operate. Consult your modem's manual to see the init string for your modem; if the string in the manual is the same as the string on the screen, you don't need to do anything.

> **CAUTION** *Modem init strings are complicated and unintuitive. If you need to type in a new string, make sure you enter it exactly as it is printed—letters, numbers, ampersands, capitalization, and all. If you enter it incorrectly, the modem will not work.*

8. Click the OK button.

   The Edit Modem Commands window closes, and the Dial-Up Configuration window reappears.

9. Click the OK button.

   The Dial-Up Configuration window closes, and the main Dial-Up window reappears.

   You've now completed configuring Dial-Up. All that's left is testing, to make sure you did everything right as you worked through the process.

Testing Your Dial-Up Configuration

Testing your configuration is as simple as making a regular connection to your ISP. If you have just completed configuring your modem, the Dial-Up window is still open on your desktop; if you closed Dial-Up, click the Application Starter icon in the Panel and select Applications I Network I Dial-Up to reopen Dial-Up.

Click the Connect button to begin the connection process. You should see a normal connection to your ISP; if your modem volume is turned up, you'll be able to hear the dial tone, the dialing, and the static-filled connection tones as your computer interacts with the ISP's computer. Once you have established a normal connection, you need not work further with Dial-Up's configuration options unless something changes, either at your ISP or with a new modem.

If you don't establish a connection for some reason, here are some basic troubleshooting tips. Connection problems are usually problems with either your setup or the ISP; test your end of the conversation first. If you did everything correctly, call the ISP and explain the problem; perhaps they are experiencing system problems that make dialing in impossible.

- Is there a working phone line plugged into the modem?

- Do you hear a dial tone on that line, either from your modem or from a telephone plugged into the line? If you hear a dial tone from a telephone but not from the modem, you may have configured the modem incorrectly.

- Do you hear a dial tone and the dialing of the number, but no connection is made? Check the telephone number you entered for the ISP; if you have the right number, check with the ISP. They may have a problem with their modems.

- Do you get a connection but cannot sign on? Did you enter your username and password correctly, especially if you're using a login script? Passwords and usernames are case sensitive, so be sure you typed them correctly.

- Do you get signed on but then receive messages concerning DNS lookup failures? Check the IP numbers you entered on the DNS tab. If you entered them correctly, check with the ISP.

Using KDE's Integrated Internet Tools

Once you have set up your ISP connection, you need to figure out what tools you want to use to take advantage of that access. KDE provides a suite of basic Internet programs that access different portions of the Internet; these programs are robust and straightforward. You may have other favorite programs for these purposes, especially if you've used UNIX-based operating systems before. To use those programs, simply locate the appropriate source package and install it. We cover installing programs from Debian packages or from source code in Chapter 22, "Administering Services."

In this section, we cover the main Internet programs that KDE offers, discussing configuration and use of each tool. Five KDE programs are covered here: Kmail, an e-mail client; Kbiff, a tool that alerts you when new e-mail arrives;

News, a newsgroup reader; JabberIM, a Web-based chat client compatible with the popular ICQ personal messaging program; and Chat, an Internet Relay Chat (IRC) client. Also, see Chapter 6, "Corel File Manager," in which we discuss using File Manager as an FTP client and a Web browser.

Kmail: KDE's Electronic Mail Client

Kmail is the KDE electronic mail client, a program designed specifically to handle e-mail. With it, you can compose new messages, reply to mail you've received, attach files to be sent along with e-mail, and organize your received mail effectively. You need to configure Kmail before you can use it; once configured, its functions are intuitive and easy to use.

> **NOTE** *You won't find Kmail in any of the Corel Linux menus, even though it's installed when you install Corel Linux. To start Kmail, click the Application Starter icon and select Run from the Start menu. When the mini–command-line window appears, type* **kmail** *and press* ENTER.

9

Configuring Kmail

Kmail's configuration screens are quite similar to those for Dial-Up. You need some basic information from your ISP, just as with Dial-Up, and you need to make changes on several tabs within the configuration window to get your e-mail connection running smoothly. Once configured, though, you won't need to change anything in the configuration unless something changes at your ISP.

1. Click the Application Starter icon and select Run from the Start menu. When the mini–command-line window appears, type **kmail** and press ENTER.

   If this is the first time you have opened Kmail, the Settings dialog box will open automatically along with the regular Kmail window. If you have opened Kmail before but haven't configured it, open the Settings dialog box by selecting File | Settings. The Settings box will open with the Identity tab selected.

2. Enter your e-mail address in the Identity tab.

   Leave the Reply-To Address field blank unless you want people to reply to a different address than the one you use to send e-mail; perhaps you are writing e-mail on someone else's behalf and want responses to go to that person directly.

3. (Optional) Enter information into the Signature File field.

   If you put something in this field, it will appear at the bottom of every e-mail message you send. Signature files usually include your full name and e-mail address and may include company name and title if you use this account for business purposes. It is never a good idea to put your home telephone number or address into a signature file since you have no control over who sees that information.

4. Click the Network tab of the Settings screen.

5. Click the button next to SMTP in the Sending Mail area of the screen.

6. Click the Add button located beneath Incoming Mail.

7. Select POP3.

8. (Optional) Select Local Mailbox if you've made arrangements with your ISP to download your e-mail directly to your computer.

9. Click the OK button.

   The Kmail Configure Account screen appears.

10. Enter the identifying information about your ISP's mail server into the Host field.

    This may be a machine name, such as mail.yourisp.com or pop3.yourisp.com. It also may be an IP number. Leave the Port field empty unless your ISP has defined a specific port for you to use.

11. Click the OK button.

    The Configure Account screen closes and the Settings screen reappears.

12. Click the OK button.

    The Settings screen closes, and Kmail builds a new set of file structures that will control your electronic mail.

   Now that you have configured Kmail to work with your ISP's mail server, you can begin to receive e-mail from the ISP. To download new electronic mail, click the Get New Mail button. Kmail contacts your ISP. To see if new mail was downloaded, click the inbox name in the upper-left corner of the Kmail screen. The subject lines and senders' names of any new mail that was downloaded will appear there. Click a message to display it in the large window at the bottom of the Kmail screen.

> **TIP** *If you want to use Kmail as your standard mail program, you may want to create a desktop icon. To do this, simply open File Manager and navigate to /usr/X11R6/bin. Find the* kmail *entry; click it with the mouse to select it, and drag the entry to the desktop. When you release the mouse button, a small menu will appear. Select Link from that menu. Now you can click the icon to start Kmail.*

Composing New Messages

Kmail makes it easy to compose and send new e-mail messages. You can also attach files from your hard drive that will accompany the message to the recipient's inbox. To compose a new message, use these steps:

1. Click the Compose New Message button.

   The New Message screen appears.

2. Enter the recipient's e-mail address in the To field.

3. (Optional) To send a carbon copy of the message, enter that person's e-mail address in the Cc field.

4. Type your message in the large text entry box at the bottom of the New Message screen.

5. When you have finished, click the Send Message button.

   Kmail automatically contacts your ISP and uploads the message to its mail server.

To attach a file from your hard drive to the message, click the Attach button (which carries the picture of a paperclip). A File Manager window appears; navigate through File Manager to the file you want to attach, select it, and click the OK button. A copy of the file is appended to the message and will be uploaded and delivered when you click the Send Message button.

Replying to Messages

Since electronic mail is two-way communication, you will need to reply to many of the messages you receive. Like composing new messages, replying to a message is a simple process.

1. Click the Reply To Author button.

   If several recipients were included in the original message and you wish to send your reply to all of them, click the Reply To All Recipients button instead.

   The Kmail composition window appears, with the e-mail address of the message's sender already placed in the To field. The complete message to which you are replying is quoted in the text entry pane.

2. Delete the parts of the quoted message that you do not wish to include in your message.

3. Type your reply in the text entry pane.

4. Click the Send Message button when you have finished the message.

Managing Electronic Mail

Once you have received and read a message, you have several options. You can delete the mail, save it to a file, or print it. It makes good file management sense to create folders for your saved mail that help you organize those messages; folders labeled "Personal," "Work," and "Linux" might be a good start.

- To delete an e-mail message, click the Delete button above the message.

- To save an e-mail message, click the Save button above the message. The Save screen appears; select the location where you want the message to be saved and click the Save button.

- To print an e-mail message, click the Print button above the message.

Kbiff: E-mail Notification

While electronic mail itself is a time-saver, you can certainly waste a lot of time clicking the Get New Mail button to see if anyone has sent you mail. KDE offers a small utility, called Kbiff, to handle that task for you. Kbiff runs in the background and sits quietly in your System Tray, checking your ISP's mail server at regular intervals to see if mail has arrived. When you do have new mail, Kbiff lets you know. You don't need Kbiff, but it is a small aid that can quickly prove its usefulness.

1. Open File Manager and navigate to /usr/X11R6/biff. Double-click the `biff` entry to open Kbiff.

2. Set the mail check interval in the Poll box.

   You can have Kbiff check your mail at any frequency you like, from mere seconds to once or twice a day.

3. Click the Mailbox tab at the top of the Kbiff screen.

4. Enter the mailbox information requested; this is the same information you used to set up Kmail. You need your e-mail address and your ISP's mail server information.

5. Click the OK button.

   The Kbiff icon appears in the System Tray. When you have new mail, the icon will change to a mailbox with the flag up.

News: KDE's Newsgroup Client

Whereas Kmail handles personal electronic mail messages, News handles messages posted to newsgroups on the portion of the Internet known as USENET. A newsgroup is a collection of messages related to a single topic, denoted by the newsgroup's name. For example, comp.x-windows.kde carries postings related in some way to the KDE desktop, while rec.woodworking carries posts related to the hobby. Messages meant for rec.woodworking are off-topic for comp.x-windows.kde, and vice versa. You can find a newsgroup for almost any concept that you can think of.

> **TIP** *News is a version of a highly reliable and popular UNIX newsreader called* rn. *If you have trouble with News, consider looking up some Internet help resources devoted to* rn; *you may find the solution there. You may also find KDE resources that refer to Krn, a program very similar to the Corel Linux News program.*

Reading News with News

News presents newsgroup posts to you in a tree format, in the same way that File Manager presents your computer's directory structure. Posts are sorted into *threads*, groups of messages that stem from the same root post, using the Subject line of the posts to organize the tree.

1. Click the Application Starter icon in the Panel and select Applications | Network | News Client from the Start menu.

   The News screen appears. If this is the first time you've read news with this computer, the screen will be blank. If you have read news on this computer before, News pulls the list of groups you read into the collapsed tree format.

> **TIP** *News looks for a file called .newsrc in your home directory. The groups to which you have subscribed are listed in .newsrc, as are the message numbers that you have viewed. You don't have to create .newsrc; once you begin reading news, your news client creates it automatically.*

2. Click the small plus sign to expand the newsgroup tree one level.

   If you have no groups showing, News asks whether you want to download a list of all newsgroups carried by your ISP's news server. Click the Yes button; depending on the speed of your modem and the number of groups carried by your ISP, this download may be brief, or it may take more than ten minutes.

> **NOTE** *You cannot read a group that your ISP itself does not subscribe to. If you know of a group that you want to read, but your ISP doesn't carry it, you can often request that it be added. For those whose ISPs do not add groups at user request, consider using a Web-based archive or purchasing a third-party Web-based news service such as those offered by* `http://www.deja.com` *or* `http://www.newsguy.com.`

3. Click the plus sign and keep doing so until you see newsgroup names in the tree, as seen in Figure 9-4.

4. Double-click the name of a newsgroup that you want to read.

The News reader window appears, as does the News Confirmation screen.

5. Enter the number of articles you want to download from that newsgroup and the order in which you want to download them into the Confirmation box.

6. Click the OK button.

News connects to your ISP's news server and downloads the requested messages. The articles appear in the upper portion of the News reader window when the download is complete.

7. Click the article you want to read first.

The text of the article appears in the lower half of the News reader window.

8. Repeat this process for each group that you want to read.

9. Select File I Exit when you have finished reading news.

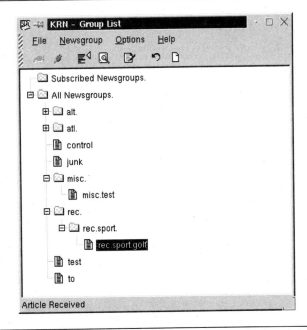

FIGURE 9-4   Reading USENET groups is simple with News's threaded presentation

Posting News with News

For many people, simply reading the posts in various USENET groups is enough. This habit is called *lurking*, and those who read but do not post are called *lurkers*. It's generally a good idea to lurk for a while before you begin to post, simply to understand how conversation happens in different groups. If you want to join the conversation in a particular group, though, you need to stop lurking and use News's posting features to participate.

1. With News open, click the Post New Article button.

   The News Composition window, shown in Figure 9-5, appears. (It looks like the Kmail Composer window; News uses Kmail's composition tools for posting purposes.)

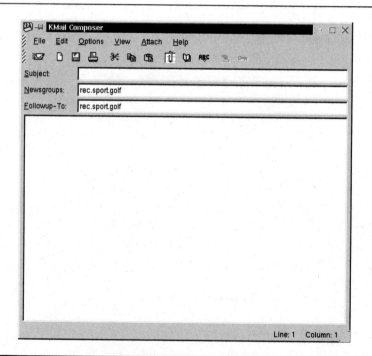

FIGURE 9-5   Post to a newsgroup with the News Composition screen

2. Fill in the Subject line.

   Use a specific and clear subject so that people will be likely to select and read your message.

3. Enter the text of your post in the text entry pane of the News window.

4. Click the Send button when you have finished the post.

   News uploads your message to the ISP news server. It is distributed to news servers around the world; it may not appear immediately, since USENET traffic is often saved in batches for bulk transfer to the Internet.

Replying to a Post with News

Like e-mail, newsgroups are a participatory medium. Threads develop because several people respond to a series of posts, building a conversation. To respond to a particular post, use the reply tools of News.

1. With the post to which you want to reply visible in the News reader window, click the Post A Followup button.

   The News Composition window opens, with many of the fields already filled in; the Subject, Newsgroup, and Follow-Up To Fields are completed. The article to which you're responding is quoted in full in the text entry pane of the screen.

2. Delete the portions of the quoted article that you don't want to address.

   It is newsgroup etiquette to trim quoted material so that you quote only parts that you are actually referring to in your response.

3. Add your response after, or interspersed with, the quoted material.

4. Click the Send button when you have finished the post.

TIP   *If you prefer to reply to an article by e-mail, use the same procedure but begin by clicking the Reply By Mail button instead.*

CAUTION *While News allows you simultaneously to send a response via e-mail and post that response to the newsgroup, this is usually a bad idea. It is not good "netiquette" to duplicate the message unless the original poster explicitly requests it (when, for example, the poster's ISP doesn't get every message for some reason). If you want to post and mail a response, make sure you mention that you've done so in the message. A line saying "Posted and e-mailed" is sufficient.*

Kvirc: Worldwide Group Chat

IRC, or Internet Relay Chat, allows you to chat with any number of people at any time of day, without planning the connection ahead of time. Kvirc is an IRC client that makes it easier to handle the often-overwhelming business of chatting on IRC.

TIP *If you haven't chatted on IRC before, it would probably be helpful for you to look through some of the help documents available on* `http://www.irchelp.org`. *IRC has its own culture, and it can be hard to understand the way in which it works or the specialized language found in the various channels.*

1. Click the Application Starter icon in the KDE Panel and select Applications | Network | Chat Client from the Start menu.

   The Server Control screen appears.

2. Select Connections | New Server to open the Connect To Server window.

3. Click the arrow next to Recent.

4. Select a server network from the drop-down list that appears.

NOTE *IRC servers are not all interconnected. Instead, they are clumped into several main networks, including EFnet, DalNet, and Undernet, as well as some smaller and more specialized networks. You may find the same channel on more than one network, but they are two independent conversations.*

5. Select an IRC server from the list under Server/Quick Connect To.

   You can often determine the server's geographical location from its name. Select one close to you to minimize lag.

6. Click the Connect button.

   The Kvirc screen appears, with a rapidly scrolling amount of text. Don't try to read it all at once; it's administrative material and not crucial to chatting. The Pick A Nick dialog box appears.

7. Type the nickname you want to use into the Pick A Nick screen.

   Since thousands of people use IRC at the same time, it's unlikely that you'll be able to simply use your first name. Keep trying until the server accepts a nickname. Once you select a unique nick, you'll be connected to the server. More text will rush past; you can scroll back if you want to read it.

8. Type the name of the channel you want to join on the text entry line, using the syntax `/join #channelname`.

   Know the channel you want to join before you connect. Literally hundreds, if not thousands, of channels are open at any time. Channel names are always preceded by the pound sign, or #. If text scrolls past yet once again, you've connected to the channel you selected; see Figure 9-6 (on the following page) for a sample of the channel #linux. Look at the right pane of the Kvirc window to see who else has joined this channel. The conversation fills the left pane of the window.

9. Send a message to the channel by entering your comment into the text entry box and pressing ENTER.

10. When you have finished chatting, type `/quit` into the text entry box.

    The Kvirc screen closes, and the Server Control screen reappears.

11. Select File | Quit to leave Kvirc.

Corel Online Services

If you want to simplify your Internet activities as much as possible, consider using some of the online services that Corel offers. These Web-based services are extremely easy to use. The two main services are e-mail and a personal messaging program, but you'll find news and information resources as well.

To use the Corel Online Services, click the Application Starter button and select Online Services from the Start menu. Select any service you'd like from the

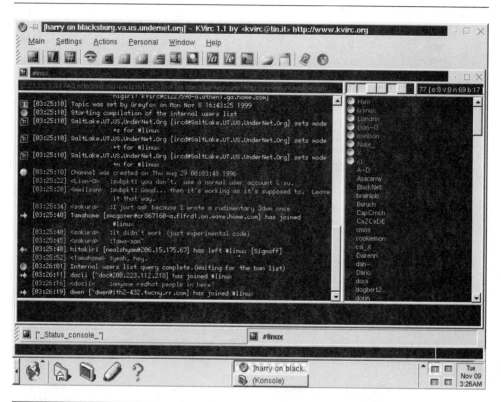

FIGURE 9-6   Kvirc lets you talk about your favorite topics in real time, with people around the world

pop-up menu; when you've made your selection, Netscape will launch to that service's home page. Available services include

- **Business Community**   News articles and services for business users.

- **Clip Art and Photos**   Download thousands of clip-art images for use in documents and Web pages.

- **Corel Printing Service**   Upload your design, art, photo, or logo and let Corel print it on a T-shirt or coffee mug.

- **Corel VDrive**   Sign up for a free VDrive (virtual drive) account and get 20 megabytes of free storage space on Corel's servers.

- **Current Events**   Headlines and articles of interest on many different subjects.

- **Designer F/X**   Create and manipulate image files.

- **eFax Service**   Allows you to create an account that sets you up with an individual phone number at which you can receive faxes. Faxes are then sent to you as e-mail attachments. Premium services include toll-free fax numbers and the ability to send, as well as receive, faxes via e-mail.

- **E-Mail**   Free Web-based e-mail.

- **Graphic Community**   News, downloads, and services for graphic designers.

- **JabberIM**   An instant messaging system similar to, and compatible with, the popular ICQ program. Use this Web page to register for a JabberIM account. When you do, a small Jabber window appears on your screen; enter your username and password to log in. Once logged into Jabber, you can communicate with other Jabber users.

  If you have an existing ICQ account (you can obtain one through `http://www.mirabilis.com`, though the software is Windows- and Macintosh-compatible only), enter your ICQ information into the Jabber account configuration options. You'll then be able to use JabberIM to communicate with ICQ users.

- **Linux Community**   News, downloads, and services for Corel Linux users.

- **New Online Services**   Use this Web page to keep up to date with the latest online services offered by Corel.

- **Search the Internet**   A search engine and Web directory.

- **Text F/X**   Create downloadable text effects with a variety of fonts, sizes, colors, and effects.

9

uploads.webspace.freeserve.net (195.92.193.198)

Username : kilnageer.freeserve.co.uk
password :   newyear 3

ftp
_____

myhome.iolfree.ie

kilnageer

belcarra

cd public-html

ls
  :
  : index.html

PART III

Running Your Corel Linux System

CHAPTER 10

Start Up and Shut Down

This part of the book addresses basic concepts about Linux operating systems, about the way in which your operating system has organized the various files on the hard drive, and the mechanics of operating a multiuser system. In this chapter, we cover the startup and shutdown processes of Corel Linux. Although it's not something that most people think about very much, the startup and shutdown processes are a crucial part of a computer's operation. Both processes are much more than a simple electrical connection; whereas a light bulb needs only the flip of a switch to become operational, a computer takes that same switch flip or button press and begins a complex process of operations that ensures the machine will continue to operate smoothly.

We use the terms start *and* boot *interchangeably because they both mean the same thing. When we mention that a certain process requires you to* reboot *before it becomes effective, we mean* restart.

Starting Your Corel Linux Computer

No matter what kind of computer you've used in the past, you've dealt with the boot-up process. However, you may not have used a computer that had a boot process that appears as complicated as that on your Linux machine. Certainly, Linux startup looks quite technical and intimidating, but it's not that much different from a Windows or Macintosh boot process. The main difference is that Windows and Macintosh screen many of the operations from the user: Windows computers show some of the data and hide the rest behind "Starting Windows..." or perform operations after the desktop appears, and Mac processes startup information behind the "happy Mac" splash screen. With a Linux computer, you see everything the computer is doing.

NOTE   *Corel Linux actually hides most of these startup messages behind the startup screen. You can see the messages by issuing the command* **dmesg** *at a command prompt after booting up, or you can select Expert Mode on the login screen to see all the messages during the boot process.*

What really happens when you press the power button on your computer case? Here's the sequence of events:

- After you press the power button, electricity goes to the power supply of the computer case and powers on the CPU.

■ The CPU tests itself briefly to make sure that it's fully operational.

■ The BIOS initializes and checks the installed RAM for problems. *BIOS* (Basic Input/Output System) is a function of the motherboard. It is the lowest level configurable software on your computer and feeds the operating system information about the various hardware devices you have installed in the computer. After BIOS initializes and tests RAM, it triggers the remainder of the startup process.

■ The CPU runs the program located in the special *boot sector* of the hard drive (or another location, if you've chosen not to start from the hard drive). In Linux, that program is called LILO; we addressed it briefly in Chapter 2, "Installing Corel Linux," and cover it in more detail later in this chapter. The *boot sector* is the first sector of the first cylinder of the physical hard drive, and computers look there first for programs that determine how the operating system will boot up.

■ LILO loads the *kernel* into system memory. The kernel is the core of your operating system; it's the code that your computer uses constantly to manage itself. By loading the kernel into RAM, the operating system ensures that it has immediate access to the kernel code for whatever functions it needs to perform (referred to as *calls*).

■ After the kernel is loaded into RAM, it calls the init process.

The init process controls your computer's configuration and initializes the system for use. The UNIX documentation that describes init calls it the "father of all processes" since it creates the environment in which all other commands will run.

■ init reads the file /etc/inittab and determines the default *runlevel* to use. A runlevel is basically a shortcut; each runlevel contains a certain set of actions. When you start up the computer, the runlevel you've chosen determines what programs and processes start. It also provides a safety feature; if you had to start all these processes by hand, you might forget one or two. With runlevels, it's automatic, so you can't forget to start something crucial. Of the seven runlevels, two are never used at startup. Corel Linux is set to runlevel 2 by default. We discuss runlevels in more detail later in this chapter, in the section "Selecting an Appropriate Runlevel."

■ Once runlevel has been determined, init runs all the scripts located in /etc/rcX.d, where *X* is the number of the runlevel. In the default installation of Corel Linux, the startup scripts are located in /etc/rc5.d. Each entry in

10

/etc/rc*X*.d is a symbolic link to a corresponding script in /etc/init.d, and each of those scripts starts a particular program or service. Most of the work of the boot process involves running these scripts. You can see the work of the scripts as the list of services being started scrolls up your screen during boot-up. The scripts contained in /etc/init.d as part of the default Corel Linux installation are described in Table 10-1. However, not all of these scripts will start on your particular machine. Corel has included a set of standard scripts to cover most known potential configurations.

■ When all services have been started, the Corel Linux login screen appears, and the system is ready for use.

Just like almost every other function of your computer, the startup process is much quicker if you have more system memory. Since the kernel lives in memory, more RAM installed on your computer means that there is more space for the kernel to operate, which means that the process is faster. Processor speed is also a component of quick startup, but adding RAM is both cheaper and easier than upgrading the chip.

A Sample init Script

Now that we've described the startup process and explained how Corel Linux uses `init` scripts to start the various processes that keep your computer running, you may be wondering what one of those scripts looks like. In this section, we show you a basic script and provide an explanation for each part of the script. If you find scripts intriguing, read Chapter 17, "The Shell Expanded: Basic Scripting."

The script we've chosen as our example is the `xfs` script, which starts and stops the X font server. This server tells the X Window System how to handle user requests for various fonts. In the following, the script appears first and the description follows.

```
#!/bin/sh
```

This line is a ritual incantation. It tells the computer that the script should be executed by the `sh` shell-command interpreter. All scripts must have a line like this, which tells the computer which shell to use to execute the various commands that follow; you can use a different shell environment to execute a given program, as explained in Chapter 17.

```
# /etc/init.d/xfs: start or stop the X font server
```

Script Name	Script Function
README	An instructional file
Xserver_setnormalmode	Starts X server in normal mode
Xserver_setsafemode	Starts X server in safe mode
apache	Web server
apmd	A power management daemon—mostly for laptops
autofs	Starts file system automounter
bootmisc.sh	Miscellaneous boot functions
checkfs.sh	Runs fsck on all disk partitions except /
checkroot.sh	Runs fsck on /
cron	Allows execution of timed, or recurring processes
detector	Updates /etc/modules file when a new network device is added
dhcpcd	Obtains IP number from DHCP server
dosplashFX	Boot time splash-screen effects
exim	Mail Transport Agent
halt	Process stopper
hostname.sh	Sets machine's hostname
hwclock.sh	Sets and adjusts hardware (CMOS) clock
isapnp	Configures ISA Plug-n-Play devices
kerneld	Kernel daemon—loads kernel modules on the fly
keymaps.sh	Configures keyboard
logoutd	Logs users out after a specified period of time
lprng	Printer daemon (print spooler)
mdutils	Enables or disables "multiple devices" (refers to RAID-type redundant devices)
modutils	Loads appropriate kernel modules at boot time
mountall.sh	Mounts all local file systems
mountnfs.sh	Mounts all network file systems
netbase	Starts/stops various networking functions
netstd_init	More networking functions
netstd_misc	Still more networking functions
netswitch	Determines if networking is static or dynamic IP
network	Sets network environment variables and brings up network devices

TABLE 10-1   Corel Linux init Scripts

Script Name	Script Function
nviboot	Recovers lost vi editing sessions after crash
pcmcia	Loads PCMCIA card devices (mostly for laptops)
pcmcia.dpkg-dist	Another version of pcmcia
ppp	Starts peer-to-peer (dial-up) networking
proftpd	Starts FTP server
rc	Starts/stops services when runlevel is changed
rcS	Determines which scripts get run for which runlevel
reboot	Executes reboot command
rmnologin	Allows logins after boot process is complete
samba	Linux/Windows file-sharing daemon
sendsigs	Sends KILL signal to all processes (used during a shutdown)
single	Configures runlevel 1 (single-user mode)
skeleton	Skeleton init script—use as an example for writing new ones
sysklogd	Starts system and kernel logging functions
umountfs	Unmounts all file systems (that is, at shutdown)
unsplashFX	More Corel splash effects
urandom	Saves "random seed" between reboots (necessary for random number generator)
xdm	Starts/stops X Display Manager
xfs	Starts/stops X Font Server

TABLE 10-1   Corel Linux init Scripts *(continued)*

This line is a comment. In UNIX-based scripting languages, the hashmark **#** at the start of a line means that the computer ignores whatever follows; it's called *commenting out* the line. Commented-out lines are intended for humans, not computers.

```
set -e
```

This command sets the shell into a protective mode; if the scripting language contains an error, the script will terminate instead of continue (and possibly cause damage).

```
PATH=/bin:/usr/bin:/sbin:/usr/sbin
DAEMON=/usr/bin/X11/xfs
PIDFILE=/var/run/xfs.pid
UPGRADEFILE=/var/run/xfs.upgrade
```

This stanza sets certain variables. For example, the variable called DAEMON now has the value /usr/bin/X11/xfs. This allows you to make changes to the daemon in question, without having to edit the rest of the script.

```
test -x $DAEMON || exit 0
```

This tests to make sure that DAEMON exists. If it doesn't, the script ends.

```
stillrunning () {
  if [ "$DAEMON" = "$(cat /proc/$DAEMONPID/cmdline 2> /dev/null)" ]; then
    true
  else
    false
  fi;
}
```

This determines if DAEMON is already running.

```
case "$1" in
  start)
   echo -n "Starting X font server: xfs"
    start-stop-daemon --start --quiet --pid $PIDFILE --exec $DAEMON ||
      echo -n " already running"
    echo "."
  ;;
```

This is the first of several possible options for running the script. If the script is called with the command xfs start, the daemon will be started. If the daemon is already running, that fact will be reported.

```
restart)
    /etc/init.d/xfs stop
    if stillrunning; then
      exit 1
    fi
    /etc/init.d/xfs start
  ;;
```

The second option: If the daemon is called as `xfs restart`, the daemon is stopped and then started again. Note that the script calls itself—this is called *recursion*. It looks weird, but it works fine.

```
reload)
    echo -n "Reloading X font server configuration..."
    if start-stop-daemon --stop --signal 1 --quiet --pid $PIDFILE --
        exec $DAEMON; then
      echo "done."
    else
      echo "xfs not running."
  fi
 ;;
```

The third option forces the reloading of the X font server's configuration file.

```
stop)
    echo -n "Stopping X font server: xfs"
    DAEMONPID=$(cat $PIDFILE | tr -d '[:blank:]')
    KILLCOUNT=1
    if [ ! -e $UPGRADEFILE ]; then
        start-stop-daemon --stop --quiet --pid $PIDFILE --exec $DAEMON ||
          echo -n " not running"
    fi
    while [ $KILLCOUNT -le 5 ]; do
      if stillrunning; then
        kill $DAEMONPID
      else
        break
      fi    done
    if stillrunning; then
      echo "not responding to TERM signal (pid $DAEMONPID)"
    else
      if [ -e $UPGRADEFILE ]; then
        rm $UPGRADEFILE
      fi
    fi
    echo "."
  ;;
```

The fourth option stops the daemon. If the daemon will not stop running, that fact is reported.

```
  *)
    echo "Usage: /etc/init.d/xfs {start|stop|restart|reload}"
    exit 1
    ;;
esac
```

Finally, if `xfs` is called any other way, the script prints a message explaining the proper usage and exits.

```
exit 0
```

This final command ends the script and exits.

Selecting an Appropriate Runlevel

How does Corel Linux know what services and scripts to run at startup? You define those items when you select the *runlevel* at which you want to boot.

On your Corel Linux system, as on all UNIX-based operating systems, are seven runlevels. Runlevels 0, 1, and 6 are predefined, while runlevels 2, 3, 4, and 5 are user-defined. See the following bulleted list for specific information about each runlevel. Most Linux computers run most of the time at runlevels 3 or 5; Corel Linux runs at runlevel 2 by default, though you can change that if necessary.

10

- **Runlevel 0** Puts the computer into shutdown mode. When this mode is invoked, all processes currently running close down. When the processes are completely stopped, Linux shuts itself down. Obviously, you don't want to set this runlevel as part of the startup process, or your computer will never actually boot.

- **Runlevel 1** Defined as "single-user mode," it's usually used as a diagnostic mode when something is drastically wrong with the system. This runlevel starts only the minimum number of functions necessary for the most basic operation of Linux, and lets you handle every other function manually.

- **Runlevel 2** Starts the computer in multiuser text mode, like runlevel 3, but does not start NFS (network file service). If you're using a solitary machine unconnected to any other computers, you won't notice a difference because you don't use NFS. If you're part of a network, this runlevel will cause your machine to behave like a standalone without any network services available. This is the default runlevel used by Corel Linux.

- ■ **Runlevel 3**   This runlevel starts the computer in multiuser mode but doesn't start the X Window System. Thus, you can operate everything on the machine that's in text mode. If you need anything graphical, you'll need to start the X Window System by hand (or switch to runlevel 5).

- ■ **Runlevel 4**   Not currently used for any particular purpose.

- ■ **Runlevel 5**   Like runlevels 2 and 3, this runlevel boots in multiuser mode. However, at runlevel 5 the X Window System starts automatically, and you'll need to use KDE terminal windows to get to text mode. This is the mode to use if you want KDE to start automatically when you boot up.

- ■ **Runlevel 6**   The final level. This runlevel is the "reboot" level. Like runlevel 0, invoking this level causes all the running programs to close down; unlike runlevel 0, when the programs have stopped, Linux reboots itself. Just like runlevel 1, you do not want to set this runlevel as part of your startup process; if you were to do so, Corel Linux would reboot itself in an infinite loop.

Shutting Down Your Corel Linux Computer

Shutting down your computer is a rare occurrence with Linux. Many people have established the habit of powering off a computer after using it, especially in office environments in which it is policy to shut down all machines before leaving for the evening. However, this is a human concern and not a computer issue. Your computer, regardless of operating system, does not need to be shut down daily (or more than once a day). Leaving a computer on uses less electricity than an incandescent light bulb, and most monitors now can shut themselves off after a period of inactivity, saving wear on the picture tube.

Linux machines can, and do, run happily for months at a time. At the time we wrote this chapter, one of our machines had an uptime of 68 days, with no reason for shutdown in sight. We are aware of several machines with over a year of continuous uptime. (Uptime becomes something of a bragging tool after a month or two.) The only reason you need to shut down your machine is to add new hardware or to upgrade the kernel. You may also fall victim to electrical surges, as we describe later in this chapter in the section "Power Outages and Other Unexpected Crises," which force your system to shut down without proper warning, but that is a different issue from the deliberate shutdown simply for the purposes of shutting down.

We do recommend that you power off your computer if you are going to be away from the house for more than a day or two, just to be safe. We take our network down for anything longer than a three-day weekend away from home. Our policy is that if we need to kennel our dogs for a trip out of town, we also need to shut down the computers.

When you do want to shut down your computer, you need to use the shutdown procedure. *Do not simply turn off the power*—this could be devastating to your file system. Linux needs to work through a shutdown to turn off all the processes that started during boot-up.

To shut off your Corel Linux computer, log out of KDE so that you are back at the Corel login screen and select Shutdown from the options along the top of the login window. You can also log in as root, or use the superuser function of File Manager to access the root account, and issue the command `shutdown -h now` at a command prompt.

When the shutdown command is issued, the computer begins to reverse the startup process. Programs that started via scripts in /etc/init.d are shut down, and file systems are unmounted. Once the shutdown process has stopped, it is safe to turn off the power.

10

Using a Boot Disk to Start Your Computer

In Chapter 2, "Installing Corel Linux," we described the process of making a boot disk. If you didn't make one at the time you installed the operating system, we highly recommend that you do so now. It's a good insurance policy; like most insurance, it may seem like a useless hassle now, but it's not a happy situation if you need it and never bothered to create one. You would use a boot disk for two reasons: Either you didn't want to put LILO on the boot sector of your hard drive (perhaps you have two operating systems installed on different hard-drive partitions), or you're using it in an emergency because something has gone wrong and Linux won't boot properly.

The boot disk contains a very small version of the Linux kernel that allows you to get the machine started. You won't run the full operating system off the disk; you just use it to get to the point that you can run the OS already installed on your computer. Here's how to use the boot disk (assuming the computer has been powered off):

1. Insert the boot disk completely into the floppy drive.

2. Turn on the computer's power.

3. The computer should begin to boot from the floppy disk.

CAUTION | *If the computer doesn't start to boot from the floppy, you'll have to open the computer's BIOS setup menu and set the floppy drive as the first boot device (that is, the device that is started first in the boot process). This process is different for different CPUs and BIOSes, so we can't provide specific instructions on opening the BIOS. Check your computer's documentation. Once you've set the floppy drive as the first boot device, shut down and restart with the boot disk inserted fully into the floppy drive. The boot process should now proceed.*

Power Outages and Other Unexpected Crises

As you know, it is never a good idea to just turn off a computer. While your computer is running—no matter the operating system—system files are open, and various processes are running in the background. Just because you can't see them in the Taskbar or the System Tray doesn't mean that they're not important; rather, they're so crucial to correct operation that they are hidden so that well-meaning users can't tamper with their work. Shutting off the power abruptly throws a wrench into this smooth operation. It leaves you vulnerable to losing those system files or may corrupt the files so thoroughly that they might as well be lost.

This danger is why we beg you to shut down the machine *properly* when you need to do so. Shutting it down cleanly involves logging out of your account and using the Shutdown button on the Corel Linux login screen. The shutdown button starts a process that closes all open system files and halts all running background processes, in addition to unmounting the various file systems. Only then will the machine shut off the power.

Sometimes, though, you don't have a choice. Power outages are an annoying fact of life, especially if you rely on the wiring in an older home or you live in a part of the world with a lot of electrical storm activity. All kinds of power outages can wreak havoc, even the miniature ones that don't even affect the clock on your microwave oven.

What does a power outage, or any other fluctuation in your electrical wiring, do to the computer? If the power is off long enough for the computer's power supply to notice the interruption, the computer reboots. Odds are that everything will be fine and that nothing was harmed. You will, however, notice that the boot process during the reboot takes much longer than usual. This is because the machine shut down uncleanly; thus, Linux checks each file system carefully to make sure there is no damage. If there is a problem, Linux reports it to you.

The single best way to avoid these problems (aside from not using a computer) is to use an *uninterruptable power supply,* or *UPS*. A UPS plugs into the wall socket, and you plug your computer into the UPS. It contains a large battery that keeps your computer running for a predetermined period of time after the AC current from the socket stops flowing; the length of that period is determined by the model of UPS you purchase, ranging from five minutes to about twenty minutes of coverage. The UPS can also be set to sound a loud and annoying alarm to alert you to loss of power, which can give you time to shut down the computer properly before the UPS battery gives out.

| NOTE | *The model rating is actually based on voltage; how many things you have plugged into the UPS, and how much load they put on the unit, will ultimately determine the length of protection.* |

We know of two UPS manufacturers, APC and Best Power, that provide Linux-compatible software for their units. This software can even be configured so that the UPS, when activated, sends a signal to the computer before the power runs out; the computer can then shut itself down cleanly. All you have to do is boot as usual when you get home and notice that the UPS has activated. You can find APC models at many computer stores in the United States and Canada; Best Power models are harder to find but are still relatively easy to locate. We use an APC Back-UPS 500 and have had no problems with it.

10

The Evils of Lightning

While lightning may not always cause a full power outage, it is hardly the computer's friend. Those who live in lightning-prone areas of the world know that lightning activity often causes fluctuations in electrical power that can be as damaging as a complete outage. The power surges caused by lightning strikes—whether near your home or office, or near the power substation that provides your electricity—can damage your computer's components or operating system just like loss of power.

Again, using a UPS can help reduce the risk of damage from power surges. A UPS unit always emits a constant voltage, and it can buffer the fluctuating voltage from the outlet before it gets to your computer. If you don't want to use a UPS, you should at the very least use a surge and voltage spike protector. Power outlet strips that contain surge and spike protection are widely available. While they won't stop your computer from shutting down if the surge or momentary loss of power is long enough, they can protect against the small fluctuations of household current that may bother your machine.

Lightning strikes also pose another danger: they can turn your modem into a useless piece of plastic. We have lost several modems to lightning strikes in the summer thunder season. The problem comes from power surges through the telephone lines and can be caused by lightning strikes miles away. We recommend that you use a small phone line surge protector, which plugs into the phone jack; many power strips with surge suppression, as well as UPS units, also have phone line voltage regulators built in.

How will you know if you've lost a modem? You'll often find out when you pick up your regular telephone and hear a lot of static, or the regular phone ring is weak and sporadic. Don't assume it's your phone; unplug all modems and test the phone again. If you call the phone company, expect them to ask if any modems are attached to the phone line; it's a major cause of service calls placed in the days after severe thunderstorms, says our phone company.

The best way to deal with lightning, if you don't have protection, is pure avoidance. At the first sign of an electrical storm in your vicinity, unplug the modem line from the wall jack and shut down your computer. You may even want to unplug it. Lightning strikes can generate megawatts of electrical voltage that can overwhelm protective devices if strong enough. We live in a lightning-prone section of the southeastern United States, and we shut down and unplug everything electronic when a bad storm hits.

When the System Locks Up

Linux is an exceptionally stable operating system. The operating system itself hardly ever "freezes," locking up so hard that it won't accept any input. This stability is one of the reasons for the lengthy uptimes we described earlier. However, the various applications that you install and use may not be so stable, especially if you're using *beta* software (prerelease versions that may not be completely finished). Even something like KDE can freeze up. When this happens, it looks like your Linux machine has crashed; the best thing to do is try to identify the offending program and shut it down.

Application Crashes

If an application crashes, you should still be able to use other applications; the keyboard and mouse should still be working properly. In this case, use Process Manager to close the offending application.

1. Open Process Manager by clicking the Application Manager icon in the KDE Panel and choosing Applications | System | Process Management from the Start menu.

2. Look at the list of processes in the bottom pane of the Process Manager window and find the one that isn't responding.

3. Click that process to select it.

4. Select Signal | Kill from the drop-down menu to terminate the process.

NOTE *Every operation that runs on your computer is assigned a process number. Some processes are constant, such as KDE, while others are temporary.*

KDE Crashes

10

If KDE itself locks up, the procedure is a little different, and you'll have to work from a text-based prompt. You can often kill an unresponsive KDE with the key combination CTRL-ALT-BACKSPACE. KDE should exit and restart, putting you back at the login prompt.

If that doesn't work, press CTRL-ALT-F1. This will switch the screen to a text-mode login prompt. Log in as root and issue the command **init 1**. This shuts down all functions and brings Linux to a single-user mode. When this process finishes, type init #, with # being whatever your previous runlevel was (probably 2). KDE will restart, and you should be able to log in again and resume whatever you were doing.

Corel Linux Crashes

In the extremely unlikely event that Linux itself actually crashes, there's only one thing you can really do: turn off the power and restart the computer. While this isn't the best thing you can do, for all the reasons we've described already, it's the only option you have. However, the odds are very good that you'll never need to do this. The stability of Linux means that lock-ups and freezes are probably not the operating system's fault and are spawned by a process closer to the user level.

CHAPTER 11

Corel Linux Directory Structure

In Linux, everything is a file. Every program, directory, and device—not to mention text, graphic, or multimedia file—is represented as an individual file and is part of the overall Linux file system. On a machine running a wide variety of applications and programs, the file system can grow to thousands of individual files, which means that managing these files can be quite a headache.

Over the years, a more or less standard way of organizing files has developed. We say "more or less" because there is no official standard that "compliant" systems must meet; the UNIX/Linux system of directory structure has evolved as a result of common practice and sensible design. This chapter is not intended to be an exhaustive catalog of the Corel Linux directory system as a whole but rather an overview of how a typical Corel Linux file system is organized. We also address the concept of *environment variables,* which are configuration settings that define certain information about your system.

Linux Directory Types

Linux directories can be grouped into two major types: *administrative* and *user.* The administrative directories hold the operating system files, applications that are available to all users, configuration files, networking information, device drivers, and so on. User files contain the specific configuration files used by each person with a user account on the computer, programs that individual users have installed for their own use, and files that users have created.

 If you are logged into the root account, you can see the contents of all the directories on the machine. If you are logged into a user account, you can see only the contents of your own directories; you may be able to see the contents of the administrative directories, but you probably won't be authorized to run any of the programs within those directories unless you log in as root. This may seem irritating, but it's a safety precaution to keep users from messing with the machine's functions.

In this chapter, we describe each of the major directories and explain what kinds of files are kept within that directory. The administrative directories that we describe here should resemble the directories created on your computer when you installed Corel Linux. If you've installed new software or tinkered with your user account since installing, your user account directory structure may look somewhat different from what is illustrated here, which is based on the default installation.

The Master Directory

At the very top of the Linux directory structure is the *master directory,* which contains all the other directories in the file system. The master directory is called the *root directory* because it is at the very root of the system. You may also hear it called the *slash directory* because the directory's path is simply / (a single forward slash). All other directories in the structure are actually subdirectories of the / directory, which is why their path names begin with a /.

 Don't confuse the / directory with the /root directory. "The root directory," or the / directory, is different from "the /root directory." If you are having an oral conversation about Linux directories, be sure you make the distinction clear.

The Linux directory structure is built around the concept that every file has a place, and that place should be obvious to the administrator. So, the root directory actually looks somewhat empty; in Figure 11-1, you can see the root directory

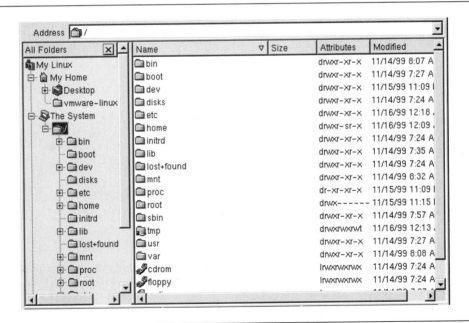

FIGURE 11-1 The root directory is the base of the Corel Linux directory structure

displayed in File Manager. Everything in the root directory is a folder, meaning that it's a subdirectory. Nothing is stored in the root directory, since every file has a better location further down in the directory structure.

Administrative Directories

The administrative directories include all system functions, applications, devices, and other components of the computer's hardware and software. The sheer number of entries in these directories can be a bit daunting. Understanding the organization of the various administrative directories can help you keep a clear idea of where certain files and programs are located. A general sense of directory layout will help you when you need to find something rapidly.

/bin

Originally, the /bin (short for "binary") directory contained binary files needed for the operating system to function. Eventually, so many binary files existed that keeping every single one in /bin would have been an organizational madhouse. Now, /bin is the directory that contains most of the basic UNIX commands, along with certain more complex programs:

- Fundamental UNIX commands (`cat`, `ls`, `cp`, and others)
- File management utilities (`tar`, `gzip`, and `gunzip`)
- Text editors (`pico`, `vi`, and `emacs`)
- Shells (`bash`, `csh`, `tcsh`, `zsh`, and others)

Generally speaking, if you're looking for a program that is an integral part of the operating system, look in /bin first.

/usr

The original function of the /usr directory was to contain all applications that users could access. As with /bin, the usefulness of a single directory was quickly outgrown, and the various functions contained in /usr were split into several subdirectories. Figure 11-2 shows the /usr directory in File Manager; the various

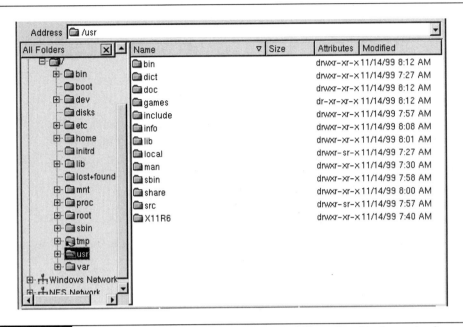

FIGURE 11-2   The /usr directory contains programs and files related to the system's individual users

subdirectories shown are described in the sections that follow. (The /usr/sbin directory is discussed later in the chapter, with the /sbin directory, rather than here in the /usr section.)

/usr/bin

This subdirectory contains a great deal of user-accessible software. It is the default location for all software that is shared across a network, as well as common programs that one expects to find on any UNIX or Linux system, regardless of the specific operating system.

/usr/local/bin

Where /usr/bin contains software that is shared across a network, /usr/local/bin is the home of most software specific to this individual machine. This is not to say that programs or software in /usr/local/bin cannot be used by other machines attached to the network, but that these programs are intended to be "local" to this machine.

/usr/bin/X11

This directory contains most of the graphics-based programs. On Corel Linux systems, this directory holds the various KDE programs.

/usr/X11R6

This directory is related to /usr/bin/X11 and also contains graphical software. Although there is no clear distinction between the two directories, files in /usr/X11R6 are generally system-oriented files, whereas files in /usr/bin/X11 are intended for individual users.

/usr/doc

This directory contains system documentation, including FAQs (Frequently Asked Questions), HOWTO files, and other miscellaneous documentation about various programs and software in the system.

/usr/man

Like /usr/doc, this directory contains documentation files. However, /usr/man contains only *man pages,* or help documents written by programmers to accompany their programs. Man pages range from incredibly helpful to arcane and cryptic.

You can read a given program's man page by typing **man <program name>** *at a text prompt. For example, to read the man page for* **adduser**, *you type* **man adduser**. *Read the man pages for* man *by typing* **man man**.

/usr/share

This directory contains files that need to be shared, whether by multiple users or by multiple programs. For example, the files that define various fonts are kept in /usr/share, since fonts are used by several different applications, which in turn are used by multiple users.

/usr/lib

This directory contains shared *libraries*. Libraries are collections of functions that programmers use. Instead of including the various functions directly in their programs, programmers create a reference to a particular library. This saves a great deal of time and effort. You must have appropriate libraries installed for various programs to work; luckily, most programs use the same libraries. If a program requires an odd library to function, the documentation will usually mention this or the library will be packaged with the program's source code.

/usr/src

Finally, this directory contains source code for various programs. Most importantly, the source code for the Corel Linux kernel is located in /usr/src.

/etc

Another important directory, /etc contains systemwide configuration files. In Chapter 10, "Start Up and Shut Down," we described the files contained in the /etc/inittab and /etc/init.d directories, which are good examples of the kinds of programs contained in this directory. See the full /etc directory in Figure 11-3.

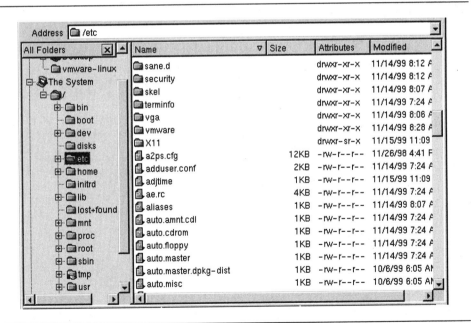

FIGURE 11-3   The /etc directory contains systemwide configuration files

Generally speaking, any program that needs to be configured for the entire system puts its configuration files in /etc. Such files usually (although not always) have names that end with the extensions .conf, .cf, or .rc. For example, the file /etc/syslog.conf controls how the program `syslog` deals with various logs generated by several operating system programs.

/var

The /var directory is a repository for files that vary in size and number; while the filename remains constant, the content changes as the computer operates. *Spool files*, which hold data until a resource is freed to handle them, are kept in /var; mail spool files, such as /var/spool/mail, news spools, and print spools are all located here. See Figure 11-4 for a display of the /var directory in File Manager.

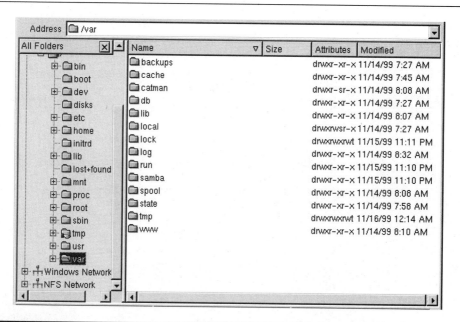

FIGURE 11-4   The /var directory holds files whose content changes constantly

Some system logs and other files that either vary in size or are transient are also kept here. For example, the subdirectory /var/lock contains *lock files*, or files that tell the operating system that certain system resources are in use. If the computer sees the file /var/lock/modem, it knows that someone is using the modem and that no other programs are to be permitted access to the modem. When the process using the modem is finished, the lock file disappears.

As the administrator of your Corel Linux system, you should pay special attention to the directory /var/log. The operating system uses this directory to house the automatically generated log files that describe system status, problems with the system, and other ongoing messages. The contents of /var/log are shown in Figure 11-5, and the function of each log file is described in Table 11-1.

NOTE *Log files are simply text files, and you can view them with a regular text editor. We discuss the Corel log tool, Event Viewer, in Chapter 14, "Corel Linux's Graphical Administration Tools."*

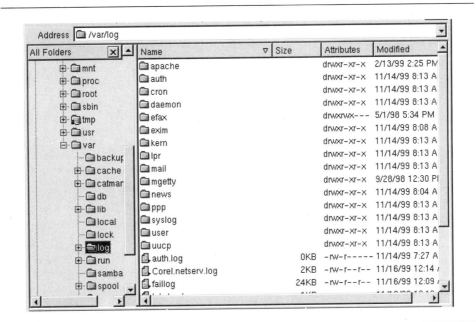

FIGURE 11-5   Corel Linux uses /var/log to give you important system messages

Log File Stored in /var/log	Log Function
Corel.netserv.log	A log containing messages from the Network File Server (NFS)
apache	A directory containing Web server logs
auth	A directory containing various security-related logs
auth.log	Primary security-related log
cron	A directory containing results of scheduled jobs
daemon	A directory containing various information about system daemons
efax	A log tracking your use of the optional eFax service (see Chapter 9, "Using the Internet with Corel Linux")
exim	A directory containing mail server logs
faillog	A log tracking all failed login attempts
kdmlog.log	K Display Manager log
kern	A directory containing kernel messages
lastlog	A log that records the device used by the last user to log in
lpr	A directory containing print server logs
mail	A directory containing more mail server logs
mgetty	A directory containing modem-related logs
news	A directory containing news server logs
nmb	Samba name server log
ppp	A directory containing dial-up networking logs
smb	Samba file server log
syslog	A directory containing logs relating to logging functions
user	A directory containing logs relating to user functions
uucp	A directory containing network-related logs
wtmp	A system function having to do with login information; *do not tamper with this log*

TABLE 11-1   Log Files and Directories in /var/log

/sbin and /usr/sbin

Both these directories contain various administrative programs used for maintenance or system upkeep. These are essential programs that help you manage your hard disk and control system operation; programs like `shutdown` and `lilo` live in these directories.

Generally, you'll want to restrict /sbin (shown in Figure 11-6) to the superuser, while users have access to /usr/sbin (shown in Figure 11-7). Note that you won't be able to execute programs in /sbin if you're logged into a user account. This is a safety precaution; because the programs housed in these directories are so critical to system function, they need to be protected from casual execution.

/dev

This is a tricky and crucial directory. The files that reside in /dev, shown in Figure 11-8, represent the various devices installed on your system; for example, /dev/hda1 represents the first partition on your primary hard disk drive. These files are used to control access to the various devices. Programmers use device files in different ways, placing them in programs so that devices can be accessed (started or stopped) as part of the program's regular operation.

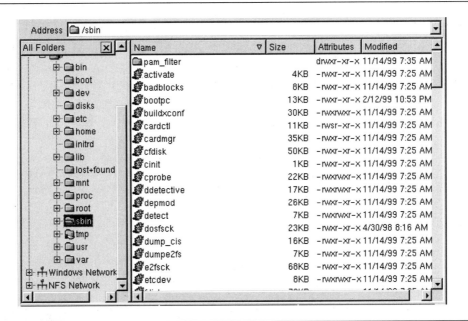

FIGURE 11-6 The /sbin directory houses systemwide maintenance functions

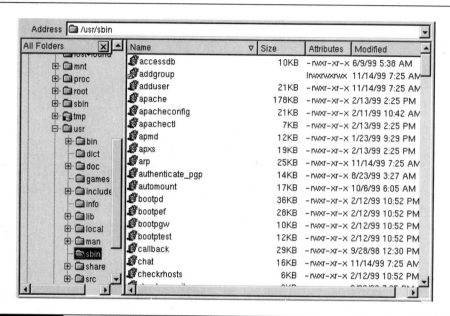

FIGURE 11-7   The /usr/sbin directory contains user account–specific functions

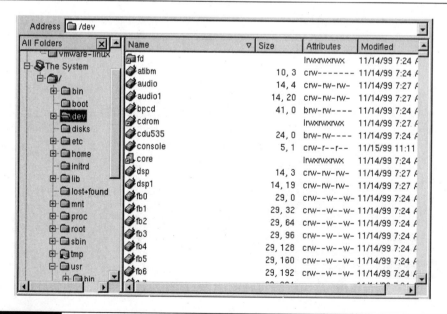

FIGURE 11-8   The /dev directory contains files related to all the physical devices of
your computer

You can use these files to manage the physical devices of your computer if you prefer text interaction to the graphical tools provided in the KDE desktop. If you want to mount a disk partition, you might issue the command `mount /dev/XXX /mnt/XXX`, where *XXX* is the device that you wish to mount. This command creates a point of access to the physical device.

 Never delete a device file or change the permissions on a device file without knowing exactly *what you are doing. Alterations in this directory could cause some of your system devices to become inoperable.*

One of the subdirectories of /dev has a special function. The directory /dev/null is basically a black hole; if you move a file to /dev/null, you have effectively deleted the file. Programmers use /dev/null frequently; if a particular program causes output that the programmer doesn't need, she can direct that output to /dev/null. No file will be created from the output, nor will the data display on the screen. You may hear /dev/null used as slang in casual conversation with other Linux or UNIX people; saying that you sent something to /dev/null is the same as saying that you didn't pay any attention and just ignored the item, person, or comment. Putting something in /dev/null is also called "bit-bucketing," as /dev/null is the bit-bucket or data garbage can.

11

/boot

The /boot directory contains the basic element that the operating system needs to start. It contains the kernel image as well as a few other files that are accessed during startup; see the complete file listing in Figure 11-9. As a rule, you shouldn't need to mess with this directory much, unless you're compiling a new kernel for some reason; kernel compilation, and reasons why you would need to do so, are covered in Appendix A, "How to Compile a Kernel."

/mnt

This directory serves as a general-purpose *mount point*. It contains subdirectories for the specific file system devices that you have installed on your computer: you might have subdirectories for floppy drives, CD-ROM drives, Zip or Jaz drives, or other storage devices, depending on your system configuration. In Figure 11-10, you can see the /mnt directory on a machine that has only a floppy drive and a CD-ROM drive installed. Note that it's not strictly necessary to use /mnt as a mount point; any empty directory will suffice.

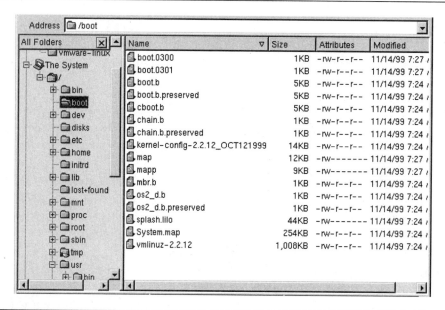

FIGURE 11-9 Within the /boot directory, you'll find the core of Corel Linux: the kernel image

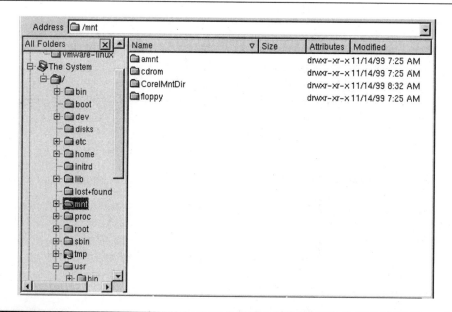

FIGURE 11-10 Links to storage devices are kept in the /mnt directory

/proc

Often called the "pseudo-file system," /proc doesn't exist on your hard disk drive. Rather, the files in /proc exist only in your computer's memory. The purpose of /proc, and the files it contains, is to contain information about your computer and the processes that are currently running on the machine. Your computer, in effect, uses /proc to talk to itself.

> *If you want to see what /proc does, open a terminal window and issue the command* **cat/proc/cpuinfo.** *You'll see more information than you ever dreamed you'd need about your computer's main processor.*

/root

This is the superuser's home directory, shown in Figure 11-11. It is kept separate from the other user directories so that, if there is a problem with the disk or partition that houses the user directories, the problem will not affect the root account. The root account will always be on the same disk partition as the / directory, regardless of where the user directories are housed.

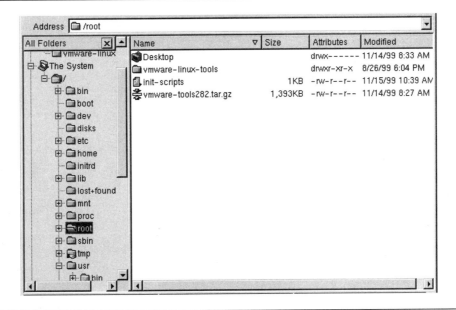

FIGURE 11-11   The /root directory contains the home account of the superuser

User Directories

User directories are directories that each individual user sees when looking at the personal account directory structure. What is contained in user Betty's account is not necessarily what is contained in user Barney's account—Betty may have added directories or programs, while Barney uses the default structure. Regardless of the changes that individual users make, the basic structure of a user account remains the same.

/home

The /home directory is the one that each user logs into at the start of a session. For example, when user Harry logs in, he is immediately placed in /home/harry, as seen in Figure 11-12. All of Harry's personal files, including his personal configuration files, are found in this directory or some subdirectory of it. If Harry desires, he can restrict permission on his /home directory so that he is the only user who has access to it.

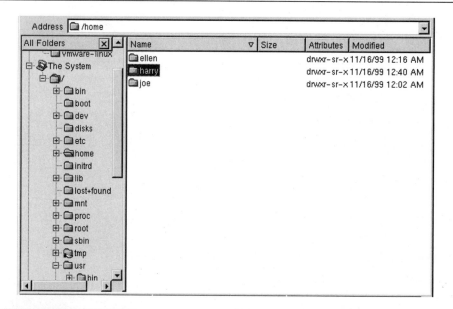

FIGURE 11-12   Harry's /home directory is the first thing he sees when he logs in

CAUTION *The superuser, or root account, always has access to all user directories regardless of the permissions set on them by the users. There is no such thing as "privacy from root" on a Linux system.*

/tmp

As the name suggests, /tmp is a place for temporary files. These can be temporary system files that Corel Linux houses in this directory, or they can be files placed in the directory by a user for temporary storage. Many system administrators make it a regular habit to delete everything in the /tmp directory at a predetermined interval to keep the disk from filling up with forgotten files. This may or may not be useful or necessary for your Corel Linux system; it depends on how many people are using the system and how much junk they tend to leave lying around. Your users should not get the idea that /tmp is a good place to store things to avoid filling up their home directories (and to circumvent any disk space limits you have imposed on your users).

Environment Variables

Once you have a basic understanding of the Corel Linux directory structure, it's useful to learn about environment variables. An environment variable is a *named value* that defines some piece of information about your system. For example, the environment variable HOSTNAME defines your computer's name. (All environment variables are completely uppercase.) If, as root, you issue the command

```
export HOSTNAME="seesaw"
```

the name of your computer becomes seesaw. Many of the graphical administration tools included in Corel Linux set these variables for you; we include them here so that you can get a better idea of how these values are defined at the operating system level.

NOTE *When you set an environment variable using the preceding syntax, you set the variable for the current session. Variables changed by the* export *command are resident in memory only; when you reboot your computer, the new variable will disappear from memory, and the default variable will reappear. If you don't reboot frequently, this isn't much of an issue. If you do reboot often, you may want to put certain variables into your shell configuration files, as explained later in this chapter in the section "User-Defined Environment Variables."*

System Environment Variables

Environment variables can be set on a systemwide level, or they can be local to a user's account. For example, the environment variable NNTPSERVER tells the computer which USENET news server to look up in order to get newsgroup postings. If root gives the command

```
export NNTPSERVER="news.isp.com"
```

news.isp.com will be the news server for all users on the system. If, however, an individual user issues the same command, only that user will access news.isp.com when she opens her newsreader. Other users on the system will still access whatever news server is set by default in the root configuration files.

REMEMBER *As we mentioned previously, systemwide variables disappear at reboot. User-defined variables, however, disappear at logout. If, for example, user Maria sets her NNTPSERVER variable to a certain news server, that value disappears when she finishes her Corel Linux session. Maria will have to edit her personal configuration files to call that news server permanently. User settings override systemwide settings, but only for the current session unless they're made part of the configuration files.*

If you want to know the current value of a particular environment variable, open a terminal window and issue the command

```
echo $VARIABLENAME
```

where VARIABLENAME is the environment variable you want to see. Be sure that you include the dollar sign ($); this tells the computer that you want to see the actual value of that variable. If you leave out the dollar sign, the computer thinks you only want to see the name of the variable, and it will simply repeat what you typed.

Environment variables are commonly set through scripts; as with the startup process, using a script ensures that all variables are set correctly and there is no room for error through forgetting to set a particular variable. Some of the scripts that run at boot-up set certain environment variables, while other scripts run only when users log into their individual accounts. The most critical environment variables are set through scripts so that the user (and root) always have these variables defined correctly.

PATH   This variable defines the *search path*, a list of directories that the computer will search automatically to find a particular command. If you have no path set, the computer will not automatically search any directories; you will have to enter the full path name for any program or command you want to execute. If you don't do so, the computer returns the result "FILENAME not found," which can be frustrating.

PATH is actually set in several different scripts, each adding to the PATH environment variable so that the list of directories is robust. This cuts down on the number of times you actually have to type a path for a given command: `traceroute` instead of `/usr/sbin/traceroute`, for example.

HOSTNAME   This variable sets the computer's name. Corel Linux needs to know the hostname so that it can handle directories properly.

DOMAINNAME   If you're connected to a network, Corel Linux needs to know the domain name to manage networking functions correctly. The domain name, even for local networks, is formed like a regular Internet domain: that is, corel.com or linux.com.

HOME   This variable sets the name of your home directory. If user Minerva is logging into her user account, this environment variable defines her home directory as /home/minerva; if you're logging into the root account, this variable's value is /root. Without this variable, your users can't access their home directories since the computer doesn't know which directories belong to which users.

11

User-Defined Environment Variables

Individual users can set environment variables that apply only to their user accounts. If the user is using the `bash` shell environment (the default shell for Corel Linux; see Chapter 17, "The Shell Expanded: Basic Scripting," for more information on shells), the variables he defines will be set in `$HOME/.bashrc`, where $HOME is the name of his actual home directory, such as /home/fred.

Assume that you have a personal directory, /home/ellen/programs, that has some programs you use frequently. Because this directory is not part of your search path, every time you want to run one of these programs, you have to specify the full path name. That is, to run the program `zoinks`, you have to type **/home/ellen/programs/zoinks** instead of simply typing **zoinks** at a command prompt. This is tiresome.

To save time and keystrokes, you can edit the PATH environment variable, as it relates specifically to your user account, to include the programs directory. Do this by editing the file /home/ellen/.bashrc, which is your individual `bash` shell configuration file. Add the line

```
export PATH="$PATH:/home/ellen/programs"
```

to the file; the next time you log in and the .bashrc file is consulted, the program's directory will be added automatically to your path, and you need type only the program name to invoke the program. Here's how that command's syntax works:

export   The command `export` specifies that the value is available outside this particular script. That is, the value affects your whole user account, not just the contents of .bashrc.

PATH   This environment variable name indicates that the value following is to be applied to the PATH variable within this user account.

"PATH: Include this statement so that the previous value of PATH is included. If you leave this part out, the other directories already in PATH will be deleted, and you'll have to type full path names for all programs except those in /home/ellen/programs.

/home/ellen/programs   Include the new directory to be added to PATH; it is appended to the old value of PATH that you kept by adding the "$PATH statement (see the preceding section).

Note that the new value of PATH will not take effect until the next time the shell is started. The simplest way to do this is just to log out and log back in again to call the new values in .bashrc.

Configuring Your Account with .bashrc

.bashrc contains all the necessary configurations to make your shell account operate as you prefer. You can set your editor preferences, your news servers, and many other external programs within .bashrc; you can also configure the behavior of regular shell commands. The Corel Linux .bashrc is quite a bit shorter than the .bashrc in other distributions; therefore, you may find yourself adding new lines if you need to change a behavior rather than editing existing lines. Corel Linux's .bashrc looks like this:

```
# ~/.bashrc: executed by bash(1) for non-login shells

export PS1='\h:\w\$ ' umask 022

# You may uncommend the following lines if you want 'ls' to be colorized:

# export LS_OPTIONS='-color=auto'
# eval 'dircolors'
alias ls='ls $LS_OPTIONS'
alias ll='ls $LS_OPTIONS -l'
# alias l='ls $LS_OPTIONS -lA'
# # Some more alias to avoid making mistakes:
# alias rm='rm -i'
# alias cp='cp -i'
# alias mv='mv -i'

export LANG=C
```

To change existing lines in .bashrc, simply uncomment them and make changes as necessary. If you plan to add information, use the environment variable method described in this chapter or consult documentation about bash.

11

CHAPTER 12

User Space and User Accounts

When you installed Corel Linux, you created both the root account and a user account for your personal use. You may want to add more users to your machine—perhaps your housemate, spouse, friend, or grandmother wants a personal account as well. In this chapter, we cover the differences between the root account and your personal account, adding new users, defining user filespace, setting file permissions on the user accounts, and the ongoing management required of user space and users themselves.

Long ago, at the dawn of the computer age, there was no such thing as a personal computer. Computing was done on huge mainframe machines, which often filled entire rooms and were used by many people simultaneously. UNIX was initially developed under these conditions; since multiple users were a routine feature of mainframe computing, the UNIX designers built a system to manage a multitude of users with a minimum of fuss.

In the early 1980s, personal computers, or PCs, began to replace the old warhorses in the mainframe rooms. The operating systems designed for these small computers—MSDOS, MacOS, and eventually Windows—were developed on the assumption that only one person would be using a particular machine. In fact, one of the selling points of the personal computer was that it was a one-person computer: no more jockeying for space or time on a mainframe.

Linux, as a UNIX-derived operating system, takes the earlier approach. Although you're running Corel Linux on a personal computer, you've installed a mainframe-based operating system on that PC. So you can take advantage of the multiple-user systems built into Linux. You may not need or want to do so, but you have that option.

| TIP | *Under Linux, individual user accounts occupy completely different sections of the hard drive. For those of you who have used the Windows 95/98 user accounts features, some transition is required. The Windows accounts are primarily used to set the visual appearance of the desktop and to handle multiple users' passwords for local networking; each user still has access to the whole hard drive and can open and alter files stored all over the computer. MacOS9 works much the same way. It's quite different in Linux, however.* |

The Root Account

With this rather cosmopolitan view of the computer comes the necessity for some form of government. Computers are extremely literal and don't deal very well with the concept of anarchy. The UNIX approach? Dictatorship. Every computer running a UNIX-derived operating system has one user who has absolute power over everything that happens on that machine. This user is called the *superuser*, and the superuser's account name is always *root*. The root account is created by default on every installation. This account can read or modify any file on the computer, issue any command, and run any program. File permissions and ownerships are not relevant to the root account.

The power of the superuser is necessary for the management of a system. If a user is misbehaving, the superuser can revoke access to certain functions. In especially severe cases, the superuser can block the user's access to the system altogether. The superuser can also dig into system configuration files to fix problems or customize the operation of the system. However, the superuser's power also carries the potential for complete disaster. For example, were the superuser to issue the command `rm -rf /` at a text prompt, the entire contents of the file system would be erased permanently. (Don't do this!) Less seriously, if the superuser were to make an error while editing a configuration file, a vital system function might fail to operate properly.

| CAUTION | *The superuser's powers also carry an ethical component. If multiple users access your machine, the temptation may be great to browse through personal files "just to see what they're doing on my machine." Don't. You have access to your users' accounts to keep them running smoothly, not to make snooping easier.* |

12

We recommend that you avoid logging in as root as much as possible. When you installed Corel Linux, you created a personal user account; use this for your daily work instead. There are several ways to get access to root functions without having to log in as root, although you can do that if you prefer to keep your root self and your user self completely separated.

The Root Password

The root password is the single most important piece of information that anyone can have about a Linux system. Anyone who has the root password can effectively hijack your machine: erasing files, changing file permissions, setting up stealth processes, or (if you're connected to the Internet) using your machine to send out objectionable material.

Your root password should be as secure as possible. It should be something that would be very difficult to guess, yet something you won't forget. It should contain a mix of letters and numbers. Once you've settled on something, keep it secret. Don't tell anybody what it is. We mean that—don't tell *anybody*. Don't write it down, don't use your favorite phrase, and don't share it; however, don't make it so incredibly complicated that you forget it. If you want to give someone some of the superuser powers, there are other ways to do it than sharing the root password; using the tools we describe later in this chapter means that you can control the level of access that person will have. Giving away the root password means that you're not the boss of your computer anymore.

> **TIP**   *We do recommend that you log in as root at least once, preferably very soon after installing Corel Linux, so that you can change the root password.*

User Accounts

Like UNIX, Linux uses a system of user accounts. When an individual user account is created, each user is given an array of information:

- A username, such as *maureen*
- A password
- A user ID
- One or more group IDs
- Some personal space in the /home directory

This information is used to build a directory structure within the user account, to enter the user into system configuration files, and to control access by password. It can also determine what files and programs the user may access.

> **NOTE** *The term* user ID *can be somewhat confusing. In the sense used earlier, the user ID is a number that is assigned to that particular account and is kept in the /etc/password file. It's rare that you'll use this numerical user ID, unless you want to write user management scripts that call sequential sets of users. The common use of this term is as a synonym for* username, *or* login ID. *You may hear someone say "What's your user ID?" That person wants to know the username. To cut down on this confusion, Linux documentation always refers to the numerical user ID as the* uid. *See the section "User IDs and Group IDs," later in this chapter, for more information.*

With the potential for a large group of users on one machine, the possibility of destruction or chaos looms large. Users need to be protected against another user's accessing their files, whether they're important system files or personal files. To deal with this problem, UNIX (and Linux) contains a robust set of file permissions that allow both root and individual users to determine who has access to a given file or directory. We discuss file permissions in detail later in this chapter.

Using Root's Powers While Logged into a User Account

12

By now, you might be perplexed. First, we say that root has a great number of powers that you need to run your system, but then we tell you not to log in as root. What's the deal? Well, there are a few ways you can get access to superuser powers without having to log directly into the root account. Some of these require that you know the root password; while your users can try these options, they can't access root powers unless they know root's password. Other options don't require that the user knows the root password, but you have to deliberately add approved users to a list of those who can access root.

File Manager's Root Mode

Corel Linux provides a graphical tool for root activity through File Manager. To use this tool, click the Application Manager icon in the KDE Panel and select Start | Applications | System | File Manager.

A small terminal window appears, as shown in Figure 12-1, and you are prompted to enter the root password. Once you have successfully entered the password, you can access files and programs with superuser status, but you can still use KDE's graphical tools to manage your system.

 If you want to let another user have superuser powers, and you use this method, you must give the user the root password. This may be an unacceptable security risk for you, or you may think it's fine. It's up to you. See Chapter 22, "Administering Services," for a detailed discussion of security risks and alternative methods of granting superuser powers to users other than you.

The su Command

Whereas File Manager's superuser mode is a graphical tool, the su command is used in a terminal window at a text prompt. You can use this command to change into another user directory if you know that user's password, or you can use it to get to the root account.

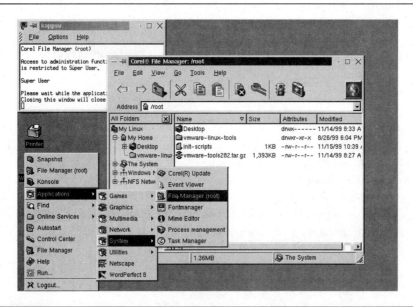

FIGURE 12-1   Use File Manager for quick access to superuser privileges

You can use the su command in several ways. One of the best reasons for using su instead of File Manager's superuser mode is to permit another user to have superuser powers without revealing the root password to that user. While using their own passwords, other users can su into the root account using another su mode.

The general form of this command is shown here, where *<username>* is replaced with the account into which you want to change:

```
su <username>
```

However, if you leave off the *<username>* portion of the command, Linux assumes that you want to su into the root account and opens the root password prompt automatically.

Configuring su

How su operates in each mode is controlled by the file /etc/suauth, another one of the many configuration files housed in the /etc directory. A sample /etc/suauth file is shown in Figure 12-2. Each entry in /etc/suauth is a line that controls the behavior of su .

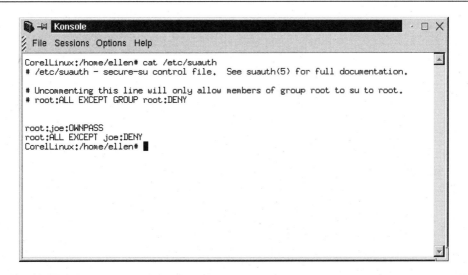

FIGURE 12-2 The /etc/suauth file controls who may log into the root account

The syntax of /etc/suauth entries is as follows:

```
to-id:from-id:action
```

Here's how the syntax works:

- **to-id**   This is the username of the account that you want to access.

- **from-id**   This field is your username as well as the usernames of all accounts that you want to make accessible to the to-id account.

- **action**   Three actions are possible: DENY, NOPASS, or OWNPASS. DENY denies the accounts in from-id from accessing the to-id account; NOPASS allows the accounts in from-id to access the to-id account without entering a password; OWNPASS requires the accounts in from-id to enter their own passwords to access the to-id account.

Given the syntax, entries in /etc/suauth look like this:

```
harry:philomena:OWNPASS
```

This means that Philomena can access Harry's account by typing **su harry** and entering her own account password at the prompt. If NOPASS had been used instead of OWNPASS, Philomena could access Harry's account simply by typing **su harry**; the computer would not prompt her for a password.

We recommend that, for security reasons, you put the following two lines in your /etc/suauth file:

```
root:<your username>:OWNPASS
root:ALL EXCEPT <your username>:DENY
```

This makes it impossible for anyone but you to `su` to the root account and will require that you enter your password at the prompt should you issue the `su` command.

Should you want to give another user access to the root account, you can change those entries in /etc/suauth to these:

```
root:<your username>,<second username>:OWNPASS
root:ALL EXCEPT <your username>, <second username>:DENY
```

Note that, with this entry, you do not have to give the second user the root password, since he will use his own password to access root with the su command.

> **CAUTION** *Changing the entries in this way is not particularly secure, even though you're not giving out the root password. If someone else gets access to the second user's account, whether through password sharing or an illicit crack, that unauthorized person now has access to root—and thereby to your entire machine, for good or for ill. A security risk is present any time the superuser permits another person to have superuser privileges. In Chapter 22, we discuss security issues in detail and offer an alternative to su or File Manager's superuser mode for multiple access to root functions.*

Using su

Once you have made all necessary entries in /etc/suauth, you can use su to access the root account. Simply type **su** at a command prompt; if you've set yourself as OWNPASS, you'll be prompted to enter your user account password; and if you've set yourself as NOPASS, you'll be placed into the root account immediately.

> **CAUTION** *Do not set yourself as NOPASS for the root account! If you did so while working through the previous section, go back and change it to OWNPASS. NOPASS is a grave security risk.*

When you've been granted access to the root account, you can issue any commands you need as the superuser. You should to know how to execute these commands in a text environment, since you have to take a couple of extra steps to use the KDE graphical administration tools if you use this method. (Use File Manager's superuser mode if you plan to use graphical tools exclusively.) You'll also have access to e-mail sent to the root account, which may be important. Check it regularly.

When you have finished issuing commands as the superuser, type **exit** at the shell prompt. The computer will return you to your regular user account, and you can continue with whatever you were doing before you changed to the root account.

> **CAUTION** *Be sure to exit out of the root account as soon as you've finished. Don't get in the habit of doing normal tasks in the root account; save root for administration alone.*

If you need to issue only one command from the root account, you can use this
syntax for the `su` command, where *<command>* is the superuser command you
wish to execute:

```
su -c "<command>"
```

You will be prompted for your password; after you enter it, the command will
execute, and you will immediately be returned to your standard user mode.

Creating New User Accounts

While you created a user account for yourself when you installed Corel Linux, the
setup program didn't give you the opportunity to create more than one. If you want to
add accounts for other users on your machine, you simply need to create the account
and assign all the appropriate identifiers and permissions. As with root account
functions, you can use either a graphical tool or a text-based tool to set up the account.

Adding New Users with User Manager

You can use a graphical tool to create new user accounts with nothing more than a
few simple mouse clicks and text entries. To use the graphical User Manager, you
must be logged in as root or have superuser privileges, as described previously.

1. Open User Manager by clicking the Application Starter icon and selecting
   Start | Applications | System | User Manager.

   The main User Manager screen appears. In the lower part of the screen,
   you'll see a list of all current users on this computer. (It may seem as
   though there are a great number, but many of these users are actually
   administrative accounts used to run programs that have customized sets of
   file permissions and user identities.)

2. Click the Add User button in the User Manager tool bar.

   The Add User screen appears.

3. Enter the user's information (at the very least, the user ID).

4. Click the Set Password button. The Password dialog box appears.

5. Type the password twice and then click OK. The dialog box closes, and you are returned to the Add User screen.

6. Select the Create Home Directory and Copy skeleton check boxes if they are not already checked.

7. (Optional) Click the Groups tab if you want to assign the new user to groups other than the default.

   The Groups tab has two panes: the left pane displays a list of all available groups. Select the groups to which you want to assign the new user, and click the right arrow button in the middle. Click the User Info tab when you have finished.

8. Verify that all entered information is correct and then click OK.

   The Add User screen closes, and the new user appears in the User Manager window.

Adding New Users at the Command Line

If you prefer to work from the command line when performing superuser functions, you can add new users in that environment simply by using the adduser program. This is a straightforward command-line program that does the same thing as the graphical User Manager; it's just a text version.

1. Click the Console button in the KDE Panel to launch a terminal window.

2. Type **su** at the shell prompt and enter your password when prompted.

   You will assume the root identity.

3. Type `adduser <username>` and press ENTER.

Replace *<username>* with the login name that you've chosen for the new account holder.

> TIP
>
> *You may decide to use a standard username format for accounts on your machine. You might restrict usernames to three to eight characters, require that people use their initials, or whatever scheme works for you. If you do enact any such restrictions, make sure you apply them evenhandedly. This consistency makes managing your user accounts easier if you have more han a few different users on this machine.*

Corel Linux adds the new user to the /etc/passwd file and creates a directory in /home for the new account. The contents of the directory /etc/skel (a skeleton directory framework) are copied to the new home directory.

4. Type `passwd <username>` and press ENTER.

5. At the prompt, enter an initial password for this user, and then retype it for confirmation. Corel Linux finishes creating the account.

> NOTE
>
> `adduser` *creates new accounts using a default set of group IDs and directory and file permissions. If you want to change permissions, or add the user to an additional group, you'll need to edit /etc/passwd and /etc/group by hand.*

Notify your new user that the account has been created. Tell the user the password you used to create the account, as well as the new username. The first thing the user should do is to change the password to something unique. This is done by issuing the command `passwd` at a command prompt. Corel Linux asks for the old password (to ensure it's really the user) and then asks for the new password twice, once to enter and once to confirm.

User IDs and Group IDs

Once you have added a new user, that user's identity is described in the file /etc/passwd. A sample /etc/passwd file is shown in Figure 12-3. The /etc/passwd entry is created as part of the `adduser` or User Manager process; you don't need to add it yourself.

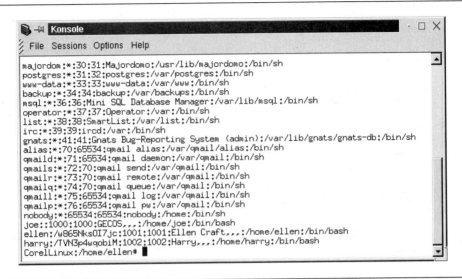

FIGURE 12-3 The /etc/passwd file contains the identities and account information for all users on your machine

CAUTION *It is critically important that the /etc/passwd file remain secure. Under no circumstances should you allow anyone but root to have write permission on this file.*

Like /etc/suauth, /etc/passwd uses a rigorous syntax to define each user account. The basic /etc/passwd entry looks like this:

```
harry:/TlknEne9:1002:1002:Harry,,,:/home/harry:/bin/bash
```

This entry uses seven elements for the user Harry; each element is separated by a colon. Here's how the /etc/passwd syntax works:

- **harry** Harry's username, created when you created his account.

- **TlknEne9** Harry's password. Passwords are encrypted in /etc/passwd to avoid the obvious security risk of having them openly displayed should someone unauthorized get access to the file. You cannot decrypt the password.

- **1002** Harry's user ID (also known as his uid). This is a unique number that identifies Harry. No other user will have the uid 1002.

- **1002** Harry's group ID (also known as his *gid*). This is a number that identifies the group to which Harry belongs. Other users can have this same gid; if they do, they are in the same group as Harry. Members of the same group share certain characteristics. For example, if one of the group members sets a groupwide file permission, all members of the group have access to the file. A user may belong to more than one group.

- **Harry,,,** Harry's personal information. He has chosen to be identified only by his first name. Had he chosen to provide his full name, office number, and so on, those pieces of data would be placed between the trailing commas. Should he want to add this information, he has to run the password program again (as he did when he changed his initial password, by typing **passwd** at a command prompt). The passwd program gives users the opportunity to identify themselves.

- **/home/harry** Harry's home directory, created when you added his user account.

- **/bin/bash** Harry's default shell program. Corel Linux uses the bash shell as the default; to change it, users need to make an entry in their configuration files.

Setting File Permissions

Linux uses a system of *file permissions* to determine who has access to a given file, and what sort of access that individual has. There are three kinds of permission:

- **Read** Anyone with the appropriate level of permission may view the file.

- **Write** Anyone with the appropriate level of permission may alter the file.

- **Execute** Anyone with the appropriate level of permission may run the file if it is a script or program. Each kind of permission can be implemented at three levels:

  - **User** Only the user who owns the file has any kind of access to it.

  - **Group** Only users who share a group ID with the user who owns the file may have any kind of access to the file.

  - **Others** All users have access to the file, including users on remote machines, via the Internet.

Any kinds of permission may be matched with any levels of access. Thus, some files may be readable by only the person who owns them (the most restrictive form of access), while others may be world-executable (the least restrictive form).

REMEMBER *The superuser can access any file on the system, regardless of the permissions set on that file.*

Permissions are changed either by using File Manager's Properties function, as shown in Figure 12-4, or by using the chmod command at a command prompt. Using chmod requires that you understand the arcane UNIX method of assigning permissions; it's usually easier to use File Manager's Properties function because the graphical interface makes clear what permissions are being assigned to the file.

TIP *If you are looking at a directory listing with file permissions shown such as that produced by entering the command ls at a shell prompt, you may find the way they are displayed a bit odd. See the ls entry in Appendix B, "A Compendium of Common Shell Commands," for a full explanation.*

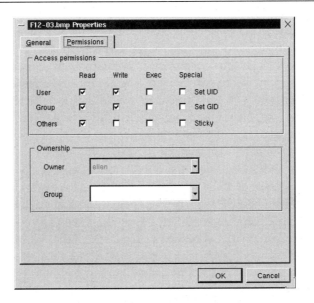

12

FIGURE 12-4 Use File Manager's Properties function to set individual file permissions

CAUTION	*It's good to be as restrictive as possible with file permissions. Great amounts of frustration can stem from leaving files too open, especially if they are executables and have execute permissions set on them. It's especially important to keep an eye on files and programs with a global execute permission, since you're essentially inviting the world to access material on your computer. This is how HTML documents are made available on the World Wide Web; they are regular documents in a user account that have been coded as globally available. The danger occurs when a document unintended for the Web is still globally available.*

Special Cases: Single- and Multiple-User Systems

One question to ask when you're deciding how to use the information in this chapter is, "Who will be using this system?" If you're the only one who will need a user account on the computer, your task is simple. Just create your own user account at installation, and use it for most of your work on the machine. Use the root account for system configuration changes. The assumption here is that you are the only person with physical access to the machine (or with a desire for physical access, in the case of a spouse or housemate who is uninterested in your Corel Linux machine) and that you don't leave your computer connected to the Internet for any lengthy unattended periods of time. While we don't recommend a lackadaisical attitude toward system security, a true single-user machine is not at much risk of being cracked and used for nefarious purposes.

However, if your Corel Linux machine is going to be used by more than one person, you need to be more vigilant about system security. Your concern for security should multiply with each new user you add, especially if you permit people to use your machine remotely via a network or the Internet. We cover system security in detail in Chapter 28, "User Management and Security," but some of the most critical concerns are worth discussing here.

In general, you should give your users as little access to the operating system as possible. That is, your users should have free access to the functions they need but no access to anything they don't need. Much of this can be done simply by being careful with file and directory permissions, and keeping those permissions as tight as possible. Restricting access to system-critical directories, such as /sbin and /boot, and restricting write permissions to directories containing configurable files, such as /etc, will go a long way toward keeping your system secure.

The overall principle by which you should abide is that users should be kept out of administrative areas; this applies to your own user account as well as to the accounts of others without superuser privileges. If a user requires access to a particular resource, he should ask the system administrator for access. This allows you to keep a close eye on what your users are doing on your system; remember the principle of dictatorship that governs Linux system administration.

12

CHAPTER 13

Disks, Drives, and File System Management

One of the most basic components of any computer system is data storage. Data can be stored in memory or on physical media. The most common physical medium is the disk, whether fixed or removable. Some systems use magnetic tape to store data; because tapes are fairly fragile for long-term use, they are primarily used to make backups for safety purposes.

In this chapter, we describe the various sorts of data storage disks, the way in which Corel Linux handles these devices, and effective methods for storing data. We also continue the discussion of file systems from Chapter 11, "Corel Linux Directory Structure," extending it to removable file systems like floppy disks or CD-ROM disks.

What Is a Disk?

At its most basic, a disk is a circular piece of plastic coated with a magnetic medium. The coating substance is actually somewhat similar to the substance used to make magnetic tapes, such as audiotapes, but it is more rigid. The substance functions in the same manner, though. By recording modulated patterns of magnetic disturbance, the surface of the disk can be used to retain and store information that is recoverable at a later time.

Floppy Disks and Hard Disks

Disks come in two major types: floppy disks, also known as *diskettes*, and hard disks, also known as *fixed disks*. Floppy disks and hard disks are similar in construction. Their names, like many computer terms, are historical artifacts. When hard disks were first developed, they were large, thick, and quite rigid. Later, when small portable disks were developed, they were thin, light, and flexible—thus, the floppy disk. As disk technology evolved, the designs of the disks themselves began to converge, but their functions remained unique. Floppy disks are removable and easily portable, while hard disks are permanently installed within a computer's case.

The real differences between fixed and removable disks are in the mechanisms used to read them and to store data on them. Every disk drive has a *head* (and sometimes more than one). The head is the component that actually makes and reads the magnetic markings on the disk's surface. Since floppy disks are removable, the heads that read these disks are much less precise; they must be protected from the constant abrasion and motion caused by disks sliding in and out of the disk slot. This lack of precision, combined with the limitation of a standardized manufacturing size, means that less information can be stored on a disk.

Hard disks, in contrast, are permanently attached to the drives that read them. The read/record head is much more precise since it is fixed to the disk. In addition, a hard disk drive often contains several disks, all readable by the same drive head(s). Because of these factors, a hard disk can store much, much more information than a floppy disk. A standard floppy disk can store up to 1.44 megabytes of data, or 1,440,000 bytes (individual data units). However, it's not uncommon to find hard drives that can hold more than 20 gigabytes of data, or 20,000,000,000 bytes—20 billion! This is almost 14,000 times what an individual floppy disk can hold.

NOTE	*You may hear it said that Linux systems don't need huge disk drives. This is true in the most literal sense: if you're running Linux in a text-only mode, you don't need much in the way of data storage. Text files are pretty small, and the kernel itself isn't that big. However, when you add a graphical interface, your storage needs grow rapidly. The X Window System requires a lot of room, as do all the graphic files used to build the interface. Add in sound files, graphics you've created or downloaded, and so on—and all of a sudden, 8- or 10-gigabyte hard drives sound just about perfect. The more things you do that require graphics, the more space you need.*

While it's technically possible to remove a hard drive from one computer and attach it to another machine, this is not a simple procedure; it's definitely not a common practice. Hard disks are not designed to be portable; floppy disks are.

13

Other Disk Types

In addition to hard and floppy disks, other types of disks have been developed in recent years. Certainly, the compact disk, or CD, has been a significant breakthrough in data storage, whether for computer or audio use. Manufacturers are also building removable disks that contain far more information than standard floppy disks. CD-ROM drives are now standard components on new computers, and Jaz or Zip drives are quickly becoming commonplace.

CD-ROM Disks

Compact disks are now common in many areas of our lives. The CD is an optical disk, a technology originally developed for audio data storage and transmission. A computer CD is often referred to as a CD-ROM, which stands for Compact Disk—Read Only Memory. This means that you can't write to the CD; it's playable only. We discuss writable CDs later in this section.

A CD is an acrylic disk, etched with a large number of microscopic prisms on the shiny side. When a laser beam is focused onto these prisms, the resulting diffraction patterns can be used to encode information; a CD-ROM drive also uses a laser to interpret the diffractions and read the data already encoded. The CD is a compromise between hard disks and floppy disks; while they have the portable nature of a floppy (although without the capability to add new information), they can store far more information: usually about 650 megabytes.

In the last year or so, the CD-RW drive has become a popular option for the home computer. This is a drive that uses specially coated CDs; with the proper CD and drive, a user can use the CD format to store information, create multimedia presentations, and so on. Writable CDs and drives are dropping rapidly in price, and it's possible to find a decent writable drive for under $200.

The disadvantage to this method is that CD data cannot be erased once encoded, and the disks themselves are still rather expensive. However, it's a great way to back up very large programs and files, such as graphic or sound files that are too big to store on floppies. It's also a good way to share these files with friends or family; most people have CD drives but many do not have a fast Internet connection. It's easier for them to view family pictures from a CD than it is to download them from a Web page over a telephone line connection.

Iomega Drives

Other newer forms of disk technology have been developed by Iomega Corporation. Iomega builds drives and disks for three different kinds of removable media: Clik!, Zip, and Jaz. The disks used with these drives hold massive amounts of data, far more than a standard floppy disk. Iomega has developed a method of file compression that allows such large amounts of storage, without quality loss from the compression.

Iomega's newest idea is the Clik! disk and drive. The Clik! drive is about the size of a credit card, while the disk itself is only two inches in diameter. The Clik! drive is designed for use with laptop and notebook computers, but it can also be used with a desktop computer equipped to use PCMCIA exchangeable device cards. Each Clik! disk holds about 40MB of information; if you want to store a great deal of information on removable media, you're better off with a Zip or Jaz drive. If you need to share files between a desktop PC and a notebook, however, a Clik! disk may be a good alternative.

Zip disks hold either 100 or 250 megabytes of data; the 100MB disk is equal to about 74 floppy disks, while the 250MB disk holds more data than 160 floppies.

| TIP | *Zip disks are excellent organizational tools. For example, all the text and image files that we created while working on this book are stored on two Zip disks; each book we write is downloaded to Zip disks and stored. Zip disks are also available in various colors, and many people use the colors as organizational tools. Back up your financial software to a green Zip disk, for example, or use red ones for critical backup files.* |

Jaz disks hold even more data; they are available in either 1 or 2 gigabytes. Many Jaz users actually use the Jaz drive as a second hard drive, storing and running applications directly from the Jaz disk. People who work in creative fields often find that even 250MB Zip disks are too small for their files or file sets; the Jaz disks are more suitable for complex graphic/audio presentations.

| TIP | *Find out more about the various Iomega products at* `http://www.iomega.com`. *Linux drivers are available for all Iomega products, but you'll have to locate them in Web file archives, since Iomega only provides Windows and Macintosh drivers at their site.* |

How Disks Are Represented in Corel Linux

13

As we have said at several points in previous chapters, every application and program in Corel Linux—as well as the output from those programs—is represented in the operating system as a unique file, or as a set of files. This includes the disks in your computer. Since disks are devices, the files that represent them are stored in the /dev directory; see Chapter 11 if you need a refresher on the structure of Linux file systems.

If you have a fairly typical computer, one that uses an IDE or EIDE hard drive (you'd know if you had something else, as non-(E)IDE hard drives are quite uncommon), the file that represents your hard drive is /dev/hda. If you have created partitions on your disk (see Chapter 2, "Installing Corel Linux," for a discussion of disk partitions), each partition has its own file as well. The first partition is represented by the file /dev/hda1, the second partition by /dev/hda2, and so on.

You may have a second hard drive (a physical drive, not a partition); if so, that drive is represented by the file /dev/hdb. The first partition on that drive is represented by /dev/hdb1, the second by /dev/hdb2, and on through the list, just as with the partitions on /dev/hda. /dev/hdb is often used to represent the CD-ROM drive, since many people do not have second hard drives. However, there is also a file called /dev/cdrom. If you do a full directory listing (by typing `ls -l` at a command prompt), you'll see that /dev/cdrom is a symbolic link to /dev/hdb.

> **NOTE**   *This use of /dev/hdb varies from system to system, even among computers running the same version of Corel Linux. The exact naming of devices depends to a certain extent on the physical configuration of your system hardware, and how that hardware is organized in the motherboard's CMOS setup. You may need to spend some time looking through the files in the /dev directory to see how your computer's device files are organized.*

The floppy drive in your computer is represented by the file /dev/fd0. If you have a second floppy drive, it will be represented by /dev/fd1.

> **NOTE**   *Numbering in UNIX and UNIX-based operating systems always begins with zero (0), not with 1.*

While dual floppy drives were very common until recently, you probably don't have dual floppies if your computer is new. The reason for dual floppies was so that people could continue to use the "old" style of floppies, the 5.25-inch black flexible floppy disks that were popular until the early 1990s when the rigid 3.5-inch floppy drives, which could hold more information, became the standard.

Devices Versus File Systems: From Representation to Use

Just because all the storage devices in your computer are represented as files in the /dev directory doesn't mean that you can work with those files in the same way that you'd work with, say, a text file. If you had some programming skills, you could read directly from the individual device files, but that doesn't really serve much purpose. For everyday use, the devices need to be *mounted* to be accessible.

The UNIX term *mount* means "to make accessible." Because one of the main philosophies of UNIX is conservation of resources, the operating system starts only the minimum number of devices necessary for operation. This usually includes the hard disk, but not floppy or CD-ROM drives; you have to instruct the operating system when you want to use those devices. The mount process converts the data in the device file into a regular file system that you can access and work with through File Manager. Although Corel Linux simplifies this process by mounting the CD-ROM drive and the floppy drive automatically, it's still a good idea for you to understand the mount process in general; the mount process is described in detail in the "Mounting Network File Systems" and "Mounting CD-ROMs and Floppy Disks" sections of this chapter.

> **REMEMBER** *A file system includes a top directory and all the subdirectories and files beneath it. The / directory is a file system, as is the /usr directory, and the /usr/sbin directory. Each file system is subordinate to, and included within, the file systems above it. Chapter 11 contains a complete description of the Corel Linux file system.*

Here's an example. Susan has a disk partition on her computer represented by the file /dev/hda6. This partition contains the /home directory of her operating system. To make the /home directory accessible to her users, Susan needs to mount the /dev/hda6 file onto the /home directory; that is, the file systems represented by /dev/hda6 need to be accessible within /home.

In ordinary practice, mounting of drives and file systems is done automatically as part of the boot process; it can also be done manually. The manual command follows, and the syntax is explained, to show the mount process's construction. To mount /dev/hda6 onto /home, Susan would issue the following command:

```
mount -t ext2 /dev/hda6 /home
```

The syntax of this command is a standard UNIX format:

13

- **mount**   The basic command that Susan wants to execute.

- **–t**   The *flag* (a command option denoted by a hyphen and a designated letter) –t defines the file system type. This flag itself does not denote the type; it tells the operating system that the next component of the command will do so.

- **ext2**   The standard Linux file system type; other types might be iso9660, used for CD-ROM drives, or msdos or FAT32 for Microsoft file systems.

- **/dev/hda6**   The file that represents the device to be mounted.

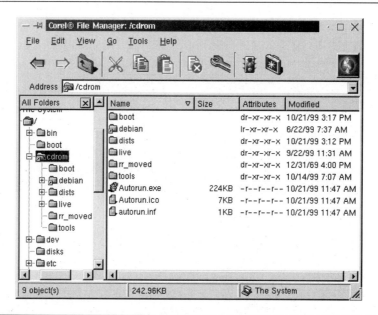

FIGURE 13-1 The contents of a mounted file system appear in File Manager's directory structure

■ **/home** The *mount point*, or location where the device is to be mounted. This must be an already existing, and empty, directory. Mount points that are either nonexistent or not empty will cause the mount command to fail.

If no problems occur during mounting, the operating system mounts the file system in the designated directory: in this case, the /home directory. Once the command has been executed, Susan can open File Manager and see the contents of the /dev/hdb1 partition displayed as the /cdrom directory's file structure, as shown in Figure 13-1.

Automatic Mounting

Although many file systems are automatically mounted at the time the machine boots up, like everything else in Linux, the behavior of this automatic mounting is configurable. You can set Corel Linux to boot as many or as few file systems as you need or want.

The file that controls the automatic mounting of file systems is /etc/fstab.

REMEMBER *The /etc directory contains the various configuration files for your Corel Linux system.*

A typical /etc/fstab file might look something like this:

```
# /etc/fstab: static file system information.

#

# <file system> <mount point> <type> <options>                    <dump>  <pass>
  /dev/hda1            /         ext2   defaults,errors=remount-ro    0       1
  /dev/hda2           none       swap   sw                            0       0
  proc               /proc       proc   defaults                      0       0
```

As you can see in this script, the single main partition called /dev/hda1 is mounted on /. This one device contains almost everything except the /proc directory.

REMEMBER *The /proc directory is a virtual directory. It is not resident on a disk, so it can't be part of the disk's file system.*

The preceding code shows that /dev/hda1 is an ext2 file system, and that it is mounted with certain options: in addition to the default options, it will be remounted in read-only mode (`ro`) mode if errors are found during mounting. The numbers that correspond to `<dump>` and `<pass>` are used for system-checking reasons. In addition to /dev/hda1 and proc, the table shows a /dev/hda2 file system that does not appear to be mounted anywhere at all. This is a swap partition, which is used by the operating system kernel for temporary storage should the system's memory fill during use.

A more complete /etc/fstab file might look like this:

```
/dev/hda1       /              ext2      defaults           1    1
/dev/hda6       /home          ext2      defaults           1    2
/dev/cdrom      /mnt/cdrom     iso9660   noauto,owner,ro    0    0
/dev/hda7       /opt           ext2      defaults           1    2
/dev/hda9       /tmp           ext2      defaults           1    2
/dev/hda5       /usr           ext2      defaults           1    2
/dev/hda8       /var           ext2      defaults           1    2
/dev/hda10      swap           swap      defaults           0    0
/dev/fd0        /mnt/floppy    ext2      noauto,owner       0    0
none            /proc          proc      defaults           0    0
```

13

In this file, you can see a number of partitions that use the ext2 file system type. The owner of this system decided to put many of the file system components on separate disk partitions. This is generally considered to be good practice because if one partition has a problem, it can be isolated from the rest of the system. (Think of it as electronic quarantine.) The file also shows that a floppy disk drive and a CD-ROM drive are mounted on this system.

By adding entries for each partition and the two additional drives to the /etc/fstab configuration file, the owner of this system has automated part of the startup process. When the machine is powered on, or Corel Linux is restarted, the drives will automatically mount into empty directories, and their file systems will be available through File Manager using those directories. This is certainly the easiest way to deal with file systems, although it is somewhat wasteful of resources if you don't use those file systems regularly.

> **TIP** *Windows and Macintosh systems mount all attached file systems on startup. If you are familiar with one of those operating systems, you might find it comforting to have your floppy and CD-ROM drives mounted on startup. If you like to pop floppies or CD-ROMs in and out of your computer, you'll want to have those drives mounted; if they're unmounted, you'll have to mount them by hand before you can use a removable disk. Corel Linux automounts the floppy and CD drives, but it's always a good idea to check that they're mounted before you try to run something. If they have become inadvertently unmounted, you'll need to remount them before use.*

Mounting Network File Systems

In addition to mounting hard disk partitions, floppy drives, and CD-ROM drives, it is also possible to mount file systems from other computers. This is done using the Network File Service, or NFS, program. Like many network functions, NFS has two components: a server and a client. The server is the machine that has the file system you want to mount, while the client is the machine you want to mount the file system onto. The server must be running the NFS server daemon, `nfsd`, and the client must be running the mounting program, `mountd`. These are started by default on most Linux systems.

> **NOTE** *We discuss NFS in more detail in Chapter 24, "File and Print Sharing."*

It is easiest to explain the process of remote mounting of file systems by walking through it with an example. Here's one: Steve runs a network of computers that are named after various well-known winds. He wants to export the /usr/local file system from the network's server, a machine called hudson-hawk, to a user machine named santa-ana.

> **TIP** *Many network administrators select machine names that fit a particular theme, to keep clear which machines belong to which network or just to make machine names easier to remember. Our network names fit a sushi theme (maguro, hamachi, fugu, umeboshi, and so forth). We've also worked on networks with a Three Stooges pattern (larry, curly, moe, and shemp), a clouds theme (cumulus, nimbus, and cirrus), and a playing cards pattern (heart, club, spade, and diamond). If you envision setting up a network, it's a good idea to pick the first machine's name in keeping with the future naming scheme. Otherwise, you'll end up with a name that doesn't quite make sense in the network context.*

To export this file system, log into the server computer as root (see Chapter 12, "User Space and User Accounts"). Edit the file /etc/exports by adding the following line:

```
/usr/local       santa-ana
```

where santa-ana is the hostname of the machine to which the file system is being exported. Then, still as root, issue the command

```
exportfs
```

On the client machine (santa-ana), make a mount point for the file system. Do this, still as root, by simply creating a directory such as /network. Then issue the following command:

```
mount -t nfs hudson-hawk:/usr/local /network
```

Once the command has been executed, hudson-hawk's /usr/local file system is available as santa-ana's /network file system. A user on santa-ana may never know that the files she uses in the /network directory are actually housed on another machine. In addition, network file systems can be added to the /etc/fstab

13

file, just as you might add a drive device, so that they will be mounted automatically at boot-up.

The syntax of this command, as well as a more detailed explanation of the Network File System, can be found in Chapter 24.

Mounting CD-ROMs and Floppy Disks

The file systems contained on CD-ROMs and floppy disks are mountable, just like the file systems in various hard disk partitions. As with the CD-ROM or floppy drives themselves, the file systems on removable disks can be mounted automatically at boot-up, or by hand whenever necessary. If you run your applications directly from a CD, for example, you might want to mount that CD's file system at boot-up so that you don't have to do it by hand every time you power up the computer.

Manually Mounting Additional Drives

If you prefer to mount CD-ROMs and floppy disks manually, you will need to shut off the automounter described in the previous section. To shut it off, log into the root account and issue the following command:

```
/etc/init.d/autofs stop
```

With the automounter stopped, you'll have to issue a mount command every time you want to use a CD-ROM or floppy disk. The format of the mount command is much the same as we described earlier in this chapter, with differences based on the type of file system being mounted and the location to which it is being mounted. For example, to mount a floppy disk, you would issue the following command:

```
mount -t ext2 /dev/fd0 /mnt/floppy
```

This assumes that the diskette was formatted for Linux. If the diskette was formatted on a DOS or Windows machine (or if you purchased a box of preformatted diskettes), the command would be

```
mount -t msdos /dev/fd0 /mnt/floppy
```

When you have finished using the floppy disk, you must unmount it before you remove it from the drive. To unmount the floppy disk, issue the following command:

```
umount /dev/fd0
```

Note that there is only one *n* in `umount`. If you don't unmount before you remove the disk, you will be unable to use the drive until you do so. If you forgot and removed the disk before unmounting, simply reinsert the disk into the drive and issue the `umount` command. Then you can remove the disk again, and the drive is ready to mount another floppy.

For a CD-ROM, the process is almost identical, except that the file system type is iso9660, which is the standard file system type used by all CD-ROM manufacturers. Thus,

```
mount -t iso9660 /dev/cdrom /mnt/cdrom
```

will mount the compact disc, while

```
umount /dev/cdrom
```

will unmount it.

Tips for Effective File Management

13

While you can run a Corel Linux system successfully without paying much attention to file management methods, you won't have much fun. There is enough to remember in administering a Linux machine, and it's a waste of time and brain space to also remember where you left important system files. It's much like putting your clothes away systematically into a dresser versus dressing out of two or three laundry baskets each morning; while you save some time in the beginning by not putting away the clothing, you lose time in the long run while you search for a matching sock or iron a shirt and pants.

Good file management techniques are those that make sense on a basic level. If you have to keep reminding yourself of your file management methods, they're too complicated. Stick to what's easy for you, as long as it's navigable.

Use a Consistent Naming Scheme

You don't have to use the directory names /mnt/cdrom or /mnt/floppy to refer to your drive mount points, but you should certainly pick some sort of consistent naming scheme. The more consistent you are with things like mount point names, the easier it will be to track down an obscure file or directory when you're looking for it in a hurry. Consistent naming is essential to a well-organized system, and a well-organized system is a joy to operate. We suspect that one of the main reasons people stop using Linux is that they don't understand the naming and directory structures, and thus don't organize their files in a systematic manner.

Get to Know /etc/mtab

The /etc/mtab file contains the names of all the file systems currently mounted on your machine. Do not attempt to edit this file (horrendous system malfunctions could occur as you inadvertently unmount running file systems). If you can't remember what's mounted, though, type

```
more /etc/mtab
```

at a system prompt to display the contents of the file and see what's mounted. A sample /etc/mtab file is shown in Figure 13-2. /etc/mtab is especially helpful if you have a large network with many shared file systems.

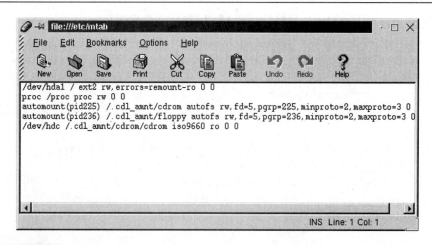

FIGURE 13-2   Use /etc/mtab to figure out what file systems are mounted

Automate Mounting with /etc/fstab

Earlier in this chapter, we described /etc/fstab, the file that contains a list of all file systems that are automatically mounted at boot-up. Keeping this file up to date can make managing your file systems a much simpler process. If you mount a lot of file systems as a routine habit, it can get tedious to mount each one by hand. In addition, you might forget to mount one or two, leading to frustration and lost time later on.

Enter each file system in /etc/fstab, using the syntax described earlier, and they will be mounted automatically at startup. If you want to add several file systems and then mount them at once, but without rebooting the machine right away, you can use /etc/fstab for that, too. Simply enter the file systems into /etc/fstab and then issue the command

```
mount -a
```

This forces the operating system to mount all file systems in /etc/fstab. Those file systems that are already mounted will be ignored during this process, so there won't be system instability.

Use the NFS Browser

Corel Linux offers a unique and helpful feature as part of File Manager—a browser that allows you to see various aspects of your networked file systems. This tool is useful for accessing file systems that you need to see, but don't need to keep mounted for lengthy periods of time.

1. Open File Manager, by clicking either the File Manager desktop icon or the File Manager icon in the KDE Panel.

2. Click NFS Network, shown in the left pane of the File Manager window. File Manager displays a list of all network file systems that are available to you.

3. Select a file system to mount it automatically, and display the contents of the file system.

13

CHAPTER 14

Corel Linux's Graphical Administration Tools

If your primary experience with computers has been with desktop systems such as Windows or Macintosh, you may be somewhat astonished by this point at the amount of behind-the-screens action going on with your Corel Linux system. You may even think that the amount of work involved in configuring and maintaining your system is somewhat overwhelming. Rest assured, though, that the situation simplifies itself quickly. Once you have your computer set up with the basic configurations, you'll find that it runs pretty smoothly without too much ongoing intervention on your part.

What's more, Corel Linux can help you with those basic administration activities. Corel Linux provides a suite of graphical administration tools that gives you an easier method of managing regular system tasks, while presenting the tasks in a simple and clear visual interface. While command-line administration seems complicated and difficult, you may find doing the same tasks easy with the graphical administration tools.

Streamlining Routine Tasks with KDE Tools

While you can manage your software and files with regular command-line programs, why not take advantage of the graphical tools that Corel Linux has provided to make system administration easier? The simplicity of these tools may mean the difference for you between keeping your computer trim and happy and letting some administrative tasks slide because of complexity or difficulty.

Update

One of the more vexing tasks of maintaining any computer system is keeping your software up to date. This is even more frustrating with open source and free software, since the very nature of open-source development tends to encourage frequent updates and releases.

You can handle this influx of new software in a number of ways. You could grab every new release as soon as it's available, and compile and install each package by hand. If you wanted to do that, though, you probably wouldn't be reading this chapter. No; what you want is to kick back, relax, and let Corel Linux do the work for you, with the Corel Update tool. The Corel Update tool allows you to access and install software packages over the Internet or from a CD-ROM.

To open the Corel Update tool, click the Applications Manager icon in the KDE Panel and select Applications I System I Corel Update.

The Corel Update window appears (Figure 14-1), showing your current software profile in the familiar tree format—the same format used in File Manager. The top level of the tree consists of several general categories: Admin (administration-specific programs), Base (the basic operating system), Corel Desktop (Corel Linux–specific programs), and so forth. By expanding the tree levels, you can view the individual packages currently installed on your system. If you click an individual package to select it, some basic information about the package appears in the lower pane.

> **TIP** *Viewing these is an excellent way to learn about your system. By reading the information presented for each package, you'll get a good idea of what software is contained in the various groups and how it works together.*

You can also use the Corel Update tool to install new software. (This is not the only method for installing new packages, however; see Chapter 21, "Adding and Removing Software," for some other options.) To install new software with Corel Update, use this procedure:

1. To open the Corel Update tool, click the Applications Manager icon in the KDE Panel and select Applications | System | Corel Update.

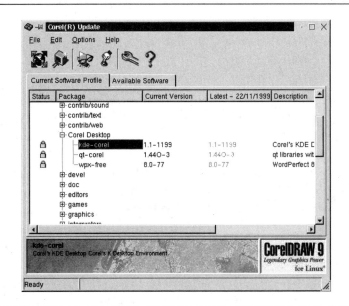

14

FIGURE 14-1   Corel Update is a wonderful way to handle software package installation

2. Click the Available Software tab at the top of the Corel Update window.

The top window contains a tree structure. The files that appear, as in Figure 14-2, are packages available to be installed. You can use any source of software for this, as long as the packages are formatted as .deb packages, the standard Debian format. If you do not set the source, you won't see any packages in the Available Software window.

NOTE   *If you want to upgrade software that is already installed on your computer, select the Current Software Profile tab instead, and continue with this process.*

TIP   *Corel Update points to a Corel FTP site by default. On that site, you'll find a number of packages correctly formatted for your use.*

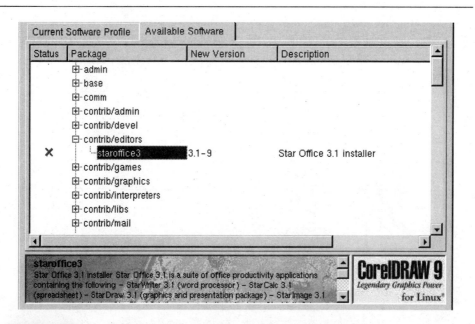

| FIGURE 14-2 | Use Update to see whether you have uninstalled packages on your machine |

3. Choose Options | Set File Sources.

In the Package Sources window, shown in the illustration, you can see the name of the default site provided by Corel Linux, where you can find new packages to download and install on your machine. You'll also see the path of the packages directory included on your Corel Linux CD-ROM.

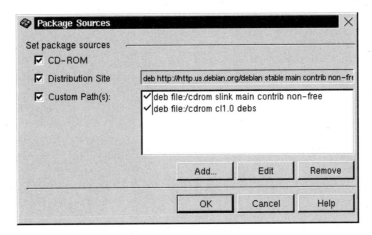

4. (Optional) Enter additional sites into the Package Sources window.

If you have favorite file archives, enter them here as a kind of bookmark for future use.

5. Check the Distribution Site check box and uncheck the Custom Paths box if it is selected.

6. Click the OK button to close the Package Sources window and return to Corel Update.

7. Click the Update Profile button in the Corel Update icon bar.

A connection message appears in the lower pane. When the connection with the remote site has been established, the list of available packages will be retrieved and will appear in the lower pane, as in Figure 14-3.

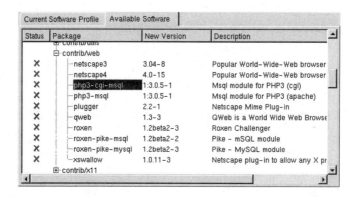

FIGURE 14-3 The available packages on the remote site are displayed in the Update window

8. Browse through the available packages until you find a package you want to install.

9. Click the package to select it.

Note that the red X to the left of the package name changes to a pair of arrows when the package is selected.

TIP *You can select multiple packages to download. Each package that is selected, with the X changed to arrows, will be downloaded and installed in turn. This is especially helpful if you update infrequently and many new versions of your software must be installed.*

10. Click the Upgrade and Install icon in the Corel Update icon bar.

Corel Update downloads and installs the package, along with any ancillary packages required by the program you selected. If any information is needed during the installation, Corel Update will prompt you to enter it. Corel Update displays a message when all packages have been downloaded and installed.

11. Click the OK button to exit Corel Update.

You can use the same process to install packages from a CD-ROM, floppy disk, or any other Internet archive or data storage device simply by setting the appropriate path in the Package Sources window.

> **TIP** *You can also click the Application Starter icon and select File | Install Deb File to install a single .deb package.*

If you need to remove an application or package from the system, you can use Corel Update for that as well. Corel Update is about as easy as software management gets, regardless of the operating system being used.

MIME Editor

MIME Editor allows you to associate particular types of files with appropriate applications. For example, you can associate image files saved in the JPEG format with Corel Linux's Image Viewer program. This association means that whenever you click a JPEG file in File Manager, Image Viewer automatically launches to display the file. MIME Editor makes these assignments based on standard file extensions; all JPEG files have the file extension .jpg, text files have the file extension .txt, and so on.

> **NOTE** *MIME stands for Multipurpose Internet Mail Extension and was originally devised as a method for sending nontext files as e-mail attachments. Its use has been extended to a general method for handling files of different types, both locally and across the Internet.*

1. To open MIME Editor, click the Applications Manager icon in the KDE Panel and choose Applications | System | Mime Editor from the Start menu.

The MIME Type Editor screen appears, as shown in Figure 14-4. In the left pane, you'll see the familiar tree view, showing the various file types available to associate with applications.

14

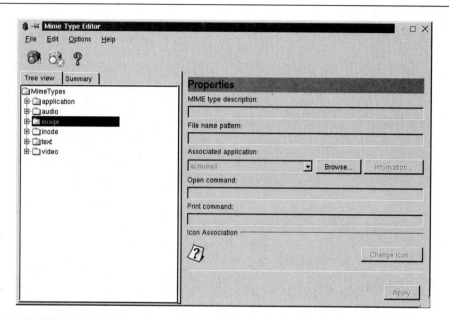

FIGURE 14-4 Use the MIME Editor to streamline the process of opening files

2. Select the file type you wish to associate with an application.

   The right pane displays a series of fields, as in Figure 14-5, that define the file type you selected. The first field contains a description of the MIME type, and the second field contains the file extensions that identify that type.

3. Set the application you want to associate with the file type, using the drop-down box in the third field.

4. (Optional) Use the fourth and fifth fields to set commands for file execution and printing of this file type, if applicable.

5. In the bottom pane, select the icon that File Manager will use to represent this MIME type in directory listings.

6. Click the OK button to save your settings and exit MIME Editor.

Most of the common file types are available as preset options in MIME Editor, and you shouldn't have to do anything special to use them. However, you may run

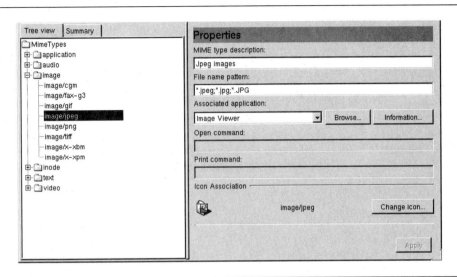

FIGURE 14-5   Associate applications with file types in the MIME Editor

across an unusual suffix for a certain file type and want to add it to your MIME Editor associations. In this case, you can simply add it to the list of types displayed in the second field in the right pane of the MIME Editor window.

You can also define new MIME types, which is useful if you work with unusual files on a regular basis. To add a new MIME type, use this process:

1. To open MIME Editor, click the Applications Manager icon in the KDE Panel and select Applications | System | Mime Editor from the Start menu.

2. Click the Local Mime Types folder in the left pane.

3. Choose File | Add New.

   A screen appears asking for the same information displayed in the right pane of the MIME Editor screen.

4. Enter the requested information.

5. Click the OK button to save your additions.

   MIME Editor adds the new file type, and future occurrences of the file type will be handled with the program you associated with the type.

14

Event Viewer

Event Viewer is an interface to your Corel Linux system's log files. Just about everything your system does is recorded in a log file, and most of these files are stored in the /var/log directory. Combing through these files to find a particular entry, or merely keeping up with the large number of regularly generated logs, can be quite irritating. Luckily, the Corel Linux Event Viewer provides a configurable method of browsing and searching your log files.

NOTE   *You must be logged in as root, or have assumed superuser powers, to use Event Viewer.*

Open Event Viewer by clicking the Applications Manager icon in the KDE Panel and selecting Applications | System | Event Viewer from the Start menu. The Event Viewer window appears, as shown in Figure 14-6.

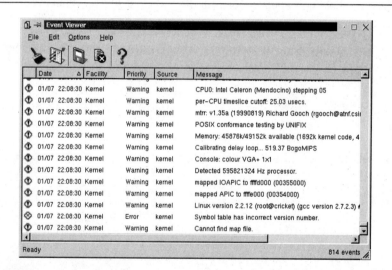

FIGURE 14-6   The Event Viewer makes reading system logs an easier process

When you first open Event Viewer, you will see a preselected cross-section of your system logs. These logs are the most critical messages from all of the subsystems that keep logs. This is a good general overview of your system, and it is probably adequate for casual browsing. If your interest in your system logs goes beyond the casual, however, you will probably want to customize the logs and log entries that Event Viewer displays.

1. Open Event Viewer by clicking the Applications Manager icon in the KDE Panel and selecting Applications | System | Event Viewer from the Start menu.

2. Open the Event Viewer Filter Manager by clicking its icon in the toolbar.

The Filter Manager screen appears, as shown in Figure 14-7, containing a grid of check boxes. Across the top are icons that denote the various categories of system log messages, ranging from simple debugging information to critical emergency warnings. Down the left side of the screen, each of the various logging subsystems is listed: Authorization, Crontab, Daemon, Kernel, Printer, Mail, News, Syslog, User, UUCP, and PPP.

Each of the check boxes in the grid refers to a specific message category for a particular subsystem. For example, if you wanted to see only emergency messages from the kernel, you would deselect all check boxes except for the far-right check box in the fourth row; this sample configuration is shown in Figure 14-8.

14

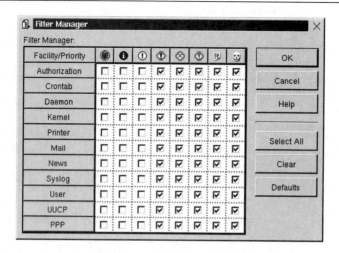

FIGURE 14-7   Configure Event Viewer with the Filter Manager's check boxes

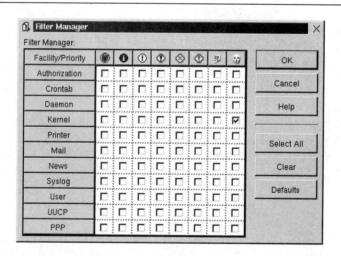

FIGURE 14-8   A minimal Event Viewer configuration

3. Click an icon in the top row or a subsystem box along the left side to select all the boxes in that row.

   If you want to see all messages from the kernel, for example, click the Kernel label. If you want to see all critical messages from all subsystems, click the last icon on the right.

4. Click the Clear button if you want to uncheck all the boxes, or click Select All if you want to display all messages.

5. Click the OK button when you have selected the profile you want.

   Event Viewer rescans the log files (which may take a minute, depending on your machine speed) and refreshes the display with the specified profile.

6. Click the Clear button to clear all log messages from the screen.

   Clearing log messages from the screen is useful if you want to keep logs to a manageable size or if you've resolved all the problems you found and you want to delete those messages. The next time you open Event Viewer, the display will generate from the point where you cleared the logs.

7. It is sometimes useful to save the log files generated by Event Viewer; these files contain the displayed messages that were shown according to the profile you set. Click the Save icon to save the log file to the hard disk.

14

Event Viewer will prompt you for a filename. Saving your log file is especially helpful when a message appears that you don't understand. You can save the file and e-mail or print it so that someone more knowledgeable can review the file and possibly diagnose the problem. You can also save log files if you want to keep certain records about your system: how many times someone tried to su into the root account, perhaps, or records from your mail logs.

Archiver

Archiver is an interface to the UNIX tar (tape archive) program. The term *tape archive* is another UNIX historical artifact: originally, the tar program was used to make backup files on magnetic tape. As the program came into widespread use, however, people discovered that tar had a lot of uses beyond the simple task of making backup tapes.

> **TIP** *Archiver can handle files compressed with the .tar, .tar.z, .tar.lzo, .lzh, .rar, .zoo, and .zip compression methods. You'll know what kind of compression was used by looking at the file extension; if it matches an extension listed in the previous sentence, you can use Archiver to open it.*

For example, most programs distributed in source code form are distributed as *tarballs*, or compressed tar files, because it's a convenient way to package source code. You can use Archiver to create tarballs of your own, to archive files that you don't need to access on a regular basis but that you don't want to delete. Tarballs retain the directory structure from which they're made; were we to make a tar archive for this book, we would first create a master directory on the hard disk, such as corel_linux, with subdirectories for each chapter that contains text and images. Then, we could run Archiver on this file system and convert all these directories and files into one tar file. The archive is now a single file and can be dealt with as one would handle any other file. However, when we *extract*, or open, the tarball, the directory structure is restored exactly as it was created.

1. To make an archive file, open Archiver by clicking the Applications Manager icon in the KDE Panel and selecting Applications I Utilities I Archiver from the Start menu.

   The Archiver window appears, as shown in Figure 14-9.

2. Click the New button.

3. At the prompt, enter the filename you want to use for the new archive.

   The filename you select must end with the extension .tar (for example, archive.tar).

4. Click the Add button

   A file browser window appears.

FIGURE 14-9 Use the Archiver to compress files and directories

14

5. Navigate through the tree structure to the files you want to include in the archive.

6. Select each file to be included by clicking it.

7. Click the OK button.

   The selected files appear in the main Archiver window.

8. Select File | Close Archive from the drop-down menus to save your archive file.

Once you have made some archive files, you'll need to extract them to access the information contained within.

1. To extract a `tar` archive, open Archiver by clicking the Applications Manager icon in the KDE Panel and selecting Applications | Utilities | Archiver from the Start menu.

2. Click the Open button.

   A file browser window appears.

3. Navigate through the tree structure to the archive you wish to extract.

4. Select the archive by clicking it.

5. Click the OK button

   The archive's files appear in the main Archiver window.

6. Click the Extract button.

   A window appears with location and extraction options, as shown in Figure 14-10.

7. Select the directory into which you want the files to be extracted and choose the extraction options you'd like to use.

8. Click the OK button.

   Archiver extracts the file. This may be rapid or slow, depending on your machine speed and the size of the archive. When the extraction is complete, Archiver displays a message with the names of the files extracted.

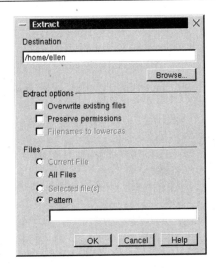

FIGURE 14-10 Select the location where you want to extract the archive

The archive file is not destroyed when you extract the files from it. The .tar file is still in the location where you found it and can be extracted again if you want.

Managing Users with User Manager

In Chapter 12, "User Space and User Accounts," we describe the process for adding a new user with User Manager. In this chapter, we explain how you can use User Manager to maintain your user accounts. To open User Manager, click the Application Starter icon, and, from the Start menu, choose Applications I System I User Manager.

- Delete a user by clicking the user's name to select the entry. Click the Delete button in the toolbar; the button shows a human figure with a circled X atop it.

- Edit a user's profile by clicking the user's name to select the entry. Click the Edit User button in the toolbar to open the Edit User dialog box, which is the same as the Add User dialog box. Edit the information as necessary and click OK.

You can use User Manager to edit groups, as well. Click the Groups tab of User Manager to show a list of available user groups. You can then add, delete, or edit groups that you've selected from the group list. When editing a group, you can select the users to be added into that group, as well as set the group name and ID number.

System at a Glance

It's often quite useful to know which processes are currently running and how much of the system's resources are being taken up by each process. Corel Linux offers two tools that provide this information: Task Manager and Process Manager. We describe Process Manager here; because Task Manager works in the same way, you should be able to use both tools after reading through the Process Manager section.

Both Process Manager and Task Manager are interfaces to the UNIX `top` (table of processes) program. This program reports every single process running on the system, the amount of CPU time and memory each process is using, and various other bits of information. The `top` program also allows you to send signals to processes and to raise or lower their priority. `top` is a dynamic program; that is, it refreshes its report at a set time interval, so that it's possible for you to see processes start and stop, or rise and fall in their system usage.

Process Manager

To start Process Manager, click the Applications Manager icon in the KDE Panel and select Applications | System | Process Management from the Start menu. Most of the Process Manager functions appear in the main window, as shown in Figure 14-11, including graphs for system load, CPU usage, memory usage, and swap usage. These are the most popular requests for system information, so they're kept at the top of the Process Manager window for easy access.

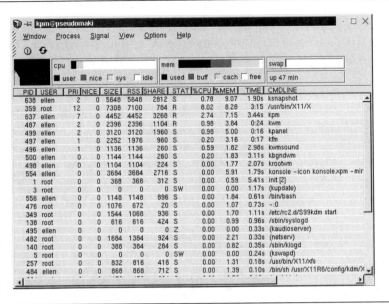

PID	USER	PRI	NICE	SIZE	RSS	SHARE	STAT	%CPU	%MEM	TIME	CMDLINE
638	ellen	2	0	5648	5648	2812	S	0.78	9.07	1.90s	ksnapshot
359	root	12	0	7308	7100	784	R	8.02	8.28	3:15	/usr/bin/X11/X
637	ellen	7	0	4452	4452	3268	R	2.74	7.15	3.44s	kpm
487	ellen	2	0	2396	2396	1104	R	0.98	3.84	0:24	kwm
499	ellen	2	0	3120	3120	1960	S	0.98	5.00	0:16	kpanel
497	ellen	1	0	2252	1976	960	S	0.20	3.16	0:17	kfm
496	ellen	1	0	1136	1136	260	S	0.59	1.82	2.98s	kwmsound
500	ellen	0	0	1144	1144	260	S	0.20	1.83	3.11s	kbgndwm
498	ellen	0	0	1104	1104	224	S	0.00	1.77	2.07s	krootwm
554	ellen	0	0	3684	3684	2716	S	0.00	5.91	1.79s	konsole –icon konsole.xpm –mir
1	root	0	0	368	368	312	S	0.00	0.59	5.41s	init [2]
3	root	0	0	0	0	0	SW	0.00	0.00	1.17s	(kupdate)
556	ellen	0	0	1148	1148	896	S	0.00	1.84	0.61s	/bin/bash
476	root	0	0	1076	672	20	S	0.00	1.07	0.73s	–:0
349	root	0	0	1544	1068	936	S	0.00	1.70	1.11s	/etc/rc2.d/S99kdm start
138	root	0	0	616	616	424	S	0.00	0.99	0.96s	/sbin/syslogd
495	ellen	0	0	0	0	0	Z	0.00	0.00	0.33s	(kaudioserver)
482	root	0	0	1664	1364	924	S	0.00	2.21	0.33s	(netserv)
140	root	0	0	388	364	284	S	0.00	0.62	0.35s	/sbin/klogd
5	root	0	0	0	0	0	SW	0.00	0.00	0.24s	(kswapd)
257	root	0	0	832	816	416	S	0.00	1.31	0.18s	/usr/bin/X11/xfs
484	ellen	0	0	868	868	712	S	0.00	1.39	0.10s	/bin/sh /usr/X11R6/config/kdm/X

FIGURE 14-11   The Process Manager provides more information about system processes

Underneath the graphs, Process Manager provides a table of processes. Each process has a number of entries:

- **PID**   The *process ID* number. Each process that runs on a UNIX-based operating system has a unique identifying number, used to distinguish that process from all other processes.

- **USER**   The user who started the process. Users can be actual users, such as mindy or bobby, or they could be system processes that assume user identities, such as daemon or nobody.

- **PRI**   The amount of time left in the process's current "time slice." This has to do with the way that Linux handles multitasking; more important processes have larger time slices, while low-priority processes have smaller slices.

14

■ **NICE**   The priority of the process. Nice values range between –20 and +19. A process with a nice value of –20 has the highest possible priority in the CPU's process schedule, while a process with a nice value of +19 has the lowest. The default nice value for most processes is zero.

> **NOTE** *Nice values are so named because processes with higher nice values are "nicer" to other processes, in that they take a lower scheduling priority and thus let other processes with higher priorities use the CPU resources first.*

■ **SIZE**   The virtual image size of the process, expressed in kilobytes. *Image*, in this context, refers to the binary file held in memory. It does not have anything to do with graphical images.

■ **RSS**   Resident Set Size, the number of kilobytes that the program currently occupies in system memory.

■ **SHARE**   Expresses the amount of shared memory used by the process, using kilobytes.

■ **STAT**   The state of the process. A process can be R (running), S (sleeping), I (idle), T (stopped), D (in uninterruptable sleep), or Z (defunct, or "zombie").

■ **%CPU**   The estimated percentage of CPU time used by the process.

■ **%MEM**   The estimated percentage of system memory used by the process.

■ **TIME**   Total CPU time used by the process since it was started.

> **TIP** *If your Corel Linux system has been running for a few weeks or more, the Time value may seem astonishing, especially if it's for a system-critical process. Don't worry about it; this value is useful mostly for entertainment purposes.*

■ **CMD LINE**   The command that started the process, which was executed by the user or system process named in the USER field.

Click any of these headings to sort the process table by that statistic; the sort is either numerical or alphabetical, depending on the variable. Click the heading again to reverse the sort.

Process Manager and Task Manager can also be used to handle some system administration processes, such as changing the nice value. We cover this kind of use of the managers in Chapter 22, "Administering Services."

PART IV

Essential Linux
System Administration

CHAPTER 15

Overview of Linux System Administration

Part IV of this book contains a great deal of technical information. While it may seem overwhelming at first, you'll probably find that you refer to this section more than others when running a Corel Linux machine. Why? Well, the programs covered in this section are those that make your machine a powerful and multifaceted computer. With these programs, you can run your own servers for Web pages, e-mail, and so on. You can write scripts to automate and speed up many routine tasks. You can configure hardware, such as printers, and you can connect several computers through a network. In short, the tools we describe in Part IV are those that make Linux computers so popular; every Linux machine has the capability to run these programs, with memory and hard disk space the only considerations.

In this chapter we provide a brief overview of the remaining chapters in Part IV. We encourage you to skip around through the chapters in this section; you may not need to know about the information contained in the networking chapters now but have a burning desire to learn to write scripts. However, reading all of the chapters may give you a better idea of the real power contained in the Corel Linux operating system. If you find yourself saying, "Huh—I didn't know I could do that myself," you're beginning to see the scope and possibilities of running a Linux machine.

What Is System Administration?

We've been using the terms *system administration* and *system administrator* a lot throughout this book, and not without some concern because we're using it in a slightly imprecise manner. Formal definitions would have to include the facts that system administration is a profession (some of our friends insist that it's a calling) and that system administrators are usually well trained and highly experienced folks.

Professional system administrators have an unenviable job. They are responsible for keeping all computers in good working order and making sure that each member of the organization has access to the information and computing services he or she needs. This often involves long and irregular working hours, tremendous workloads, and dealing with various sets of requests and orders that are often at odds with each other. Calling yourself a *sysadmin* because you happen to use a computer running Corel Linux may raise the ire—or at least the disdain—of a sysadmin who manages Linux machines for a living.

> **TIP**
>
> *If you are a sysadmin, you'll find lots of helpful information in this part of the book. We assume that you're looking for the ways in which Corel Linux handles standard services that you're familiar with already; if you're coming from a Windows NT background instead of a UNIX-based background, you'll probably need to study this section more carefully since NT services work differently. Corel Linux uses regular UNIX/Linux services, such as Apache, Samba, and C News.*

That said, we do use these terms in this book. Many of the tasks involved in installing, configuring, and maintaining a Corel Linux system echo those tasks performed by professional system administrators, and there really is no better way of describing them than to call them "administrative tasks." Whether or not you're a professional, these tasks require basic knowledge of your system and how best to administer the programs that keep it running well. Certainly installing and configuring Corel Linux is key, and so are regular maintenance and upgrades, user management, and service installation and maintenance.

Shell Use and Programming

One of the greatest Corel Linux assets that you have at your disposal is simply the operating system. It seems obvious since that's what the whole book is about, right? Well, yes. We refer here, though, to an often-overlooked component of the operating system that can give you an incredible amount of power in an efficient and often elegant manner: the shell interface to the operating system.

> **NOTE**
>
> *A shell interface is both a user interface and a programming environment. Shells convert your commands into language that the operating system understands, much like the graphical tools in KDE convert your mouse clicks into operating system commands. There are several different kinds of shell environments, and we discuss the various shells in Chapter 16, "The Administrator's Tools: Shells and Text Editors," with primary focus on the* bash *shell, which is used as the default Corel Linux shell environment.*

15

Throughout the previous chapters, we provided some shell commands (also referred to as *command-line* or *text commands*) as alternatives to various KDE or Corel Linux graphical tools. In Chapter 16 and Chapter 17, "The Shell Expanded:

Basic Scripting," we show you how to take advantage of some of the advanced features that make the shell interface such a powerful tool.

Thousands of Linux users around the world still haven't switched to a graphical user interface. The various text-based shell interfaces are so powerful that people haven't found a real need to change to something visual. We aren't advocating a total rejection of KDE—far from it. Using a blend of KDE and shell commands will make your Corel Linux machine a more powerful and useful tool.

In Chapter 16, we show you some of the common shell commands and how to use command-line modifiers, such as flags and switches, to customize the command behavior. We also show you how to redirect input and output, and how to make compound commands by using pipes. (An extensive list of shell commands is located in Appendix B, "A Compendium of Common Shell Commands.")

In Chapter 17, we show you how to write shell scripts, which are programs that use shell commands. The shell's built-in program interpreter allows you to create full-fledged programs that can perform complex tasks automatically. We also describe how to run these programs automatically or how to start them only when needed.

Networking

If you connect more than one computer together, you've got a network. Networking is a big topic, one that could easily fill a book of its own.

For more detailed information on networking, we suggest Networking: A Beginner's Guide, *by Bruce Hallberg, published by McGraw-Hill.*

In Chapter 20, "Networking," we cover some of the basics of Linux networking. We explain how to connect to the Internet, either via an Ethernet connection or through a dial-up link. (Chapter 9, "Using the Internet with Corel Linux," contains an extensive discussion of dial-up networking, and Chapter 20 contains only the basics; see Chapter 9 for an explanation.)

We also teach you how to build a local network of machines, whether or not they are all Linux computers. For those non-Linux computers on your network, we introduce a highly useful program called Samba, which allows you to share files between Linux and Windows computers on the same network. (We use Samba for our own home network and think it's a fantastic solution for a multiple–operating system network.) We also introduce `netatalk`, a Samba equivalent for MacOS computers.

Software Management

Most people want to have the latest and greatest software running on their systems, and we assume you're no exception. In addition, you may want to upgrade various packages for security reasons; if a new hole (security risk) is found, you'll want to install a patch (a small upgrade that fixes the problem) before someone can exploit the hole and compromise your machine's security.

In Chapter 21, "Adding and Removing Software," we show you how to locate, install, upgrade, and uninstall software packages, whether from source code or a particular package format. We discuss various package management tools, including the Debian `.deb` and Red Hat `.rpm` formats, which are the two most popular package formats and the ones in which you're likely to find software that you want to install. We finish the chapter with a complete discussion of source code and how to install programs from source code (it's not as complicated as it sounds).

Hardware Management

Just as they do with software, many people want to keep their hardware upgraded to the cutting edge. You may want to install a larger hard drive or an ancillary storage unit, like a Zip drive; you may want to attach a printer to your Corel Linux computer; or you may want to add a new video or audio card to improve the gaming experience. All these hardware components are controlled by software drivers within Corel Linux.

In Chapter 19, "Dealing with Hardware," we cover hardware installation and management. We discuss obtaining and configuring various drivers and provide some hints on troubleshooting installations (especially important with printers).

15

Administering Services

Whether you're having a conversation about computers or listening to someone else talking about them, you're likely to hear the terms *server* and *workstation* thrown about, almost randomly. Like our use of *system administration* and *administrator*, these terms are often used imprecisely. Following is the technical definition of each term.

Servers

As the name suggests, the server provides services—anything from housing a Web site to routing e-mail throughout an organization, managing printing, or coordinating any other kind of service imaginable. Servers are often dedicated machines: that is, they are configured to do one thing, and that's all they do.

Servers are often the biggest and fastest pieces of hardware in the organization, and they handle a heavy and continuous workload. Some servers are so powerful that they generate an immense amount of heat and must be kept in special temperature-controlled rooms that are locked so that the environment stays chilled and stable. Servers are primarily intended to be accessed by other, smaller, computers that are referred to as *client* machines.

Workstations

Workstations are the desktop computers that most people use on a day-to-day basis. The software found on a workstation tends to be productivity-oriented applications, such as word processors, databases, spreadsheets, Web browsers, e-mail programs, and so forth (games, too, but those aren't technically productivity oriented).

In this technical sense, these definitions really hold true only in fairly large organizations. In smaller environments, computers often have mixed purposes. For example, a household Corel Linux computer, like yours, may function primarily as a workstation but may also host a low-traffic Web site and handle electronic mail for all family members.

Corel Linux, by virtue of its largely graphical interface, is primarily oriented toward workstation implementations. That doesn't mean that your Corel Linux computer can't be used as a server, only that the user interface tends to be oriented toward desktop users. Remember, though, that any Linux machine can be configured to function as a server, a workstation, or some blend of the two. It all depends on what services you choose to run.

In Chapters 22 through 27, we describe the various services available to you and explain how to configure and run them. Breaking each service down into its own package means that you can install only the services you need; if you don't want to run a Web server, you don't have to install and run Apache.

Mail Services

Chapter 23, "Mail Services," provides an overview of the various mail transport agents, or MTAs, available in the Linux environment. We concentrate on `exim` and `qmail`, the default MTAs provided with Corel Linux.

File and Print Sharing

Chapter 24, "File and Print Sharing," covers the methods through which you can share files between computers (over a network) and the basics of NFS, the Network File Service. We also discuss the software side of printing, from both standalone and networked computers.

INET Services

Chapter 25, "INET Services," contains thorough coverage of the various Internet-related services that you might choose to run: Telnet, FTP, `rlogin` and `rsh`, and `ssh` (a secure replacement for `rlogin` and `rsh`). We also explain `inetd`, the master network daemon used with these services.

Web Services

Chapter 26, "Web Services," covers Apache, the UNIX/Linux Web server program. This is described separately from other Internet services because it is not controlled by `inetd`. (Apache is not controlled by `inetd` because of its complexity and because it functions slightly differently from the other Internet services.)

Managing Users

Once you have the proper packages and services installed and working smoothly, the second step in effective system administration is user management. You will need to decide who can use your computer and what level of access to the system each user will have. We covered some of the issues of user management in Chapter 12, "User Space and User Accounts"; in Chapter 27, "Miscellaneous Network Services," we go into more detailed discussion of the concerns that administrators should have.

Chapter 27 offers more information about the /etc/passwd file, setting default environment variables for your users and defining user groups, among other topics. We also cover the important issue of educating and communicating with your users, a part of system administration that is often covered only as an afterthought.

A Look Ahead

As we said at the start of this chapter, you don't have to learn everything in this part of the book to run your Corel Linux computer. However, you may find yourself consulting these chapters as a reference when you want to add some services to your computer or automate some processes. Don't be intimidated by what might seem "too advanced"; we've given you straightforward explanations and some sources for more detailed information.

CHAPTER 16

The Administrator's Tools: Shells and Text Editors

Although you can do a great deal in Corel Linux using the KDE graphical administration tools, it's a good idea to familiarize yourself with the shell environment and the text editors used in that environment. At times you may not be able to use the graphical environment, or you may simply prefer working in character mode for some tasks.

In this chapter, we describe the concept of a shell environment and provide some tools for using `bash`, the Corel Linux default shell, in an effective way. We also explain the differences between some of the popular text editors and give more detailed descriptions of the `vi` character-mode text editor and the KEdit graphical text editor.

What Is a Shell?

When you open a terminal window and issue a command at the text prompt, it is convenient to think of those commands as being UNIX or Linux commands. However, this is not technically the case (although we're guilty of using the terms in that way). The only true Linux commands are *system calls,* which are used by programmers to access system services from within a given program. The commands that you issue at a terminal prompt are more correctly called *shell commands*.

A shell is, in fact, partially a command interpreter. It takes the commands that you enter at the prompt and translates them into a language that the kernel can understand and act upon. The shell also performs several other tasks; in fact, if a shell environment weren't running, no command prompt would be available for you to work with. So in addition to being a command interpreter, the shell also provides the environment you use to interact with the operating system.

As with KDE and other parts of the Corel Linux system, you can customize your shell environment to your liking. It will still be a text-based environment, and it won't look much different, but you can tinker with the way in which the shell responds to your commands and its general behavior. Among other options, you can set your preferred text editor, include various directory paths as default search paths, and even change to a different shell if you don't like the one you're using.

The most commonly used shell across various Linux distributions is the Bourne Again Shell, usually referred to as `bash`. It's so named because it is a rewrite of an old UNIX shell called the Bourne shell; the Bourne shell, also known as `sh`, was a proprietary program and was one of the programs that was rewritten and re-implemented in a free version as part of the GNU Project. (See Chapter 1, "Why Linux, and Why Corel Linux?," for more information about GNU and the free software movement.)

But `bash` is not the only shell available. Far from it. There are many shell environments, and all have their adherents. `csh` is also included as part of the Corel Linux distribution, and you can find other shells at `http://www.freshmeat.net` if you'd like to try them.

> **TIP**
>
> *You won't be able to distinguish between shell environments easily just by looking at the command prompt. If you have a new account on a UNIX or Linux system, it's wise to ask your system administrator what shell is used as default; you can change your shell if you don't like the default. It's quite frustrating to go into a new environment and notice that your usual habits don't work very well; but, unless you're programming heavily or writing scripts, you may not notice a lot of difference between the various shells. (You may find those differences when you start setting environment variables, though.) To see what shell is running, type **echo $SHELL** at a text prompt; if the shell is a bash-style shell, the current shell name will print on the screen.*

The following shells are the most popular ones that you're likely to find running on other Linux systems if the administrator hasn't chosen to run `bash`.

- **ksh** The Korn Shell is similar to `bash`. It differs primarily in the way that it handles variables, mathematical functions, and process control.

- **csh and tcsh** The C Shell, and the `tcsh` version of the C Shell, use a command syntax that is similar to the C programming language. If you're comfortable in C, you may like using this shell. (Kate likes `tcsh`, though she's not a C wizard by any stretch of the imagination.)

- **zsh** The Z Shell resembles `ksh` but with many added features. In fact, many people think of `zsh` as a compromise between `ksh` and `csh`. This is a powerful and advanced shell; it's used mostly by programmers because of the efficient way in which it works with the operating system.

Still other shells exist in addition to these four. For the purposes of this book, though, we are going to concentrate on `bash` since it is the most commonly used shell (and the default shell in Corel Linux). In all likelihood, you'll never need to use another shell unless you're a hard-core programmer or your programming background is in C or one of its derivative languages. If you do decide to use another shell, see the sidebar "Changing Your Shell" for help on switching and use the Web or your local bookstore to get more specific information on working with the new shell environment.

16

Changing Your Shell

To change your shell environment, simply type the name of the new shell at the command prompt. Corel Linux changes the shell, and the prompt used by the new shell environment appears. In this example, switch to `tcsh` by typing its name; Corel Linux supplies the `tcsh` prompt, which is a right angle bracket. To exit the new shell and get back to `bash`, simply type **exit** at the prompt.

```
bash>$ tcsh
>
> exit
bash>$
```

Preferred shell environments are controlled by the /etc/passwd file. As we've mentioned in other chapters, only someone with access to root powers can edit /etc/passwd; if you want to make another shell your default environment instead of `bash`, you need to log in as root and edit your user entry in /etc/passwd to reflect the new shell. (Just replace `bash` in your user entry with the new shell name.)

The Bourne Again Shell

Because `bash` is the default shell for Corel Linux, we spend a major portion of this chapter describing it and giving some basic commands to operate easily within the `bash` shell. You'll find many of these commands familiar UNIX commands if you've worked in a shell environment before. For those of you new to UNIX/Linux shells, commands tend to be oddly abbreviated versions or acronyms of the words they represent. Be careful if you decide to wing it and type something you *think* is right—you may end up typing something that you did not intend to invoke.

Common Commands

There are dozens of `bash` commands. We provide a few here; but if you're hungry for more, we also provide a long list of commands that work with `bash` in

Appendix B, "A Compendium of Common Shell Commands." Here are some of the most useful commands, and the ones you'll probably use a few times a day:

- **ls** The ls command lists the contents of a directory. If you don't specify the directory path, ls returns the contents of the current directory.

- **cd <directory path>** The cd command changes the directory to the specified directory. If you don't give a path, cd doesn't do anything. To get into /etc/passwd, for example, you'd type **cd /etc/passwd** at the prompt.

- **pwd** If you forget where you are, use pwd. The pwd command prints the name of the current directory.

- **cat, more, less, head, and tail** All these commands are used to print the contents of a file to the screen. They differ in the format; cat scrolls the entire file content at once, more and less go through the file a screen at a time, and head and tail show you either the first or last few lines of the file contents.

- **mv** Use mv to move files from one directory to another or to change the name of a file. The syntax for this command is mv <filename> <directorypath>, as in mv jimbob.txt /usr/jimbob/. You can use mv to rename a file in the same directory by using the syntax mv <oldfilename> <newfilename>, or mv jimbob.txt donnasue.txt.

- **cp** Use cp with the same syntax that mv uses. Instead of moving the file (and deleting it from the original location), cp simply places a copy in the new location.

- **grep** The grep command is useful for searching for a particular character string or expression in a given file. grep has a flexible syntax; the most common use of grep is with the syntax grep -e <expression> <filename>. So, if you're searching for the user Beeble in your /etc/passwd file, you'd type **grep -e beeble /etc/passwd**. Corel Linux scans the file and returns the lines in which the expression "beeble" occurs.

16

■ **apropos** If you're not sure what command you need in any given situation, try using the apropos command. apropos searches an internal database for any text string contained in the command you issued and outputs the shell commands that contain that string in their descriptions. For example, typing the command **apropos copy** returns the following (we include only part of the output):

```
COPY (1)                      - Copies data between files and tables
bcmp, bcopy, bzero, memccpy, memchr, memcmp, memcpy, memfrob, memmem, memmove,
memset (3)                    - byte string operations

bcopy (3)                     - copy byte strings
copysign (3)                  - copy sign of a number
cp (1)                        - copy files and directories
cpio (1)                      - copy files to and from archives
dd (1)                        - convert and copy a file
dvicopy (1)                   - produce modified copy of DVI file
fcopy (n)                     - Copy data from one channel to another.
gl_copybox (3)                - copy a rectangular screen area
gl_copyboxfromcontext (3)     - copy rectangular area from another context
gl_copyboxtocontext (3)       - copy a rectangular area to another context
gl_copyscreen (3)             - copy the screen contents of contexts
```

Command Syntax

Because each command is actually a separate program, syntax may differ from command to command. In general, though, the syntax of a shell command is this:

```
<command> <flags> <source> <destination>
```

How does this work in a real command situation? We'll use the cp command as an example. Here is a common use of cp:

```
cp -v /home/ellen/program1 /tmp/program1
```

This command breaks down nicely:

■ **cp** The *<command>* is cp, which copies a file to a new location.

■ **-v** The expression -v is a *flag*, also called an *option*. In this case, the flag tells the command that it should be *verbose*, reporting everything that it does.

TIP	*Flags are indicators to the operating system; they indicate that an optional part of the program should be run. Some flags are used routinely, such as the -e flag with the* grep *command:* -e *tells the operating system what expression to search for. Other flags are rarely used but exist just in case someone wants to use the command for an unusual function.*

- **/home/ellen/program1** The *<source>* is the file program1 in the user Ellen's home directory; this is the original file to be copied.

- **/tmp/program1** The *<destination>* is in the /tmp directory. Ellen has chosen to use the same filename for the copied file; she could also change the name of the copied file at this time.

The total operation of this program consists of making a copy of the program1 file from Ellen's home directory, naming it /tmp/program1, and printing a message to the terminal that it has done so. Had Ellen left the -v flag out of the command, cp would have operated in the default manner; it would have done its job silently and simply returned another command prompt when it was finished.

If you want to find out the exact syntax for any given command, you can use the man program to help. This program displays the UNIX *manual page*, or *man page*, for the particular command requested. For example, the manual page for cp looks like this:

```
$man cp
CP(1)                    FSF                    CP(1)
NAME
      cp - copy files and directories
SYNOPSIS
      cp [OPTION] ... SOURCE DEST
      cp [OPTION] ... SOURCE... DIRECTORY
DESCRIPTION
      Copy SOURCE to DEST, or multiple SOURCE(s) to DIRECTORY.
      -a, --archive
           same as -dpR
      -b, --backup
           make backup before removal
      -d, --no-deference
           preserve links
```

In the remainder of the cp man page, the rest of the flag options are listed, and some description of each command's behavior is given. Manual pages range from

16

incredibly helpful to absurdly cryptic, but the Synopsis section will always give the exact syntax for the command.

Input and Output Redirection

The individual command is only one part of the shell's story. Shell commands can be modified to behave in certain ways, including one of the most useful ways— input and output redirection. Normally, when you issue a command to the shell, the command handles input and output in a standard way: in most cases, the input is taken from the keyboard and the output is printed to the terminal window. For example, consider the following command:

```
ls /etc
```

This command will print the contents of the /etc directory. The command is `ls`, and `/etc` is the input, which was typed on the keyboard. The output is the directory listing and will appear on the computer's screen; see the output for an `ls` run on a random directory on our system in Figure 16-1. The input device—the keyboard— is called the command's *standard input*. Likewise, the computer screen—the output device—is called the command's *standard output*.

```
bash-2.01$ ls /etc
X11                    gateways           mtools.conf
a2ps.cfg               gnuplot.conf       netscape4
adduser.conf           group              networks
adjtime                group-             news
ae                     gs.Fontmap         nsswitch.conf
ae.rc                  harddrive.inf      pam.conf
aliases                host.conf          pam.d
alternatives           hostname           papersize
apache                 hosts              passwd
apm                    hosts.allow        passwd-
apt                    hosts.deny         pcimap.inf
auto.amnt.cdl          hosts.equiv        pcmcia
auto.cdrom             im                 porttime
auto.floppy            inetd.conf         ppp
auto.master            init.d             printcap
auto.master.dpkg-dist  inittab            profile
auto.misc              inputrc            proftpd.conf
bootparams             ioctl.save         protocols
bootptab               isapnp.gone        psdevtab
build.conf.inf         issue              pwdb.conf
chatscripts            issue.net          rc.boot
checksecurity.conf     joe                rc0.d
conf.modules           kbd                rc1.d
conf.modules.old       ld.so.cache        rc2.d
conf.modules.org       ld.so.conf         rc3.d
conf.modules.vm        ld.so.conf.old     rc4.d
cron.d                 lilo.conf          rc5.d
cron.daily             lilop.conf         rc6.d
cron.monthly           limits             rcS.d
cron.weekly            locale.alias       resolv.conf
crontab                localtime          rmt
csh.cshrc              login.access       rpc
```

| FIGURE 16-1 | After you issue the `ls` command, you'll get a listing of all files in the specified directory |

However, just because an output or an input device is the standard device doesn't mean that you have to use it. Suppose you wanted to issue the `ls` command and capture the output into a file so you could edit or print it. This is quite simple; just alter the command to look like this:

```
ls /etc > etc-list.txt
```

This compound command creates a file called etc-list.txt and directs the output of the `ls` command into the new file. If you view the contents of that file, you'll see the directory listing that would have otherwise been printed in the terminal window.

In addition, you can use the double redirection operator (`>>`):

```
ls /etc >> etc-list.txt
```

Because of the double redirection operator, the output of this `ls` command is appended to the end of the etc-list.txt file, instead of replacing the existing contents of the file. This is especially useful if you're executing a series of commands and want the output contained in one file for later use.

Although we've given you examples of ways to handle the output of a given command, you can also redirect the input. Consider the shell command `sort`, which takes a list of items and sorts them into numerical or alphabetical order. Here's an example of `sort` at work:

```
sort
tom
dick
harry
```

Press CTRL-D when you have finished entering the items to sort. Typing CTRL-D tells the shell that you have completed the list of items to be sorted and produces the output

```
dick
harry
tom
```

Now assume that you have a file called input.txt, which contains the entries

```
tom
dick
harry
```

16

If you were to issue the command

```
sort < input.txt
```

you would see the following output on the screen:

```
dick
harry
tom
```

You can also combine input and output redirection. Thus, issuing

```
sort < input.txt > output.txt
```

sorts the content of the file input.txt and places the output of the sort into the file output.txt (and creates the file output.txt if one did not already exist).

Pipes

Pipes can be considered another form of input and output redirection. A *pipe* takes the output of one command and feeds it to the input of another command. Pipes in action usually look like this:

```
command1 | command2
```

 The term pipe *refers to the upright bar character, or |. The pipe character is usually found as a SHIFT character on your keyboard. Try looking near the BACKSPACE key or the right SHIFT key; these are common locations for |.*

Say you wanted to see whether a particular program was running on your Corel Linux machine. At the prompt, enter this command: **ps aux**.

TIP *The* aux *portion is a trio of command flags that direct the* ps *command to show all processes running, owned by all users, even those running in the background. It's the most complete listing of processes that you can get from* ps.

However, running ps aux can produce quite a barrage of output. On our (moderately small) system, it routinely generates two or three screenfuls of text; one of those screens is shown in Figure 16-2. In many cases, it's impossible to scroll back far enough to find the exact process you're looking for.

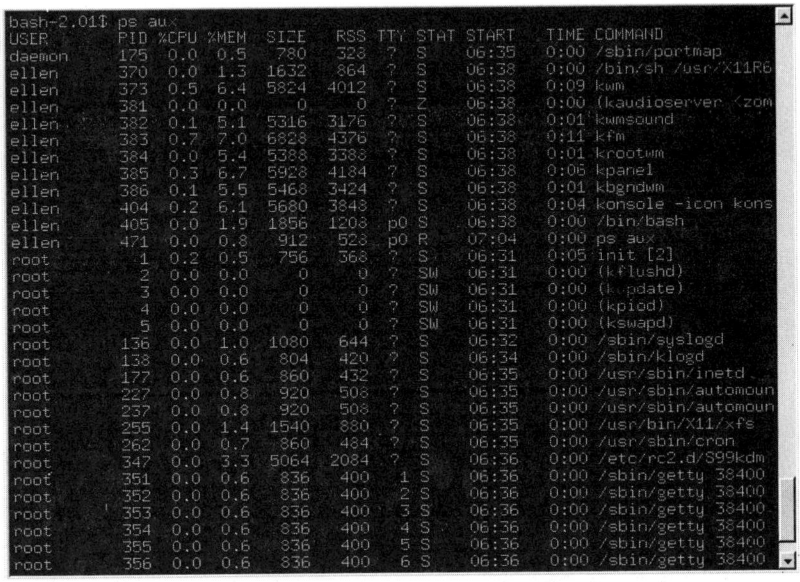

```
bash-2.01$ ps aux
USER        PID %CPU %MEM   SIZE   RSS TTY STAT START   TIME COMMAND
daemon      175  0.0  0.5    780   328  ?  S    06:35   0:00 /sbin/portmap
ellen       370  0.0  1.3   1632   864  ?  S    06:38   0:00 /bin/sh /usr/X11R6
ellen       373  0.5  6.4   5824  4012  ?  S    06:38   0:09 kwm
ellen       381  0.0  0.0      0     0  ?  Z    06:38   0:00 (kaudioserver <zom
ellen       382  0.1  5.1   5316  3176  ?  S    06:38   0:01 kwmsound
ellen       383  0.7  7.0   6828  4376  ?  S    06:38   0:11 kfm
ellen       384  0.0  5.4   5388  3388  ?  S    06:38   0:01 krootwm
ellen       385  0.3  6.7   5928  4184  ?  S    06:38   0:06 kpanel
ellen       386  0.1  5.5   5468  3424  ?  S    06:38   0:01 kbgndwm
ellen       404  0.2  6.1   5680  3848  ?  S    06:38   0:04 konsole -icon kons
ellen       405  0.0  1.9   1856  1208 p0  S    06:38   0:00 /bin/bash
ellen       471  0.0  0.8    912   523 p0  R    07:04   0:00 ps aux
root          1  0.2  0.5    756   368  ?  S    06:31   0:05 init [2]
root          2  0.0  0.0      0     0  ?  SW   06:31   0:00 (kflushd)
root          3  0.0  0.0      0     0  ?  SW   06:31   0:00 (kupdate)
root          4  0.0  0.0      0     0  ?  SW   06:31   0:00 (kpiod)
root          5  0.0  0.0      0     0  ?  SW   06:31   0:00 (kswapd)
root        136  0.0  1.0   1080   644  ?  S    06:32   0:00 /sbin/syslogd
root        138  0.0  0.6    804   420  ?  S    06:34   0:00 /sbin/klogd
root        177  0.0  0.6    860   432  ?  S    06:35   0:00 /usr/sbin/inetd
root        227  0.0  0.8    920   508  ?  S    06:35   0:00 /usr/sbin/automoun
root        237  0.0  0.8    920   508  ?  S    06:35   0:00 /usr/sbin/automoun
root        255  0.0  1.4   1540   880  ?  S    06:35   0:00 /usr/bin/X11/xfs
root        262  0.0  0.7    860   484  ?  S    06:35   0:00 /usr/sbin/cron
root        347  0.0  3.3   5064  2084  ?  S    06:36   0:00 /etc/rc2.d/S99kdm
root        351  0.0  0.6    836   400  1  S    06:36   0:00 /sbin/getty 38400
root        352  0.0  0.6    836   400  2  S    06:36   0:00 /sbin/getty 38400
root        353  0.0  0.6    836   400  3  S    06:36   0:00 /sbin/getty 38400
root        354  0.0  0.6    836   400  4  S    06:36   0:00 /sbin/getty 38400
root        355  0.0  0.6    836   400  5  S    06:36   0:00 /sbin/getty 38400
root        356  0.0  0.6    836   400  6  S    06:36   0:00 /sbin/getty 38400
```

FIGURE 16-2   The `ps` command can often generate multiple screenfuls of information

This is where pipes come into play. Using a pipe and the shell command `grep`, which searches for a particular character string, you can identify the specific processes you're looking for with a couple of simple commands.

Perhaps you want to know if your Web server is running, since you're having trouble pulling up pages from your domain. To find out, you want to search the output of a regular `ps` command for the expression `httpd`, which is the name of the Web server process. The command-line entry looks like this:

```
ps aux | grep httpd
```

This makes the output of the `ps` command serve as the input of the `grep` command. On our system, the final output looks like this:

```
root      393  0.0  0.0  2560   52  ?        S    Nov25  1:58 httpd
nobody    397  0.0  0.0  2748    0  ?        SW   Nov25  0:00 [httpd]
nobody    398  0.0  0.0  2748    0  ?        SW   Nov25  0:00 [httpd]
nobody    399  0.0  0.0  2748    0  ?        SW   Nov25  0:00 [httpd]
nobody    400  0.0  0.0  2748    0  ?        SW   Nov25  0:00 [httpd]
nobody    401  0.0  0.0  2748    0  ?        SW   Nov25  0:00 [httpd]
nobody    402  0.0  0.0  2748    0  ?        SW   Nov25  0:00 [httpd]
```

16

```
nobody     403  0.0  0.0  2748    0 ?        SW   Nov25   0:00 [httpd]
nobody     404  0.0  0.0  2748    0 ?        SW   Nov25   0:00 [httpd]
nobody     405  0.0  0.0  2748    0 ?        SW   Nov25   0:00 [httpd]
nobody     406  0.0  0.0  2748    0 ?        SW   Nov25   0:00 [httpd]
joe       3323  0.0  0.4  1244  512 pts/0    S    11:28   0:00 grep httpd
```

This output shows that we have one master `httpd` process and ten subprocesses currently running. (This is standard `httpd` behavior; it means that our system can handle up to ten page requests to `httpd` at one time.) You can also see the `grep` command just issued since it contains the character string `httpd` as part of our request.

Now, consider the following command-line entry:

```
ps aux | grep httpd > output.txt
```

Using a combination of a pipe and output redirection, we have created a complex command that creates a file called output.txt and then fills that file with the output of a `ps` command as filtered through `grep`.

Multiple pipes are also possible:

```
ps aux | grep httpd | mail alex
```

This command sends an e-mail to the user Alex that contains the output of `ps` as filtered through `grep`.

As you can see, the `bash` shell's command syntax offers an enormous degree of power and flexibility. If you want to know the specific command syntax for any given command, we suggest that you first try the man page, by typing **man <command>** at the command prompt.

> | TIP | *It's always a good idea to install the* man *pages, even if you think they'll take up too much space. Without the* man *pages, you'll have to do too much searching to find the quick answer to a syntax or flag question.* man *pages are installed by default with Corel Linux; if you install new software and are prompted to choose whether or not to install* man *pages, install them. You'll be glad you did when you need them later.*

Setting Environment Variables

We've discussed environment variables in earlier chapters. Since they are a shell function, it's important to include a section in this discussion of the shell environment that explains how to set the variables that affect that environment.

Environment variables are *named values*: that is, each value that affects the shell environment is associated with a particular name. These values tell the operating system something about the environment that you've configured. Most environment variables are preset and should not be changed, but you can alter some variables to your taste.

You can generate a full listing of all your environment variables by issuing the `set` command at a text prompt. The output will look something like this:

```
[harry@fugu harry]$ set
BASH=/bin/bash
BASH_ENV=/home/harry/.bashrc
BASH_VERSION=1.14.7(1)
BOOT_IMAGE=linux
COLUMNS=80OSTYPE=Linux
PATH=/usr/bin:/bin:/usr/X11R6/bin:/usr/local/bin:/opt/bin:/usr/X11R
6/bin:/home/joe/bin:/usr/X11R6/bin:/home/joe/bin
PPID=6276
PREVLEVEL=N
PS1=[\u@\h \W]\$
PS2=>
PS4=+
PWD=/home/joe
QTDIR=/usr/lib/qt-2.0.1
RUNLEVEL=5
SESSION_MANAGER=local/fugu:/tmp/.ICE-unix/6197,tcp/fugu:1348
SHELL=/bin/bash
SHLVL=3
TERM=xterm
UID=500
USER=harry
USERNAME=
WINDOWID=20971553
XAUTHORITY=/home/harry/.Xauthority
_=.bashrc
CONSOLE=/dev/console
DISPLAY=:0
EUID=500
HISTFILESIZE=1000
HISTSIZE=1000
HOME=/home/harry
HOSTNAME=fugu
HOSTTYPE=i386
```

All these values have some effect on the shell environment on Harry's computer; if he changes them, the environment will change.

An environment variable, in and of itself, is not particularly special. Any variable can be made an environment variable with the `export` command. A general form of the command is

```
export VARNAME="var-value"
```

where `VARNAME` is the variable name, and `var-value` is the value. Note that all the environment variable names are capitalized. This is not strictly necessary, but it is an established UNIX convention; we recommend it highly as it helps to avoid confusion. You must, however, use the quotation marks around `var-value`.

If you want to see the value of a particular environment variable without searching through the entire output of `set`, use the `echo` command:

```
echo $SHELL
```

Note the `$` in front of the variable name. This tells the `echo` command that you want to see the value of the variable, not the name of the variable. If you omit the `$`, you'll get the name of the variable, which you've already entered (that is, SHELL).

An environment variable, as we stated previously, can be anything. This concept becomes more important when you begin to write your own scripts, as described in Chapter 17, "The Shell Expanded: Basic Scripting." Assume that you want to set an environment variable called, for some reason, CHAMP, and you want to give it the value "Hart". Use `export` to do this:

```
export CHAMP="Hart"
```

If you then issue the `echo` command for the CHAMP variable, Corel Linux will show the value Hart.

If you need to change the value of a given variable later, simply repeat the process with a new value:

```
export CHAMP="Goldberg"
```

This changes the value of the CHAMP variable and will be shown if you issue the `echo` command.

Why would you want to do this? Well, you may be using the value of that variable in a script or program that you write. In this case, we're just pointing out that you can create any kind of environment variable you like and name it anything you want.

Environment variables last only as long as your current bash session, though: that is, they are created when you log in or when you start a new instance of bash. (In KDE, you start a new instance of bash when you open a new terminal window.) The variables are destroyed when you log out or close that session.

If that's the case, then, why do some environment variables exist without your having set them? In fact, most environment variables operate that way. The answer to this lies in bash's startup procedure. When you first start an instance of bash, it runs two scripts. One is called /etc/profile, and the other is called .bash-profile, which should exist in your home directory. export commands can be placed in these files to set various environment variables:

- export commands placed in /etc/profile affect the bash environments of all users on the system.

- export commands placed in your home directory's .bash-profile affect only the environment of your personal account.

Text Editors

If you plan on doing anything more complicated than superficial configuration of your Corel Linux system, you will need to learn to use at least one UNIX text editor. For most purposes, you can use the KDE default text editor, KEdit; we cover KEdit thoroughly in this chapter. However, we strongly recommend that you also learn at least one text-mode editor. The reason for this is simple: Should you have a system failure that affects your ability to run the X Window System, the only way to correct the problem is to boot your machine into text mode (which may involve changing the machine to single-user mode or booting from a rescue disk). You'll have to use a text editor to edit the configuration files and correct the problem.

So, what is a *text editor* anyway? A text editor is sort of a stripped-down version of a word processor; some folks say that a word processor is just a tarted-up version of a text editor. (Count Kate in the former camp and Joe in the latter.) Instead of producing documents intended for printing, a text editor is concerned only with producing text files.

16

TIP   *If you've ever used the Windows Notepad or Macintosh Teachtext programs, you've used a text editor. They're faster and simpler than word processors, but the text doesn't look fancy.*

There are several UNIX character-mode text editors. The dominant ones are vi (pronounced *vee-eye*, not *vye*), GNU emacs, and pico. Others include jed, joe, mutt, elvis, le, and ped. Of all of these, the most important is certainly vi. We consider it to be so important because it's the only one you can be almost 100 percent sure of finding on any given system or rescue disk. Other editors may be more popular or easy to use (pico, for example), or arguably technically superior (emacs), but vi is the only text editor that could be considered standard. It's also the default editor in Corel Linux.

NOTE *Hey, we said* arguably! *The "One True Editor" concept is one of those things that UNIX and Linux people like to argue endlessly about. For the record, we're* pico *people by preference, but we use* vi *for a lot of system maintenance. If you choose to learn a text editor that isn't* vi, *you pretty much have to learn* vi *as well since you can't guarantee that your preferred editor will be available in a crisis or on another machine.*

vi

The name vi is actually an abbreviation of "visual editor." vi was the first UNIX text editor that could deal with more than one line of text at a time. That doesn't seem like a huge achievement in these days of desktop publishing, but when vi was first devised, it was quite a breakthrough. In fact, vi is a *full screen editor*, which means that, if it's used when the computer is in character mode (or in a terminal window), vi uses the entire area of the screen or window for its display.

Unfortunately, vi is a fairly complicated program and could easily fill a book of its own. Our aim in this section is to give you enough information to open the program, do basic file editing, save files, and exit vi; consider this a cheat sheet, not an exhaustive manual, for vi.

Starting vi

Like other UNIX text commands, vi is started from the command line. There are two ways to start it; simply typing **vi** at a shell prompt starts vi with an empty file, as shown in Figure 16-3. When you save the file, you can give it a filename, and then you'll have a new file with the new filename.

If you want to start vi in order to work on an existing file, just type **vi** **<filename>** at a command prompt, and vi will open with the named file on the screen.

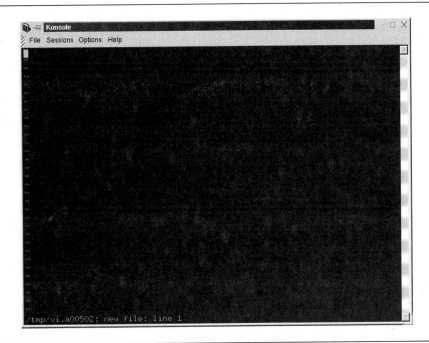

FIGURE 16-3   When you start vi, it opens with an empty file

  TIP   *If you type* **vi <filename>** *but use the name of a nonexistent file to replace <filename>, you will open an empty file. When you save the file, it will already have the filename you used to open it. So, if you type* **vi schmozz.txt** *but no schmozz.txt file already exists, vi will save it as schmozz.txt when you execute the* save *command or exit* vi.

vi's Modes

When you work with vi, it is important to remember that it has two modes of operation: *command mode* and *insert mode*. When you first start vi, you'll be in command mode. In command mode, everything you type is interpreted by vi as a command. This often confuses people new to vi because they expect to be able to just start typing (as in a word processor or some text editors). If you do just start typing, vi will give you a string of error commands because it sees no text upon which to execute the "commands" you have just entered.

When you open vi, then, you need to change to insert mode before you can start entering your text. You do this by typing **i** as soon as you enter the editor.

Once you've typed i, vi places a cursor at the beginning of the screen's first line. At this point, you can begin typing. Type anything you want; for test purposes, you could type this paragraph.

Notice that the cursor doesn't wrap to the next line when you hit the end of the first line. If you want the line to break, you'll have to press the ENTER key. In a narrative text file (blocks of text broken into paragraphs), it doesn't matter whether or not you do this; it makes a difference, though, if you're writing shell scripts or programs where each line must end with a carriage return.

To use the command mode of vi, you'll need to exit from text mode and get back into command mode. Do this by pressing the ESC key. You can alternate between modes by pressing ESC when in the text mode, and i when in the command mode.

Pattern Matching and Replacing

Once you've entered some text into your file, you may want to move around the text to edit it. You can always move around the screen using the arrow keys on your keyboard.

NOTE   *You can't use the mouse in most text-based programs, including text editors, because the mouse drivers do not load in text-only mode. Replace mouse clicks with command-key sequences and the arrow keys—as it was done before the mouse became so popular.*

You can also use pattern matching to move around the document. This is especially helpful when you're searching a large document for a single phrase.

Suppose you've been typing about your new Corel Linux machine, and you want to advance the cursor to the next occurrence of the word "Corel." To do this, just type **/Corel**. If you want to search backward to an occurrence before the current cursor position, type **?Corel** instead. vi searches the document and places the cursor at the next (or previous) occurrence of "Corel" in the document.

Now, assume that you've searched for the word "Corel" and you realize that you've forgotten to capitalize it. You can correct that mistake by entering the command

```
:s/corel/Corel
```

Note the leading colon. vi searches the document for the character string "corel" and replaces it with "Corel".

What if you've been happily typing along and you forgot to capitalize "Corel" in several places? You could perform the previous commands repeatedly until you got all the mistakes, or you could use a global search and replace command to take care of the problem all at once. To do a global replace, enter the command

`:s/corel/Corel/g`

The trailing g indicates that the change needs to be made globally.

Table 16-1 shows the various search and replace patterns that you'll use frequently when you're editing files in vi.

Deleting Characters and Strings

Unless you are a prodigy both in typing and in composition, sometimes you will have to delete characters or portions of text. vi has a number of commands that provide various deletion options. Table 16-2 provides a brief summary of these commands; note that they are all case sensitive.

> **TIP** *Don't forget that you can always position the cursor with the arrow keys and use the BACKSPACE key as well.*

Moving the Cursor Around the Screen

As mentioned previously, the easiest way to move the cursor around the screen is to use the arrow keys on your keyboard. However, there are other ways to move the cursor around, including ways to traverse large blocks of text quickly. When vi was developed in the 1970s, arrow keys were not a standard feature on most keyboards, so substitute key commands had to be invented. Even today, many vi users prefer to use these alternative movement key combinations because they

Command	Action
/<pattern>	Searches forward for the character string *<pattern>*
?<pattern>	Searches backward for the character string *<pattern>*
:s/<pattern1>/<pattern2>	Replaces the first instance (after the current cursor position) of the character string *<pattern1>* with the character string *<pattern2>*
:s/<pattern1>/<pattern2>/g	Replaces all instances of the character string *<pattern1>* with the character string *<pattern2>*

TABLE 16-1   vi Search and Replace Commands

16

Command	Action
x	Deletes the character under the cursor.
dd	Deletes the current line (in which the cursor is positioned).
D	Deletes everything from the cursor to the end of that line.
:D	Deletes the current line (same as dd).
:D$	Deletes to the end of the current line (same as D).
:U	Undoes the last deletion.

TABLE 16-2   vi Deletion Commands

don't have to move their hands off the main keys of the keyboard; this allows them to write and edit more quickly with less wasted motion. Table 16-3 shows the various keystroke combinations that you can use to move around your document when using vi.

Saving and Exiting

In many ways, the ability to exit vi is the most important piece of information you can have about the program! Without knowing this, you can find yourself trapped in vi, not knowing what to do. (Don't laugh—it happens to the best of us, especially if you use another text editor as your regular editor and use vi only in emergencies.)

Command	Action
0	Moves the cursor to the beginning of the current line in which the cursor is located
$	Moves the cursor to the end of the current line in which the cursor is located
w	Moves the cursor to the beginning character of the next word
nG	Moves the cursor to the beginning of line *n*, where *n* equals a number
n|	Moves the cursor to the beginning of column *n*, where *n* equals a number
G	Moves the cursor to the last line of the file
^D (CTRL-D)	Scrolls the document forward one half page
^F (CTRL-F)	Scrolls the document forward one full page
^U (CTRL-U)	Scrolls the document back one half page
^B (CTRL-B)	Scrolls the document back one full page

TABLE 16-3   vi Cursor Movement Commands

The simplest way to exit `vi` is to type `:q` in command mode. (Note the leading colon.) There is some danger in doing this because you haven't saved the file yet; however, `vi` generally refuses to quit if you haven't saved the file. To be safe, though, establish the habit of saving first and then issuing the `quit` command.

To save your file, whether you're quitting or just saving changes while you work—always a good idea—simply issue the `:w` command. Again, note the leading colon.

You can also save a few strokes and issue these commands together using the `:wq` command. An easy way to remember this command is to think "*w* for write, and *q* for quit." Other options for saving a file and quitting `vi` are shown in Table 16-4.

More About vi

As promised, the preceding sections provided only the most basic features of the `vi` text editor. If you are interested in learning about its more advanced features, we suggest that you investigate the many `vi` resources on the Web, especially the very comprehensive "vi Lover's Home Page" at `http://www.cs.vu.nl/~tmgil/vi.html`.

> **NOTE** *You may prefer books to Web pages. In that case, we recommend the only book in print that is completely about* `vi`*:* Learning the vi Editor *by Linda Lamb and Arnold Robins (6th edition, O'Reilly & Associates, 1998). This book is exhaustive; there is nothing about* `vi` *you won't know after working through it.*

We strongly recommend that you spend some time practicing using `vi` before you need to rely on it in a critical situation. Some people find certain aspects of its behavior idiosyncratic (to put it kindly), especially if they are accustomed to using

Command	Action
`:w`	Saves (writes) the file to the specified filename.
`:q`	Quits `vi`.
`:wq`	Saves the file and then quits `vi`.
`:q!`	Forces `vi` to quit. This option allows you to quit an unsaved file, so don't use it if you want to save changes to the file.
`ZZ`	Saves the file and then quits `vi` (same as `:wq`).

TABLE 16-4   `vi` Save and Quit Commands

16

word processors or text editors, such as `pico`, that behave somewhat like word processors. There are many good reasons why `vi` behaves the way it does, but they're not always obvious to the beginner.

KEdit: The KDE Text Editor

If there's no particular reason that you need to be in character-only text mode to perform a task, a nice alternative to the somewhat inscrutable `vi` is KDE's text editor KEdit. KEdit is designed to run within the KDE interface and has the usual graphical features that make editing text files a bit more intuitive. In addition, since you can choose the colors and fonts you want KEdit to use, it's also a bit easier on the eyes than the average white-on-black text-mode editor.

Start KEdit by clicking the Applications Manager icon in the KDE Panel and selecting Applications | Utilities | Text Editor from the Start menu. You can also access it by clicking the text editor icon in the KDE Panel.

The KEdit screen, as shown in Figure 16-4, contains a menu bar, a tool bar, and a text area. To get started, simply click in the text area and start typing. Most of the familiar word processing features should apply here; try out your favorite keyboard shortcuts or mouse clicks and drags.

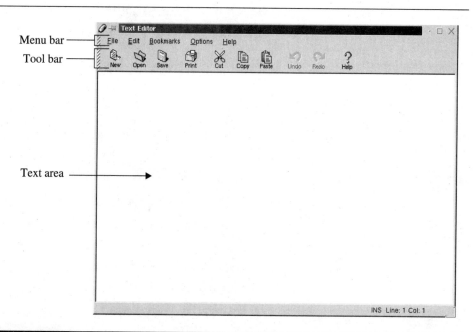

FIGURE 16-4   KEdit is an excellent and full-featured graphical text editor

You can move the cursor within the document by using the arrow keys on the keyboard or by positioning the mouse pointer and clicking to set the cursor in a new location. In addition, you can press the HOME key to move the cursor to the beginning of the current line or the END key to move the cursor to the end of the current line. The PAGE UP and PAGE DOWN keys also function in KEdit.

KEdit File Operations

KEdit works like many other word processors you may have used. Some of the more advanced features are not available since KEdit is intended to be a stripped-down version of a robust word processor like WordPerfect, but the standard features are available. You can initiate file operations from either the tool bar or the drop-down menus.

FILE OPERATIONS FROM THE KEdit TOOL BAR   Use the icons in the tool bar to perform the three most common file operations:

- **New**   Click the New icon to open a new unnamed file.

- **Open**   Click the Open icon to open a File Manager window, from which you can select an existing file to edit within KEdit.

- **Save**   Click the Save icon to save the current file. If the file does not yet have a name, KEdit prompts you for a filename and location.

16

FILE OPERATIONS FROM THE DROP-DOWN MENUS   As with other KDE programs, you can use the drop-down menus to perform various operations on your files. Table 16-5 shows the various operations available in the File drop-down menu of KEdit.

File Menu Selection	Action
Insert	Inserts the contents of another file into the current file
Open Recent	Provides links to the most recently edited files
Save As	Saves the current file with a different filename or location
Close	Closes current file without exiting KEdit
Print	Sends current file to print spool (only if you have a printer attached and configured properly)
New Window	Opens a new KEdit window containing an empty file
New View	Opens a new KEdit window containing a second copy of the current file

TABLE 16-5   File Menu Options in KEdit

Editing Functions in KEdit

KEdit provides most of the standard editing functions found in other text editors and word processors. As with word processors, many of KEdit's editing functions (available from the Edit drop-down menu and described in Table 16-6) operate on selected text, which is highlighted by positioning the cursor at the beginning of the desired text, clicking, and dragging to the end of the desired text. Once the text is selected, editing functions may be selected and will execute on the highlighted text.

 Many of the descriptions in Table 16-6 refer to the paste buffer. Think of the paste buffer as a temporary storage area for text, like the Clipboard in Windows. Anything in the paste buffer disappears when you exit KEdit.

All of these functions are quite intuitive, especially if you've used a standard word processor like WordPerfect or Word. With a little practice, you should be able to edit files efficiently and quickly in KEdit.

Other Text Editors

Besides vi and KEdit, there are a number of other character-mode and graphical text editors in the UNIX/Linux world. In this section, we introduce you to two other popular character-mode text editors: GNU emacs and pico. We do not go into detail about using them (partially because they are not provided as part of the default Corel Linux installation), but they are in sufficiently wide use that you ought to at least know about them.

Edit Menu Selection	Action
Cut	Copies selected text into the paste buffer and deletes it from the text area
Copy	Copies selected text into the paste buffer and leaves it in the text area
Paste	Copies the text in the paste buffer to the text area at the cursor location
Find	Finds a particular character string in the text
Replace	Finds a particular character string in the text and replaces it with a second character string
Find Again	Repeats the previous Find operation
Go to Line	Moves cursor to the beginning of the specified line
Undo	Undoes the last edit
Redo	Redoes the last edit
Indent	Indents the selected text
Unindent	Removes the indentation of selected text
Select All	Marks all document text as selected
Deselect all	Removes all selected text
Invert Selection	Marks all selected text as unselected and all unselected text as selected

TABLE 16-6   Edit Menu Options in KEdit

 Should you wish to install either emacs *or* pico *on your Corel Linux system, refer to Chapter 21, "Adding and Removing Software," for more information on installing software packages.*

GNU emacs

If you find vi proponents to be vocal about their happiness with their text editors, you should meet the emacs crowd. GNU emacs was one of the first programs created by Richard Stallman when he conceived the GNU Project, and it is almost as popular as vi—more so in some circles. (See Chapter 1 for some background on the GNU Project and Richard Stallman.)

Like vi, emacs is a full-screen text-mode editor with multiple modes; unlike vi, it has an enormous number of other functions. See Figure 16-5 for a glimpse of emacs in operation. emacs has a built-in mail reader and a built-in news reader, and it also has the abilities to edit multiple files simultaneously and to interact with the shell, an extensive suite of keyboard macros, and a built-in scripting language based on the LISP programming language. In fact, GNU

16

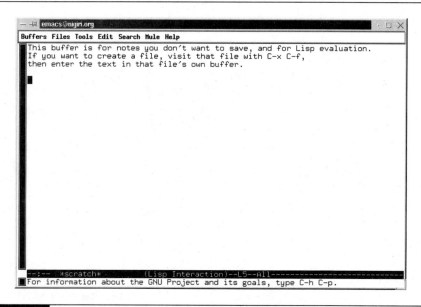

FIGURE 16-5   GNU `emacs` is a powerful and popular text editor

`emacs` has so much built-in functionality that some UNIX users use it as their entire operating environment!

All this functionality comes with a significant downside, though. GNU `emacs` is a very large program. It can take up a good chunk of disk space, and when in operation, it uses a significant portion of system memory. Thus, it might not be the best choice on systems with tight resources. Also, like `vi`, `emacs` is not a very intuitive environment. (We suspect that part of the reason for such devoted feelings about `emacs` is due to the amount of time spent on learning the program.) If you're looking for a simple single-use program, `emacs` is not for you; if, however, you thrive in complicated environments that let you do far more than a regular editor would, give GNU `emacs` a try.

GNU `emacs` is not distributed with Corel Linux, but packages in the Debian `.deb` format are available from the Debian FTP site, at `http://www.debian.org/distrib/ftplist`.

pico

Our personal favorite text editor is `pico`, shown in Figure 16-6. This dooms us to eternal weeniehood in some people's eyes. We don't care—it's simple and intuitive, and we suggest you give `pico` a try. It's a lightweight and straightforward

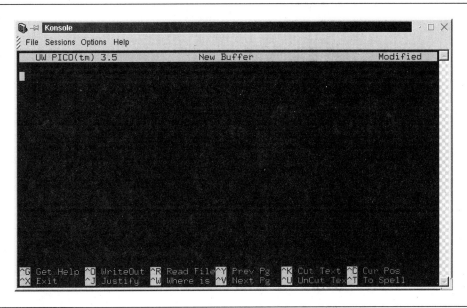

FIGURE 16-6   Use pico if you want an intuitive and simple character-mode text editor

character-mode text editor that uses CTRL-key sequences for editing commands and cursor movement. Unlike `vi` and `emacs`, it has only one mode; you can enter text and edit it without changing modes. In addition, we find the `pico` interface to be extremely intuitive. Kate has taught `pico` to people who've never used Linux or UNIX before, and she finds that they pick it up in less than 15 minutes. (Try that with `vi` or `emacs`—it's simply not possible.)

`pico` was developed at the University of Washington as part of the `pine` e-mail program; in good UNIX fashion, `pine` stands for Pine Is Not Elm, a joke at the expense of the `elm` mail reader. Unfortunately, because of licensing restrictions, the `pine` (and therefore `pico`) packages cannot be distributed with either the Debian or Corel distributions of Linux.

You can, however, obtain packages that will enable you to build a "Debianized" version of `pine` that will work on your Corel Linux machine. These packages are available at the Debian FTP site.

16

Read the accompanying documentation carefully before you attempt to install the `pine` packages. Because of the changes to make `pine` acceptable as a entirely Open Source program, the installation is tricky and can cause some problems with your system if it goes wrong.

CHAPTER 17

The Shell Expanded: Basic Scripting

 One of the advantages of running Linux on your computer is that you can use some of the tricks and methods developed over the years for use on UNIX-derived operating systems. Perhaps the most powerful tool available to you is the *shell script. Scripts* are small programs that you can run either manually or automatically and that you can use to handle frequently repeated operations, build custom commands, or perform any tasks that keep your system running to your liking.

In this chapter, we delve into the heart of the scripting process and provide some methods with which you can begin to build your own scripts. It is far beyond the scope of this book to go deeply into programming itself; if you find yourself enamored of scripting, and you don't already know much about programming in the shell environment, we suggest that you look at more narrowly focused books or take an introductory course. You can write decent scripts with a smattering of programming experience, but if you want to get really complicated, it might be helpful to understand how programming languages work.

If you'd like to read a complete book on scripting for bash, *we suggest* Learning the BASH Shell *by Cameron Newham and Bill Rosenblatt (O'Reilly, 1998), or* UNIX Shells by Example *by Ellie Quigley (Prentice Hall, 1999).*

What Is a Shell Script?

At its most basic, a shell script is nothing more than a set of shell commands intended to be run as a unit. Any command that you can use at a shell environment text prompt, as described in Chapter 16, "The Administrator's Tools: Shells and Text Editors," can be used in a script. However, the shell environment itself also provides certain advanced features that can turn a simple list of commands into a full-fledged computer program.

A shell environment functions as an interpreter between your commands and the operating system. Although several popular shell environments are available, in this chapter (and throughout this book) we focus on the bash *shell, which is the default shell in the Corel Linux distribution.*

Scripts Versus Programs

If a script is a program, why is it called a script and not a program? Some people like to draw distinctions between small programs like shell scripts, and large, complicated programs like Netscape or WordPerfect. The criteria for the distinction vary depending on who you ask.

Some people make the distinction based on the language used to write the programs: Some programming languages, including that used in the bash shell, are *interpreted languages*. An interpreted language runs directly from text files with a command interpreter (that is, the shell environment) translating the commands into machine language. Interpreted languages include bash, TCL/Tk, and JavaScript. Other programming languages are *compiled languages*, meaning that, before they can be used, programs written in these languages must be processed through a *compiler* that converts the written instructions, or *source code*, into machine-readable binary files. Compiled languages include C/C++ and Java.

Others distinguish between programs and scripts using the size and function of the program, rather than the language in which it is written. Scripts tend to be short single-function items and are usually used for system administration tasks, while programs are large multipurpose applications that embody a huge array of individual operations.

In any case, the distinction is largely semantic. Scripts can have the features of programs, and vice versa. *Shell script* is the common way to refer to the kinds of programs we offer in this chapter, but most people will know what you mean if you choose to use the term *shell program* instead. We tend to use *script* more than *program*, but we do use both.

Shell Scripting

This chapter is accumulative; that is, we start with an extremely basic script and build scripts of increasing complexity as we go along. Shell scripting is extremely flexible, and much of the flexibility is based on various combinations of commands and terms.

17

A Basic Shell Script

Jump in and get started with shell scripting by writing a simple one-line program.
To work through this chapter, you'll need to be working in a shell environment.
Click the KEdit button in the KDE Panel to start KEdit, or click the Terminal
Emulator button (shown in the following illustration) to open a terminal window
and invoke your favorite text editor (see Chapter 16 for some help on selecting
an editor if you don't already have a preference).

Type the following line into your text editor:

```
echo "Hello world!"
```

Save the file, using the filename hello. Now, type the following at the shell prompt:

```
chmod u+x hello
```

This command gives you *execute permission* on the hello file, meaning that you
have permission to run this file as a program, as well as look at it as a text file.
(File permissions are covered in Chapter 12, "User Space and User Accounts.")

 *You will need to set execute permissions for yourself on every script you
write, or you won't be able to use the scripts for their intended purpose.*

Still at the shell prompt, type the following:

```
./hello
```

The ./ element tells the shell that you're executing a script in the current directory.
You should see the words "Hello world!" appear on your monitor.

Congratulations! You've written your first shell script. This particular script
is one that is used as the first programming assignment in many, if not most,
programming classes; tell a fellow programmer that you've written a "hello world"
script, and you'll probably get a knowing smile.

A Multiline Example

Now that you have had a successful scripting experience, you can add some complexity to the script. Open the hello file in your text editor and change it like this:

```
echo "Hello world!"
echo "It's good to see you."
```

Save the file and exit the text editor. At the shell prompt, run the script by typing

```
./hello
```

On your monitor, you'll see the following output:

```
Hello world!
It's good to see you.
```

This script, admittedly basic, illustrates a major feature of shell scripting in bash. You can combine multiple commands into a single script that is executed by a single command. This becomes increasingly useful as you add commands to a script.

Variables

In Chapter 16, we discussed *environment variables* in some depth. Variables in a script behave in much the same way. However, script variables are not exported like environment variables, so script variables are always specific to the script in which they're created. To use the same script variables in multiple scripts, you have to define those variables in each script.

> **TIP** *You can create environment variables in the shell environment and then use those variables in scripts. This is a useful way to get your scripts to interact more closely with the operating environment. However, if you want to use those environment variables in more than one script, you'll have to set them in your .bash-profile configuration file. Just exporting the variable isn't enough to make it constantly available. Don't go overboard with this, though; every additional variable you define in .bash-profile is an additional system memory load. Just include the variables you know you will use frequently.*

17

As with environment variables, script variables—also called *regular variables* or *local variables*—are *named values:* that is, a value is assigned to a name, as with

```
CAR="toyota"
```

In this example, the value toyota has been assigned to the variable named CAR. It is customary, as we mentioned in Chapter 16, to make variable names uppercase, so that they're easy to spot in a script.

If you want to change the value of a given variable, you simply need to re-assign it:

```
CAR="porsche"
```

When this is done, the old value of toyota is destroyed, and the new value of porsche takes its place.

The value of a variable can be determined by typing the $ character in front of the variable name when used with a command such as echo. Thus, if you want to know the value of CAR, you could type the following at a shell prompt:

```
echo $CAR
```

The value of the variable—in this case, porsche—is printed to the screen. You can use this concept to make a slight variation on the reporting of the variable. At a shell prompt, type

```
echo "My car is a $CAR"
```

Corel Linux prints the output "My car is a porsche" on the screen.

This is an important concept because it allows you to use the variable name in any location where you need to include the actual value of the variable. If the value of the variable changes, you won't have to rewrite the script. For an example, open your text editor and enter the following script:

```
CAR="toyota"
echo "My car is a $CAR"
CAR="porsche"
echo "My car is a $CAR"
```

Save the script with the filename **cars** and exit the text editor. Run the script by typing the following at a shell prompt:

```
./cars
```

The output prints to the screen:

```
My car is a toyota
My car is a porsche
```

The two output lines differ, even though the second and fourth lines of the script are the same, because the value of CAR has changed.

The $ character is the key to this flexibility; it lets you substitute the name of the variable for the value of the variable. If you don't include the $ sign, your output will simply repeat the variable name instead of the variable value: that is, you'd get "My car is a CAR". You can use this character to simplify nested variables; if you set a certain value as

```
TRANSPORTATION="$CAR"
```

the current value of CAR, whatever it may be, will be printed to the screen when you issue the command

```
echo $TRANSPORTATION
```

Now, try this in a small script:

```
MYCAR="saturn"
BRO_CAR="dodge"
echo "My car is a $MYCAR but my brother drives a $BRO_CAR."
```

The output will print to your screen:

```
My car is a saturn but my brother drives a dodge.
```

Any time you change the value of either MYCAR or BRO_CAR, those new values will reflect when you issue the echo statement.

Taking Input from the Keyboard

Many times, though, you won't have the information needed to define variable values. If you want to write a script that prompts the user for more information, you can use the read scripting command to get that information. When a script contains the entry read VARIABLE, the script pauses until some input is typed

17

on the keyboard and the ENTER key is pressed. The script then assigns the entered data as the value of VARIABLE and continues its work.

Rewrite the cars script to use this feature:

```
echo "What kind of car do you drive?"
read MYCAR
echo "What kind of car does your brother drive?"
read BRO_CAR
echo "You drive a $MYCAR but your brother drives a $BRO_CAR."
```

Save the script and exit the text editor. Execute the script by typing **./cars** at a shell prompt. The first line will echo the following to the screen:

```
What kind of car do you drive?
```

Type the name of your car (if you don't own a car, make one up) and press ENTER.

Saturn

The next line echoes to the screen:

```
What kind of car does your brother drive?
```

Again, type the name of the car.

Dodge

and press ENTER. The final line of the script echoes to the screen:

```
You drive a Saturn but your brother drives a Dodge.
```

There is no restriction on the type on input that is entered; the computer doesn't know the difference. If you got silly and typed Lobsterfish and Oops, the output would say

```
You drive a Lobsterfish but your brother drives a Oops.
```

Flow Control

The term *flow control* refers to the ability of programs to make decisions about how to execute themselves. More specifically, you can use flow control to create sections of code that execute only if a particular condition is met. You can also create optional sections that are executed only if the condition is not met.

Flow control comes in two flavors: *conditional flow control* executes a section of code if the condition is met and skips the section if it isn't; *iterative flow control* causes a section of code to repeat until (or unless) a condition is met.

Conditional Flow Control

The two major commands for conditional flow control are the *if-then statement* and the *case statement*. The if-then statement marks a section of code so that it is executed only if a certain condition holds true, while the case statement comes into play when the script must select between several alternatives, usually in response to user keyboard input.

THE IF-THEN STATEMENT   The general form of the if-then statement is this:

```
if condition
then
        commands to execute if condition is true
fi
```

If the condition is not true, the code included between `then` and `fi` is simply skipped, and the script resumes execution with the next line of commands after `fi`.

> **NOTE** `fi` *is just* if *spelled backward, and it's used to denote the end of the if clause in the script.*

Try this out by modifying the `cars` script again to include an if-then block:

```
echo "What kind of car do you drive?"
read MYCAR

if test $MYCAR = "Saturn"
then
        echo "The best Saturns are the red ones."
fi

echo "What kind of car does your brother drive?"
read BRO_CAR
echo "You drive a $MYCAR but your brother drives a $BRO_CAR."
```

17

In this example, the sentence "The best Saturns are the red ones." will print to the screen only if the value entered for MYCAR is Saturn. If anything else is entered, the script skips directly to the next line of commands after the entry fi.

Note that we have used the test command to evaluate the expression $MYCAR = "Saturn". The test command returns a value of true (actually a value of 0) if the data entered for MYCAR equals "Saturn", and a value of false (a value of 1) if it does not equal. The return value of test is what triggers the if command.

The if-then construct can be extended using the else statement. else designates a section of code that is executed only if the condition named in the if statement is untrue. Test this by modifying the cars script again:

```
echo "What kind of car do you drive?"
read MYCAR

if test $MYCAR = "Saturn"
then
     echo "The best Saturns are the red ones."
else
     echo "That's a very good car."
fi

echo "What kind of car does your brother drive?"
read BRO_CAR
echo "You drive a $MYCAR but your brother drives a $BRO_CAR."
```

With the addition of the else statement, the message "That's a very good car." will be printed to the screen if the value entered for MYCAR is anything other than Saturn.

You can introduce subsequent conditions using another extension to the if-then construct, the elif statement. For example, modify the cars script again:

```
echo "What kind of car do you drive?"
read MYCAR

if test $MYCAR = "Saturn"
then
     echo "The best Saturns are the red ones."
elif test $MYCAR = "Chevy"
then
     echo "Fords are better."
else
     echo "That's a very good car."
```

```
fi
```

```
echo "What kind of car does your brother drive?"
read BRO_CAR
echo "You drive a $MYCAR but your brother drives a $BRO_CAR."
```

Using the `elif` statement is more or less like adding another `if` statement, except that you can put all the `elif` statements into the same block as the initial `if` statement without having to create new blocks ending with `fi`. You must use a `then` statement after an `elif`, just as you would with an `if` statement; you don't need to enter a `fi` statement until you are finished with all the `elif` statements that associate with the `if` statement.

THE case STATEMENT   Another way of doing conditional flow control is to use the `case` statement. This statement is designed to be used in situations with multiple alternatives; the `case` statement tells the script which data to use and which to ignore. Using the `case` statement is more or less like using multiple `elif` statements, but `case` is both more elegant and easier to keep track of—especially when there are more than two or three alternatives from which the script must select.

To use the `case` statement, modify the `cars` script yet once again:

```
echo "What kind of car do you drive?"
read MYCAR

case $MYCAR
in
     Saturn)
          echo "The best Saturns are the red ones."
     ;;
     Dodge)
          echo "Dodge makes nice trucks."
     ;;
     Chevy)
          echo "Fords are better."
     ;;
     *)
          echo "That's a very nice car."
     ;;
esac

echo "What kind of car does your brother drive?"
read BRO_CAR
echo "You drive a $MYCAR but your brother drives a $BRO_CAR."
```

17

As you can see, the user will get a customized response if she enters Saturn, Dodge, or Chevy when prompted. If she enters any other answer, the script selects the default case, signified by the `*)` entry, and prints the generic response "That's a very nice car." The double semicolon after each entry indicates the end of that particular case; at the end of the full case block, the term `esac` is used to denote the end of the conditional section. (As with `fi`, `esac` is simply case spelled backward.)

> **NOTE**   *You've probably noticed that we indent certain lines of code, while others remain flush to the left margin. This is a traditional element of programming style that we recommend you use when writing your own scripts. Indent a line when it contains elements that are dependent on the line above it; that is, if the line contains information necessary for the previous line to operate, it is indented. Observing the examples in this chapter should give you a good idea of how this works.*

Iterative Flow Control

Iterative flow control, also called *looping*, repeats a given section of code as long as a given condition is true. When the condition is no longer true, the code stops repeating. There are several different ways to implement iterative flow control: the *while loop*, the *until loop*, and the *for loop*.

THE WHILE LOOP   Consider this script:

```
echo "What kind of car do you drive?"
read MYCAR

while test $MYCAR != "Saturn"
do
      echo "Wrong. Try again."
      read MYCAR
done

echo "Saturn is correct."
```

In this script, the correct answer to the initial question, "What kind of car do you drive?" is Saturn. If the user enters anything other than Saturn, she is told to try again. This continues until she types Saturn.

The question will repeat as long as the value of MYCAR is *not* equal to **Saturn**; the != construction means "not equal."

> **TIP** *The ! is a negation operator, which reverses the value of whatever follows it. For example, you could write the expression "Two plus three does not equal four" as 2 + 3 != 4.*

As long as the values are not equal, the code between the do and done lines is repeated. As soon as the condition stops being true—in this case, when MYCAR finally equals Saturn—the script skips to the line immediately following done and continues from that point.

THE UNTIL LOOP   *While loops* can be a bit confusing; the true/untrue definitions may seem backward to you. (They do to us.) You can use another kind of iterative flow control to get the same results; the *until loop* repeats the code block until the condition is false, rather than positive. Here's how the script would look using an *until loop*:

```
echo "What kind of car do you drive?"
read MYCAR

until test $MYCAR = "Saturn"
do
        echo "Wrong. Try again."
        read MYCAR
done

echo "Saturn is correct."
```

As you can see in this example, the syntax is almost identical to the previous script using a while loop. The only difference is that you have replaced the negative condition, !=, with a positive one, =. This makes the script less confusing to many people.

> **CAUTION** *Any time you create a loop, make sure that you also create a condition that will end it. If you don't, you'll end up with an infinite loop that will cycle nonstop until you kill the process manually. Infinite loops are syntactically valid, so they won't cause the command interpreter to complain, but they do cause your program to misbehave. Infinite loops are a common programming error and are something you should always be aware of.*

THE FOR LOOP   The *for loop* is a slightly different way of handling iterative flow control. The *for loop* takes a range of values as a single argument and does an iteration of the loop for each value. Here's a sample script using a *for loop*:

17

```
for CAR in "Saturn" "Dodge" "Plymouth" "Ford" "Chevy"
do
        echo $CAR
done
```

The output for this script will look like this:

```
Saturn
Dodge
Plymouth
Ford
Chevy
```

As you can see, the code between the do and done lines is executed for each value of CAR that is listed in the for line.

Tying It Together

Using these various control structures, it is possible to write programs of nearly unlimited complexity. Control structures can appear anywhere in the program—even inside other control structures—and create the possibility for very complicated behavior. Take a look at this slightly more complex version of the cars script:

```
echo "What kind of car do you drive?"
read CAR

while test $CAR != "Saturn"
do

        echo "What color is your $CAR ?"
        read COLOR

            case $COLOR
            in

            blue)
                echo "Blue is a good color for a $CAR"
            ;;
            yellow)
                if test $CAR = "Dodge"
                then
                        echo "Yellow Dodges are ugly."
                else
                        echo "I've never liked yellow cars."
```

```
            fi
        ;;
        green)
            echo "Green looks good on a truck, but not on a $CAR"

        ;;
        *)
            echo "$COLOR certainly is a color for a $CAR"

        ;;

        esac

    echo "$CAR is not the car I'm thinking of. Try another one."
    read CAR
done

echo "Saturns look great in any color."
```

This example shows some of the complexity that can be achieved by nesting control structures inside one another. In this script, an `if` block is nested inside a `case` block, which in turn resides in a *while loop*. As a matter of good programming style, try to keep your nesting to as few levels as possible. Programs with five, six, or more levels of nested levels are very difficult to read and, therefore, difficult to debug. This doesn't mean that you should never nest deeply, but you should be sure it's absolutely necessary when you do choose to do so.

> **TIP** *To debug something is to find and fix the errors in a program. Programming errors have been called* bugs *since the dawn of computer time.*

More About the test Command

You've probably noticed that almost every control structure that we have used in these scripts has employed the `test` command to determine whether the controlling condition is true or false. While this is not strictly necessary, as there are other ways to evaluate a controlling condition, use of the `test` command is very common.

You can use a number of operators with the test command to gain greater flexibility; you've already seen two of them, the comparison operator = and the negation operator !. Both = and its negative, !=, are *string tests*; that is, they determine the equality or inequality of *text strings*. A text string is any sequence of characters; = and != only determine if the characters in both strings are exactly the same.

If you're comparing strings of numbers, instead of strings of characters, you can't use = and !=. Rather, you use the numeric equality operator, -eq. This

17

operator determines the mathematical equality of two integer expressions. Doing math in the shell environment is a little tricky, so we've devoted a section of this chapter to basic math operations. See the next section, "Shell Math," for details.

In addition to string tests and integer tests, there are also file tests. The `test` command can check to see if a file exists, what type of file it is, and what permissions it has, as well as some other file characteristics. See the section "System Programming," later in this chapter, for more on file test commands. For future reference, Tables 17-1, 17-2, and 17-3 contain a breakdown of some common test operators.

Shell Math

Doing math in the shell environment is fairly tricky, especially in `bash`. The difficulties stem from the fact that shell variables take only strings as their values, not actual integers. Thus, if you assign a variable value that looks like VAR=1, you have assigned the *string* 1 to $VAR, not the actual integer 1. This is quite inconvenient because, even in a script that doesn't involve math at all, it's often useful to keep a running count of something (files checked, entries made, and so on). For example, a very common programming structure looks like this:

```
i=0
while test $i -ne 9
do
        <some action>
        i=$i+1
done
```

Operator	Format	What It Means
=	$VAR = "string" or $VAR1 = $VAR2	$VAR is the same as "string" or $VAR1 and $VAR2 have the same string value
!=	$VAR != "string" or $VAR1 != $VAR2	$VAR is not the same as "string" or $VAR1 and $VAR2 do not have the same string value

TABLE 17-1 Common String Operators

Operator	Format	What It Means
-eq	$VAR -eq <integer> or $VAR1 -eq $VAR2	$VAR is equal to the quantity <integer> or $VAR1 and $VAR2 represent the same value
-ne	$VAR -ne <integer>	$VAR is not equal to the quantity <integer>
-lt	$VAR -lt <integer>	$VAR is less than <integer>
-le	$VAR -le <integer>	$VAR is less than or equal to <integer>
-gt	$VAR -gt <integer>	$VAR is greater than <integer>
-ge	$VAN -ge <integer>	$VAN is greater than or equal to <integer>

TABLE 17-2   Common Integer Operators

In a programming language with native math functions, this script would be a quick and easy way to get the code block to loop ten times. Unfortunately, `bash` doesn't interpret this script in that way; instead of having the 1 added to the $i each time the block is repeated, the string "+1" is added to the string value of "$i". Thus, the second time through the loop, the value of $i would be "0+1", the third time would result in a value of "0+1+1", and so on. We could edit the condition to look something like this,

```
while $1 != "0+1+1+1+1+1+1+1+1+1"
```

but it would be extremely cumbersome and confusing. It would be a lot easier if we could deal directly with numerical quantities.

Operator	Format	What It Means
-e	-e <filename>	File <filename> exists
-s	-s <filename>	File <filename> contains at least one character
-r	-r <filename>	You have read permission for <filename>
-w	-w <filename>	You have write permission for <filename>
-x	-x <filename>	You have execute permission for <filename>

TABLE 17-3   Common File Operators

17

Luckily, there is a way to do this. The `expr` command forces the shell to evaluate a string for its numerical value. So, to make the preceding code fragment work properly, we could rewrite it like this:

```
i=0
while test $i -ne 9
do
      <some action>
      i= `expr $i + 1`
done
```

Note the backtick (`` ` ``) characters surrounding the `expr` expression. These are necessary to make the entire line work as a unit.

What happens in this script, and with the `expr` statement in general, is that `expr` is passed to a subshell for evaluation, and the value of the expression is returned to the current shell. In addition to addition (+), the `expr` command can also subtract (–), multiply (*), divide (/), and take the modulus (%) of any two integers.

 The `bash` *shell can work only with integers, or positive whole numbers. The command returns an error if you try to use a number that isn't an integer.*

This, obviously, is a limited form of mathematics, but it's sufficient for basic flow control functions. We assume that's all you'll really use `bash`'s mathematical capabilities to do. If you have the burning need to do more advanced math, several command-line based calculator programs are available that you can incorporate into your scripts, using their output as a given variable value for your needs. This is kind of cumbersome; if you want to write mathematically intensive scripts, we suggest that you learn a programming language with strong math support, such as C or C++.

Handling Input Through Arguments

In addition to taking input directly from the command line, you can also pass input in the form of command-line arguments. This is done through a set of special variables, $0 through $9, which represent discrete items on the command line ordered from left to right. $0 always represents the name of the script being executed. Here's an example, using a script called `param`:

```
echo $0
echo $1
echo $2
echo $3
echo $4
```

After you make this script executable (see the beginning of this chapter), if you type the following line at the shell prompt

```
./param this is a test
```

you should see the following on your monitor:

```
./param
this
is
a
test
```

This capability is quite useful, allowing you to write a script that uses command-line arguments and executes differently depending on what those arguments are, such as

```
case $1
in
    option1)
        <action 1>
    ;;
    option2)
        <action 2>
    ;;
    *)
        <action 3>
    ;;
esac
```

You can also use values provided on the command line in the course of executing a script, such as this:

```
echo "You drive a $1."
```

With this script, if you type `./cars Saturn` at the shell prompt, the script outputs the following line:

```
You drive a Saturn.
```

Comments

One important feature of the `bash` language, and of most programming languages, is the ability to insert *comments* into the body of a script. A comment is simply a line that is ignored by the command interpreter but that is readable by anyone who looks at the text file of the script itself. Comments are used to identify sections of code or to explain how they work. They are present solely to make the script more understandable to someone reading it. This may seem superfluous, but we assure you it is not. It is quite easy to write a script, put it aside for a few days, and come back to it only to realize that you have no idea why you wrote what you wrote (or, in fact, what the script is meant to do).

 If you share your scripts with others, good commenting habits will make your code intelligible to them, and vice versa. Establish the habit of including a comment for each function in your script; unless it's glaringly obvious, use your comment to explain how the function does what you intend it to do.

A comment is a line of text that begins with the # character, called the *hashmark* in general programming talk:

```
# This is a comment.
This is not a comment.
```

Comments can also begin in the middle of a line, causing the command interpreter to ignore everything after the hashmark:

```
This is not a comment  # This is a comment.
```

The comment includes everything from the hashmark to the end of the line. If you want your comments to span more than one line in the script, you need to begin each of the comment lines with a hashmark:

```
# This is an example
# of a multi-line
# comment.
```

Here's how our old friend, the `cars` script, might look with appropriate comments:

```
#  CARS - a script that provides a biased assessment of automotive preferences
#
#  Revised Dec 3, 1999

echo "What kind of car do you drive?"
read CAR

# If CAR is not a Saturn, evaluate user's color preference.

while test $CAR != "Saturn"
do

     echo "What color is your $CAR ?"
     read COLOR

          case $COLOR
          in

          blue)

               echo "Blue is a good color for a $CAR"
          ;;
          yellow)

               # We especially dislike yellow Dodges.

               if test $CAR = "Dodge"
               then
                    echo "Yellow Dodges are ugly."
               else
                    echo "I've never liked yellow cars."
               fi

          ;;

          green)
               echo "Green looks good on a truck, but not on a $CAR"
          ;;
```

17

```
        *)
                echo "$COLOR certainly is a color for a $CAR"
        ;;

        esac

    # Keep going until user enters "Saturn".

    echo "$CAR is not the car I'm thinking of. Try another one."
    read CAR
done
# Success!
echo "Saturns look great in any color."
```

The Magic bash Invocation

The scripts that we've developed in this chapter are specific to the bash shell
environment. While they might work in other bash-like shells, there is no guarantee
that they will. Since we've been working in the bash shell by default, the scripts
have worked properly. However, if you want to use a different shell environment,
you probably want a way to make sure that your scripts written for bash will still
work in the new environment, regardless of the current shell environment.

You can make sure that your scripts are executed by the bash shell, no matter
what shell you're using, by including the "magic invocation" at the start of your
scripts:

```
#! /bin/bash
```

This command invokes the bash shell to execute the script. While the leading
hashmark may lead you to believe that this is a comment, the combination of #
with ! is a specific instruction to Linux to use the named shell for this script. Use
this as the first line of any script you write that you intend to be executed in
bash (probably all of your scripts unless you are somewhat advanced in your
scripting skills).

System Programming

So what good is all this scripting, anyway? Is there nothing more useful we can
do with shell scripts besides write stupid Saturn-centric programs about our cars?
Well, think back to the beginning of this chapter. We said there that any command

that can be used at the command line can be used in a script. This includes not only common commands like `ls` or `pwd`, but administrative commands like `ifconfig` (the command that configures network devices) and `insmod` (the command that loads kernel modules).

In fact, all of those initialization scripts that we talked about in Chapter 10, "Start Up and Shut Down," are nothing more than complex shell scripts. For example, the file /etc/init.d/apache is the script that starts the Apache Web server:

```
#! /bin/sh
#
# apache    Start the apache HTTP server.
#

NAME=apache
PATH=/bin:/usr/bin:/sbin:/usr/sbin
DAEMON=/usr/sbin/apache
SUEXEC=/usr/lib/apache/suexec
PIDFILE=/var/run/$NAME.pid
CONF=/etc/apache/httpd.conf
APACHECTL=/usr/sbin/apachectl

trap "" 1
trap "" 15

test -f $DAEMON || exit 0
test -f $APACHECTL || exit 0

if egrep -q -i "^[[:space:]]*ServerType[[:space:]]+inet\>" $CONF
then
      case "$1" in
      start)
            echo -n "Starting web server: $NAME"
                  if $APACHECTL start > /dev/null 2>&1
                  then
                        echo "."
                  else
                        echo "... failed."
      fi
      ;;

      stop)
            echo -n "Stopping web server: $NAME"
            $APACHECTL stop > /dev/null
            echo "."
      ;;
```

17

```
        reload)
                echo -n "Reloading $NAME configuration... "
                if $APACHECTL graceful > /dev/null 2>&1
                then
                        echo " done."
                else
                        echo " failed."
        fi
        ;;

        reload-modules)
                echo -n "Restarting $NAME daemon."
                $APACHECTL stop > /dev/null
                start-stop-daemon --stop --quiet --oknodo --pidfile $PIDFILE >\
/dev/null
                echo -n "."
                sleep 4
                echo -n "."
                test -u $SUEXEC && echo
                if $APACHECTL start > /dev/null 2>&1
                then
                        echo " done."
                else
                        echo " failed."
        fi
        ;;

        force-reload)
                $0 reload-modules
        ;;

        *)
                echo "Usage: /etc/init.d/$NAME {start|stop|reload|reload-\
modules|force-reload|restart}"
                exit 1
        ;;
esac
exit 0
fi
```

Take a minute to look over this script carefully. Based on the information you've learned already, most of the script will be somewhat familiar to you. Once you've read it through, you can begin to break it down section by section:

```
#! /bin/sh
```

This line is that magic invocation that sets the appropriate shell environment in which to execute the script. Notice that it says /bin/sh instead of /bin/bash. On Linux systems, /bin/sh is a symbolic link to /bin/bash, but this construction preserves compatibility with other UNIX systems that may use the sh shell instead of the bash shell.

```
#
# apache       Start the apache HTTP server.
#
```

The preceding is a comment list that identifies and describes the program.

```
NAME=apache
PATH=/bin:/usr/bin:/sbin:/usr/sbin
DAEMON=/usr/sbin/apache
SUEXEC=/usr/lib/apache/suexec
PIDFILE=/var/run/$NAME.pid
CONF=/etc/apache/httpd.conf
APACHECTL=/usr/sbin/apachectl
```

The preceding section defines a few variables. Note that these are all files and path names; this allows for easy modification of the script. Should a particular file need to be moved, you need change only the variable definition, not each mention of it in the body of the script.

```
trap "" 1
trap "" 15
```

The preceding are *signal traps*, which allow for a particular kind of system control. Don't worry about them; it is an advanced topic, and not something you need to change in your initialization scripts.

```
test -f $DAEMON || exit 0
test -f $APACHECTL || exit 0
```

Here, the script tests to make sure that these two files exist. $DAEMON is the Apache program itself, and $APACHECTL is the Apache control file, which is necessary in order for Apache to run. The || operator is a *logical or* operator, which causes the program to exit if the files in question don't exist. So, if either of these files are missing, the script stops and exits.

17

```
if egrep -q -i "^[[:space:]]*ServerType[[:space:]]+inet\>" $CONF
then
```

This if statement searches for a particular expression in the $CONF file (the apache configuration file, which controls how apache runs). If that expression is contained in the $CONF file, the script will proceed.

```
case "$1" in
start)
      echo -n "Starting web server: $NAME"
            if $APACHECTL start > /dev/null 2>&1
            then
                  echo "."
            else
                  echo "... failed."
      fi
      ;;

stop)
      echo -n "Stopping web server: $NAME"
      $APACHECTL stop > /dev/null
      echo "."
      ;;

reload)
      echo -n "Reloading $NAME configuration... "
      if $APACHECTL graceful > /dev/null 2>&1
      then
            echo " done."
      else
            echo " failed."
      fi
      ;;

reload-modules)
      echo -n "Restarting $NAME daemon."
      $APACHECTL stop > /dev/null
      start-stop-daemon --stop --quiet --oknodo --pidfile $PIDFILE >
/dev/null
      echo -n "."
      sleep 4
      echo -n "."
      test -u $SUEXEC && echo
      if $APACHECTL start > /dev/null 2>&1
      then
            echo " done."
      else
            echo " failed."
```

```
    fi
    ;;

force-reload)
    $0 reload-modules
    ;;

*)
    echo "Usage: /etc/init.d/$NAME {start|stop|reload|reload-
    modules|force-reload|restart}"
    exit 1
    ;;
esac
```

The preceding lengthy code block defines six cases. The variable used is $1, which tells you that these cases are going to be executed depending on the value of the first command-line parameter. The alternatives are start, stop, reload, reload-modules, force-reload, and * (a default case that prints a message explaining the proper usage of the script).

```
exit 0
```

This entry defines the *return value* of the script; if there is another script that depends on the successful execution of this script in order to make a decision, this script returns the value 0, or true.

```
fi
```

This entry, of course, is the end of the earlier if statement.

If you look at any other script contained in the /etc/init.d directory structure, you'll find a similar architecture. Shell scripts are used to control basic system functions, and once you have a handle on how they operate, you can read the various scripts on your system to get a better sense of what your computer is doing when it executes various commands.

17

Automatic Execution with cron

Perhaps you are not satisfied. Sure, you can perform complex operations with a single command if you write a script including various actions, but that's still too much work. You want these actions to happen by themselves without any intervention from you. Maybe you want to run some system diagnostics in the middle of the night when load is low, or you want to execute certain scripts while you're at work. Fortunately, UNIX and Linux cater to the laziness inherent in the sysadmin!

It was for precisely this reason that the `cron` program was born. `cron` is a program that runs other programs, triggered by the system clock's date and time. `cron` starts when you boot up your machine and runs continuously as long as the machine is running. In order to schedule a job to run at a certain time, you need to edit the file `crontab`, which you do by using the following command at a shell prompt:

```
crontab -e
```

When you give the preceding command, a text editor opens. For each program you want to run automatically, enter a line using this syntax:

```
<minute> <hour> <day of the month> <month> <day of the week> <command>
```

Suppose that you want to run a script called `whizbang` every day at 10:30 in the morning. Your `crontab` entry would look like this:

```
30 10 * * * whizbang
```

The * character in the preceding line means "every possible value"; for example, placing * in the *<day of the month>* field means "every day in the month."

Here are some things to keep in mind when you create a `crontab` entry:

■ Days of the week are numbered 0 (Sunday) through 6 (Saturday).

■ Times are specified as a 24-hour value; thus, 1:00 P.M. would be represented as 13 in the hour field.

■ You can place more than one value in a given field. If you want to run `whizbang` every 15 minutes, the *<minute>* field would contain 0,15,30,45.

■ You can also have a range of values. If you want to run `whizbang` every 15 minutes on weekdays only, your entry would look like this:

```
0,15,30,45 * * * 1-5 whizbang
```

Using Scripts

If you enjoy writing scripts, you may soon find yourself adrift in a sea of scripts that have automated almost every part of your administrative tasks. Those who use multiple scripts should be sure to check for conflicts; do you have two scripts that affect the same file in different ways? Will that cause an error? While it can be great fun to write scripts, and while the time saved is useful, the best use of these administrative scripts is not for entertainment, but to handle ongoing and repetitive tasks with `crontab`. Rare things should be done by hand; if you automate too much, you lose the easy familiarity with your system that's part of the fun of Linux (and that will save you if you have a significant system problem).

17

CHAPTER 18

Runlevels and the Boot Process

W hen we discussed the startup process used by Linux in Chapter 10, "Start Up and Shut Down," we introduced the concept of *runlevel*. Linux uses runlevels as a way to designate certain sets of services and activities performed at startup; each runlevel contains a different set of services, and you can configure your runlevels to be used for different purposes. Chapter 10 contains a list of the basic runlevels generally used in Linux. However, every Linux distribution—including Corel Linux—uses a slightly different runlevel configuration. In this chapter, we discuss Corel Linux runlevels and explain how you can configure these runlevels for your own purposes.

Basic Runlevel Concepts

When a Linux machine begins the boot process, the first program that's started is the init program. init is responsible for starting all other processes during boot; in fact, those other processes are called the *child processes* of init since it was init that started them. Using the /etc/inittab file as a guide, init determines the runlevel to enter and starts all processes associated with that runlevel.

Each runlevel is defined by the initialization scripts in a unique directory called /etc/rc*X*.d, where *X* is the number of the runlevel: that is, /etc/rc2.d contains the scripts for runlevel 2. The "scripts" in these directories are actually *symbolic links* to scripts contained in the /etc/init.d directory.

 A symbolic link is simply a file that points to another file. Thus, the file /etc/rc2.d/S20samba is a symbolic link that points to the actual Samba initialization script found in the file /etc/init.d/samba.

These links are used for two reasons: first, they avoid duplication of identical scripts in different directories; and second, they are used to control the order in which processes start and stop during boot. We describe both of these reasons in more detail in the section "The Runlevel Directories," later in this chapter.

The Inner Workings of Runlevels

Because init relies on the contents of the /etc/inittab file to run, it's a good idea to understand how /etc/init.tab is structured and the syntax of its entries. It's also important to understand the way in which each runlevel directory (those named

Corel Linux and Runlevels

Traditionally, the different runlevels are associated with specific functions. For example, the X Window System is traditionally associated with runlevel 5. Corel Linux does not use the standard system by default; Corel Linux uses runlevel 2 as the default runlevel, running everything—including server functions and the X Window System—in that runlevel.

While this differs from runlevel usage in other Linux distributions, Corel designed its Linux distribution with desktop users in mind and configured an all-purpose default desktop runlevel in the /etc/rc2.d directory. This decision doesn't cause problems for you, and Linux will run just fine at runlevel 2. For desktop users, and people who use their computers for one particular set of functions (such as office and Internet applications), the default runlevel need not be changed.

However, if you're planning to use a Corel Linux machine as a workhorse—running many different kinds of applications—or if you plan to use your machine as a single-purpose server for a network, you'll probably want to reconfigure your runlevels so that they're more appropriate to your needs. We encourage you to read through this chapter to determine what path you take with your machine's runlevels.

/etc/rcX.d, where X equals the number of the runlevel) is constructed. Finally, we describe KsysV, a graphical runlevel editor that you can use to make runlevel configurations more easily.

/etc/inittab

/etc/inittab is not tremendously large, but the small file size is not proportional to its importance. Here is the default Corel Linux /etc/init.tab file:

```
# /etc/inittab: init(8) configuration.
# $Id: inittab,v 1.8 1998/05/10 10:37:50 miquels Exp $

# The default runlevel.
id:2:initdefault:
```

18

The `id:2:initdefault:` line was discussed in Chapter 10. This line identifies the default runlevel. To change the default runlevel, you simply need to change the 2 to the number of the runlevel you want to use by default.

```
# Boot-time system configuration/initialization script.
# This is run first except when booting in emergency (-b) mode.
si::sysinit:/etc/init.d/rcS
```

The last line of the preceding code describes the first script to be run upon startup. /etc/init.d/rcS is a file that sets certain basic operating parameters, such as the hostname, some environment variables, directory paths, and so on, without which the rest of the boot process could not continue.

```
# What to do in single-user mode.
~~:S:wait:/sbin/sulogin
```

The second line in the preceding code tells the machine what to do when it is booted into single-user mode. In this case, it invokes the `sulogin` program, which allows only the superuser to log in. This is an effective first-level security precaution.

The next listing shows the heart of the file. These lines instruct the `init` program to run the script /etc/init.d/rc. They then pass the number of the requested runlevel to that script for use as an operating parameter in the script's successful operation. The /etc/init.d/rc script then locates the directory that matches the runlevel (the /etc/rcX.d mentioned previously) and executes every script in that directory.

```
# /etc/init.d executes the S and K scripts upon change
# of runlevel.
#
# Runlevel 0 is halt.
# Runlevel 1 is single-user.
# Runlevels 2-5 are multi-user.
# Runlevel 6 is reboot.
l0:0:wait:/etc/init.d/rc 0
l1:1:wait:/etc/init.d/rc 1
l2:2:wait:/etc/init.d/rc 2
l3:3:wait:/etc/init.d/rc 3
l4:4:wait:/etc/init.d/rc 4
l5:5:wait:/etc/init.d/rc 5
l6:6:wait:/etc/init.d/rc 6
```

```
# Normally not reached, but fallthrough in case of emergency.
z6:6:respawn:/sbin/sulogin
```

And the next bit:

```
# What to do when CTRL-ALT-DEL is pressed.
ca:12345:ctrlaltdel:/sbin/shutdown -t1 -a -r now

# Action on special keypress (ALT-UpArrow).
kb::kbrequest:/bin/echo "Keyboard Request--edit /etc/inittab
    to let this work."
```

The last two lines define special keyboard sequences that affect `init`.

```
# What to do when the power fails/returns.
pf::powerwait:/etc/init.d/powerfail start
pn::powerfailnow:/etc/init.d/powerfail now
po::powerokwait:/etc/init.d/powerfail stop
```

If you have an uninterruptible power supply, or UPS, the preceding lines will trigger a clean shutdown if the power fails. We encourage you to use a UPS for peace of mind and discuss its use in Chapter 10.

The following lines invoke the `getty` program, which is the program that listens for input from terminals. In effect, `getty` is the program that makes it possible for you to log into your computer. The "respawn" attribute ensures that the machine will continue to listen for input after the user has logged out. (This is what makes it possible for you to re-login without completely shutting down the machine.)

```
# /sbin/getty invocations for the runlevels.
#
# The "id" field MUST be the same as the last
# characters of the device (after "tty").
#
# Format:
#   <id>:<runlevels>:<action>:<process>
1:2345:respawn:/sbin/getty 38400 tty1
2:23:respawn:/sbin/getty 38400 tty2
3:23:respawn:/sbin/getty 38400 tty3
4:23:respawn:/sbin/getty 38400 tty4
```

18

```
5:23:respawn:/sbin/getty 38400 tty5
6:23:respawn:/sbin/getty 38400 tty6
```

The following lines are optional `getty` configurations. If you're planning on using a terminal connected via a serial line, or allowing dial-up access to your machine, you would use these. See the `getty` and `mgetty` documentation for details on how to use these configurations; you can find these documents by typing **man getty** or **man mgetty** at a shell prompt.

```
# Example how to put a getty on a serial line (for a terminal)
#
#T0:23:respawn:/sbin/getty -L ttyS0 9600 vt100
#T1:23:respawn:/sbin/getty -L ttyS1 9600 vt100


# Example how to put a getty on a modem line.
#
#T3:23:respawn:/sbin/mgetty -x0 -s 57600 ttyS3
```

As you can see, the /etc/inittab file directs `init` to begin a chain reaction that starts quite a few child processes. In general, you shouldn't mess with this file unless you know exactly what you intend to do, with the sole exception of changing the default runlevel. Configuration is far easier, and less dangerous, when done within the various runlevel directories.

The Runlevel Directories

As we explained at the beginning of this chapter, each runlevel has its own directory, designated as /etc/rcX.d, where X stands for the runlevel's number. Each of the runlevel directories contains a set of symbolic links to scripts actually contained in the /etc/init.d directory, and each script is responsible for starting or stopping a particular service or set of services. We listed all the scripts contained in /etc/init.d in Chapter 10; consult that chapter if you're curious about a particular script or service and how it's controlled by `init`.

| NOTE | *New initialization scripts should always be placed in the /etc/init.d directory. Don't put actual scripts into a numbered runlevel directory; put the script into /etc/init.d and create a symbolic link in the numbered runlevel directory.* |

Why use symbolic links at all? One consideration is that it saves on duplication of effort. If the same service is started by more than one runlevel, you need to place links to the same script in each of the affected runlevel directories only; were you not to use links, you'd have to copy the identical script in each directory. Links are also used to streamline Linux's efforts during startup; if all scripts are kept in a central location, the operating system doesn't have to scramble all over the disk to find each one when needed.

However, the main reason that symbolic links are used in these directories is because they help in the use of a specific naming convention. This convention makes it easier to manipulate the order in which various services are started and stopped during startup. To understand how this convention works, consider the symbolic link that governs the operation of Samba, the Linux/Windows file-sharing program described in Chapter 24, "File and Print Sharing."

The Samba symbolic link is called *S20samba*. Each part of the filename is important.

■ The S tells `init` (or, more accurately, informs the /etc/init.d/rc script) that this is a script to be started during boot-up. Thus, running `init` on this file is the same as issuing the command /etc/init.d/samba start.

> **TIP**
>
> *If this is a service to be stopped, the link uses the capital letter K to replace the S. So, to stop Samba, the link would be named K20Samba. Think "S for start, K for kill."*

■ The number immediately following the *S* dictates the order in which services will be started or stopped during startup, using a range of two-digit numbers from 00 to 99. Samba, with the position of 20, will be started before the process S89cron.

> **TIP**
>
> *If two links have the same priority number (S20samba and S20exim, for example), they will be started in alphabetical order. That is, S20exim would start before S20samba. In addition, K links are always executed before S links, regardless of priority number.*

■ The final component of the link is the service name itself, such as `samba` or `exim`.

This naming convention offers a great deal of flexibility if you want to configure your startup process carefully. You can control startup quite closely if you name the symbolic links in the numbered runlevel directories appropriately.

18

How to Create a Symbolic Link

Create a link with the `ln` command. Symbolic links, a particular kind of link that you'll use often, require the use of the `-s` flag with `ln`. The full syntax of the command is

```
ln -s <name of linked-to file> <name of link>
```

Thus, for the Samba link example, you might issue the command

```
ln -s /etc/init.d/samba /etc/rc2.d/S20samba
```

The next time you look into the /etc/rc2.d directory, you'll see the symbolic link that starts the Samba server at boot-up.

KsysV

If you find the idea of configuring your own runlevels to be a bit intimidating, don't worry. You're right; it can be quite complicated. Luckily, the KDE component of your Corel Linux distribution offers a secret solution! One of the KDE tools included with Corel Linux is KsysV, a graphical tool used to configure runlevels with mouse clicks.

> **TIP** *You won't find KsysV in the Corel Linux menus. Instead, start it by clicking the Application Starter icon in the KDE Panel and selecting the Run option from the Start menu. In the mini-command line window that appears, type* **/usr/X11R6/bin/ksysv** *to start KsysV.*

Configuring KsysV

To use KsysV with Corel Linux, you'll first need to configure KsysV properly. The following procedure shows you how. Different distributions arrange the numbered runlevel directories in slightly different ways, and KsysV's default configuration doesn't quite match the way in which Corel built the runlevel directories.

1. Click the Application Starter icon in the KDE Panel and select Run from the Start menu.

2. In the mini–command-line window that appears, type **/usr/X11R6/ bin/ksysv**.

   The main KsysV window appears, as shown in Figure 18-1. (Note that some KsysV windows, like this one, may be entitled "SysV Init Editor.")

3. Use the drop-down menus to select Options | Configure.

   The KsysV Preferences dialog box appears.

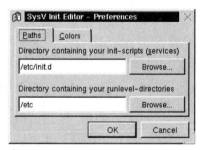

4. In the top field, type **/etc/init.d**.

   This field defines the directory that contains your initialization scripts.

5. In the bottom field, type **/etc**.

   This field defines the directory in which your numbered runlevel directories are located.

6. Click OK to close the Preferences window closes, and you return to the main KsysV window.

You can now use KsysV to configure the runlevels of your Corel Linux machine.

Using KsysV

Once you have configured KsysV to work with Corel Linux, it can be used as a quick and simple way to configure runlevels. The KsysV window, as shown in Figure 18-1, is divided into multiple panes. The left pane, Available Services, shows a complete list of services with scripts located in the /etc/init.d directory.

18

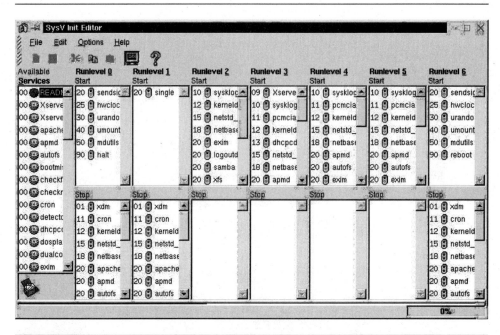

FIGURE 18-1   Use KsysV to configure runlevels graphically

To the right of the Available Services window are seven sets of panes, and an upper and lower pane for each runlevel. The upper pane contains services started in that runlevel, while the lower pane contains services stopped in that runlevel.

It's a good idea to study the services listed in the Available Services window, just to make sure that you know which ones you want. You have less chance of leaving something out, or including services you don't want, if you have a clear idea before you begin configuring with KsysV.

To configure runlevels with KsysV, use the following procedure:

1. Identify the runlevel you want to configure.

   For the remainder of the configuration, you will need only the upper and lower pane for that runlevel, as well as the Available Services pane.

2. In the Available Services pane, right-click a service you want to start or stop in your selected runlevel.

3. Select Cut from the pop-up menu.

4. Right-click in the desired runlevel pane. Right-click in the upper pane to start the service at boot-up in that runlevel, and right-click in the lower pane to stop the service.

5. Select Paste from the pop-up menu.

6. (Optional) To remove a service from a runlevel, right-click the service in the appropriate runlevel pane and select Cut from the pop-up menu.

7. Click the Save icon when you have finished configuring your runlevels.

The next time `init` is invoked, it will use the new configuration.

Why Use Multiple Runlevels?

The most obvious reason to have more than one runlevel is so that you can bring up different sets of services, or shut them down, in stages during the startup process. If you have multiple users, employing multiple runlevels is frequently a blessing. For example, you could bring down certain services, such as news and FTP, without having to shut off access to others, such as mail and Web. Another good use for runlevels is in the case of access levels; you may need or want to shut off access to the Internet for a while (perhaps you're switching service providers or your upstream is having trouble), but you still want your users to be able to use local network functions.

Imagine that you're setting up a server that will be used for file and print sharing, as well as allowing users access to telnet and FTP into the machine via the Internet, and that you want to define a set of runlevels that enables you to shut down certain services without affecting others. Suppose that your basic runlevel scheme looks like this:

- **Runlevel 1**   Single-user mode. All services are off, and all file systems are unmounted. Only root can log into the machine.

- **Runlevel 2**   Multiple-user mode. User logins are allowed but only local logins (not across a network or via the Internet). File systems are mounted, and e-mail is available.

18

■ **Runlevel 3**   Multiple-user mode and the default runlevel. File and print sharing services are enabled.

To accomplish this set of runlevel configurations, you need to start the following services in each runlevel:

■ **Runlevel 1**   `single` (/etc/init.d/single)

■ **Runlevel 2**   `network`, `netstd_init`, `netstd_misc`, `mountall`, `sh`, and `exim`

■ **Runlevel 3**   All services from Runlevel 2 plus `mountnfs.sh` and `samba`

In runlevel 2, note that you should put in symbolic K links for `mountnfs` and `samba`, so that they will be stopped when switching from runlevel 3 to runlevel 2. (See the section "The Runlevel Directories," earlier in this chapter, for an explanation of symbolic links.)

Any of these runlevels can be entered at any time by issuing the following command at a shell prompt, while logged in as root:

```
init <number of runlevel>
```

Using this command means that you can shift from runlevel to runlevel without having to physically reboot the machine each time you want to change the array of services running or stopped.

CHAPTER 19

Dealing with Hardware

The essence of any operating system is the interaction between hardware and software. The operating system enables software (and, by extension, you the user) to use the computer's hardware—not only the monitor or the printer, but the actual chip itself. How does the operating system manage the hardware? Through the use of various *drivers* included in the kernel. Drivers are sets of procedures that direct the flow of data to and from various hardware devices; they format the data in a way that the individual device can comprehend. Each driver works slightly differently, depending on the unique characteristics of the hardware device itself and the way in which various electrical signals are interpreted and processed by the device.

In Corel Linux, as in most current Linux distributions, device drivers are provided by *modules*, sections of code that can be loaded into system memory by the kernel only when needed. Most of the time, this loading happens automatically and is directed by the kernel daemon, a server process that is responsible for the management of modules.

 It is also possible to load and unload modules by hand as well as compile them permanently into the kernel code. If you want to add them to the kernel, see Appendix A, "How to Compile a Kernel," for information on kernel recompilation.

In the great majority of cases, you should not have to mess with device drivers. Corel Linux is able to detect a great deal of hardware automatically and can configure itself to use that hardware. However, one sometimes runs across an especially tricky piece of hardware that requires some hand-tweaking; in that case, it's good to have a grasp of the drivers concept and an understanding of what needs to be done.

Choosing Hardware

One of the most fun aspects of being a computer owner is adding new hardware. New toys are always being released: faster scanners, cheaper digital cameras, hand-held computers, better printers, more advanced video or sound cards, and so on. Once you decide you want a new piece of hardware, though, you need to do some work. It's not quite as simple to buy hardware when you're using Linux as it is when you use MacOS or Windows.

Express Yourself

If you see a great piece of hardware that you're dying to use, but you know that it's unsupported under Linux, write to the manufacturer! Mention that you'd like to see Linux support for its products, whether they be drivers that the company develops or simply the release of product specifications. If a manufacturer receives some requests for Linux-friendly information or drivers, it is often prompted to release its interface specifications to developers. Once the specs are available, it's usually not long at all before someone writes a reliable driver for the item.

Finding Supported Hardware

Because of the nature of Linux and related free software, Linux users expect to have access to source code and specifications for the programs and devices they use. Unfortunately, not all hardware manufacturers agree. Many are reluctant to release the specifications of their products in fear that they will be "giving away" trade secrets to their competitors. Thankfully, with the increased popularity of Linux over the last few years, this situation is changing; however, certain pieces of hardware are still simply impossible to use with current kernel versions because Linux developers simply don't know how those items work.

If you want or need to know whether a piece of hardware is supported under Linux, you should consult the authoritative source: the Hardware Compatibility HOWTO, located at `http://www.linuxdoc.org/HOWTO/Hardware-HOWTO.html`. Be aware that this document refers only to individual hardware components (cards, printers, scanners, and so on) and not to preassembled systems. If you bought a system off the shelf, you need to consult your documentation to find out what the components inside the box actually are. Any time you are contemplating a new purchase for your Linux system, though, you should check this document to make sure that you're getting a piece of hardware that is well supported. You can also consult the list of hardware that's specifically supported under Corel Linux at `http://www.linux.corel.com`.

19

TIP   *Don't assume anything! In particular, don't assume that, because some items from a given manufacturer are supported, all are usable with Linux. Joe recently decided to buy a new printer for the main Linux workstation. Because Kate gets great results from a Hewlett-Packard DeskJet 720C attached to the Windows 98 computer, Joe bought an identical model. About eight minutes after unpacking and connecting the printer, Joe discovered that the 720C is one of the few DeskJet models that isn't supported under Linux. After consulting the Hardware Compatibility HOWTO, he exchanged the 720C for a 612C, which is fully supported and works just fine. The moral of the story is check the document first and save yourself a return trip or two to the computer store!*

Understanding What Hardware You Need

Whether you have a Linux computer or one running another operating system, you have to know what you need. Before you rush out and buy a new sound card, for example, make sure you understand its specifications. Does it require a PCI or an ISA bus slot? Most modern (Pentium and higher) computers use primarily PCI bus slots and have only one or two ISA slots available. If your ISA slots are already full, then you must find PCI hardware, or you cannot use it. Likewise, some older computers (386s or 486s) have only ISA slots.

TIP   *Buy a book about hardware. We particularly like* The Hand-Me-Down PC, *written by Morris Rosenthal and published by McGraw-Hill. Rosenthal gives helpful explanations of various hardware components and breaks down his suggested upgrades into price categories. While the book was published in 1997 (and a lot has changed in the last few years), the concepts are still valid. You can learn more about the book at Rosenthal's Web site,* http://www.daileyint.com.

One thing to be quite wary of in the Linux environment is the USB (Universal Serial Bus) interface. It seems as though almost every cool peripheral on the shelves these days requires a USB port, and that most new systems use USB ports instead of serial or parallel ports. Unfortunately, the USB protocol is not currently (as of winter 2000) supported under Linux, and you won't be able to use either the port or the peripherals if you already have USB hardware. If you're looking for a scanner, digital camera, or webcam, be especially careful; you may have to order a non-USB version from a catalog since large computer stores seem to be stocking fewer non-USB multimedia peripherals.

Support for USB is being worked on by Linux developers. USB should have some level of support in future versions of the Linux kernel and of Corel Linux itself. We assume you want to use the peripherals you buy, not store them in anticipation of support down the road.

Researching the Options

Once you've determined what you want, and have gotten some idea of the particular model or manufacturer, it's time to fire up Netscape. Most hardware manufacturers maintain Web sites with tons of information about their various products. An hour or two of surfing these sites, as well as some sites operated by hardware retailers, can often yield a great deal of information about which product is right for you and how much you should expect to pay for it. Informed buying helps keep prices down and quality high.

CAUTION *If you shop at computer mega-stores, enter the store fully aware that the employees probably know very little about Linux. Asking whether a component is Linux compatible may very well be answered "yes" because the employee needs to sell the item to meet a sales quota; the actual answer might be "no," and you'll have to return it. Do your homework.*

We can't let a discussion of hardware purchases go by without some mention of online auction sites. A lot of writers and Web pundits warn against buying hardware from a seller on eBay or Yahoo! and Amazon's auction sites. We can see the point; there's often no recourse if you buy a lemon from an individual. Still, we have to admit it: most of our hardware is stuff we bought on eBay.

We've had the best luck buying from companies who happen to do business on auction sites; these companies often accept credit cards. If your credit card has purchase protection, you're safe.

TIP *If the seller provides a link to his company's Web site, check it out before you bid. We've found that eBay bidders often inflate the bid price above the regular retail price at the company's site or store. Why pay an extra $50 or $100 just to get something at auction? If it's cheaper at the regular price, don't bother with the auction. (You could leave a nice feedback entry if you found the seller at an auction site, though.)*

Buying from individuals is trickier, though we've done that, too. Look for someone with a high feedback rating as a seller and who offers a great deal of

19

information about the item. We especially like sellers who provide links to manufacturer information as well as information about the actual item you're buying: Is it refurbished? Is it under warranty?

Finally, as with any auction transaction, figure out your personal panic threshold: Are you comfortable with the risk on a $15 scroll mouse? A $75 sound card? A $250 monitor? A $400 hand-held computer? If you're worried about losing your money on a low-priced peripheral like a mouse, auction sites may not be for you. If they are, though, you can usually find lower prices for the same items you'd buy from a catalog or a store.

Auto-Detection

After you install a new piece of hardware, the first thing you should do is reboot; actually, since you should never ever add hardware with the power on, you need to boot up the computer. Corel Linux can often auto-detect a new piece of hardware and configure itself to load the appropriate driver automatically.

However, Corel Linux's auto-detection powers have some exceptions:

- **Video cards**   An improperly configured video card can cause actual physical damage to your computer. This is because video displays, unlike other peripherals, use relatively high voltages. If the video card attempts to pass signals that are incorrect or mistimed, these voltages can damage the motherboard or the card itself.

- **Printers**   Printers do not work straight out of the box. You have to do some additional configuration, even if Corel Linux recognizes the printer. This is probably the aspect of Linux least like Windows; Plug-n-Play works fine with printers under Windows. See Chapter 24, "File and Print Sharing," for information on installing a printer with Linux.

- **Modems**   Modems also require additional configuration after installation, and you have to be quite careful with the kind of modem you buy.

Both printer and modem issues are addressed later in this chapter.

Configuring a Video Card

As we explained in Chapter 3, "The X Window System," the video card and monitor settings are contained in the /etc/X11/XF86Config file. To create a new version of this file with the proper settings for your new card, use this procedure:

1. Boot your machine into single-user mode.

   To do this, reboot the machine and select the Linux Console option from the LILO menu.

2. Back up the existing configuration file. At a shell prompt, issue the command

   ```
   cp /etc/X11/XF86Config /etc/X11/XF86Config.bak
   ```

3. Start the Corel Linux hardware probe. At a shell prompt, issue the command

   ```
   /usr/X11R6/bin/XF86Setup
   ```

   This causes Corel Linux to probe the video hardware to determine what settings to use. Your display will flash a few times during the probe, and then a basic X session will begin with the main XF86Setup screen appearing on the monitor, as shown in Figure 19-1.

4. Click the Card button at the top of the screen.

   The Video Card Setup screen appears, as in Figure 19-2.

5. Click the Card List button at the lower right of the screen.

   The Card List screen, as in Figure 19-3, appears, with a list of video cards.

6. Scroll through the list and select your video card.

   If you bought a supported video card, it should be on this list. If it is not, select Generic VGA Compatible.

7. Click the Done button.

8. When the confirmation screen appears, verify the information and click Done.

19

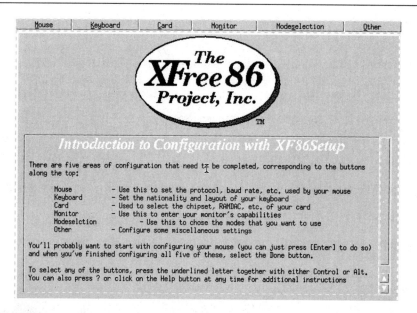

FIGURE 19-1   Corel Linux determines your video hardware setup with the XF86Setup tool

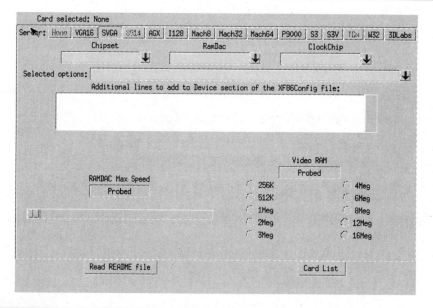

FIGURE 19-2   Configure your video card on this screen

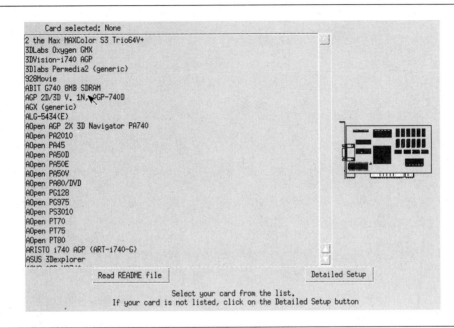

FIGURE 19-3   Select your video card from the Card List

After you click Done, XF86Setup attempts to start the X server. It will fail because it attempts to use the X Display Manager, which has been removed from Corel Linux and replaced with the K Display Manager.

9. Press CTRL-C to kill the attempt at starting the X server.

10. At the shell prompt, issue the command `init 2`.

Your machine reboots to runlevel 2 (see Chapter 18, "Runlevels and the Boot Process," for more information on runlevels). When the machine completes booting, KDM should start with the correct video settings.

Configuring a Modem

Purchasing and configuring a modem for a Linux system is a bit more complicated than configuring other hardware peripherals. The first hurdle is finding a modem that actually works under Linux; this can be somewhat difficult to do if you are trying to shop at a local computer or office supply mega-store. Then you need to configure and test the modem before you can actually use it.

Beware the WinModem!

Some modems simply cannot be used with Linux, no matter how much configuring you try to do. These are the modems often referred to as "WinModems" or "software modems." These modems use part of the Windows 95/98 operating system software to emulate the hardware used by a more standard modem. Since these modems are designed to be used with Windows, the drivers are written with Windows programming routines; since Microsoft does not make these routines public, equivalent routines cannot be used to write Linux drivers.

WinModems can be recognized by their small size; they're about half the size of a regular modem, roughly the size of a pack of extra-long cigarettes. They're also extremely cheap. While it's unfortunate that Linux users can't take advantage of low-cost hardware, regular modems are more reliable anyway. You'll make up the extra cost in a longer lifespan of the unit.

Internal or External Modem?

Before you begin to shop for a modem, you'll have to decide whether you want one that goes inside the computer's case—an *internal modem*—or one that plugs into a port and has a separate container—an *external modem*. Both have advantages and disadvantages and are usually comparable in price. It's easier to find a non-WinModem external modem, for some reason, but you do have to find room for another external peripheral.

Internal modems plug into a slot inside the computer case. Recently manufactured modems usually fit into an ISA slot. They look like a regular circuit board, with two phone jacks on the flat silver end. External modems are usually small flat boxes with a panel of lights on the front; phone jacks are on the back, along with a cord that connects to a serial port on the back of the computer case. While many internal modems are perfectly adequate for the job of getting you connected to your Internet service provider, the conventional wisdom holds that external modems are sturdier and more reliable.

| CAUTION | *If you buy an internal modem, check to see that it is not a Plug-n-Play modem. Plug-n-Play capability is not as crucial to avoid as the WinModem, but it is still impossible to use with Linux. Many Plug-n-Play modems allow the feature to be disabled by changing the tiny dip switches or jumpers on the modem itself. If you can't tell from the box whether a modem is Plug-and-Play, ask the salesperson to open the box and show you the manual.* |

Connecting the Modem

When you connect your new modem to the computer, you'll need to decide which serial port to put it on. If you're adding an external modem, this is as simple as deciding which external serial port to plug the cord into. If you're using an internal modem, however, you need to assign the port yourself. Again, check your modem's manual. Most modems either come with a preassigned port setting or have a jumper or dip switch that you can set to determine the port. If the latter is the case, the manual will have a chart showing the settings.

| CAUTION | *Make sure you choose a port that isn't already being used by another device. For example, if you have a serial mouse plugged into the first serial port, you cannot assign the internal modem to /dev/cua0 or /dev/ttyS0 (the Linux designations for that first serial port).* |

You also need to avoid *IRQ* conflicts. The IRQ number relates to the order in which the microprocessor handles requests, and each device has its own. You should be able to set the IRQ number on the modem itself; check the file /proc/interrupts to see what IRQ numbers are already in use. Normally, you'll use IRQ 3 or 4 for a modem, depending on which port you select. If you think that you need to use another number or a different serial port, check the HOWTO for modems at `http://www.linuxdoc.org/HOWTO/Modem-HOWTO.html`. (It's a good idea to read this anyway before you add a new modem.)

Once you have the modem installed and connected to the proper serial port, you can use the instructions in Chapter 9, "Using the Internet with Corel Linux," to establish a connection to your ISP.

19

Kernel Modules

A new piece of hardware occasionally won't be recognized by the kernel daemon, and it will be necessary for you to load the driver module by hand. If you install a piece of hardware and it is not detected at boot, this may be the case. The first thing you need to do is to locate the appropriate driver. Kernel modules are kept in the directory /lib/modules/2.2.12/<type>, where <type> is the category of driver (such as "net" for network cards, "sound" for sound cards, and so on). A sample directory listing for the /lib/modules/2.2.12/net directory is shown in Figure 19-4.

When you've located the proper file, you can load it with the `insmod` command. For example, suppose you installed a 3Com 3c509 Ethernet card

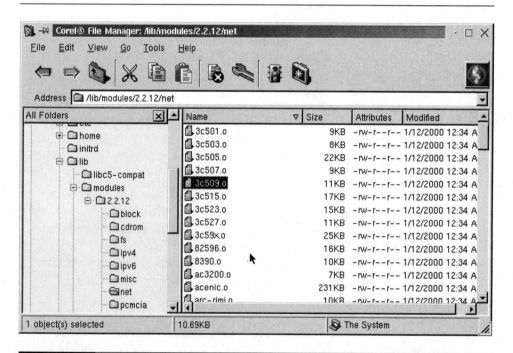

FIGURE 19-4 The various /lib/modules/2.2.12 directories contain drivers for specific component types

that didn't show up when you rebooted. Load the module by issuing the following command at a shell prompt:

```
insmod /lib/modules/2.2.12/net/3c509.o
```

Since modules follow a standard format, you can also use the shorthand command

```
insmod 3c509
```

If this command gets the hardware working—and it should—you'll need to make sure the driver module gets loaded every time the machine boots. Do this by adding the following entry to the /etc/conf.modules file:

```
alias net 3c509
```

Obviously, you can't use that line for every piece of hardware. Entries in /etc/conf.modules use the syntax

```
alias <type> <driver>
```

So, for an Ensoniq 1371 sound card, you'd use the entry

```
alias sound es1371
```

and so on.

 As an alternative to editing /etc/conf.modules, you can recompile the kernel and include the driver as a static addition to the kernel code, rather than as a module. See Appendix A for instructions.

19

CHAPTER 20

Networking

If you've read straight through this book, you remember that we have already discussed networking in Chapter 9, "Using the Internet with Corel Linux." That chapter, though, was devoted to dial-up networking used to connect to an Internet service provider, so that you can use your computer for Internet access. In this chapter, we cover some of the more advanced aspects of networking, including how to set up a Local Area Network, or LAN. No Internet connection information is presented here; see Chapter 9.

This chapter is devoted to networking with 10/100BaseT Ethernet cable, since that is the most common kind of networking equipment in use. Other kinds of networking hardware are much less common, and you're likely to require the services of a specialist should you want to use them. We assume you want to build a LAN in a home or a small office; 10/100BaseT is both fastest and most economical for those purposes.

Basic Networking Concepts

Before you begin to build a network, it's a good idea to know the basic concepts behind networking. Basically, a network is a group of computers connected together that can share files and devices, such as printers. Networks usually have a main server machine, which may or may not be one of the user machines attached to the network.

> **TIP** *When you are building a small network with a Linux machine as the server, you don't have to purchase a high-powered and fancy new computer for the server. Save the fireworks for the user machines; Linux servers can quite happily plug along on an old machine destined for the garbage heap. Our server is a 1995 Gateway 486 with a 1-gigabyte hard drive, and it runs fine. We have heard of people running servers from 386s, though we'd probably not do that. You can use a smaller, older machine unless your network is destined to serve more than 15 or 20 computers or users.*

TCP/IP Versus Dial-Up

When we discussed networking in Chapter 9, we covered only dial-up networking. Dial-up networking is done using the Peer-to-Peer (or Point-to-Point) Protocol, or PPP, which describes how data is to be sent over a serial line (telephone line).

> **NOTE** *In this context, a* protocol *is a description of how information is passed between systems. Programmers use these protocols to design the programs that actually do the work. These programs can differ greatly in how they implement the protocol; but as long as the information is handled in the prescribed manner, the different programs all "speak the same language."*

Once we step away from phone lines and modems, however, we move from PPP to the TCP/IP protocol. TCP/IP (Transmission Control Protocol/Internet Protocol) is the main language of the Internet. It is a set of protocols that manage how information is sent among the machines that make up the Internet, a wide array of hardware that varies wildly in its design and operation. Since the Internet and TCP/IP were originally designed to network UNIX machines, it shouldn't be any surprise that Linux—a UNIX derivative—handles networking very well.

The form of networking that we describe here involves the use of TCP/IP via Ethernet cable, which is a common configuration. As we noted earlier, we assume that you are building a network in a home or small office and that you already have some form of Internet connection (probably that dial-up connection you configured in Chapter 9).

Unlike dial-up connections, Ethernet connections are always active. There is no need to dial into the server machine because the network is always functioning unless you disable it. If you have a 24-hour connection to the Internet that uses Ethernet cable for the hook-up (DSL or a cable modem, or a similar workplace connection), the Internet is always on for you. Ethernet connections are also a good deal faster than dial-up connections. In theory, a 10BaseT connection should transfer data at the rate of 10 million bits per second; the fastest modems currently permitted by the U.S. Federal Communications Commission (FCC) transfer data at a maximum rate of 56,000 bits per second. Thus, Ethernet is approximately 178 times faster than the fastest dial-up connection.

> **NOTE** *These are theoretical speeds. Rarely will you actually get the highest possible speed on your modem or on your 10BaseT connection. All sorts of factors contribute to the actual speed of your network connection, including the quality of the equipment you've used, the quality of the equipment at your Internet provider's office, the type and length of cables you've used for your network, and so on. Congestion on the Internet itself delays any connection regardless of the mechanism used. Still, it's not inaccurate to say that an Ethernet connection is at least 100 times faster than a perfect modem connection.*

Static Versus Dynamic IP

Another concept that's important to understand is that of static versus dynamic IP. Every computer on the Internet is identified by a unique number, called an Internet Protocol (IP) address or number. They are so called because the use of these numbers is required by the Internet Protocol (the IP part of TCP/IP). Every IP number has this form:

qqq.xxx.yyy.zzz

where *qqq*, *xxx*, *yyy*, and *zzz* are numbers between 0 and 255.

This unique number can be assigned to a given computer in one of two ways. It can be *static* if the computer's IP number is assigned once and is a permanent association with that machine. Or it can be *dynamic* if the computer is assigned a new and different IP number each time it connects to the Internet. Static IPs are far easier to work with, but dynamic IP numbers are far more common.

Dynamic IP numbers are immensely popular with Internet providers because they allow the ISP to sign up many more users than they actually have IP addresses for. Since not every user is connected to the Internet at the same time, the pool of dynamic IP numbers can be assigned as necessary. If your ISP uses dynamic IP numbers, your IP number will change each time you log in; this is handled using DHCP, the Dynamic Host Configuration Protocol. As long as the DHCP servers and clients are set up properly, you won't find dynamic IP numbers to be a problem. We discuss DHCP clients later in this chapter and DHCP servers in Chapter 27, "Miscellaneous Network Services."

NOTE	*In some regions, PPPoE (PPP Over Ethernet) is beginning to overtake DHCP as the dynamic IP protocol of choice by ISPs. If this is the case in your area, take a look at the PPPoE HOWTO document, at `http://sidhe.folkwolf.net/~chris/pppoe-howto/`. The next major version of the Linux kernel (version 2.4) should include kernel-level PPPoE support.*

For the purposes of setting up your network, we concentrate on static IP numbers; we'll discuss how to handle dynamic IP numbers from your ISP when we discuss DHCP clients.

Anatomy of an IP Number

It looks fairly arbitrary: four sets of numbers, each ranging from 0 to 255. Why are IP addresses structured in this fashion? It's because each IP address is a 32-bit number. A *bit* is the basic unit of information in the digital world. Each set of numbers within the IP address represents 8 bits, or one *byte*; in binary format, a 32-bit number looks like this:

xxxxxxxx.xxxxxxxx.xxxxxxxx.xxxxxxxx

with each *x* representing either 0 or 1 (binary format uses only ones and zeros). Because each segment contains eight bits, the units are sometimes called *octets*.

Because each digit has two possible values, a 32-bit number has more than 4 billion possible values (expressed by the equation $2e^{32}$). That's a cumbersome number to work with, so it's usually split into four 8-bit numbers. An 8-bit number has 256 possible values ($2e^8$). Because UNIX always starts counting from zero, possible values range from 0 to 255.

Network Devices

Under Linux, network connections are managed by *network devices,* a name assigned to a particular kind of network connection. For example, if you have a dial-up line that uses PPP as well as an Ethernet connection, the dial-up line is designated as `ppp0`, while the Ethernet connection is designated as `eth0`. A second Ethernet connection would be `eth1`, and so on.

Note that these are not devices in the traditional UNIX sense; that is, they are not entries in the /dev directory. Rather, they are software constructs that direct the flow of information through the connections. The physical devices—the modem or Ethernet card—have entries in /dev. A modem is usually in /dev/cua0, for example.

Because the network devices are not contained in the /dev directory, you might wonder how to see the configuration of the network devices. For this, you can use the `ifconfig` command, which displays the current setup for each device running. Here's a sample `ifconfig` output:

```
eth0    Link encap:Ethernet  HWaddr 00:8C:FB:D5:7E

        inet addr:192.168.0.5  Bcast:192.168.0.255  Mask:255.255.255.0
```

```
UP BROADCAST RUNNING MULTICAST  MTU:1500  Metric:1

RX packets:638389 errors:261 dropped:0 overruns:263 frame:261

TX packets:446938 errors:0 dropped:0 overruns:0 carrier:1

collisions:3069 txqueuelen:100

Interrupt:9 Base address:0x300


lo        Link encap:Local Loopback

          inet addr:127.0.0.1  Mask:255.0.0.0

          UP LOOPBACK RUNNING  MTU:3924  Metric:1

          RX packets:18 errors:0 dropped:0 overruns:0 frame:0

          TX packets:18 errors:0 dropped:0 overruns:0 carrier:0

          collisions:0 txqueuelen:0
```

This sample output shows that two network devices are currently configured: an Ethernet device, eth0, and the *loopback device*, lo. A loopback device is a special network device that lets Linux talk to itself; its IP number is always 127.0.0.1. Many processes use the loopback device for interprocess communication, so always leave it alone. The entry for eth0 shows, among other things, the IP number (192.168.0.5) and the fact that the interface is UP, or working.

Routing

Routing refers to the practice of directing traffic on a network. Any network that connects to another network, such as the Internet, needs to have a way of getting information from the internal network to the outside world. In such cases, a particular machine may be designated as a *gateway* or *router* machine. Very large networks may require two or three of these specialized machines. It is the job of the router to determine where to send each piece of information received across the connection, depending on its destination. On very small networks, such as the one you are building, routing is a fairly simple task since there is generally only one place where external information is sent. For large networks, though, the process is significantly more complicated.

Routing can be a full-time job. There are people whose entire work life is taken up with configuring and maintaining routers; several professional certifications are available that proclaim the recipient to be capable of handling various sticky routing situations. For our purposes here, we deal only with very simple routing configurations.

Setting Up a Network

Bearing some of these basic concepts in mind, get ready to work your way through setting up a simple network. We begin with a basic network of Linux machines; once that's set up, we show you how to connect it to the Internet. After that's accomplished, we explain how to add a Windows machine to the network, and then a Macintosh.

Getting Your Hardware Together

For each machine that you want to add to the network, you'll need a properly configured 10BaseT Network Interface Card, or NIC. See Chapter 19, "Dealing with Hardware," for configuration information for your Linux computers; for Windows or Macintosh computers, consult the relevant documentation that came with the network card.

In addition, you need a network hub. These are available at any computer supply shop and can also be found in most office supply mega-stores. Small hubs with four or five ports can be had for as little as $40; if you can afford it, get a hub from a reliable manufacturer like 3Com or Linksys.

You also need a piece of cable for each computer you want to connect to the hub. Twisted-pair cable, which is what the *T* in 10BaseT stands for, comes in two grades: Category 3 and Category 5. Category 3 cable is lighter and cheaper; while it's perfectly adequate, we suggest you splurge a little and get Category 5 cable instead. It's more expensive, but its heavier construction means that less data will be lost per foot of cable, which means that you have faster data transfer over your network. Twisted-pair cable has a plug on each end that resembles an oversized phone plug. The cable plugs into a socket on the network card in your computer on one end, and into the hub on the other end. A schematic diagram of network configuration is shown in the following illustration.

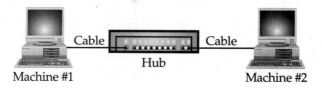

Networking Linux Machines

Once you have all your hardware together, it's time to begin setting up the Linux network. We assume that you have at least two computers running Corel Linux that will form the core of the network.

Begin by assigning each machine an IP number. Because you are building a private network, you can assign any IP number you want to the machines. However, the Internet Protocol has reserved certain blocks of IP numbers for use in private networks, such as the one you're building now, and you should use these numbers. (It helps when you want to expand your network in the future.) These IP numbers range from 192.168.0.0 to 192.168.255.255. Numbers that end with 0 and 255 (for network and broadcast addresses) are reserved.

Assign Computer #1 the IP number 192.168.0.1 and assign Computer #2 the IP number 192.168.0.2. Use the `ifconfig` command to make these assignments:

```
ifconfig eth0 192.168.0.1 netmask 255.255.255.0 up
```

The part of the command that reads `netmask 255.255.255.0 up` is used for the routing setup; it will be the same for all machines on the network. Repeat the process for Computer #2:

```
ifconfig eth0 192.168.0.2 netmask 255.255.255.0 up
```

At this point, your network should be up. Check to see if this is the case by issuing this command from Computer #2:

```
ping 192.168.0.1
```

You should see output that looks like this:

```
PING 192.168.0.1 (192.168.0.1) from 192.168.0.2 : 56(84) bytes of data.
```

```
64 bytes from 192.168.0.1: icmp_seq=0 ttl=64 time=1.0 ms
64 bytes from 192.168.0.1: icmp_seq=1 ttl=64 time=0.9 ms
64 bytes from 192.168.0.1: icmp_seq=2 ttl=64 time=0.8 ms
64 bytes from 192.168.0.1: icmp_seq=3 ttl=64 time=0.9 ms
64 bytes from 192.168.0.1: icmp_seq=4 ttl=64 time=1.1 ms
64 bytes from 192.168.0.1: icmp_seq=5 ttl=64 time=0.8 ms
64 bytes from 192.168.0.1: icmp_seq=6 ttl=64 time=0.9 ms
64 bytes from 192.168.0.1: icmp_seq=7 ttl=64 time=0.8 ms
64 bytes from 192.168.0.1: icmp_seq=8 ttl=64 time=0.8 ms
64 bytes from 192.168.0.1: icmp_seq=9 ttl=64 time=0.9 ms
64 bytes from 192.168.0.1: icmp_seq=10 ttl=64 time=0.9 ms
64 bytes from 192.168.0.1: icmp_seq=11 ttl=64 time=0.9 ms
```

Press CTRL-C to make the output stop; `ping` sends a closing statement to the screen:

```
--- 192.168.0.1 ping statistics ---

12 packets transmitted, 12 packets received, 0% packet loss

round-trip min/avg/max = 0.8/0.8/1.1 ms
```

Repeat this process but from Computer #1 to Computer #2 to test the network in the other direction:

```
ping 192.168.0.2
```

If you can successfully ping both machines, your network is functioning. You should now be able to use all regular network functions between both machines.

Before you get too carried away, though, do something that will make your life a lot easier: name your computers. In this example, we will name Computer #1 homer and Computer #2 bart. Use the `hostname` command to name the computers. On Computer #1, enter this command:

```
hostname homer
```

and enter this command on Computer #2:

```
hostname bart
```

Now, each machine knows its own name, but you still need some way for the machines to know each other's name. The file /etc/hosts serves this purpose; it contains a list of known IP numbers and associates them with the computer's given name. On homer, open /etc/hosts in your favorite text editor and edit it to look like this:

```
127.0.0.1     homer localhost
192.168.0.1   homer
192.168.0.2   bart
```

Do the same on bart, but notice that the first line of /etc/hosts on bart looks different, because /etc/hosts applies to the machine on which it resides:

```
127.0.0.1     bart localhost
192.168.0.1   homer
192.168.0.2   bart
```

Once you have edited these files, the computers can recognize each other both by IP number and by name. This makes it easier for you to issue network commands, since you don't have to remember which IP number matches each machine. Names are both easier to remember and more friendly.

Connecting Your Network to the Internet

At this point, you can connect your network to the Internet. In the first scenario of this section, we connect to the Internet via a dial-up connection with your service provider, while the second scenario describes connection through an existing TCP/IP connection, whether it's provided by a cable modem, DSL, or the owners of your office building.

Using a Dial-Up Connection

We have arbitrarily designated homer to be the machine that dials up, so make sure you've configured homer's dial-up networking properly as described in Chapter 9. Note that when you dial up, the ISP will assign a separate IP number to your PPP device so that it can identify your computer on the Internet; this means that homer will have two IP numbers while the connection is operative.

Before you dial up, though, do a little work so that both computers will be able to use the connection once it is established. On homer, issue these commands at a shell prompt:

```
/sbin/ipchains -P forward DENY
/sbin/ipchains -A forward -s 192.168.0.0/24 -j MASQ
```

Still on homer, issue the command

route add default ppp0

On bart, issue this command at a shell prompt:

route add default gw 192.168.0.1

Now, both computers on your network will be able to access the Internet. The /sbin/ipchains commands set up an *IP masquerade*, a situation in which all signals from the network that are intended for the Internet are sent through the gateway device: in this case, homer's ppp0 device. To the outside world of the Internet, it looks like all data is coming directly from homer; the ipchains program on homer, however, knows the origin of each piece of data and routes data that arrives in response to the correct machine. For example, if your daughter is sitting at bart and requests a Pokèmon Web page, ipchains will route both the request and the incoming page data to bart, even though it's homer that is connected to the service provider.

Using a TCP/IP Connection

If you have a TCP/IP connection instead of a dial-up connection, the configuration process is a little different. On your gateway machine, which we've defined as homer in this example, you need to have two Ethernet devices. There are a couple of ways you can do this: you can install two Ethernet cards, one for the internal network and one for the external network, or you can bind a second IP address to the single card that you have already installed. If you choose the second option, you'll use a process called *IP aliasing* to set up the second address. Using IP aliasing is as simple as configuring a second network device using ifconfig:

```
ifconfig eth0:0 qqq.xxx.yyy.zzz netmask 255.255.255.0 up
```

where *qqq.xxx.yyy.zzz* is homer's IP number for the external network. Note the slight difference in the Ethernet device number, eth0:0, as opposed to the eth0 you used in setting up the network. The appended :0 indicates that it is the first alias for the eth0 device. (You need to have configured eth0 properly in order for this to work.)

20

Once you've done this, you can issue the `ifconfig` command again to see what your network device configurations look like:

```
lo        Link encap:Local Loopback
          inet addr:127.0.0.1  Bcast:127.255.255.255  Mask:255.0.0.0
          UP BROADCAST LOOPBACK RUNNING  MTU:3584  Metric:1
          RX packets:25945413 errors:0 dropped:0 overruns:0 frame:0
          TX packets:25945413 errors:0 dropped:0 overruns:0 carrier:0
          collisions:0

eth0:0    Link encap:Ethernet  HWaddr 00:XX:8C:XX:D0:0B
          inet addr:209.167.40.5  Bcast:192.168.0.255  Mask:255.255.255.0
          UP BROADCAST RUNNING MULTICAST  MTU:1500  Metric:1
          RX packets:14522548 errors:12750 dropped:0 overruns:12504 frame:12750
          TX packets:13373566 errors:0 dropped:0 overruns:0 carrier:15
          collisions:40439
          Interrupt:10 Base address:0x300

eth0      Link encap:Ethernet  HWaddr 00:XX:8C:XX:D0:0B
          inet addr:192.168.0.1  Mask:255.255.255.0
          UP RUNNING  MTU:1500  Metric:1
          RX packets:0 errors:0 dropped:0 overruns:0 frame:0
          TX packets:0 errors:0 dropped:0 overruns:0 carrier:0
          collisions:0
```

Both Ethernet devices act as if they are separate and independent from each other, even though they make use of the same hardware.

Next, set up IP masquerading for the aliased device:

```
/sbin/ipchains -P forward DENY
/sbin/ipchains -A forward -s 192.168.0.0/24 -j MASQ
```

Then set up routing so that it recognizes the new alias. On homer, issue this command at a shell prompt:

```
route add default eth0:0
```

and on bart, issue this command at a shell prompt:

```
route add default gw 192.168.0.1
```

Now both computers on the network should be able to use the TCP/IP network connection.

If you're interested in using TCP/IP connections with a network, we recommend that you read some of the documents produced by the Linux Documentation Project. You can find the LDP at their home site of `http://www.linuxdoc.org`. *A series of documents produced by LDP and called* HOWTO *documents address various subjects useful to Linux users. In particular, we recommend the ipchains HOWTO, the IP Masquerade HOWTO, and the Networking HOWTO as invaluable references. These documents are written for the general Linux audience, not specifically for Corel Linux, but you should be able to figure out any Corel-specific requirements.*

Adding a Windows Computer to the Network

To connect a Windows computer to your Linux network, you just need to configure the Windows networking client correctly. We assume that you installed a TCP/IP driver when you installed your network card; if not, see your network card's documentation. Use this procedure:

1. Choose Start | Settings | Control Panel.

2. Double-click the Network icon in the Control Panel.

   The Network screen appears, as seen in Figure 20-1, opened to the Configuration tab.

3. Select the TCP/IP network component in the top window.

4. Click the Properties button.

   The TCP/IP Properties screen appears, opened to the IP Address tab.

5. Enter the IP address that you want to assign to this machine and the subnet mask: **255.255.255.0**.

6. Click the WINS Server tab.

7. Select the radio button for Disable WINS Resolution.

8. Click the Gateway tab.

9. Enter the IP number of the gateway computer and click Enter.

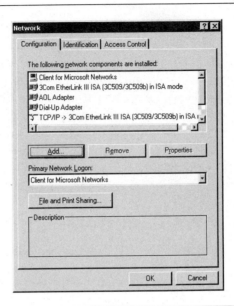

FIGURE 20-1   Use the Network utility to add your Windows machine to an existing network

The gateway IP appears in the bottom window.

10. Click the DNS tab.

11. Select the radio button next to Enable DNS and enter the DNS server IP addresses that you want to use.

12. Click OK. You can ignore the Bindings, Advanced, and NetBIOS tabs.

13. On the Network screen, click OK to save your entries and exit Network configuration.

14. Close the Control Panel.

15. Reboot the Windows computer.

Once you have rebooted, the network functions will be available to you. Other machines on the network will not show up in the Network Neighborhood folder unless you are running Samba, but you will be able to use the network's Internet connection from this machine, as well as FTP and Telnet.

A Word About Samba

Samba is a useful program that allows UNIX/Linux machines to share files, directories, and printers with Windows 95/98 machines. Essentially, it presents itself as a Windows NT file server and allows your Linux machine(s) to appear in the Windows Network Neighborhood folder. Samba makes file sharing between Linux and Windows simple and easy to do.

Corel Linux has integrated Samba functions into File Manager in an effort to make the connection between Samba and the network almost seamless. We discuss Samba in detail in Chapter 24, "File and Print Sharing." If you want to add a Windows computer to your Linux network, you should investigate Samba; it makes the daily use of the network much simpler.

Adding a Macintosh to the Network

The procedure for adding a Macintosh to your network is similar to that for adding a Windows machine:

1. Click the Apple menu icon at the top-left corner of the screen.

2. Select Control Panels | TCP/IP from the drop-down menu. The TCP/IP dialog box appears, as shown in Figure 20-2.

3. Choose Edit | User Modes and switch to Advanced or Administration to get the most access.

4. Click the pop-up menu at the top of the User Modes dialog box.

5. Select Ethernet for network type and Manually for method.

6. Enter the appropriate information as requested.

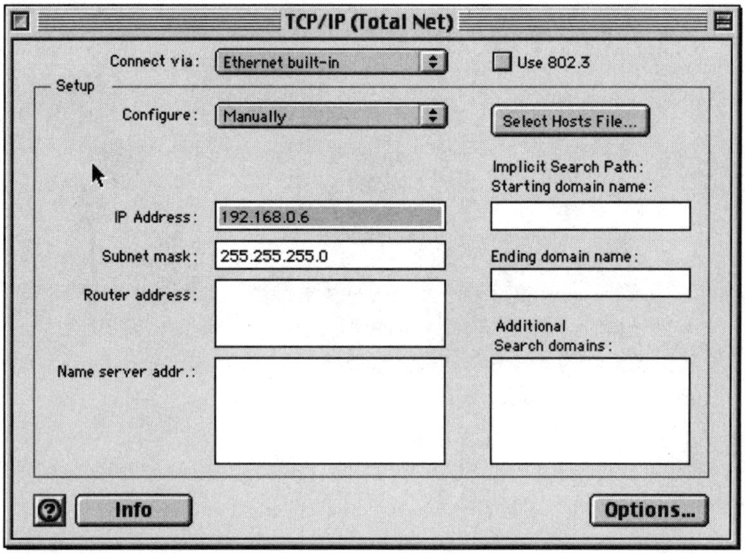

FIGURE 20-2 Macintosh computers can be added to your network as well

DNS: The Domain Name Service

When you set up your network, you used the /etc/hosts file to associate IP numbers with machine names. This is suitable for a small local network, but think about all the millions of IP numbers used by computers attached to the Internet! For associations on this scale, /etc/hosts is simply inadequate. This is why the Domain Name Service, or DNS, exists. DNS is a program that allows computers to query other computers for the IP numbers that correspond to a given computer name.

When you connect your network to the Internet, you need to make sure that each machine on the network knows where to find at least one Domain Name Server. Normally, you'll get this information from your Internet Service Provider; however, in Chapter 27, we explain how to set up and run your own DNS server, should you be so inclined. The address for each DNS server goes in the file /etc/resolv.conf. This file should look something like this:

```
search <domain name>
nameserver qqq.xxx.yyy.zzz
nameserver qqq.xxx.yyy.zzz
```

where <domain name> is the name of your domain (for example, yourisp.com), and *qqq.xxx.yyy.zzz* are the IP addresses of each name server you want to use. You can enter as many name servers as you want, but two is standard.

On Windows and Macintosh machines, you'll enter the DNS information in the network setup dialog boxes you used to add those machines to the network.

DHCP

As we mentioned earlier, the Dynamic Host Configuration Protocol, or DHCP, is used to allocate IP numbers "on the fly." Using DHCP requires both a server and a client; we discuss running a DHCP server in Chapter 27. Here we discuss running the DHCP client.

The DHCP client daemon, dhcpd, is the program that connects to a DHCP server, obtains an IP number, and configures the local network device based on that number. To run dhcpd, you need only issue the command

`/sbin/dhcpd`

Optionally, you can specify the name of the network device where you want the obtained IP address to be bound; the default is eth0.

 If you prefer to use the Control Center, you can select Network | TCP/IP and specify "Dynamic IP."

You can also configure dhcpd to run at boot. Simply link /etc/init.d into your default runlevel, and dhcpd will automatically start when you boot the computer.

CHAPTER 21

Adding and Removing Software

No matter what kind of operating system is being used, every computer user needs to manage software on an ongoing basis. Managing software can be as simple as checking for upgrades or as complex as installing a new operating system. New software is constantly flooding the store shelves and the online file archives, and existing software is upgraded nearly as often. Just keeping up with what's new and available for your platform can sometimes be a daunting task.

As we discussed in Chapter 1, "Why Linux, and Why Corel Linux?," software for Linux computers is usually *free*—even though you may pay for it, as you paid for your copy of Corel Linux. Remember the snappy statement we used in that chapter? It's common for free software folks to say that the concept is "Free speech, not free beer." In this context, *free* means that the software is licensed under the Free Software Foundation's General Public License (GPL) or something similar. Software released under the GPL has its code available, and anyone talented enough to do so can write patches and release them.

The Corel Linux License

Your Corel Linux distribution contains software released under a variety of licenses. While most of the software included in the distribution is licensed under the GPL, some of the programs have more restrictive licenses. Corel recommends that you consult the online documentation that accompanies each program in the distribution to see the license under which it is released. In general, non-Linux programs (WordPerfect, Netscape, and Bitstream fonts, for example) are probably released under a more restrictive license than the Linux components. Always check licenses before sharing programs with friends or coworkers; you may be able to do so under some licenses, while others grant you permission for only a single personal copy.

Corel Linux is released under a number of different licenses. The code written by Corel is released under one of three licenses: GPL, LGPL (Limited GPL), or CPL (Corel Public License). The CPL is a slightly modified version of the license used by Netscape for its Mozilla open-source project. KDE portions of Corel Linux are released under either the GPL or the QPL (Qt Public License, which affects some of the code components of KDE).

Anyone can download and use free software, as long as whatever cost is associated with the program is paid. It's important to remember, though, that free software comes without any guarantees. If it doesn't work, there's not much you can do about it except hunt around on the Web to see whether there's a fix. That said, much of the free software available for Linux computers is extremely well made and comparable—in some cases, superior—to its commercial counterparts.

A good example of the best of free software is a graphics program called The GIMP (GNU Image Manipulator Program). The GIMP serves more or less the same purpose as Adobe System's immensely popular Photoshop program, which retails for several hundred dollars per copy. Photoshop and The GIMP share many of the same functions, and it's nearly impossible to tell from a final version what program was used to create a given image. If you look at The GIMP and what can be done with it, it's hard to believe it's free. (The GIMP is free in both senses: it's covered by the GPL and it's downloadable at no cost. See `http://www.thegimp.org` for downloads and more information.)

> **NOTE** *Much of the available downloadable software is* shareware. *Shareware is software that the owner permits you to download free of charge; if you use it and like it, you're supposed to send a small fee to the developer. Some shareware has an annoying opening screen that reminds you that your version is unregistered; this type is often called* nagware. *Other shareware is time limited and will no longer operate after the time period has expired (usually 21 or 30 days from first installation); this type of shareware is often referred to as having a* time bomb. *Finally, you may find shareware that includes only a partial set of the program's full capability; this is a* demo *version, irreverently called* crippleware. *When you register your shareware, if it has one of these reminder functions, you'll receive a key to turn off the function and change your program to a fully functional version. Register your shareware; it's the decent thing to do.*

Due to Linux's tremendous leap of popularity in the last few years, a number of commercial software manufacturers have created, or are in the process of creating, Linux versions of their software; Corel, for example, will soon release a Linux version of the popular WordPerfect Suite 2000. Some of these programs are competitors of other free products; some have no free analogs; and still others are mainstays of the business world in their Windows, Macintosh, or commercial UNIX formats. The choice of software on your machine is entirely up to you; the possible array of selections is growing monthly.

Do Your Homework

Most of the more common pitfalls in software installation and configuration can be avoided with one simple procedure: read the documentation that comes with the software. When you are installing from source code, this documentation almost always comes in a file called README. If you are installing a binary package, such as Debian or Red Hat packages, look on the software's Web page for documentation; there will usually be a clear link to it. The documentation that accompanies software is written by the people who wrote the software and is generally considered to be the authoritative source for information and answers.

The importance of reading the documentation cannot be overstated. In fact, techie culture has spawned a specific acronym that addresses this very situation. If you ask someone a question that is already answered in the documentation, you may be told to *RTFM*. This stands for *Read The [expletive deleted] Manual*. It should not necessarily be taken as a hostile suggestion but as a reminder that you already have the answer to your question.

In this chapter, we discuss general procedures for installing and upgrading software. We expand our discussion of Corel Update, the Corel Linux package management tool, covered briefly in Chapter 14, "Corel Linux's Graphical Administration Tools," and the Debian package manager upon which it's based. In this chapter, we also discuss the Red Hat Package Manager, RPM. Finally, we cover the process of installing software directly from source code—it's not nearly as intimidating as it sounds.

Corel and Debian Package Management

In Chapter 14, we discussed the Corel Update tool, which is the Corel Linux package management program. While it is not our intent to reprint that discussion in this chapter, we do want to talk a little bit about the Debian package management tools upon which Corel Update is based. You may find that you want to use both Update and dpkg to manage your software.

What Is a Software Package?

Throughout this chapter, we use the term *package* to describe the software that you're installing. A piece of software is usually more than a single program; it may be several programs that work together, even though they appear to the user as a single item. A piece of software also usually includes such things as documentation, configuration files, various data files, and so on. When these items are all bundled together, they become a package.

Obtaining, bundling, customizing, and installing each file by hand is an overwhelming and tedious process. Therefore, bright programmers conceived of packaging so that users could download one file guaranteed to have all the ancillary programs needed to install the main program. *Package management systems*, such as the Debian and Red Hat package managers, soon followed; packages in these formats are configured to make software installation even more automated than before.

Debian Packages

Since Corel Linux is based on the Debian Linux distribution, it follows that Debian packages are often the most trouble-free way to install new software on your computer. Debian packages can be found in the Debian FTP archive at `http://www.debian.org`.

dpkg

The simplest, and possibly the most useful, of the Debian package management programs is `dpkg`. This is a basic command-line tool that installs, uninstalls, and upgrades software packages. It is simple to use, though you must be logged in as root to use it.

To use `dpkg`, first log in as root or assume superuser privileges (see Chapter 12, "User Space and User Accounts") and open a terminal window. Type the following to install a package:

```
dpkg -i <name>_<version>-<build>.deb
```

Debian Package Naming Conventions

In general, Debian package names are formatted as

```
<name>_<version>-<build>.deb
```

Thus, a package name like

```
foo_1.1-2.deb
```

means that this package is the second *build* of the `foo` program's version 1.1. The build number identifies each unique compilation of the source code by the developers; in general, you don't need to worry about builds until you get into quite advanced levels of software updates. (See Chapter 22, "Administering Services," for a more detailed explanation of builds and when you need to worry about them.)

and type the following to remove a package:

```
dpkg -r <name>
```

You will receive output that resembles that shown in Figure 21-1. When removing a package, you need only give the name of the package; you do not need to supply the version number, build number, or .deb suffix. The package name remains the same after installation, simply without suffixes. (This is one reason to keep track of packages you have installed.)

If you are using `dpkg` to install a newer version of a program that's already been installed, `dpkg` simply upgrades the existing package instead of reinstalling from scratch. If you are using `dpkg` to remove a package that has installed files required by other programs, those cross-utilized files will not be removed unless you use the `--purge` option, as in

```
dpkg -r --purge <name>
```

If you use the `--purge` option to remove cross-utilized files, you may find that programs relying upon those files no longer operate properly. Use `--purge` with care.

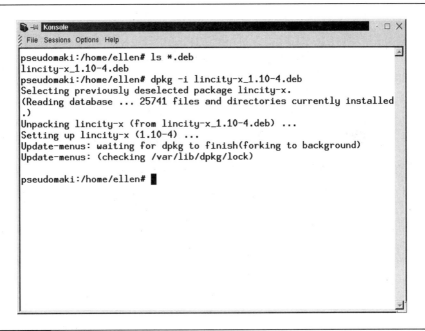

FIGURE 21-1   Use dpkg to install Debian packages from the command line

dselect

The dselect program is a *front end* to dpkg. Like dpkg, it is invoked from the command line; unlike dpkg, dselect is a full-screen, menu-driven program. The graphical interface provides a friendlier initial appearance to the user, from which derives the term *front end*.

Use the various menu options in dselect to install, remove, and upgrade packages. You can also use dselect to browse a list of packages available for installation and to see what is currently installed on your computer. In fact, dselect works in a fashion quite similar to Corel Update; the only difference is that dselect is not X-based (not graphics intensive and is operable from a command-line prompt). This can be quite handy if you're having trouble with the X Window System, or if you simply want to use a program that is lightweight and quite fast.

Open dselect by typing **dselect** at a command-line prompt. As shown in Figure 21-2, you'll be presented with a menu of items:

■ Access

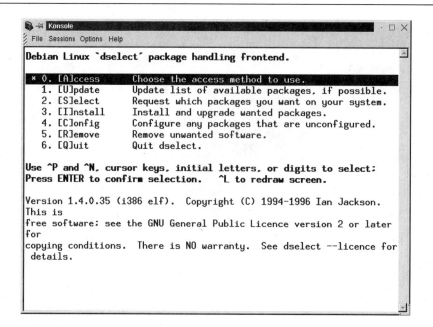

FIGURE 21-2   dselect provides a friendlier interface to dpkg

- Update
- Select
- Install
- Config
- Remove

Each item has an explanatory note. Make your selection using the arrow keys or typing the item's menu number, and then press ENTER. That item's menu appears; make selections until you have completed the installation procedure.

You can use dselect to install packages from local media, such as CD-ROMs or your local hard disk, across a network, via FTP or HTTP, or any other storage device.

Red Hat Package Management

Along with the Debian package managers and the Corel Update program, your Corel Linux installation includes RPM, the Red Hat Package Manager. RPM is similar to `dpkg` in that it provides a simple interface to installing binary packages. RPM, however, provides an extended set of options that allows for advanced dependency checking, version tracking, and package querying. These are advanced options that scan your installed programs to determine whether you have already installed a version of this program or whether you have files installed that conflict with the needs of the package you are going to install. RPM also has options that allow for the installation and compilation of source code packages.

Since Corel Linux is based on the Debian Linux distribution and not the Red Hat distribution, you should approach the installation of Red Hat packages with a

RPM Package-Naming Conventions

RPM packages have a particular naming convention that is slightly more complicated than the Debian naming structure described earlier. Each RPM package is named like this:

```
<name>-<version number>-<build number>.<architecture>.rpm
```

Thus, `gnucash` (a money management program) has the package name

```
gnucash-1.2.5-1.i386.rpm
```

This shows that the name of the package is `gnucash`, the version number is 1.2.5, the build number is 1, and the architecture is i386; this is the Intel 386 architecture. i386 packages also work on 486 computers and all versions of the Pentium processor.

Once the package is installed, you need refer only to the package's name. Thus, if you wish to uninstall `gnucash`, you simply need to issue the command **rpm -e gnucash**.

bit of caution. There is no danger involved—if a Red Hat package is incompatible with your system, the installation will simply fail—but you should not get the impression that Red Hat packages are always perfect substitutes for Debian packages.

> **NOTE** *We don't mean to imply that Red Hat packages are unreliable: in fact, they're quite the contrary. However, Red Hat packages are built on the assumption that they will be installed on a Red Hat Linux system, and that assumption leads to certain configurations that are not always compatible with non–Red Hat Linux distributions. Not every Red Hat package is incompatible with a Corel Linux system, and not every package is compatible. Try it out; you can't hurt your system by trying to install an* `.rpm`*. But, if you have the choice between a Red Hat package and a Debian package, try the Debian package first.*

RPM is a command-line program and, like `dpkg`, must be used from the root account or with superuser powers. To install a Red Hat package with RPM, type the following at a command prompt:

```
rpm -i <name>-<version number>-<build>-<architecture>.rpm
```

To upgrade a Red Hat package, type the following at the command prompt:

```
rpm -U <name>-<version number>-<build>-<architecture>.rpm
```

RPM commands are case sensitive, so be sure to type them exactly as printed.

> **NOTE** *For the preceding two commands, it is often useful to append* `vh` *to the command-line flags, as in* `rpm -ivh <etc.>`*. This causes RPM to operate in* verbose *mode, which causes it to print system messages on the screen, and to show installation progress by printing a row of # characters across the screen, as seen in Figure 21-3. The addition of* `vh` *can give you a better idea of what's happening as the package installs; however, you'll only see system messages if the installation fails (hopefully you won't see them often).*

To uninstall a Red Hat package, type the following at the command prompt:

```
rpm -e <name>
```

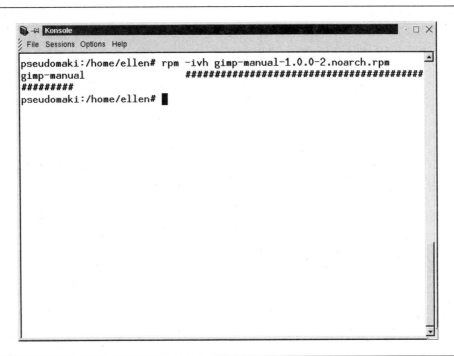

FIGURE 21-3   Run RPM in verbose mode to track the installation's progress

RPM keeps a database of all packages that are installed on the system and allows you to query that database to see if a particular package is installed. You can also query an uninstalled package to see what files are included in it and whether it requires the installation of other files or packages to function properly. You can invoke these options with the command

```
rpm -q <name>
```

Issuing this command will output the full package name if the package is installed on your system.

Append various options to the q in order to get more specific information:

- **-a** runs the query action on all installed packages. The output contains full package names for every package you have installed on the computer.

21

- **-f <filename>** Identifies the package containing <filename> and runs the query action on that package (useful for libraries and other required files that aren't the program itself).

- **-p <packagename>** Performs the query action on the named uninstalled package. You will need to know the full package name for this operation. You can also use flag options to tell RPM which information you want to have displayed when you query packages. The following flag options are technically called the Information Selection Options:

  - **-i** This flag produces output containing basic package information, such as the name, release number, size, and description.

  - **-l** This flag produces output containing a full list of all files contained within the package.

  - **-s** This flag produces output describing the current state of all files within the package.

  - **-d** This flag produces a list of all files within the package that are documentation files, such as manual pages or README documents. (This is especially useful before you install the package.)

  - **-c** This flag produces a list of all files within the package that are configuration files, which you may need to edit after installation so that the programs operate properly.

> **NOTE** *As with many other commands issued in the shell environment, these flag options can be used in combination. To use more than one when you issue an rpm command, simply place all the flags you wish to use together, as in rpm -qils. RPM will return all the output requested at one time; see Figure 21-4 for a sample.*

As you can see, RPM is a powerful tool with many options. If you want to learn more, consult the RPM HOWTO document at http:// www.linuxdoc.org or the full documentation at http://www.rpm.org. You can also view the manual pages already installed on your Corel Linux system by issuing the **man rpm** command at a command prompt.

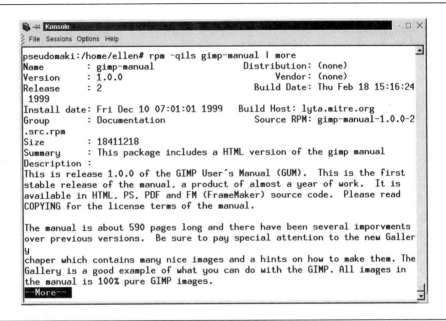

```
pseudomaki:/home/ellen# rpm -qils gimp-manual | more
Name        : gimp-manual              Distribution: (none)
Version     : 1.0.0                          Vendor: (none)
Release     : 2                          Build Date: Thu Feb 18 15:16:24
 1999
Install date: Fri Dec 10 07:01:01 1999   Build Host: lyta.mitre.org
Group       : Documentation            Source RPM: gimp-manual-1.0.0-2
.src.rpm
Size        : 18411218
Summary     : This package includes a HTML version of the gimp manual
Description :
This is release 1.0.0 of the GIMP User's Manual (GUM).  This is the first
stable release of the manual, a product of almost a year of work.  It is
available in HTML, PS, PDF and FM (FrameMaker) source code.  Please read
COPYING for the license terms of the manual.

The manual is about 590 pages long and there have been several imporvments
over previous versions.  Be sure to pay special attention to the new Galler
y
chaper which contains many nice images and a hints on how to make them. The
Gallery is a good example of what you can do with the GIMP. All images in
the manual is 100% pure GIMP images.
--More--
```

FIGURE 21-4   If you combine several RPM query flags, you'll get more output

> **NOTE**   *A program called Alien converts packages from the RPM to the Debian format, and vice versa. Alien is included with Corel Linux; use* **man alien** *to see the various options available. Be aware, though, that the Alien development team warns that its program is now, and probably always will be, experimental software. There is no guarantee that a given package will convert cleanly with Alien.*

Installing Software from Source Code

When all else fails and you just can't locate a Debian or Red Hat package for the program you want to install, you can always install directly from *source code*. Source code is the set of raw instructions that the programmer writes while coding the program. Most Linux programs are written in the C or C++ language, or some combination of the two. These source code files must be *compiled*, or activated, before they can be used. Fortunately, this is usually not too difficult.

21

There are no constant procedures for creating and distributing source code files. Practices vary from one package to the next. What we describe here are the most common practices and should help you get started at the very least.

Source code packages are usually found in the form of *tarballs*, or compressed archives produced by the archiving program `tar`. Tarball package names usually look like this:

```
foo-1.0.tar.gz or foo-1.0.tgz
```

Either the `tar.gz` or the `.tgz` extensions indicate tarred source code packages that are also compressed with the compression program `gzip`. Like Debian or Red Hat packages, source code packages contain code files, documentation, and configuration files.

When you begin to work with source code packages, you should be in a directory where you have some disk space to work with. The resulting files from the decompression of a tarball can be quite large, and your home directory may or may not have enough space to contain them. We like to work with source code in the /tmp directory.

Once you have the tarball in an appropriate directory, issue the following command at a command prompt:

```
tar xvfz <filename>
```

This command decompresses and extracts the files from the tarball. You should see a list of filenames scroll up the screen. Now, if you issue the directory listing command `ls`, you'll see a new subdirectory with a name somewhat resembling the name of the package you just untarred.

Change to that new subdirectory with the command

```
cd <directory name>
```

and do another directory listing with `ls`. Look for a file named README or INSTALL or something similarly imperative. Read this file and follow the directions contained within it. You will find the specific practices used by the package creator in that file; only the documentation contained in that file is truly and completely authoritative for that package.

In general, though, the process of installing from source code involves three steps:

1. *Configure the package.* This is usually done by running a script called `configure`, `configure.sh`, `configure.pl`, or something similar. (The exact name of the script will be given in the README file or its equivalent.) This script runs a few simple tests on your system to ensure that you have certain necessary files installed, that certain directories already exist, and so forth. It then creates a file called Makefile.

2. *Build the package.* Do this by typing **make** at the command prompt. `make` is a standard interface to `gcc`, the GNU C Compiler (the program that runs the code instructions to create the program). Using Makefile as a blueprint, `make` runs `gcc` on the various source code files and then links the resulting output into an executable binary file.

3. *Install the package.* When the package has finished compiling, type **make install** at the command prompt. This moves the binary into its proper directory and also installs any configuration or documentation files that were included in the package.

At this point, the package is installed. You may have to edit or create a configuration file before you can run it, though. The only way to know if you have to do this is to read the documentation. If a directory called /doc is in the package, move into that directory and read all the relevant files.

Once you have the package installed and working, there is no further need for the source code unless you decide that you need to recompile the package. You can do whatever you want at this point: delete the source code or keep it. If you want to keep it, consider moving it into the /usr/src directory. This directory is the default UNIX location for source code packages, and keeping source code in /usr/src is a good habit to develop.

Other Types of Installation

Some software packages come with their own methods of installation. This is fairly unusual, but it's not wholly unheard of. In these cases, you can usually run a script or program that will handle the entire installation process. Again, read the available documentation and follow the instructions provided within it.

CHAPTER 22

Administering Services

The remaining chapters of Part IV deal with administering services of various kinds. Linux can function both as a server and as a workstation; in this chapter, we describe some of the many server functions that are available to you. We also present some information that may help you decide which services are appropriate to run on your own system. At the end of the chapter, we discuss the general procedure for installing services.

In general terms, a *service* is a function that is available to one or more *clients*. Clients are machines or programs that make use of the service as part of their function. For example, the e-mail programs most people run on their desktop computers connect to a *mail server* to actually send and receive the e-mail messages. With few exceptions, most servers are in the business of transporting and/or distributing information. Some services, such as the X Font Server (xfs), are essential for almost all Linux systems; others, such as the Domain Name Service or DNS, covered in Chapter 20, "Networking," are generally run only on fairly sizable networks.

Servers can serve a small local network, such as an NFS server that makes shared disks available within an office, or they can serve the entire world, such as a World Wide Web server that provides Web pages to anyone connecting from the Internet. Most services, though, have no inherent limitation on who can be served. It is up to the administrator to define the terms of access.

To some extent, the decision about which services to run is an individual one. You should select services based on what you need or want your computer to do; each person's needs are slightly different. A single user using her system for workstation-type tasks, for example, could probably get away with a fairly minimal suite of services, whereas she would need to run a number of major services if she were providing network connections to various other computers.

You may be tempted to run a lot of services just because you can (hey, we all fall into this trap). Unless you're doing this because you want to learn all about systems administration, we don't recommend running services just because you can. Each service runs constantly and consumes a portion of your system resources in terms of CPU time and memory. Unless you have a super-fast and powerful computer—and sometimes even if you do—running certain services can make a noticeable difference in the speed with which your computer operates. Our advice is to run only those services that are necessary for the smooth functioning of your system. If you run a minimal configuration, you can always add necessary services later.

What Kind of User Are You?

The easiest way to figure out which services you should run is to figure out what class of user you fall into. These "classes" are not formally defined in any way—they're simply a way to think about how different types of people use their computers. You'll get slightly different definitions of these types of users, depending on whom you ask, but here is a general breakdown of Linux users.

Home Users

Home users use their computers primarily for simple productivity tasks: letter writing, bookkeeping, schoolwork, and Internet access. If this describes you, you can probably get by with a minimal installation of services. Corel Linux does install a suite of services by default; if you wish to shut down some of these services and regain that portion of system resources, you can probably turn off NFS (Linux file sharing), Apache (the Web server), C News (the news server), and Samba (the Windows file-sharing device). You need not add any new services to your system.

 If you are running a home network with several machines, we do recommend that you retain NFS and Samba if you plan to share files between machines (and you will, since it is far simpler than any other file transfer method for a local network).

Office Users

Office users cover a wide range of territory. In general, office users perform the tasks of the home user (productivity, Internet, perhaps a little bit of solitaire) but also need to use more intensive applications that handle document and image processing, file sharing, and print sharing. Offices may even want to run their own small Web server to publish corporate Web pages to the world. In an office environment, you'll probably want to run NFS, Samba, and Apache to fill your service needs.

Power Users

Power users are a special breed. A power user is someone who needs a specific set of computing services to perform a given specialized task or set of tasks. Power

users demand a lot from their computers and generally know what they need.
(If you are a power user, chances are much of the material in this book is already
familiar to you, and you know precisely what services you want to run.) Power
users should read the chapters on the specific services they require, to see if there
are any differences between the Corel Linux implementation of those services and
the versions they may be accustomed to running.

Autodidacts

An *autodidact* is a person who is self-educated—a person who enjoys teaching
himself new things and who is using Corel Linux as a vehicle to learn about
UNIX, Linux, or any of the software that runs on these platforms. Autodidacts are
usually experimenters and should read the chapters on the software they wish to
run to learn its basic configuration options. This provides a good starting point for
further experimentation; just be careful. Autodidacts get pretty good at rescuing
their systems from crashes—don't ask us how we know!

Installing Services

The procedure for installing services on a Corel Linux machine is much like the
procedure for installing software, in that specific installations will vary from
service to service; but the general procedure is the same.

1. Install the software.

   You can install a service from a package or from source code. The
   procedure for installing new software is described in Chapter 21, "Adding
   and Removing Software."

2. Configure the software.

   This is the tricky part—configuration can vary widely between programs
   and ranges from simple to enormously complex. Generally, it involves
   editing (and, in some cases, actually writing) one or more configuration
   files. It may also require some system adjustment, such as creating or
   editing various environment variables.

> **NOTE**   *In the case of packaged versions of service software, many of these
> configuration requirements may be performed automatically during
> installation. As always, read the documentation included with the package
> before you install it. Basic configuration options are described in the
> chapter related to each type of service.*

22

3. Configure the system.

You'll need to place an initialization script in /etc/init.d and create the appropriate symbolic links in the desired /etc/rcX.d directory (where *X* is the appropriate number for the directory you want), so that the service can be started by `init`. See Chapter 18, "Runlevels and the Boot Process," for more information. If the service is something more properly handled by `inetd`, you'll have to configure `inetd` to start the service; this is described in detail in Chapter 25, "INET Services."

NOTE *Many packaged versions of software will install initialization scripts automatically. After installing a package, it's always a good idea to check the /etc/init.d file to see if a script has been added, before you go to the bother of adding one yourself.*

In most cases, you're ready to start the service at this point. It is a good idea to do a few tests to determine if everything is running properly; simply demand something of the server to see if it delivers the proper information. If it's working, you can let it run in the background. If it's not, you can attempt to correct the problem.

Removing Services

You may find that you've installed a service you never use, or you may simply want to remove some of the services installed by default so that you have more system resources available for the programs that you do want to run. Removing services is even simpler than installing them.

1. Remove any references to the service from system scripts.

If the service starts from `init`, go to the directory /etc/init.d. If you know that you will not use the service again, you can delete the file that contains the script that executes the given service.

However, you may want to use the service later; in that case, you won't want to remove the script from /etc/init.d. You simply need to delete symbolic links to the service in the /etc/rcX.d directory, where *X* is the number of the runlevel directory in which the symbolic links are located. In this case, the `init` scripts will not run because they are not contained in the startup files for that runlevel. You can always add the symbolic link back to the runlevel directory later, and the existing script will be called at startup.

If the service starts from `inetd`, you will need to remove entries referring to the service from /etc/services and /etc/inetd.conf. See Chapter 25 for more information on configuring these files.

2. Decide whether or not you want to delete the program.

   In general, we recommend that you leave services installed, although not running. This makes it easier if you eventually decide that you want to run that service. If you know that you won't want to run a Web server, for example, you can delete Apache from your system. In the event that you do want to run it in the future, however, you'll have to download a new version and install it from scratch.

CHAPTER 23

Mail Services

Electronic mail is the driving force behind the Internet's rapid popularization during the last few years. For some people, e-mail is the sole reason to get access to the Internet. They don't care about Web pages, newsgroups, or file transfers; they just want easy, instant mail service.

True to the Linux model that we've explained throughout this book, Corel Linux gives you a couple of options when it comes to handling your mail. Most Corel Linux users will use a standard POP (Post Office Protocol) mail client such as Kmail, which we discussed in Chapter 9, "Using the Internet with Corel Linux." Others will want to set up a system to handle incoming mail connections directly on their Corel Linux computers, using either `exim` or `qmail`, the two mail transport agents included with the Corel Linux distribution.

Do You Need a Mail Transport Agent?

As with a number of the other services we discuss in this part of the book, we begin this chapter by explaining some of the reasons you might *not* want to run a mail server. We don't do this to be discouraging but rather to save you a good deal of time and trouble in dealing with complicated software that you don't really need. Also, when it comes to networked services, remember that you aren't operating them in a vacuum. A single misconfigured server can cause huge headaches for system administrators all over the world, when they have to deal with output from your servers. So, for the sake of your own sanity—as well as the sanity of others—it is worth giving some thought to exactly how you want to handle networked services, such as electronic mail.

If you already have a mail server at your disposal, such as one at your Internet Service Provider or through your work, use that. There is no reason to deal with the hassle of setting up and maintaining a mail server when someone else has already done it for you. In addition, an ISP or workplace mail server is likely to be more reliable, since it probably runs on a faster and more robust computer than you can afford to run at home. If you're going to use someone else's mail server, simply configure your mail reader as described in Chapter 9, and use that freely.

The only reason you need to run a mail server is if you are responsible for providing mail services to a number of other users. In this case, your Corel Linux machine will be the server to which other clients (and possibly other computers) connect to download their incoming mail and upload their outgoing mail.

| CAUTION | *If you run a mail server, you will be handling incoming mail connections, and there can be a lot of those. Consider the effect that these connections (one for each piece of incoming mail) can have on your network's available bandwidth, especially if your users are prone to sending and receiving lots of e-mail or participating in mailing lists with heavy traffic.* |

How a Mail Transport Agent Works

Internet electronic mail is handled through a protocol called *SMTP*, or *Simple Mail Transport Protocol*. Check out the following illustration of the mail-handling process. When you write an e-mail message, you do so using a program that's generally called an MUA, or *mail user agent*; this is Kmail or a similar program. You enter the text of your message and click the Send button; when you give this send command, your MUA alerts an *MTA*. This is the mail server program running on the machine that you specified when you configured your mail program's SMTP Server attribute. The MUA hands the message off to the MTA (and usually saves it to a Saved Messages or Sent Mail folder).

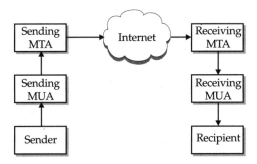

The MTA then makes an SMTP connection to the MTA at the receiving computer: that is, if you sent e-mail to Corel, your MTA would connect to the MTA at corel.com. The two MTAs engage in a dialog in which they establish such information as who the sender is, who the intended recipient is, and whether the recipient is a valid user at the receiving site. After all of this information is verified, the sending MTA gives the message to the receiving MTA. The receiving MTA then places the e-mail message in the recipient's mailbox. When the recipient fires up her own MUA, she will download and read the message.

Using exim

`exim` is one of the MTAs that comes with Corel Linux. It is installed by default when you install the Corel Linux operating system. `exim` should work reasonably well "out of the box," but you will need to do some configuration to get it just right for your personal needs and system.

The main configuration file for `exim` is /etc/exim.conf. This file is well-commented, and most options should be evident.

Do not change the order in which elements of the configuration file appear. exim *is very picky about this.*

You will need to set two options for exim to function. Locate the qualify_domain entry and modify it like this:

```
qualify_domain = <your.domain.name>
```

This appends your domain name to e-mail from local users. Next, locate the local_domains entry and modify it like this:

```
local_domains = <your.domain.name>
```

This specifies the domains that are considered "local."

When you have edited these two entries, you can start exim by issuing the command

```
/etc/init.d/exim start
```

When mail is received for a user on your system, exim places the message in the file /var/spool/mail/*<user>*.

 Encourage your users to clean out their incoming mailboxes frequently. Keeping messages in /var/spool/mail/<user> means that they are storing their messages in the directory used for everyone's incoming mail. Mail saved to specific folders is stored in the user's home directory and does not affect everyone else's e-mail.

exim supports a large number of configuration options. If you are interested in finding out more about the various ways in which you can configure and use exim, take a look at the documentation in the /usr/doc/exim directory. You can also consult the exim project's Web page at http://www.exim.org.

Using qmail

If you want to try an alternative to exim, we recommend qmail. (In fact, we recommend qmail over exim, because it has a couple of features that add a lot to the user experience.) If you did a server installation of Corel Linux and you selected mail services during the installation, qmail was installed at the same time that exim was installed.

If you have security concerns, run qmail. *It is a very secure program, so much so that there's a standing cash offer to anyone who can find a verifiable* qmail *security hole—and nobody has done so yet.*

qmail is a robust mail transfer agent. It's more configurable than exim and can handle mail traffic higher than anything you're likely to generate from your Corel Linux computer; in fact, qmail is used by several Web-based mailing list or e-mail sites, including Hotmail and Onelist/eGroups. There are security and reliability advantages to using qmail, as well. The downside to this wonderful program is that qmail can be rather tricky to set up properly. Luckily, Corel has designed a qmail configuration wizard that simplifies the process and reduces the complication to five screens of questions.

To configure qmail, you must be logged in as root or have assumed superuser powers. Once you have done that, click the Application Starter icon and select Applications | Servers | Mail Server Setup Assistant.

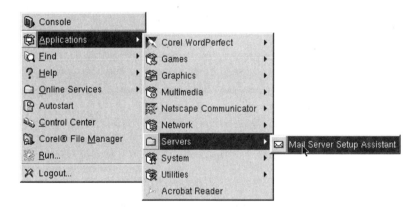

The Setup Assistant appears, as shown in Figure 23-1.

At this point, you'll need to decide whether you want to configure the server to provide mail via the POP or IMAP protocol. We suggest that you select POP; most e-mail clients, including Kmail, use the POP protocol. IMAP is also supported by most clients, but POP is a bit simpler to maintain.

Select the protocol you want to use, and click Next. On the next screen, as shown in Figure 23-2, enter your server's *Fully Qualified Domain Name,* or

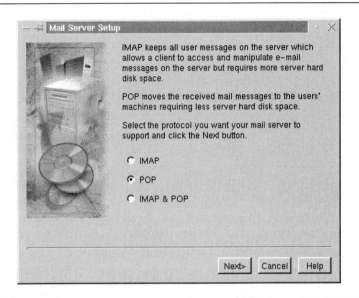

FIGURE 23-1 Use the Setup Assistant to configure qmail

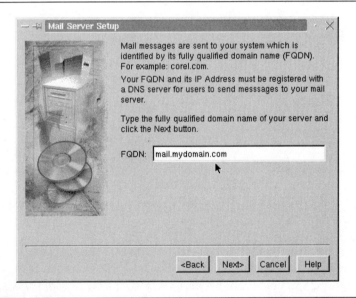

FIGURE 23-2 Enter your domain name on the second screen of the Assistant

FQDN. The FQDN is the full host and domain name of your computer, like mail.cnn.com. Click Next when you have finished.

| CAUTION | *The full domain name of this machine, plus the IP number that corresponds to it, must be listed in your domain's DNS record as a Mail Exchanger (MX). If this is not the case, contact your upstream ISP to configure the MX record properly.* |

The third screen of the Setup Assistant prompts you to enter contact information for the mail server, as in Figure 23-3. This information includes the user names of the people who will receive various status and error messages from qmail. You can enter the same name in all the fields, but you should never enter "root" (it's a security issue). The three contact fields are

- **postmaster**   Mail addressed to postmaster@yourdomain.com will be delivered to the user designated here.

- **MAILER-DAEMON**   Mail that, for any reason, cannot be delivered to its destination will be bounced to the user designated here.

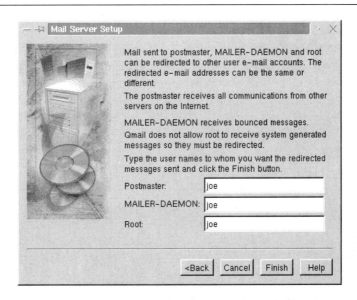

FIGURE 23-3   Enter contact information on the third screen of the Assistant

■ **root**   System status and error messages will be delivered to the user designated here.

Finally, enter the contact information and click Finish.

Assuming that everything went well, you'll see the confirmation message shown in Figure 23-4. Click OK, and you're finished. The mail server should start itself; if you open a terminal window and issue the command **ps aux | grep qmail**, you'll see several lines representing qmail processes.

As with any other service, you can stop qmail by issuing the command

```
/etc/init.d/qmail stop
```

Start qmail with the command

```
/etc/init.d/qmail start
```

and restart it with

```
/etc/init.d/qmail restart
```

You can reload the configuration files after editing them with the command

```
/etc/init.d/qmail reload
```

Once invoked, qmail runs constantly in the background. You can configure various options with the package; see the qmail Web site at http://www.qmail.org for the most up-to-date options and packages.

FIGURE 23-4

23

Instant Mailing Lists with qmail

One of the great user features of `qmail` is that your users can create their own small mailing lists, without your having to install the majordomo list-server package. To create a mailing list, simply create a file in your home directory called .qmail-*listname*, replacing *listname* with the name of the list (avoid periods or capital letters). In that file, enter all the e-mail addresses of the people you want on the list, save the file, and exit. You can now e-mail to all those people simultaneously by sending a message to *yourname-listname@yourdomain.com*.

For example, assume you want to create a `qmail` list for your high school buddies. Create the file .qmail-buddies in your home directory and enter the addresses of the people you want to add to the list—make sure to include yourself. Now everyone on the list can send messages to *yourname-buddies@yourdomain.com*, and the messages will be distributed to all subscribers.

Use these lists only for small groups of people. Individuals cannot subscribe and unsubscribe themselves—you have to edit the file—so it's not suitable for the kind of lists where people drop in and out. These are great lists for family and friends, though, or for announcements that you send regularly.

Setting Up a POP Server

Once you have your mail transfer agent set up, you need to give your users a way to retrieve their e-mail. If you allow remote users to telnet directly into your computer, they can simply use a local mail client such as `elm` or `pine` to read their mail. If they want to download mail to their local machines, though, you will need to set up a POP, or Post Office Protocol, server to let them use their local clients.

NOTE *If your users are using graphical mail readers, it's likely they'll need a POP client even if they use the same computer you do. Also, if you manage a network comprising computers running multiple operating systems, it's easy for clients using each of the operating systems to locate a compatible POP mail reader.*

To set up the POP server, you need to install the `ipopd` package. You can find this package at the Corel download Web site; use the Corel Update tool to locate, download, and install the package. `ipopd` is controlled through the `inet` service; see Chapter 25, "INET Services," for more information on `inet` and how it works. Once you have `ipopd` installed and operating correctly, your users should be able to download their e-mail directly from your machine.

 You will have to give your users the POP server address so that they can configure their mail readers correctly.

Other Mail Transfer Agents

A number of other programs serve the same function as `exim` or `qmail`, and they all emphasize slightly different features of the MTA function. We provide a partial listing here, describing the four most popular MTAs being used in the Linux community, and include Web sites where you can learn more if you're interested in running an MTA other than `exim` or `qmail`.

sendmail

`sendmail` is the "granddaddy" of Internet MTAs. Despite its reputation for being difficult to configure and maintain, `sendmail` is probably the most popular MTA in use today. Part of the reason for this popularity is that a number of client programs are configured specifically to work with `sendmail` in transferring electronic mail. However, it is common now for other MTAs to mimic `sendmail`'s behavior, making this less of a problem.

`sendmail` often comes preconfigured, and once you have it running, it should not be necessary to tinker with it much. You can learn more about `sendmail` at `http://www.sendmail.org`.

smail

`smail` was the first serious attempt to replace `sendmail`. It is much simpler to configure than `sendmail`, and it has some improved security features. Newcomer MTAs such as `qmail`, `exim`, and Postfix have caused `smail`'s popularity to decline somewhat, but it is still used by quite a few systems.

Learn more about `smail` from the FAQ for the USENET newsgroup `comp.mail.smail`, located at `http://www.sbay.org/smail-faq.html`.

Postfix

Postfix aims for performance and ease of administration, while still being fairly secure. The author claims to have taken some design ideas from Web servers, such as Apache, that allow the program to do more work while placing less of a load on the system.

Like `qmail`, Postfix also has support for filtering junk e-mail before it reaches your users. Learn more about Postfix at `http://www.postfix.org`.

CHAPTER 24

File and Print Sharing

One of the greatest advantages of having a networked system of computers is the ability to share resources over the network. Corel Linux offers a number of ways to share resources: you can share files among different computers without actually having to e-mail or transfer the document, or you can send documents to printers attached to other computers. This is especially helpful if you have splurged on one expensive printer, perhaps a color laser printer, and need to share that resource. In this chapter, we describe the mechanism behind sharing hard disks and printers and explain how to set up file and printer sharing on your own network.

File Sharing

File sharing is a convenient way to make documents available to a variety of users, all working in different locations and on different computers connected only by a local network. It is also a good way to customize your network with some machines specialized in function (gateway servers and database servers) and others less specialized but able to use the specialized functions as if they were local to each computer.

How does this work? Consider the example of our home network. We connect our home network to the Internet using an old 486 PC running Linux as the central network server. We also have a rather high-powered Linux workstation and a mid-level off-the-shelf Windows 98 machine as our primary personal machines. The Linux and Windows computers use the 486 as a gateway to the Internet, but they also use it as a way to share files with each other. When Joe, sitting at the Linux computer, wants to make a file available to Kate on the Windows machine, he moves the file into a directory mounted via the Network File System (NFS) from the 486.

Because that directory is NFS-mounted onto the Linux workstation, it seems as though the file is simply being moved into a local directory. In fact, the file is actually being placed on the 486's hard drive. This directory on the 486 is also shared with the Windows computer via the SMB service (Samba) and appears in the My Computer folder on the Windows desktop as a local directory.

> **NOTE**   *If you look up a shared directory in Windows Explorer, Windows labels it a "network (virtual) drive." You can deal with it just as you would a physical drive, though.*

24

The end result is that, once the file has been moved into the shared directory on the 486, it is available to all machines on the network just as if it had been physically copied to each hard drive.

Since the 486 is the central server, it is also the machine that receives our e-mail. Instead of using the POP protocol to download his mail messages individually from the ISP, Joe has saved a step. He has his mailbox file NFS-mounted from the 486 to the Linux workstation; when mail arrives at the 486, it triggers the "new mail" icon (a biff program, as described in Chapter 9, "Using the Internet with Corel Linux"). His mail program reads the messages just as if it were reading them from a local mailbox file. This saves him from having to transfer the mail from one machine to another.

Even in the smallest of home networks, like ours, file sharing can be a useful and efficient way of conserving resources and effort. Imagine the benefits on a larger network!

Sharing Files Linux-to-Linux

Sharing files among Linux systems is fairly simple. You simply export the files by listing them in the /etc/exports file and then issue the `exportfs` command, which mounts the files on the client machine. We discussed this procedure in depth in Chapter 13, "Disks, Drives, and File System Management," but it's helpful to review it when discussing file-sharing services.

Assume that you have a machine named *zeus*, which you wish to use as a file server. On zeus, you want to set up a directory that will act as a publicly shared workspace for documents. If your network is properly configured and running well, the first thing you'll need to do is to check that the `nfs-server` package is installed. Check the /etc/init.d directory to see if a script called `nfs-server` is there. If it isn't, use the Corel Update package management tool to download and install the package. Once `nfs-server` is installed, you can follow this procedure to get your directory installed:

On zeus's hard drive, create the directory to be shared.

1. To create the directory and name it /usr/public, issue the following command at a shell prompt:

   `mkdir /usr/public`

2. Change the file permissions on the directory.

You need to make sure that anyone on the network can read and write to files in this directory, so set the permissions with the command

```
chmod a+rw /usr/public
```

TIP

Learn more about chmod *in Appendix B, "A Compendium of Common Shell Commands." You can also change file permissions with File Manager if you don't want to use a command-line tool; this process is described in Chapter 12, "User Space and User Accounts."*

3. Edit the /etc/exports file.

To do this, you need to know the name of the machine to which the directory will be exported. To keep the Greek gods theme, let's call that machine *apollo*. Open the /etc/exports file in a text editor and add the entry

```
/usr/public apollo(rw)
```

Notice that no space appears between the end of the machine name and the opening parenthesis. The rw means that network clients will be able to read and write the exported directory. You could use ro instead, which would grant read-only access. If you don't use either variable, the directory will be read-only by default.

NOTE

The /etc/exports file contains a lot of configuration options, Read the manual page for exports (use the command **man exports***) for a full description.*

If you wanted to export the directory to more than one machine, you could list them in a single entry, as in

```
/usr/public apollo(rw) athena(rw)
```

You could also export the directory to the entire network with the entry

```
/usr/public *.local.domain(rw)
```

The * character is a *wildcard*, which will match any entry in that position.

4. Export the directory by typing **exportfs** at a shell prompt.

5. Check the `nfs-server` daemon. Issue the command

```
/etc/init.d/nfs-server start
```

The directory should now be exported and available for mounting on a client machine. Next, you need to configure that client machine (in this case, apollo) to recognize the shared directory.

1. Create a mount point.

A *mount point*, as we explained in Chapter 13, is simply an empty directory in which a given file system can be mounted. For this example, name the mount point /mnt/zeus. (Joe really wanted to call it /mnt/olympus, but there's a limit to the lengths we'll go for a bad pun.) For the simplest method of mounting a remote directory, issue the command

```
mount -t nfs zeus:/usr/public /mnt/zeus
```

Once you issue this command, zeus's /usr/public directory will be available on apollo, as /mnt/zeus, just as if it were a file system on apollo's hard drive. In other words, if you wanted to read the file called mythology, which exists on zeus in the file /usr/public/mythology, you'd have to open a text editor on apollo and view the file /mnt/zeus/mythology.

2. (Optional) Edit the /etc/fstab file.

However, if you want to automatically mount this exported file system every time you boot up apollo, you will need to add an entry to apollo's /etc/fstab file:

```
zeus:/usr/public   /mnt/zeus    nfs    defaults    0 0
```

Although you don't see them in the entry above, you should know that tabs appear between each component except the final zeros, which are separated by a single space. When you boot up apollo, all the file systems listed in /etc/fstab will be mounted automatically.

NOTE *If you boot up apollo, but zeus is not running or the network is down, apollo's boot-up procedure will delay while it tries to mount a file system that it can't find. This will not harm apollo, but the time lag can be irritating.*

One thing to be aware of is that you cannot re-export a mounted network file system. If you really wanted the /usr/public directory to be available on a third machine, you'd have to handle that on zeus; you couldn't export it directly from apollo.

Sharing Files Linux-to-Windows Through Samba

Life would be so much simpler if we could all share files among Linux machines and Windows machines just by using NFS. Unfortunately, that's not the case; Windows uses a different protocol to share files. That protocol, called Session Message Block (SMB), is not a protocol that Linux understands without some tinkering. Luckily for those of us with mixed-OS networks, there is a solution.

One of the greatest successes of the free software movement is a suite of programs called Samba. Samba allows Linux, and other UNIX-derived operating systems, to make use of the SMB protocol. It can also emulate certain functions of a Windows NT file server. Without Samba, it would be difficult to have true file-sharing capabilities across a mixed network.

Corel Linux makes extensive use of Samba, and the Samba package should have been installed when you installed Corel Linux. Just to be sure, check that the script /etc/init.d/samba exists. If it doesn't, use Corel Update to install the Samba package, either from your Corel Linux CD or from the Corel or Debian software distribution sites.

Once you have installed the Samba package, you need to edit the /etc/samba/smb.conf configuration file. This file is simply organized and is easy to read and edit. Lines beginning with a semicolon are comments (unlike the usual comment marker, #) and are ignored by the program when it runs. The file contains several sections, each beginning with a header enclosed in square brackets. At the very minimum, you'll need a [global] section and a section for each directory you want to share with the Windows machine. A minimal global configuration might look like this:

```
[global]
    workgroup = NETWORK
    server string = Zeus
    encrypt passwords = Yes
    update encrypted = Yes
    log file = /var/log/samba/log
    max log size = 50
    socket options = TCP_NODELAY SO_RCVBUF=8192 SO_SNDBUF=8192
    dns proxy = No
```

24

In this example, `workgroup` is the name of the workgroup that will appear in the Windows machine's Network Neighborhood folder. `server string` is the name that the server machine will have in its icon. `log file` is the name of the file where Samba will log its activity.

Now for each directory that you want to share with the Windows machine, you'll have to add a section to /etc/samba/smb.conf that looks like this:

```
[public]
      comment = public workspace
      path = /usr/public
      guest ok = yes
      writable = yes
      printable = no
      public = yes
```

This directory will show up as an icon labeled "public" in the Windows Network Neighborhood folder. To change the name of the directory, substitute the new name between the square brackets at the top of the entry. Repeat this entry for each directory that you want to share among the Linux and Windows machines.

At this point, you can restart the Samba server to make the changes take effect. Do so by issuing the following command at a shell prompt:

/etc/init.d/samba restart

To see these shared directories on the Windows machine once you restart Samba, you'll need to edit the Network settings in the Control Panel. Make sure that you have the correct Gateway and DNS IP numbers in the Properties settings of your network connection, and put the machine name and network name (usually NETWORK) on the Identification tab.

CAUTION *Windows 98 and later versions of Windows 95 use a password encryption program that makes life a bit more difficult for Samba users. In fact, it may require that you hack the registry a bit to get Samba working properly. Since we're not comfortable telling you to blithely go in and tinker with the Windows registry, we recommend that you read the Samba HOWTO document at `http://www.linuxdoc.org/HOWTO/ SMB-HOWTO.html`. In addition, you should read the ENCRYPTION.txt, Win95.txt, and WinNT.txt files in the Samba documentation. Samba does work with Windows 98; it just requires a bit more effort to get it working properly.*

For a far more in-depth treatment of Samba, the Samba development team recommends *Using Samba*, published by O'Reilly & Associates. Although the book was not written by the Samba team, its documentation is so accurate and exhaustive that the team has designated it the official documentation for the Samba package.

NOTE   *Samba may be configured automatically during the installation process. Check to see whether the various files described here are on your system, and edit them if necessary. Corel Linux uses Samba so that Corel File Manager can access shared drives on other machines. Even if Samba runs smoothly from installation, it's a good idea to understand how it works and to know where the relevant files are located.*

Sharing Files Linux-to-Macintosh with netatalk

Macintosh computers do not use the SMB protocol to share files. Instead, they use a protocol called Appletalk, which serves the same purpose. Samba doesn't work with Appletalk, so Mac users need another option. `netatalk` is a Linux server program that allows your Linux machine to communicate with a Macintosh using the Appletalk protocol.

To get `netatalk` working, you first need to install the `netatalk` package with the Corel Update tool (be sure to point Update to an FTP site that contains the application packages; try the Debian site first). Once you have it installed, you'll need to edit the configuration files found in the /etc/netatalk directory. These files are well-commented, and you should be able to figure out easily what you need to do.

TIP   *It's possible that you won't have to make any edits at all. Read through the file, and see if the comments direct you to change anything. If they don't, just leave the file as it is.*

When you have finished editing the `netatalk` configuration files, you can start the `netatalk` server by issuing the following command at a shell prompt:

```
/etc/init.d/netatalk start
```

Once the server is started, you should be able to communicate among the machines. See your Macintosh documentation for more information on using Appletalk correctly and for any changes you need to make to the network settings on your Macintosh.

If you need more information about `netatalk`, we suggest the `netatalk` HOWTO document located at `http://thehamptons.com/anders/netatalk/`.

Printer Sharing

As with disks and directories, it is possible to share printers over a network. This can be convenient if you have several computers but want to buy only one printer, for example. It's also convenient if you have one really great printer (perhaps a high dots-per-inch laser printer) and want to share it among the users on your network without having to dedicate a machine to the printer.

Sharing Printers Linux-to-Linux

Using Linux, it is possible to share a printer attached to the Linux machine with other Linux machines on the network. To make this work, you'll need to install your printer as described in Chapter 19, "Dealing with Hardware." Make sure that the printer is working properly and that you can print from the Linux machine to the local printer.

Once your printer is working properly, edit the /etc/hosts.equiv file by entering the names of the Linux machines with which you want to share your printer. Restart the printer daemon by issuing the command

```
/etc/init.d/lpd restart
```

Now you can set up the printer on a remote Corel Linux machine. Use the procedure described in Chapter 19, with one exception: instead of selecting the Locally On My Computer option, choose the Remotely On The Network option. You'll be prompted for several pieces of information:

- Printer Name: choose anything you like

- The hostname of the machine to which the printer is physically attached

- Network Type: select Unix

- Manufacturer and model of printer

When you've entered this information, click Finish. You should now be able to use that printer, provided your network is up and running.

Sharing Printers Windows-to-Linux

To print from a Windows computer to a printer attached to a Corel Linux machine,
you'll need to use Samba. To do so, you'll need to edit the /etc/samba/smb.conf
file again, as you did when you set up Samba. Find the section of the configuration
file that looks like this:

```
[global]
        workgroup = NETWORK
        server string = Zeus
        encrypt passwords = Yes
        update encrypted = Yes
        log file = /var/log/samba/log
        max log size = 50
        socket options = TCP_NODELAY SO_RCVBUF=8192 SO_SNDBUF=8192
        dns proxy = No
```

Add this entry to that section:

```
        printing = bsd
        printcap name = /etc/printcap
        load printers = yes
        log file = /var/log/samba/log
        lock directory = /var/lock/samba
```

Next, you need to add a section for the systemwide print options:

```
[printers]
        comment = All Printers
        security = server
        path = /var/spool/lpd/lp
        browseable = no
        printable = yes
        public = yes
        writable = no
        create mode = 0700
```

And add a section for each printer:

24

```
[ljet]
     security = server
     path = /var/spool/lpd/lp
     printer name = lp
     writable = yes
     public = yes
     printable = yes
     print command = lpr -r -h -P %p %s
```

NOTE *Depending on the kind of printer you have, the commands in the print command entry may be different. The preceding code block will work with a Hewlett-Packard LaserJet printer. You should always be able to print with the plain* lpr *command; to learn the various options that you can use with* lpr, *type* **man lpr** *at a shell prompt. In addition, you can name the printer whatever you want; we've called this one "ljet" because it refers to a LaserJet, but you could call it "HP" or "Fred" for that matter.*

Once you've made these edits, restart Samba with the command

`/etc/init.d/samba restart`

Configure the printer on your Windows machine as a network printer, using the Printers folder (Start | Settings | Printers), and you should be able to send files from the Windows machine to the printer on the Linux machine.

Sharing Printers Linux-to-Windows

If you want to print files from the Corel Linux machine to a printer attached to a Windows computer, you'll need a slightly different configuration. First, you need to configure printer sharing on the Windows machine.

1. Open the Network tool in the Control Panel.

2. Select the network component you use for the network (probably a network card).

3. Click the File And Print Sharing button shown in Figure 24-1.

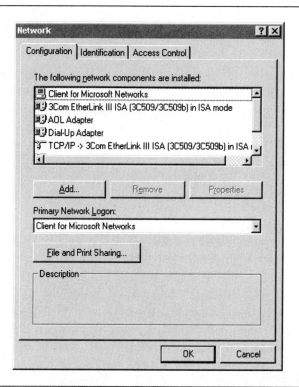

FIGURE 24-1   Begin configuring printer sharing with the Windows Network tool

The File And Print Sharing dialog box appears, as shown in the illustration.

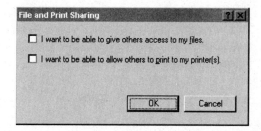

4. Select the I Want To Be Able To Allow Others To Print To My Printer(s)
   check box.

5. Click OK.

The dialog box closes and you are returned to the Network tool.

6. Click OK.

The Network tool closes and saves your settings.

Back on the Corel Linux machine, open the Control Center by clicking its icon in the KDE Panel.

1. Select Printers in the Control Center.

The printer configuration dialog box appears, as shown in Figure 24-2.

2. Configure the printer as a network printer.

3. To define the printer type, select Windows. This enables the Browse button.

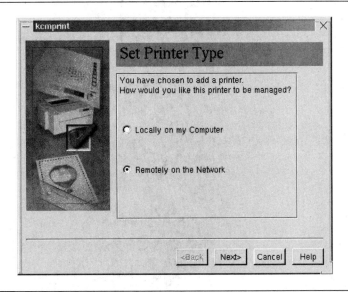

FIGURE 24-2   Use the Control Center to configure a network printer

4. Click the Browse button.

5. Search the Windows Network, and select the printer you want to use.

6. (Optional) Provide a username and password if prompted to do so.

These should be the same username and password you use to log into the Windows Network Neighborhood.

7. Click Finish.

The Printer Configuration dialog box closes.

8. Click OK.

The Control Center closes, saving your changes.

The Windows printer should now be available for your use across the network.

## CHAPTER 25

INET Services

If you plan on connecting your computer to the Internet and allowing other people to make use of resources on your computer, you need to understand how the `inet` daemon works. `inet` handles requests made to your computer from the outside world; examples of requests handled by `inet` are requests for FTP files or Web pages housed on your computer. With `inet`, you can configure your computer so that the servers responsible for answering those external requests start up and operate only upon demand. This saves you some network load and also provides a mild security benefit because you don't have a variety of communicable services running unattended.

inetd—The Master Network Daemon

A number of network services are placed under the umbrella of the `inet` daemon. `inet` runs at boot, like many other services described in this book. It "listens in" on certain ports, as defined in the /etc/services file, for incoming connections. When a connection is requested, `inetd` starts the appropriate service, which then handles the connection. (`inetd` does not handle the connections itself; it only directs traffic.) This reduces overall system load by causing certain services to run only when they're needed.

While a certain set of services is almost always run from `inetd`, other services can be added or removed to the /etc/services file so that they will be run from `inetd`. For example, `httpd` (the World Wide Web server) usually runs on its own and is started at boot time. If you don't use `httpd` frequently, though, you can add it to /etc/services and let `inetd` control it. This does slow the speed with which Web pages are served, but it conserves your total machine resources because `httpd` runs only when necessary.

| NOTE | *See Chapter 26, "Web Services," for a discussion of* `httpd`. |

`inetd` is controlled by two files. The /etc/services file associates port numbers with their respective services, while /etc/inetd.conf identifies the actual program that will be used when a connection is detected, the protocol to be used, and other information about the service. In this chapter, we look at both /etc/services and /etc/inetd.conf and discuss some of the services controlled by `inetd`.

Ports

In network-speak, a *port* (also called a *socket*) is a sort of subaddress that identifies which program handles any given incoming network connection. For example, FTP connections are almost always handled by port 21. When you use a client program to connect to an FTP server, the client is programmed by default to make a connection to port 21 on the server machine. When the server machine detects a connection request to port 21, it knows that the incoming request is an FTP connection and hands off that connection to the FTP program for appropriate handling.

While it is possible to assign nonstandard port numbers to services (for example, assigning port 5678 to FTP services), it is not a good idea; any client who tries to connect to your machine must know the unusual port number before a successful connection can be made. To continue the example, most FTP clients permit a user to specify a given port—but the user must first know what the port is. If the user does not know the special port, the FTP client defaults to port 21.

In addition to serving Internet purposes, many programs use sockets for inter- and intraprocess communications. A program may set up a socket for itself, or for another program, to pass information that may affect how the program itself operates. These programs also often use /etc/services to find the service they need in order to continue working properly.

The /etc/services File

As we previously noted, the /etc/services file is the file that associates port numbers with the services assigned to them. The /etc/services file is rather long; we encourage you to look at the file on your computer to familiarize yourself with the location of services on your machine. Here is an excerpt from an /etc/services file:

```
tcpmux      1/tcp       # TCP port service multiplexer
echo        7/tcp
echo        7/udp
discard     9/tcp           sink null
```

```
discard      9/udp         sink null
systat       11/tcp        users
daytime      13/tcp
daytime      13/udp
netstat      15/tcp
qotd         17/tcp        quote
msp          18/tcp        # message send protocol
msp          18/udp        # message send protocol
chargen      19/tcp        ttytst source
chargen      19/udp        ttytst source
ftp-data     20/tcp
ftp          21/tcp
fsp          21/udp        fspd
ssh          22/tcp        # SSH Remote Login Protocol
ssh          22/udp        # SSH Remote Login Protocol
telnet       23/tcp
```

The left column contains the name of the service. The center column holds the port number and the specific protocol needed to invoke the service: either TCP (Transmission Control Protocol) or UDP (UNIX Datagram Protocol). (Note that most of the services have entries for both protocols, to cover all the bases.) The final column contains other information about the service, such as an alias or a comment.

Some of the services in this file, such as FTP and Telnet, are used to interact with other networks, such as the Internet. Others, such as echo and discard, are primarily for the use of various internal programs.

The /etc/inetd.conf File

The primary configuration file for the inet daemon is /etc/inetd.conf. This file provides information to the inet program, which allows it to start its various subservers in the proper way. An excerpt from the /etc/inetd.conf file looks like this:

```
#
ftp        stream    tcp nowait    root      /usr/sbin/tcpd    in.ftpd
telnet     stream    tcp nowait    root      /usr/sbin/tcpd    in.telnetd
#
# Shell, login, exec, comsat and talk are BSD protocols.
#
```

```
shell     stream   tcp   nowait   root        /usr/sbin/tcpd   in.rshd
login     stream   tcp   nowait   root        /usr/sbin/tcpd   in.rlogind
#exec     stream   tcp   nowait   root        /usr/sbin/tcpd   in.rexecd
#comsat   dgram    udp   wait     root        /usr/sbin/tcpd   in.comsat
talk      dgram    udp   wait     nobody.tty  /usr/sbin/tcpd   in.talkd
ntalk     dgram    udp   wait     nobody.tty  /usr/sbin/tcpd   in.ntalkd
```

To better understand the construction of entries in /etc/inetd.conf, consider a single line in detail:

```
ftp     stream    tcp    nowait    root     /usr/sbin/tcpd    in.ftpd
```

- **ftp** The service being configured in this entry.

- **stream** This column defines the type of socket being used. Socket types generally correspond to the TCP and UDP protocols; most entries in /etc/inetd.conf use either the stream (TCP) or dgram (UDP) types (dgram is shorthand for *datagram*). Stream implies that the service deals with streams of data, as in the TCP protocol; dgram implies that the service deals with discrete message units, as in the UDP protocol.

- **tcp** This column defines the protocol being used; although you can generally extrapolate the protocol type from the socket type, /etc/inetd.conf requires that the protocol be stated explicitly.

- **nowait** The *flags* column, which generally applies to datagram sockets only; it concerns how datagram sockets manage connections that pass individual data units. You will usually see "wait" or "nowait" as the entries in this column.

- **root** The *user* column. The entry here is the name of the user under whose environment the program is run. If the user is "root," for example, the program runs with all the superuser's privileges. Some servers may be run as regular users, with lesser privileges, for security reasons.

- **/usr/sbin/tcpd** The directory path to the actual server's location. You need to specify this path so that inetd knows where to find the service being invoked.

- **in.ftpd** The actual filename of the server and the program that inetd invokes when the appropriate request is made. Without this, inetd won't know what to do.

Each service that you want to run from `inetd` must have an entry in the /etc/inetd.conf file. If there is no entry, the service won't run. Assume that you have decided that you don't want to handle incoming FTP connections at all; you could either delete the FTP entry (or entries) from /etc/inetd.conf, or you could simply comment them out by placing a # symbol at the start of those lines. After you have finished either method, you need to restart the `inetd` program. Do so by issuing this command at a text prompt (you must be logged in as root or have assumed superuser powers):

```
/etc/init.d/netbase restart
```

The `netbase` script starts a number of networking daemons, including `inetd`.

inet's Subservices

In this section, we take a closer look at some of the services controlled by `inetd`. Note that `inet` handles only a certain selection of what we might call "Internet services." Apache, the World Wide Web server, and INN, the USENET news server, are not traditionally handled through `inetd`. (Some people do run Apache via `inetd`, but there is a trade-off in terms of response time.)

Telnet

Telnet is the service that allows remote users to log into a shell account on your computer from another machine. Telnet is a TCP/stream service because it is interactive in nature. The program that handles incoming Telnet connections is `in.telnetd`, which runs on port 23 by default.

FTP

FTP is the service that allows files to be moved between machines. Like Telnet, it is a TCP service. FTP is controlled by the file `in.ftpd`, and its default port is 21.

rlogin and rsh

`rlogin` and `rsh` are services similar to Telnet. `rlogin` is actually almost identical to Telnet, in that it allows remote users to log into your computer and use the shell environment interactively. `rlogin` is handled by the file `in.rlogind`, and its default port is 513.

rsh, the *remote shell*, is slightly different. `rsh` allows commands to be executed on remote machines, without actually having to log into that machine. `rsh` is controlled by the file `in.rshd` with the default port 514.

ssh

`ssh` is a replacement for `rlogin`, `rsh`, and Telnet. One problem shared by those three services is with the security of passwords; under `rlogin`, `rsh`, or Telnet, passwords sent by users to authenticate their connections are sent across the network as plain text. This means that, if some unscrupulous soul is using a program designed to spy on network connections—a program called a *sniffer*—those passwords are easily captured and can be used to break into the computer being accessed. `ssh` solves this problem by replacing the plain-text connection with an encrypted connection; if someone is sniffing the `ssh` connection, the result will be an encoded password that cannot be used as found.

> **CAUTION** *`ssh` is not distributed with all Linux distributions because U.S. export laws prohibit the international distribution of certain types of cryptographic software. In the United States, `ssh` packages can be downloaded from `ftp://metalab.unc.edu/pub/packages/security/ssh`. The main `ssh` Web page is at `http://www.ssh.org`; check the FAQ page at that site to ensure that it is legal for you to download and use `ssh`. We do not want you to be arrested for illegal export of cryptographic software. Those users outside the United States and Canada may have access to other forms of cryptography usable for secure login connections; you ought to be able to find more information about what you can use via the ssh.org Web site.*

sshd, the `ssh` daemon program, is not always run from `inetd`. Frequently, it simply runs by itself, whether you invoke it manually or via an initialization script. However, it is possible to run `ssh` from `inetd`. Simply add this line to /etc/inetd.conf:

```
ssh    stream   tcp   nowait   root   /usr/sbin/sshd   sshd -i
```

Then add this line to /etc/services:

```
ssh    22/tcp    # SSH Remote Login Protocol
```

To force your remote users to use this secure method, it's a good idea to disable `rlogin`, `rsh`, and maybe even Telnet. Do this by deleting or commenting out those lines in /etc/inetd.conf.

> **NOTE**   *We discuss system security in more detail in Chapter 28, "User Management and Security." If you are planning to frequently use your computer on the Internet, or if you have a constant Internet connection such as a cable modem or DSL, we strongly encourage you to use some sort of encrypted login.*

CHAPTER 26

Web Services

In this chapter, we discuss Apache, the World Wide Web server. You probably won't run this server unless several users on your network expect personalized Web service; since your ISP probably provides space for your Web pages as part of your account service, you may choose to use those services instead.

 If you do not have a 24-hour connection to the Internet, via a cable modem or DSL, you won't want to run Apache; it assumes a constant connection to operate effectively.

However, if you do want to host your own Web pages, you will find Apache useful and appropriate. Even if you don't choose to run it, we suggest reading this chapter for a better understanding of how Web pages flow back and forth between your computer and the network of computers that makes up the Internet.

Apache: The Open Source Web Server

A number of Web servers run on Linux, and many of them are free software. Such programs as `boa`, `dhttpd`, `fhttpd`, `jigsaw`, and others are widely available, and many people do use them. However, one Web server towers above all other available servers: Apache.

Apache is the most popular Web server in the world, bar none. Apache's closest competitor, the Microsoft Internet Information Server (IIS), serves only about half the number of Web sites served by Apache. (If there were any doubt about the ability of free software to compete with its commercial counterparts, the success of Apache should lay that doubt easily to rest.)

Apache is included in your Corel Linux distribution, and in this section, we discuss the basics of getting a Web server up and running. However, you should be aware that Apache is a large and powerful program with an enormous number of configuration options. It is beyond the scope of this book to offer a full treatment of the subject; if you are interested in running a Web site for anything more than personal or rarely accessed use, you need to read the Apache documentation. This documentation is thorough and comprehensive and can be found in the /usr/doc/apache directory. Actually, anyone using Apache—even for small personal sites—should read the documentation. It's amazingly good.

Where Does Apache Come From?

Apache was originally produced by the Apache Group, a loose confederation of developers with a common interest in creating a Web server that would be released under Free Software Foundation licenses. In 1999, the success of Apache prompted the Apache Group to adopt a more structured organization, so they formed the Apache Software Foundation. As a not-for-profit organization incorporated under U.S. law, the ASF can act as a legal entity in such capacities as entering into contracts and managing donated funds.

You can learn more about Apache and the Apache Software Foundation at its home page: `http://www.apache.org`.

26

Basic Apache Configuration

The basic configuration file for Apache is the /etc/apache/httpd.conf file. You can learn a lot about this configuration file just by reading the comments contained within it; although—as the comments themselves state—that's not enough for a real understanding of Apache configuration.

NOTE *Corel Linux refers to the Apache Web server as* `apache`*. Some Linux distributions use the more generic name* `httpd` *instead. We use the two terms interchangeably.*

The /etc/apache/httpd.conf file includes a lot of lines, each configuring a different aspect of the server. You will probably never need to touch most of those entries, but you must edit at least one before you can use Apache:

```
ServerName    <new.host.name>
```

Replace `<new.host.name>` with the name of your machine. This name must be a valid name for your network; if you want the machine to be accessible from the Internet at large, it must also be a name that is registered in your network's DNS server. For testing purposes, you can use the name `<localhost>` to fill this space. You will be able to serve only Web requests coming from the machine you're working on, but it is a good way to find out whether Apache is running properly.

> **NOTE** *Ask your system administrator whether your machine name is located in the Domain Name Service. If you're the administrator, see Chapter 27, "Miscellaneous Network Services," for more information on configuring and running DNS, or finding someone who will host your DNS entry for you.*

HTML documents, the Web pages that will be served by the machine running Apache, should go into the /var/www directory. This directory is called the *document root*. For security reasons, Apache treats this directory as the root directory, and you should not be able to see the parent /var directory from the Web or any other directories above it in the machine's full directory structure.

> **CAUTION** *You can change the location of the document root by editing the DocumentRoot line in /etc/apache/httpd.conf, but we don't recommend it. It's easy to create an inadvertent security hole if you use a nonstandard document root directory.*

With the minimal setup provided by default, you should be able to start the Apache server and see the default home page contained in the file /var/www/index.html. This page was created during setup. If you want a more personalized page, you can edit that document with whatever HTML editor you prefer. For now, though, leave the default page for testing purposes.

Start the Apache server by issuing the following command at a shell prompt:

```
/etc/init.d/apache start
```

You must be logged in as root, or have superuser privileges, for this to work. Note that your network connection must be up and functioning to start Apache. If it's not, the Apache startup script will fail. Dial in with your modem, if you need to do so, before issuing the start command.

Now start Netscape (click the Netscape icon on the Corel Linux desktop) and type the following in the Location field:

```
http://localhost
```

You should see the default Apache home page, as shown in Figure 26-1; it begins "Welcome to Your New Home in Cyberspace!"

FIGURE 26-1 Apache provides this page as a way to test your configuration

Additional Configuration Options

While you can run Apache with the extremely minimalist configuration described in the preceding section, chances are that you'll want to tinker with various configuration files a bit more in order to meet your own Web server needs. In this section, we'll address various entries in these configuration files, showing how you might want to change each line to change Apache's behavior.

 We provide the various entries exactly as they appear in the default Apache configuration that's provided with your Corel Linux distribution; should you want to download and install a later version of Apache at some point, these lines may no longer work as described here. As always, read the documentation before you begin to edit configuration files.

/etc/apache/httpd.conf

The main configuration file for Apache is /etc/apache/httpd.conf. When you want to change something about Apache, chances are the entry you seek is contained in this file. Here are some of the major entries in /etc/apache/httpd.conf:

- **ServerType standalone**   This line specifies that Apache will be started on its own, rather than automatically started by `inetd` (as described in Chapter 25, "INET Services"). If you want to use `inetd` to start Apache, edit this line by replacing `standalone` with `inetd`; then edit /etc/inetd.conf to include a control line referring to Apache.

 The Apache documentation warns that `inetd` mode is "no longer recommended and does not always work properly." We recommend that you stick with standalone mode and start Apache by hand when you need it.

- **Port 80**   This entry says that Apache will listen for http requests on port 80, which is the default port for this service. You can change this to another port if you like, but everyone trying to access your Web pages will need to know the new port number to see your site. Many Web administrators use a port such as 8000 or 8080 as a test port, where they can view new pages before making them publicly available.

- **User www-data and Group www-data**   These two entries specify the user and group IDs under which the Apache process runs. For security reasons, it's not a good idea to have Apache run as root, since this would give root privileges to Apache-spawned processes. The `User` and `Group` items allow the server to be started as root but to run as another user with plain user privileges.

- **ServerAdmin root@localhost**   The ServerAdmin attribute of this entry specifies where Apache will send critical e-mail messages. If you want this e-mail to go to the root account on your machine, you can leave this line alone. If, however, you want to designate a certain user—such as your regular user account—as the recipient of Apache messages, change `root@localhost` to that user's e-mail address.

- **ServerRoot /etc/apache**   The ServerRoot attribute specifies the directory that contains the configuration and log files. While you can change this entry if you want, there's no reason to do so.

- **LockFile /var/run/apache.lock** This is the name of Apache's *lock file*. The lock file, among other things, tells the system that a current Apache process is running. While you should not change this entry, you should be aware of it; in the unlikely event that Apache crashes, you may need to remove this file before you can restart Apache. (Apache will create a new one when it restarts.)

- **MinSpareServers 5, MaxSpareServers 10, and StartServers 5** These three attributes determine the number of incoming connections that Apache will allow. When you start Apache, it *forks off* a number of subprocesses, with each subprocess being a sort of clone of the original process. Apache can handle as many simultaneous incoming requests are there are processes available. The number of servers that are started is determined by the value of the StartServers attribute. Thus, in the default case, when Apache is first started, it will create five server processes.

  The MinSpareServers attribute, however, determines that there must always be at least 5 more server processes than active processes; therefore, when an http connection is made to one of the active servers, Apache will create another process. This means that you will have 6 processes, though only 1 is active. Now assume that you get a flurry of incoming requests, and 10 requests arrive simultaneously. Apache creates 10 more server processes, so that 16 processes are running with 11 active. Once all those requests are served and the clients disconnect, there will be 16 processes with none active. At this point, the MaxSpareServers attribute takes over and kills off 6 of those processes, leaving only 10 processes in existence—that is, the value of MaxSpareServers.

  The default values given for these attributes are probably fine for most small installations. If you expect your Web server to be used only rarely, you might want to lower these numbers to conserve system resources. Likewise, if you expect Apache to be very busy, you may want to increase these numbers to increase the speed of the server; creating spare server processes takes time, and that time will be experienced as a delay by the user calling up your pages.

- **MaxClients 150** Related to the preceding values, the MaxClients attribute determines the maximum total number of server processes that can exist at any given moment.

- **#Listen 3000** The Listen attribute enables you to tell Apache to use another port in addition to the one specified in the Port attribute. This value is commented out by default and is therefore inactive. You may choose to uncomment the entry if you publicize the additional port as a way to access pages on your server; if you don't let people know that the port is available, though, having an additional port listened to by Apache doesn't accomplish anything.

These are only a few of the many attributes controlled in the /etc/apache/httpd.conf file. Carefully read the documentation for this file and choose the Apache configuration that provides the best mix of security, performance, and conservation of system resources for your specific Web server needs.

/etc/apache/srm.conf

Another Apache configuration file can be found at /etc/apache/srm.conf. This file allows you to define the *name space* of your Web site; instructions in this file relate to the locations of various files and Web pages within your site. While you probably won't want to change any of these defaults, you should be aware of a few items contained in this file; the most important ones are shown in the following list.

- **DocumentRoot /var/www** The DocumentRoot attribute defines the root directory for the Web site. The main home page HTML document should be placed here, and Apache creates the basic index.html file for your site in this directory upon installation. The server will never be able to access pages above this directory, even if requested directly by a client.

- **UserDir /home/*/public_html** If you allow your users to have personal Web space, this attribute defines where their Web pages should be located in their personal directories. For example, if Miranda creates the directory /home/miranda/public_html and puts her Web files in this directory, those files will be served by Apache in response to requests for http://www.yourdomain.org/~miranda.

- **DirectoryIndex index.html** This attribute specifies the name of the default file to serve. Thus, the page /var/www/index.html will be the page served when a user's client requests the page http://www.yourdomain.org.

/etc/apache/access.conf

The third Apache configuration file that you should know about is /etc/apache/access.conf. As its name implies, this file contains instructions for controlling access to your computer's file system.

> **CAUTION** *If you're disturbed by the phrase "controlling access to your computer's file system," perhaps you should not run Apache. That's an accurate description of how the World Wide Web works; when you call up a page with a browser, you're accessing that computer's file system. You don't have to run a Web server; you can find Web hosting services or free Web page providers to host your pages if you're not comfortable having external and unknown visitors to your personal machine.*

The structure of this file can be quite complex, and we won't get into it deeply. For basic purposes, you should be aware of one major thing in this file:

- **`<Directory /var/www>`** This entry should have the same value as the `DocumentRoot` attribute in /etc/apache/srm.conf. Double-check this entry to make sure you've closed a potential security hole.

You'll find many other access options in this file. We cannot stress strongly enough that, should you want to run Apache, you should read the Apache documentation in the /usr/doc/apache directory on the Apache CD for the proper syntax to use in /etc/apache/access.conf and the various options available. Yes, Apache is complicated, but for the amount of power and flexibility it provides, it's about as simple a program as it can be.

26

CHAPTER 27

Miscellaneous Network Services

Throughout this part of the book, we have discussed various servers that you might want to run on your Corel Linux computer—some simple and some quite complex. The last two servers that we bring to your attention are the Domain Name Service, or DNS, and the Dynamic Host Configuration Protocol, or DHCP. Running these servers is truly optional, and in fact, most people will not choose to run them since you can use identical services from your ISP.

However, it can be useful to run these services—especially DNS—if your upstream provider is slow or if you run a network of computers that can benefit from a shared local resource. Running these servers will release some of the bandwidth strain between you and your ISP. For many people, that strain is negligible; but for some folks, running a DNS server can speed IP address resolution significantly. In much the same way, those who have a large network but only a few IP addresses assigned to them may want to run a DHCP server to share those IP addresses upon demand.

 Even if you don't plan to run either of these services, we encourage you to read this chapter anyway. Your ISP runs identical services, and if you plan to use their DNS or DHCP services (which you do simply by logging in), it's useful to know how those services operate.

DNS: The Domain Name Service

In Chapter 20, "Networking," we discussed the Domain Name Service from the client side—that is, we discussed how to use other computers that provide DNS to look up IP addresses and names for still other computers on a network such as the Internet. In this section, we discuss DNS from the server side, describing how to set up a basic DNS server on your home computer.

How DNS Works

As described in Chapter 20, the DNS is the service that associates domain names with IP numbers. Any time a domain name is registered and paid for, the registrant is required to provide the IP number of at least one DNS server. This information becomes part of the master DNS directory, which is organized in hierarchical fashion.

When you fire up your browser and request a connection to a particular domain name, such as `http://www.corel.com`, your computer first makes a connection to the local DNS server and requests *resolution* to the corresponding IP number. *Resolution* is the process by which the DNS server searches its directory and finds a match. If the local server doesn't have the information in its directory, it passes the request to your upstream provider's DNS server. If that server doesn't have the information, the request is passed yet further up the line, and so on. Eventually, if no server in the chain has the information you need, the request will reach a DNS server that has a copy of the master DNS directory (a server owned by one of the agencies permitted to register domain names). The master directory server provides the correct IP number for the requested domain, and that number is passed back to the original DNS server your computer contacted. The miracle is that all this takes mere seconds!

27

> **TIP** *DNS servers retain information. If you look up* `http://www.`
> `userfriendly.com` *for the first time, it may take a second for the DNS server to resolve the address—perhaps requiring the help of upstream servers. The next time you want to read User Friendly, though, the DNS server will remember the IP number. (User Friendly is a great comic strip dealing with the travails of working at an ISP and running free software.)*

In ordinary practice, the process of DNS resolution isn't that complicated. Some DNS servers synchronize with the master directory servers at regular intervals, and most other DNS servers synchronize to their upstream servers regularly. In this way, DNS records propagate to many servers, and the number of upstream requests is thereby cut down.

Do You Need a DNS Server?

Most home users have access to the DNS servers maintained by their ISPs. It is quite rare for single users, who work on a single computer, to need to run DNS locally. Likewise, most office networks have DNS services available from their upstream service providers.

However, you might want to run a DNS server if you have a very slow provider and you want to take some of the load off your connection to the ISP, or if you have a slow connection to your ISP (less than a 33.6 modem on the ISP end). Also, if you are setting up services for a domain of your own, a DNS server might be useful if it is too unwieldy for you to maintain and synchronize local records by hand, using the /etc/hosts file (as described in Chapter 20).

Running your own DNS server won't make your ISP connection magically faster, but you will probably notice minor speed increases when you visit your usual Web pages.

Setting Up Your Own DNS Server

In this section, we describe the setup for a simple type of DNS server called a *caching server*. This type of server simply remembers every single hostname/IP number combination that it looks up, saving the results in a *cache file*. The server does not obtain records through synchronizing with other servers on a regular basis; it requests resolution when necessary and saves the results in the cache.

The Caching DNS Server

The caching DNS server is the simplest type of DNS server possible. It is usually used in conjunction with an upstream server, such as the DNS servers of your ISP.

When you configured your ISP account, as described in Chapter 9, "Using the Internet with Corel Linux," you entered two DNS server IP numbers in the configuration process. Those numbers, provided by the ISP, are the same DNS servers you'd use if you were to set up a caching DNS server.

Local clients, such as Netscape, will check your local caching DNS server first; if no record is found for the desired hostname resolution, the request moves to the upstream server at the ISP. If no record is found there, the request proceeds as described previously.

When a record is found at an upstream DNS server, the local caching server remembers the record by placing it into the cache file. The next time a local client requests that domain name, the IP number will be provided instantly, without having to contact any upstream DNS servers for the information. Over time, the cache file will develop into a fairly comprehensive list of your most commonly requested domain name records, and the majority of local client requests can be handled locally (reducing the load on the connection to your ISP).

Setting Up a Caching Server

Domain Name Services are handled by a program called `named`. This program is part of the Berkeley Internet Name Domain package, or BIND, which is contained in the Corel Linux distribution. If the BIND package isn't already installed on your computer, install it now. (See Chapter 21, "Adding and Removing Software.")

Once BIND is installed, you need to edit the /etc/named.conf configuration file. This file tells named where to look for information. For a caching DNS server, /etc/named.conf should look like this:

```
// generated by named-bootconf.pl

options {
        directory "/var/named";
        /*
         * If there is a firewall between you and nameservers you want
         * to talk to, you might need to uncomment the query-source
         * directive below.  Previous versions of BIND always asked
         * questions using port 53, but BIND 8.1 uses an unprivileged
         * port by default.
         */
        // query-source address * port 53;
};


//
// Boot file for name server
//
// type     domain      source     file
zone "." {
        type hint;
        file "named.root";
};



// Zone boot information and daemon options are kept in other files
// (autoincluded from boot.zones)
//
// Name server zone boot file
// See named(8) for syntax and further information
//
// type          domain          source          file
// (autoincluded from boot.options)
//
// Options for name server
// Use `bindconfig' to automatically configure this file
//
// type          domain          source          file
```

```
zone "localhost" {
      type master;
      file "named.local";
};

zone "127.in-addr.arpa" {
      type master;
      file "named.rev-local";
};

// Custom configurations below (will be preserved)
```

Note that the configuration files for named use a different style of comments than the ones you've seen in other configuration files. named uses C/C++ programming language style for its comments. Anything following the double slashes (//) up to the end of a line is a comment (where you've seen #, or a hashmark, before) as is anything enclosed between /* and */.

The line

```
directory "/var/named"
```

tells the server that all files named subsequently are located in the /var/named directory. Thus, when the file named.root is mentioned later in the configuration file, the full path name of the file is actually /var/named/named.root. The named.root file contains the addresses of the *root servers*, servers that contain copies of the master directories. This file changes over time, and you should maintain it regularly. (See the sidebar titled "Maintaining named.root.")

Now that you have an idea of what /etc/named.conf should look like, you need to add the IP addresses of your local server to the /etc/resolv.conf file. Put them in as the first entry. Thus, /etc/resolv.conf would look something like this:

```
nameserver 192.168.0.1
search mydomain.com
nameserver 110.2.15.15
nameserver 110.2.15.17
```

In this entry, 192.168.0.1 is the IP number of the local server, and the other two numbers are the IP addresses of two upstream servers. This way, any requests will be checked on the local server first, before going upstream for resolution if the local server doesn't have the correct information.

Maintaining named.root

You can see a copy of the current named.root file used by your upstream DNS server by using the `dig` command. Issue the command

```
dig @nameserver > named.root.new
```

where `nameserver` is the IP number of your upstream DNS server. Then copy your current named.root file to named.root.old by issuing the command

```
cp named.root named.root.old
```

and copy named.root.new to named.root by issuing the command

```
cp named.root.new named.root
```

When you restart your local DNS server, it will read the new named.root file. Do this on a regular basis, perhaps every month or two, to keep your local DNS server running smoothly.

27

NOTE *The new entry needs to be placed first in the list because you want your requests to check the local DNS server first. If you put it at the end, your requests will be checked through a remote server first, which negates the purpose of running a local server. Also, you need to use an IP number beginning with 192.168.x.x, because those first two sets of numbers signify that you are using a private Class C network.*

Now start the DNS server by running the initialization script:

```
/etc/init.d/named start
```

Place a symbolic link in the appropriate runlevel directory if you want the server to start at boot-up. See Chapter 18, "Runlevels and the Boot Process," for a discussion of runlevels.

DHCP: Dynamic Host Configuration Protocol

As with DNS, DHCP was covered from the client side in Chapter 20. Now in this chapter, we discuss how to set up a simple DHCP server. Not everyone needs to do this, but it's useful to have the information at hand should you find yourself with a plethora of computers and insufficient IP numbers to supply them all. It's also a good idea to read through this section even if you don't intend to run a DHCP server; you'll learn the process through which your ISP allocates IP numbers and thus know a bit more about what's happening when you log in.

How DHCP Works

The Dynamic Host Configuration Protocol server program allows you to reserve a range of IP numbers that can be assigned to clients. It also allows you to define a *lease period*, which is the period of time that a particular client may have a given IP number before it has to re-register itself with the DHCP server. As numbers are assigned to clients, a record is kept of each assignment, and that IP number is removed from the pool of available numbers. When a client's lease period expires, its IP number is returned to the pool and can be assigned to another machine.

Do You Need a DHCP Server?

As with many of the server programs we've described in this part of the book, it's a judgment call whether you need—or even want—to run the DHCP server. If you are running a single computer, you don't need it. If you have only a few machines on your local network, and you have IP numbers for all of them, you probably don't need DHCP. Small home or office networks are probably better off assigning IP numbers by hand.

> **NOTE** *Discussions of local networks recently have turned to the argument that there are certain benefits to using DHCP in small networks, especially if the network includes laptop computers that connect to the network on a regular basis. As laptops are moved from network to network (for example, from a work network to a home network or to networks in different offices), some people find it easier to use DHCP rather than having to manually reassign IP numbers every time the laptop is connected to a different network.*

If a large number of computers are attached to your network, or if you have more computers than available IP numbers, DHCP may carry quite a bit of benefit.

Setting Up Your Own DHCP Server

Once you've decided to set up a DHCP server, it's a simple process. However, DHCP is not part of the regular Corel Linux distribution; so if you want to use it, you'll have to download it first. You can find DHCP at any Debian FTP site; look for the DHCP packages at `ftp://http.us.debian.org/debian/dists/slink/main/binary-i386/net/`.

Install the DHCP packages using the process described in Chapter 21. If you got the packages from a Debian site, chances are pretty good that you got a Debian package, so use those instructions. You may need to install from source code if you got DHCP elsewhere or couldn't find a Debian package.

Once you have installed the DHCP packages, type `ifconfig -a` at a shell prompt. You should see several lines scroll up your screen, looking much like this:

```
eth0      Link encap:10Mbps Ethernet  HWaddr 00:C0:4B:D9:C4:62
          inet addr:183.214.19.43  Bcast:183.217.19.255  Mask:255.255.255.0
          UP BROADCAST RUNNING MULTICAST  MTU:1500  Metric:1
          RX packets:2875542 errors:0 dropped:0 overruns:0
          TX packets:218647 errors:0 dropped:0 overruns:0
          Interrupt:11 Base address:0x210
```

Check the third line to be sure that it says MULTICAST. If it doesn't, you'll need to recompile your kernel to make sure that you have enabled multicast support. Don't panic; you will not have to do this in most cases. If you do, just see Appendix A, "How to Compile a Kernel," for more information on kernels and how to recompile them.

Once you've run `ifconfig` and checked for multicast support, you need to do some configuring. To configure the DHCP daemon, DHCPd, you need to edit /etc/dhcpd.conf. This file may exist already, having been created during installation, or it may not. If you don't see that file, just create it in a text editor.

The most common setting for DHCPd is to assign IP addresses randomly in order of request from computers on the network. This maximizes IP number availability because no numbers are reserved, nor do sequential assignment processes need to be used. To set DHCPd for random assignment, edit /etc/dhcpd.conf so that it looks like this:

```
# Sample /etc/dhcpd.conf
# (add your comments here)
default-lease-time 600;
max-lease-time 7200;
option subnet-mask 255.255.255.0;
option broadcast-address 192.168.1.255;
option routers 192.168.0.1;
option domain-name-servers 192.168.1.1, 192.168.1.2;
option domain-name "mydomain.org";

subnet 192.168.1.0 netmask 255.255.255.0 {
      range 192.168.0.10 192.168.1.100;
      }
```

These settings cause your DHCP server to give the requesting client machine an IP address in the range 192.168.0.10 to 192.168.0.100. The DHCP server sets the lease time for each IP address at 600 seconds if the client doesn't ask for a specific time frame in the initial request for an address; otherwise, the maximum lease time permitted is 7200 seconds.

> **TIP** *If you want to set DHCP to give endless leases to the computers on your network, set both the default lease and the maximum lease settings to something immense, such as the number of seconds that elapse in ten years (315,360,000,000 seconds, if you were wondering). DHCP does not permit you to use an "infinite" setting, but it's highly unlikely that you won't reboot in ten years!*

The DHCP server also provides the client with a set of IP numbers that should be used for general network requirements:

- 255.255.255.0 should be used as the subnet mask.
- 192.168.1.255 should be used as the broadcast address.
- 192.168.0.1 should be used as the router/gateway address.
- 192.168.1.1 and 192.168.1.2 should be used as the DNS server addresses.

If you install DHCP from the Debian DHCP package, you'll find that the /etc/dhcpd.conf file contained with that distribution is quite thoroughly commented, and any additional options that you want to configure will be well described in those comments. We encourage you to read the file carefully to see what else you can do with DHCP. You'll probably need to delete, or comment out, a number of configurations that you don't need to use with your network.

Running the DHCP Server

Before you start the DHCP server, but after you've edited the configuration files, you need to create an empty file called /etc/dhcpd.leases. This is the file in which the server stores its lease information, and it is rewritten by dhcpd constantly. Create this empty file by issuing the command

```
touch /etc/dhcpd.leases
```

> **NOTE** *The* `touch` *command is used to update the* timestamp *on a given file; the timestamp is a bit of information that tells you the time the file was last accessed. It has the side effect of creating an empty file if the target file, named in the* `touch` *command, doesn't already exist.*

The last thing you need to do before starting the DHCP server is to edit the initialization script, contained in the file /etc/init.d/dhcp. In this file, you'll see the line

```
#run_dhcpd=0
```

If you want the DHCP server to start at boot-up, change the 0 to a 1 and put a symbolic link to the script in /etc/rcX.d, where X is the number of the runlevel at which you want DHCP to run automatically.

You can now invoke the DHCP server by issuing the command

```
/etc/init.d/dhcp start
```

At this point, you should test your server. Configure another computer on your network to obtain an IP address through DHCP. If you're using another Corel Linux machine to do this, follow the procedure described in Chapter 20. If you're using a different operating system on that other machine, follow the normal procedure used by that system for obtaining an IP address from a remote server.

If you receive an IP address successfully, you've configured DHCP properly. You can leave it running; it will restart at boot-up and run quietly in the background. If you do not receive an IP address, check that your request was correctly formatted. If it was, reconfigure DHCP using the previously described method. You may also want to check the DHCP HOWTO file or read the DHCP man page if you need more information.

CHAPTER 28

User Management and Security

Although it's tucked back here at the end of the book, this chapter covers an important topic for anyone running a Linux machine: computer security. Security issues range from your teenagers downloading copyrighted music files to someone in another country using your computer as a storage unit or as home base for further illegal entry into larger systems. A computer—with any operating system—can be compromised in many ways; luckily, with Linux, you have some simple ways to block most of those security holes.

You're unlikely to get an e-mail virus while using Linux. Most e-mail viruses are designed for people using Windows mail readers, like Outlook or Eudora, and are designed to attack the Windows OS. You should, of course, be careful when confronted with an attachment of unknown derivation, but you don't have to panic.

Why Does Security Matter to You?

It seems as if we hear something about computer security every day. Whether it's a new e-mail virus or the defacing of a large company's Web site, nobody can ignore the fact that hostile elements are on the Internet, just as in the "physical world." Just as you probably wouldn't leave the front door of your house open while you slept, neither should you leave your computer unguarded.

"Sure," we bet you're saying. "I can understand security concerns for governments and big corporations, but I'm just a person with a computer. I don't have any sensitive data." No, you probably don't have data as sensitive, say, as that which the Central Intelligence Agency must handle. But you may use a computerized money management program, trade stocks on the Internet, or use your home computer to work on documents from your job. Your data might not be globally interesting, but it's interesting to you.

Besides, the type of data you have is not usually why a *cracker* would want to get into your system. Crackers usually look for open systems (those that are easily accessed) that they can use as a base of operations while cracking other, more important, systems. This adds a layer of IP numbers to their activity and makes it look like *you* are doing the cracking, not them. Compromised computers are sometimes used as storage places for illegally obtained files, such as pirated software or music. And people sometimes break into computers just because they can.

NOTE
Many people use the term hacker *to refer to someone who breaks into computer systems. Though popular, the usage is incorrect: such a person is a* cracker, *or one who cracks into a computer illegally. A hacker is simply a clever and dedicated programmer who hacks away at computer code. Real hackers resent being lumped in with criminals.*

Don't panic, though! Linux is a very secure operating system as long as it's properly configured and managed. In this chapter, we introduce the basic concepts of Linux security and point you to further resources.

How Secure Do You Need to Be?

There is no such thing as perfect security, and trying to attain perfection will just waste time you could use to do more enjoyable things; increasing levels of security require increasing amounts of time and effort to achieve and maintain. So, before you decide what you need to do to secure your system, you should decide how secure you really need to be.

For example, if you're running Corel Linux on your home system and connect to the Internet via a dial-up connection with a dynamic IP number, and you aren't running any services on your machine, you can probably get away with a minimal level of security. However, if you're maintaining an FTP server for your company's confidential internal files, with a computer connected to the Internet by a T-1 line (a high-powered connection usually available only to corporate users), tight security is an absolute must. If you're a home user connected to the Internet via DSL or a cable modem, you'll probably need to be somewhere in between, depending on what you're actually using your computer to do.

CAUTION
Why do we keep talking about the Internet in a security chapter? Because the Internet is the single largest security risk for those of us who use it. Millions of computers, with millions of users connected via a decentralized web of electrons, present a great opportunity for mischief and not enough concern for security. A lot of crackers run mindless scripts that search the Internet endlessly, seeking computers left unguarded. Many of these scripts perform port scans, *a glance through your assigned ports to see if anything has been left open that can be exploited for illegal activity. You don't have to leave the Internet for good; you just have to be careful.*

28

Common sense applies here. The more access to the Internet you have, the more security you need. The more sensitive the information on your computer, the more security you need. If you're not sure, use more security measures than you think you need.

Physical Security

Before you think about any other kind of security measure, consider the most overlooked (and yet critical) aspect of computer security: physical access to the machine. If someone has access to your machine, he or she has access to your data. The most extreme example would be someone coming into your home or office and simply stealing the computer. Sure, that lacks a certain amount of finesse, but it is quite effective.

Another aspect of physical security to consider is that of rebooting. Someone could simply reboot the machine into single-user mode and then edit the /etc/passwd file to create an entrance to be exploited later. Alternatively, that same person could install special hidden software that leaves a *back door* open permanently; the cracker can then use this new entrance at leisure.

Regardless of the scenario, it's important to consider where your machine will be located and how it will be protected. In the work environment, it is not uncommon for servers to be kept in a locked room, to which only trusted administrative personnel have the key. If you're using Corel Linux on your only computer, that's probably not the best solution. However, you can do a couple of things to make tampering more difficult:

- If your computer can assign a password in the BIOS setup (most machines sold in the last few years do have this capability), do so. With password protection enabled, you will have to enter the separate BIOS password at boot-up.

- It is also possible to configure LILO to require a password. Place the following in the /etc/lilo.conf file:

```
restricted
password=<some-password-here>
```

Then issue the **/sbin/lilo** command. You should also change the permissions on the /etc/lilo.conf file so that it is not world-readable.

These methods won't stop a knowledgeable and determined cracker, but they will slow down a nefarious attempt to log into or reboot your computer.

Just remember that anyone with physical access to your machine has the potential to compromise it, so set your access accordingly.

Basic User Security

You need to consider your own users when you plan security procedures for two reasons. It is possible that one or more of your users may be using your system for illegal or nefarious purposes. More likely, it is possible that one or more of your users, through simple ignorance or carelessness, may create a weakness in your system that could be exploited by some external agent.

While you don't have to—and shouldn't—treat your users like criminals without any evidence to support that accusation, it's a good idea to enforce some basic security rules that are applicable to anyone using your system:

- *Require strong passwords.*   A password is "strong" if it contains numeric as well as alphabetic characters, is of mixed case, and is not a word that can be found in the dictionary. `w56ExP4` is a strong password; `mommy` is not.

- *Require secure network connections.*   If users log into your machine from remote locations, consider requiring them to use the `ssh` program instead of Telnet or `rlogin`. `ssh` uses an encrypted connection so that, if anyone is using a *packet sniffer* program to "listen in" on a user's connection, he won't get any useful information. A variety of `ssh` clients are available for almost all platforms; Kate regularly uses a Windows `ssh` program called SecureCRT to connect to remote Linux machines. (It's available at `http://www.vandyke.com`.)

- *Give users as little access to the system as possible.*   Always make sure that critical system files are not writable by ordinary users, and that administrative commands, such as the ones in the /sbin directory, are not executable by ordinary users. (See Chapter 12, "User Space and User Accounts," for more information on file permissions.)

- *Use quotas.*   A user account can be used effectively in an attempt to "lock up" the system, by consuming all available system resources. It's a fairly trivial task to write a script that will do one of the following:

  - Fill up all available disk space.

  - Fill up all available memory.

  - "Max out" the number of running processes that the system can handle.

You set quotas by editing the /etc/security/limits.conf file; read the comments included in that file for the exact syntax to use and the options available to you. Alternatively, you can use the `ulimit` function of the `bash` shell to set many of the same limits; type **help ulimit** at a command prompt for a description of this command, or see Appendix B, "A Compendium of Common Shell Commands."

In addition to enforcing rules and limits, it's a good idea to keep an eye on your users. While you should never snoop on them for no good reason, do check your log files periodically for unusual activity from any user account.

For example, you should keep track of bandwidth usage. One of the simplest ways to do this is to use the accounting functions of the `ipchains` command (we cover `ipchains` more fully in the section "ipchains," later in this chapter). Be alert for large transfers of data, especially at strange hours.

> **CAUTION** *Finding such transfers does not automatically mean that a user is doing something wrong. In fact, a considerate user may have used* cron *to schedule a large download for a time when general network usage is low, or you may have a user who works from home and regularly transfers documents and other files to her employer's computers. When in doubt, ask the user.*

If you suspect that one of your users is up to no good, or that a user's account has been hijacked by a cracker, you may want to monitor that user more closely before making an accusation. A number of tools are available for doing this, and a search of the Web using the string *+linux +security +tools* ought to turn up the latest versions rather quickly.

Be warned, though! There are ethical and legal implications to "spying" on users. Before you do anything out of the ordinary for your system, be sure you have just cause. To be safe, we recommend that you consult an attorney experienced with electronic issues to be sure you're on solid legal ground. We also recommend that you have a written policy available to all users that explains your security concerns and the steps you take regularly.

Passwords

One of the most common ways in which systems get compromised is through the /etc/passwd file. Because of the way in which this file is used, it must be kept world-readable. Therefore, it is fairly simple for any user to grab a copy of it. The encryption mechanism used to encode the passwords is not very complex; a variety of deencryption tools can be used to crack the weaker passwords. (One of the most popular ones checks the password list against a complete dictionary listing. Do not let your users use dictionary words as passwords, even if they're unusual or obsolete. You never know if the cracker is using the *Oxford English Dictionary*.)

It's often helpful to run a password-cracking program against your /etc/passwd file to determine any problem with weak passwords; this is an especially good idea if you have a large number of users or if you're concerned about your users' habits. One popular program for this purpose is John the Ripper, available at `http://www.openwall.com/john/`; if it finds a problem, you can alert the user before the problem goes further. Programs are even available that check passwords against the Crack libraries while someone is using `passwd` to change a password. In addition, you can find a Windows version of Crack at `http://www.l0pht.com`; if you are running a mixed-OS network, this is worthwhile.

If you are seriously concerned about password security, beyond simply setting up good policies and enforcing them, you may want to look into using *shadow passwords*. This is a scheme in which passwords are kept in an alternate location, where only privileged users can access the password file. The downside of this option is that a number of programs aren't compatible with shadow passwords and will need to be recompiled before you can use them. If you're interested in shadow passwords, read the documentation at `http://www.linuxdoc.org/HOWTO/Shadow-Password-HOWTO.html`.

Network Security

When most people think of computer security, they are usually thinking of network security: they envision a cracker using her wiles to compromise a system from the outside. This is the sort of thing that's involved when you hear of people cracking the Pentagon's system, for example. This type of crack is fairly rare, especially when compared to the exploitation of weak user accounts as described previously; however, outside cracking does exist and you should take some precautions to keep your entire network secure.

■ *Turn off unnecessary services.* Every service that you run is a possible mode of access into your system. If you're not using a particular service, such as Apache or `exim`, make sure the server is turned off. If you turn off a server, delete its entry from the /etc/services file or make sure it's commented out.

■ *Keep your software up to date.*   Many of the minor revisions of
various software packages are actually *security updates*, which fix newly
discovered weaknesses in the software that could be exploited to gain entry
into a system. A good source of information about security updates for
Linux packages is the Linux Weekly News journal, found at `http://`
`www.lwn.net`. The Weekly News staff compiles a list of all the updates
released each week and provides links to updated packages (including
the Debian packages—if they exist—that are most easily installed on Corel
Linux). The Linux Weekly News is posted each Thursday; daily updates
are at `http://www.lwn.net/daily`.

TCP/IP Wrappers

One of the most fundamental methods of keeping a Linux machine secure is the use
of *TCP/IP wrappers*—a rather simple system that lets you allow or deny access to
particular services based on the hostname or IP address of the requester. If, for
example, you are the target of a *ping attack* (a flood of ping requests intended to
overload your machine and shut it down; it's one form of a larger category called
denial of service attacks), you can set up a wrapper to block ping requests from that
particular IP number.

TCP/IP wrappers are configured using the /etc/hosts.allow and /etc/hosts.deny
files. These files are fairly easy to configure. The general syntax of an entry in one
of these files is

```
daemon list : client list [: shell command]
```

The `[: shell command]` portion is optional. So, if you type the entry `ALL :`
`ALL` in /etc/hosts.deny, access to all daemons would be denied to all clients unless
a specific entry for those clients was in /etc/hosts.

> **TIP**   *If you're concerned about remote user access to your computer, place the*
> `ALL : ALL` *entry in /etc/hosts.deny and make specific entries for each*
> *user in /etc/hosts.allow, as described above. The major drawback is that*
> *if a user is logging in from a different machine than usual, he won't be*
> *able to log directly into your machine because you have permitted only*
> *one particular IP address from him. He'll have to ask you to add the new*
> *machine into /etc/hosts.allow so that he can access his account.*

Suppose that you want to grant access to your FTP server to any user from the `foobar.com` domain. Place this entry in /etc/hosts.allow:

```
in.ftpd : .foobar.com
```

Note the leading dot before `foobar.com`. That indicates that anyone from that domain, regardless of the specific machine name, can access your FTP server.

This is a simple example, but these files can actually be used to create complex access patterns. To use TCP/IP wrappers most effectively, read the man pages for hosts.allow and hosts.deny (they're actually the same man page) to get a better idea of what wrappers can really do for you.

Other Kinds of Security

A number of other security tools may be useful to you. Anything more than a cursory description of each of these tools is beyond the scope of this book, but we mention them here in case you want to do some further research or your security concerns haven't been fully addressed yet.

ipchains

The same `ipchains` program that you used to set up IP masquerading in Chapter 20, "Networking," can be used to build network *firewalls*. These firewalls filter network traffic based on the source and destination of the packets in that traffic. For information on effective use of `ipchains` for security purposes, we recommend that you read several pieces of documentation:

- **The ipchains HOWTO** `http://www.linuxdoc.org/HOWTO/IPCHAINS-HOWTO.html`

- **The firewall HOWTO** `http://www.linuxdoc.org/HOWTO/Firewall-HOWTO.html`

- **The ipchains manual page** Type **man ipchains** at a command prompt

Proxies

Several programs are designed to filter content over network connections. Of these, `socks` and `squid` are probably the best known. A proxy generally runs on a network firewall computer and can be configured to permit or deny various sorts of connection requests depending on your needs.

■ `socks`, a general-purpose proxy, can be found at `http://www.socks.nec.com/`

■ `squid`, a Web proxy, can be found at `http://squid.nlarn.net/`

■ Other proxy programs are available from the Freshmeat archive at `http://www.freshmeat.net/appindex/daemons/proxy.html`

Intrusion Detection Programs

If you're not comfortable with your skill at reading logs, and you want to run a program that will alert you if your system has been compromised, we suggest that you check out one of these programs. Tripwire is probably the best known, but PortSentry also has a strong user base.

■ Tripwire can be found at `http://www.tripwiresecurity.com/`

■ PortSentry can be found at `http://www.psionic.com/abacus/portsentry/`

Security Auditing Tools

It's a good idea to have more than one set of eyes check your system for security risks. If you don't have a security-savvy friend to help you out—or even if you do—try one of these programs that will perform a security audit and give you a report of what's wrong or missing.

■ `check.pl` is a script written in the Perl programming language that audits file permissions. It can be found at `http://opop.nols.com`.

■ Nessus is a multifaceted security scanner that will check several different segments of your system. It can be found at `http://www.nessus.org`.

Encryption

One of the most common ways that ordinary users can help enforce security is to use an encryption program for their e-mail, USENET posts, and data files. The most popular of the encryption programs is PGP, for Pretty Good Privacy. However, PGP has run into some problems with software patents. We recommend that you try the GNU Privacy Guard instead; as with all products released by the GNU project (see Chapter 1, "Why Linux, and Why Corel Linux?"), it is completely open source and patent-problem free. GNU Privacy Guard can be found at `http://www.gnupg.org`.

 Because of software export laws, readers outside the United States and Canada may not be able to obtain "strong encryption" software developed in the United States. While we think that laws restricting the use and distribution of secure encryption software are counterproductive, the fact remains that it's the law in the United States. Do not lie to obtain encryption software, and do not break any laws to get it. Look for local alternatives if you're ordering from another country.

28

Further Reading

As you can see, security is a huge topic with many facets that are constantly evolving as new technologies become available. As with most technological topics, the Web is the best resource for up-to-the-minute news as well as the most recent releases of the software you use. We especially recommend that you check out these resources to learn more about security:

- *The Linux Administrator's Security Guide* This document, which is constantly being revised to keep on top of changes, is quickly becoming the definitive resource for Linux security issues. Find it at `http://www.securityportal.org/lasg`.

- *The Linux Security HOWTO* The HOWTO isn't quite as comprehensive as the Security Guide, but it's shorter and filled with excellent information. Find it, as you can find all HOWTO documents, at `http://www.linuxdoc.org/HOWTO/Security-HOWTO.html`.

In addition to these two documents, we recommend that you keep an eye on a few of the Web sites devoted to the latest in security news. You should know, though, that some security sites have a high "attitude quotient"; this usually derives from either an attitude of security paranoia or of "hacker pride." You may even find some sites hard to read since they're written in a particular typographic convention common among hackers, crackers, and *warez-traders* (people who seek and share illegal copies of copyrighted software). If you see letters mixed with numbers, phonetic spellings, and so on, you've stumbled onto one of these sites. The information is still good; it's just not written in standard English.

- `http://www.rootshell.com`
- `http://www.10pht.com` (that's a lowercase *L* and a zero)
- `http://www.cert.org`

We strongly recommend CERT's page. This is the page to check if you receive a virus warning via e-mail. All these folks do is security, and they do it extremely well.

PART V

WordPerfect 8 for Linux

CHAPTER 29

Using WordPerfect 8 for Linux

WordPerfect 8 is a robust and powerful word processor that is provided free of charge to the Linux community. If you purchased the boxed retail versions of Corel Linux (either Standard or Deluxe), Corel WordPerfect 8 is included on the CD. If you downloaded Corel Linux from the Corel Web site, you can also download WordPerfect 8 there; however, you will have to do some preinstallation to make sure that the word processor works correctly. See the section "Installing Corel WordPerfect 8 for Linux" for more information.

 Because of space constraints, we cannot go into great detail here about the many features of WordPerfect 8 for Linux. We recommend the WordPerfect for Linux Bible (IDG Books, 1999) to get the most out of this program.

WordPerfect's release for Linux marked a real watershed for the community. Sure, there are other word processors available for Linux users, but Corel's decision to port WordPerfect to the Linux platform was the first time that an office application—one already extremely successful for Windows—had been made available for Linux users. What does this mean? It means that Linux is one step closer to being a completely valid alternative office desktop solution. Without Linux versions of the same applications being used on Windows or Mac computers, Linux will remain on the sidelines. WordPerfect 8 for Linux is something we wholeheartedly endorse and suggest you try.

NOTE *In the interests of full disclosure, you should know that we are also co-authors of a book about the WordPerfect Office 2000 integrated office suite for Linux (WordPerfect Office 2000 for Linux: The Official Guide— another fine book published by Osborne/McGraw-Hill), and that we've also co-authored more than one book about Sun's StarOffice, another integrated office suite for the Linux and Windows platforms. We suggest that you check out both of those suites, as well as the Applixware suite, and make your own decision. We use both WordPerfect Office 2000 and StarOffice for our office application needs.*

What can you do with WordPerfect 8? The return question is, what do you need to do? You can work with plain text, create tables or columns, incorporate graphics or sounds, draw new images, or insert complicated mathematical equations. You can use built-in tools to check your spelling or grammar, convert text to hyperlinks, or work with multiple versions of the same file. We've even devoted a separate chapter (Chapter 30, "Creating Web Pages with WordPerfect 8) to the HTML publishing tools included with WordPerfect 8. In short, you don't lose any features by using the Linux version of WordPerfect; if you've never used WordPerfect before, you're in for a treat.

Installing Corel WordPerfect 8 for Linux

If you bought Corel Linux over the counter in a boxed version, WordPerfect 8 should have installed by default when you installed Corel Linux. (Wow—that was easy, wasn't it!) If you downloaded Corel Linux and WordPerfect 8 from the Corel Linux Web site, though, you won't be able to install WordPerfect 8 and have it work without doing some initial labor.

> **NOTE** *The problem lies with a particular set of libraries. The xlib6 package, which is installed by default with the boxed versions of Corel Linux, doesn't install by default with the download version. However, xlib6 is needed to run the downloadable WordPerfect 8. So you need to install xlib6 first.*

29

Here's what you need to do, direct from Corel.

1. Click the Application Starter icon and select Applications | System | Corel Update.

   The Corel Update screen appears.

2. Choose Options | Set File Sources.

3. Select Distribution Site, and unselect Custom Path(s).

4. Click OK.

5. When the File Manager screen appears, select the Available Software tab.

6. Choose File | Update Profile.

7. Choose Edit | Find.

8. Enter **lib6** into the search box (Figure 29-1) and click OK.

   Update should locate the package "xlib6 3.3.5-1.0.1 shared libraries required by libc5 X clients."

9. When the package is found, click the X in front of lib6 so that it becomes two arrows.

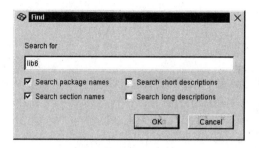

FIGURE 29-1   Use the Update tool to install the required libraries

10. Choose File | Upgrade/Install Packages.

The library will install automatically.

Once you've gotten the library installed, you can install WordPerfect 8. Open Netscape or File Manager and go to `http://linux.corel.com/ products/linuxproducts_wp8_download.htm`. Click the link called **Click Here To Continue With The Download Process** and follow the steps to download the package.

 You must download several files—and optional modules if you want to use language files that aren't U.S. English.

When you have downloaded the software (we suggest downloading all WordPerfect files into a separate directory), open a terminal window and issue the following command for each file:

```
gunzip <filename> ; tar -xvf <filename>
```

This will open each file and prepare it for installation.

When you've finished, you simply need to issue the command that starts the installation program. At the system prompt, type **./Runme**.

If you downloaded language modules, this is the time to install them; directions for module installation can be found on the Corel Web site. If you don't need language modules, WordPerfect 8 is now ready for use.

Working with WordPerfect Documents

Once you have WordPerfect 8 installed, you can begin to work with documents. WordPerfect has a fairly intuitive interface, meaning that you can usually figure out what a given button does without much trouble. (You can also hover your mouse pointer over any button for a moment to see a small pop-up label.) The main WordPerfect document screen, as shown in Figure 29-2, has a large area for the document being worked on and a variety of tools contained in tool bars underneath the standard menu bar.

> **TIP** *If you don't like the way that WordPerfect displays its options, choose Tools | Settings | Customize, or Tools | Settings | Display. In the Display Settings box, you can configure the various bars and icons to your heart's content.*

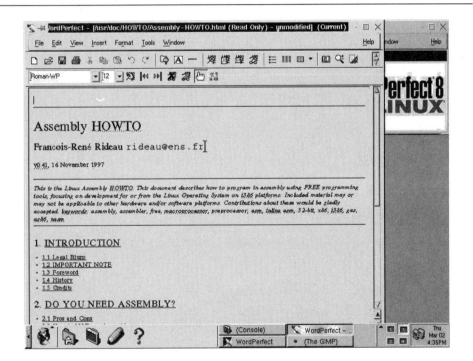

FIGURE 29-2   WordPerfect is laid out in an understandable manner

Opening a WordPerfect Document

Before you can begin to work on a document, you need to have one open. You can either create a new document or open an existing one, but you must have a document open to use the various WordPerfect tools. If you're connected to a network, you can open files from other machines in your WordPerfect window, as long as the file permissions are set to allow you to do so. Once the file is open, continue to the next sections, "Working with Text" and "Page Formatting," to learn how to work with the file itself.

Opening an Existing File

To open an existing WordPerfect file, choose File | Open. You can also click the Open File button on the tool bar. The selected document opens in the main area of the WordPerfect window, ready for you to edit or add material.

> **TIP**   *If you're not sure whether a particular file is the one you need, use the View menu command in the Open dialog box. You'll be able to preview the contents of a given file without actually placing a load on your system while the file is opened in WordPerfect.*

Creating a New File

If you want to create a new file, choose File | New, or click the New File button on the tool bar.

The new document appears in the WordPerfect window, with gray lines indicating the margins, as shown in Figure 29-3.

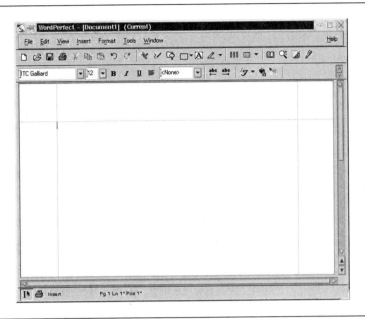

FIGURE 29-3 A new document is ready to be edited

Working with Text

At its most basic, entering text into a WordPerfect document is just like using a typewriter. Just click the mouse pointer inside the document to set the cursor point, and type away! We figure that you'll want to do a bit more than that, though. In this section, we explain how to set fonts, justify your text, set tabs, create lists, insert special characters, and use the unique QuickFormat tool. Again, we can provide only a basic introduction to these tools; they are far more flexible and powerful than we have room to show you here!

Fonts

A *font* is a particular set of characters that are designed to look good together. Fonts can be either fixed width, such as Courier, or proportional, such as Times. In WordPerfect 8, fonts are controlled with the Font Selector tool located at the left side of the property bar.

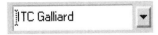

Click the arrow button in the Font Selector to see a drop-down menu listing all the font choices you have. (These are fonts that you've installed on your computer; if you don't see very many choices, you don't have very many fonts installed.) Select the font you want to use by clicking it. From the cursor point on, anything you type will appear in that font.

If you want to change the font of something you've already written, select the block of text to be changed by clicking and dragging. Then use the Font Selector to choose a different font. When you release the mouse button, the selected text's font will be changed to the new font.

To the immediate right of the Font Selector tool, you'll find the Font Size Selector tool.

This tool works in the same way as does the Font Selector, but it controls the size of the type rather than the font itself. Click the arrow button to see a list of available type sizes, and click the desired size to apply it to selected text or to affect all new typed data.

Alignment

Alignment is the process by which text is made to align on the page. Text can be aligned to the left margin, to the right margin, or centered. Left-aligned text will be *ragged* on the right margin, meaning that the ends of the sentences won't line up cleanly. Right-aligned text will be ragged on the left margin. In center-aligned text, both the left and right margins will be ragged.

You can also choose to fully justify your text, which makes it align with both the left and right margins. This is accomplished through changing the spaces between letters and words so that the lines of text align evenly along both margins. Justified text looks neat and clean; however, especially if you have a lot of long words, the added spaces can be jarring to the eye.

 WordPerfect offers two types of full justification: fully justified text is aligned along both margins, except for the last line; all-justified text is aligned along both margins, including the last line. Be careful with all-justified text, as that last line can get pretty ugly if it's a short line.

Left alignment is the most common option, and it's the default option in WordPerfect documents. If you want to change the alignment of a selected portion of text, select the text and then click the alignment button on the property tool bar.

A box will drop down with the alignment options; select the one you want, and the selected text will be reformatted accordingly.

Tabs

Tabs provide a shortcut for indenting text a fixed number of spaces. The default tab spacing in WordPerfect is five spaces; if you press the TAB key on the keyboard, the cursor jumps five spaces to the right. Note that the tab unit is a discrete unit and is not five actual spaces; you can't click in the middle of a tabbed space and enter more text. If you indent a line using the TAB key, and then position the cursor at the beginning of the text and press the BACKSPACE key, the text will move all the way back to the left margin, not back one space to the left.

Most of the time, the default five-space tab is sufficient. However, you may want to set your own tab spacing for some documents, especially if you're trying to format some text more attractively. To do so, choose Format I Line I Tab Set. The Tabs dialog box appears, as in Figure 29-4.

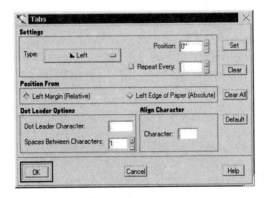

FIGURE 29-4   Define your own tab distances in the Tabs dialog box

In the Tabs dialog box, you can specify customized positions for your tabs—whether you want to define the position of a single tab or of a whole set of tabs—by using the repeat function. If you want your tabs to be preceded by a line of dots, for example, select the Dot Leader options. Click OK when you've made all your selections; the tab characteristics will apply to this document alone. You will have to redefine tabs for each new document unless you create a template with these tab spacings.

Lists

Anyone who does much writing, especially for work reasons, is familiar with bulleted and numbered lists. We've used both in this book; we use numbered lists for step-by-step processes and bulleted lists for various unordered information. WordPerfect 8 makes it simple to create both kinds of lists.

The basic process is the same for both lists. Choose Insert | Bullets & Numbering; the Bullets & Numbers dialog box appears, as in Figure 29-5.

Select one of the numbering or bullet styles in the window. You can choose from regular numbers or letters, several outline formats, or Roman numerals. If you choose

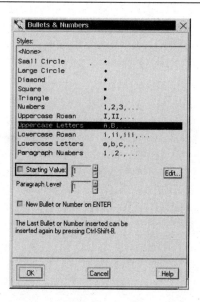

FIGURE 29-5   Use the Bullets & Numbers dialog box to set up different kinds of lists

a numbering style, you can specify the starting number's value and the amount by which it increments with each new entry; you can also choose to continue a previous numbered list or start numbering anew.

Return to the document and enter your first item. Each time you press ENTER, a bullet or number will be inserted at the start of the next line. To end the list, press BACKSPACE to delete the last bullet or number and return the cursor to the left margin. Then press ENTER to advance to a new line with no bullet or number.

QuickFormat

If you think document formatting is a bore, you might want to give the QuickFormat tool a try. QuickFormat is a WordPerfect feature that lets you quickly copy the format of one section of text to another, including fonts, tabs, styles, and other formatting options. This is especially useful if you forgot to select the entire document before you made formatting changes that affected only one paragraph!

To use QuickFormat, follow this process:

1. Position the cursor anywhere in the paragraph that has the formatting you want to copy.

2. Choose Format | QuickFormat.

   The QuickFormat screen appears, as in Figure 29-6.

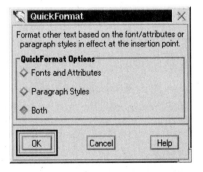

FIGURE 29-6   Use QuickFormat to copy the format of one text section to another

3. In the QuickFormat screen, select one of the following options:

■ **Characters**   Copies only fonts and attributes of the selected text

■ **Headings**   Copies styles applied in the selected text as well as fonts and attributes

4. Click OK when you have made your selections.

If you chose the Characters option, the cursor turns into a paintbrush; if you chose Headings, the cursor turns into a paint roller.

5. With the new cursor, select the text that you want to format.

When you release the mouse button, the transferred format will be applied to the selected text.

We suggest that you experiment with QuickFormat for a while before you try to use it for anything important. While it's a useful tool, it can be somewhat confusing. A bit of practice will go a long way toward demystifying QuickFormat's behavior.

Special Characters

Special characters are characters not found on the regular keyboard. Some special characters include diacritical marks for non-English languages; currency symbols for other monetary systems that don't use the dollar symbol; and certain graphic characters like stars, bullets, or pointing fingers. Corel WordPerfect contains a good selection of special characters, and it is easy to insert them into your documents.

To insert a special character, use this process:

1. Choose Insert | Symbol.

The Symbols selection screen appears, as in Figure 29-7.

2. From the drop-down box in the upper-left corner of the Symbols selection screen, select the kind of symbol you're looking for.

You can choose from various language character sets such as Arabic or Cyrillic, math and scientific symbols, icons and dingbats, or typographic symbols. The selected symbol set will fill the grid in the Symbols selection screen; Figure 29-8 shows the Math/Scientific set.

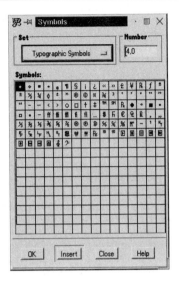

FIGURE 29-7   Insert special characters with the Symbol Selection tool

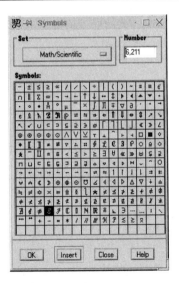

FIGURE 29-8   Insert mathematical and scientific symbols into your document

29

Don't plan to use the Symbols selection screen to type long documents in another character set. Download the appropriate language module from the Corel Web site instead.

3. Click the desired symbol, and then click Insert.

The character is inserted into your document at the cursor location.

Page Formatting

While you can have a lot of fun with text formatting, and make a drastic difference in the way your information is presented in the document, it's page formatting that determines how the finished product will appear. Corel Linux has a wide variety of page formatting options, including easily configured margins and text spacing, various types of headers and footers, a watermark option, several kinds of page numbering, a detailed chart creation tool, and the ability to divide text into several columns.

Margins and Spacing

In the default configuration for WordPerfect documents, the margins are set at 1 inch all around the page. That is, there is 1 inch of space between the edge of an 8.5×11-inch sheet of paper and the outer edge of the text itself. However, you might need to change those margins, depending on the kind of document you're working on; you may need to increase the inner margins so that the full document can be bound, or you might want to lower the top margin and raise the bottom margin to accommodate your company's letterhead design.

In the WordPerfect window when a document is open, margins display as gray lines that surround the work area. You can't click in the area outside the margins, but you always know where they are. If you don't want the default margin configuration, you can use one of two methods to control their position; the first method is not as quick but is far more accurate, while the second method is fast and simple but can lead to errors.

The most accurate way to change margins is to choose Format | Page | Page Setup | Margins. The Margin dialog box appears, as shown in the following illustration. On this screen, you can set each of the four margins to a specific distance from the edge of the paper. Using the dialog box means that the margins will be accurate and the settings will apply to the complete margin.

TIP *If you set margins smaller than 1 inch, your printer may cut off text when the pages print. Check your printer's manual to see what the absolute margin limits are; many printers won't print complete documents when the margin is smaller than half or three-quarters of an inch.*

The faster way to change margins is to click and drag the gray margin lines that appear on the screen while you're working on a document. Be aware, though, that if you click a margin inside the work area, the placement of the margin is only changed from the position of the cursor downward—that is, if you click on the segment of the right margin that falls between the top and bottom margins, the margin position will be affected only from the cursor insertion point on. You could end up with stairstepped margins that will make your document look quite odd. Avoid this problem by clicking and dragging only margin lines that are outside of the intersection between margins.

Headers and Footers

If you're old enough, you took typing in high school—not keyboarding, but actual typing on actual typewriters! Remember how much of a pain it was to insert headers and footers into a typed document? All that measuring, subtracting lines, and so on. Luckily for everyone (except for Miss Cobb, who now has nothing to do in typing class except run the *Mavis Beacon Teaches Typing* CD-ROM), word processors take all the fuss out of headers and footers.

NOTE *Why use headers and footers? Because they are probably the easiest way to handle page numbering, especially if you want to include a document title or chapter heading on each page. They're also good for identifying the author of the document. If you don't staple multiple-page business letters, using a header to identify yourself or your company may make it easier to sort out a letter after it's been dropped!*

To insert a header or a footer into a document, choose Insert | Header/Footer. The Headers/Footers dialog box opens, as seen here.

Select Header A and click Create. The dialog box closes, and a small area appears at the top of the document page. Click inside that area and enter the information you want on each page. Whatever you put in the header will be repeated on every page of the document. If you want to stop using the header, re-open the dialog box and click Discontinue. The header will disappear.

The process is the same for creating a footer, except that you would select Footer A in the Headers/Footers dialog box.

Watermarks

A *watermark* is a shadow design that is printed in a light grayscale behind the actual text of your document. Watermarks are used to identify the author or company producing the document, to denote a draft version or a document that requires security clearance, or simply as a graphical element of the overall document.

 Watermarks work best with a laser printer. If you use an inkjet to print a watermarked document, the ink is doubled when text prints over the watermark, and the page may buckle or smear. Laser printers handle the grayscale a lot better.

To add a watermark to a document, choose Insert | Watermark. The Watermark dialog box appears, as shown here.

Click Create. A new WordPerfect window opens; create your watermark in that window, entering whatever text or image file you want to use as the watermark. When you have finished designing the watermark (keep it simple so it doesn't distract from the actual text of the document), choose File | Close. The watermark will be transferred into the original document. To stop using the watermark in this document, re-open the Watermark dialog box and click Discontinue.

29

 If you create a lot of documents that need a particular kind of watermark, such as draft documents that must be circulated through a department and have a DRAFT watermark, consider building a document template that includes the watermark. That will save you time, since you won't have to build the watermark every time you want to use it.

Page Numbering

Next to margin placement, page numbering is probably the most frequently used page formatting option. Everyone likes page numbers on longer documents; they help the reader to know where she is in the document, and, in larger documents, they help track various chapters or sections if the document is not stapled or bound. The benefit of numbering pages with a word processor is that, if the document changes, the page numbers change to reflect any added or deleted material.

To add page numbers to your document choose Format | Page | Page Numbering | Numbering. (Odd that a crucial formatting tool is buried so deep in the menus, but that's the way it is.) The Page Numbering dialog box appears, as seen in Figure 29-9.

In the dialog box, click the drop-down box in the Position box to see a list of options for the location of the page number. When you select one of these locations, the preview window below the list will show a corresponding number in the proper location.

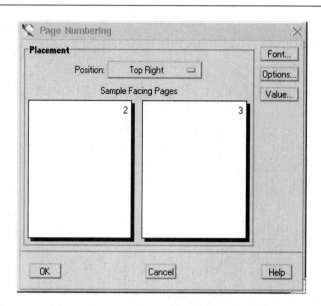

FIGURE 29-9   Number your pages accurately with the Page Numbering tool

Click the Options button to open a screen on which you can determine the page-numbering format. You can select the type of number to use, whether to use chapter or volume numbers, and so on. You can also select options such as Roman numerals or letters, or enter text to accompany the page number, such as "Page" or "Your Name—Page." When you've made your selections, click OK to return to the main Page Numbering dialog box.

Click the Font button to set the font, size, and style of the page numbers. Be aware that if you change your document font from the default, the page number font won't change unless you set the new font on this screen. It can be unattractive to see various types of fonts on a single page, so be careful to change fonts here as well. Click OK when you have made your selections, to return to the main Page Numbering dialog box.

When you have made all your selections, and used the Options and Font screens if necessary, click OK. The page numbers will be applied to your document as you formatted them, and they will change as you add or delete material. If you decide to stop using page numbers, re-open the Page Numbering dialog box and select No Page Numbering, and then click OK. The page numbers will disappear from the document.

Columns

Many people find it easier to read large amounts of data when it's presented in columns, since the shorter lines require more frequent eye movement and are thus less tiring to read. Others simply like the flexibility of columns, since it's easier to insert small images or text boxes and make a more attractive graphical presentation of the text; think of a newsletter that's just stapled pages of text, compared to one laid out with columns and graphics.

If you're interested in working with columns in your WordPerfect documents, you can select from a variety of columnar styles. It's easiest to work with columns when you've already entered the text, since you can see what the columns will look like immediately, rather than watch them develop as you type more. (It's a matter of preference. We're instant-feedback junkies, so we prefer to do column formatting last.)

To apply columns to your document text, choose Format I Columns. This opens the Define Columns dialog box, shown in Figure 29-10.

Use the Define Columns dialog to set the attributes of your columns. You can select the style of column, the number of columns on the page, and the amount of

29

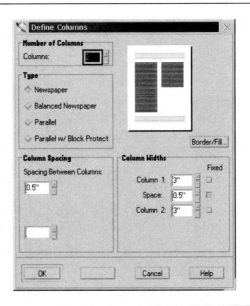

FIGURE 29-10   Arrange document text attractively with the Columns tool

space between columns (use more white space on the page to make it easier to read). When you make a selection, your choices are reflected in the preview box at the upper-right corner of the Define Columns dialog.

Make your selections and click OK to apply the column formatting to your document. You can turn off columns by reopening the Define Columns dialog box and clicking Discontinue. You can turn columns off and on throughout the document if you want to have certain blocks of text span the entire page, and other blocks of text divided into columns.

Other WordPerfect 8 Tools

In addition to formatting features, WordPerfect 8 offers several advanced assistants that will help you create the most accurate and attractive documents possible. In this section, we introduce six of these tools; for a more detailed explanation of their multiple features, we suggest consulting a book devoted to WordPerfect 8 for Linux to get the most information possible. The six most useful WordPerfect tools, in our opinion, are Find & Replace, Spellcheck, Thesaurus, Outlining, Styles, and WordPerfect's resident grammarian, Grammatik. (Which is, obviously, misspelled. We always get a giggle out of that.)

Find and Replace

No matter how smart you are, or how good your typing skills, there are times when you make an error consistently throughout a document. Perhaps you've mistyped someone's name, or referred to the wrong product. Never fear! You can use Find and Replace to locate and edit those mistakes.

To use Find and Replace, choose Edit | Find And Replace. In the Find and Replace Text dialog box, as shown in Figure 29-11, enter the word or text string that you want to find into the Find box. If you want WordPerfect to automatically replace the text, enter the replacement text in the Replace With box. Click Find Next to find the first occurrence of the word, or click Replace to automatically replace the next occurrence. You can also click Replace All if you want WordPerfect to locate and change all the occurrences of the text.

 Replace All may not be the best option all the time. You may have used that text string correctly in some places, so you don't want those spots changed to the new text. It's always a good idea to do a final edit of your document when you've finished replacing text, just to catch those embarrassing mistakes.

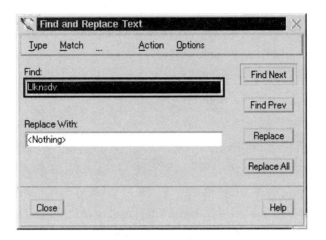

FIGURE 29-11   Search and replace all those pesky errors

29

Spell Checker

Use the Spell Checker function. Really. We mean it. Nothing conveys a lack of professionalism like a document riddled with misspellings. No matter how good a speller you think you are (and Kate's the queen of "I'm A Good Speller"-land), there's probably a word that you misspell or mistype consistently. Just so you feel among peers, Kate's is "publicly" and Joe's is "navigate."

To use the Spell Checker function in WordPerfect, choose Tools | Spellcheck. This opens the Spell Checker dialog box, as shown in Figure 29-12.

Spell Checker compares each word in your document to the dictionary installed when you installed WordPerfect. For each word that the program flags as misspelled, you'll be given the option to replace it, and you'll usually be offered a list of alternative spellings or words. If you know you spelled the word correctly, you can elect to add it to the dictionary so it won't be flagged again; if you know you spelled it correctly but you don't use it often enough to add to the dictionary, just click Ignore.

When you have reviewed all the words that Spell Checker thinks are misspelled, and corrected or ignored them as necessary, you'll be prompted to close the Spell Checker dialog box. Click Yes, and you'll be returned to the main document window, with all the corrections automatically made for you.

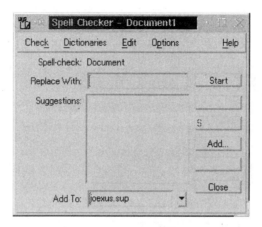

FIGURE 29-12 Use Spell Checker to save you from future embarrassment

Thesaurus

Tongue-tied? Can't think of the right word, or used the same word too many times in a single paragraph? It happens to everyone; that's why most word processors include a thesaurus program now. When you can't remember *le mot juste* (the perfect word), let the computer do it for you.

To use the thesaurus function of WordPerfect, choose Tools | Thesaurus from the menu bar. The Thesaurus screen appears, as in Figure 29-13.

If you had selected a word in your text before you opened Thesaurus, the program will automatically search for synonyms and antonyms for that word and display them. If you didn't select anything, you can type the word you need into the Word box, and click Look Up. Thesaurus scans its files for a moment and presents you with a number of alternatives to the word you entered. You can keep doing this all day, but when you get bored or find the word you need, click Close to exit Thesaurus.

Grammatik

If the thought of grammar lessons scares you stiff, or you slept through English class in high school, you may find Grammatik to be of some help to you. Grammatik is WordPerfect's grammar tool. It scans your document, considers the structure of each sentence, and offers alternatives to the sentences it flags as being in error. You can use Grammatik's offerings, provide your own, or ignore what Grammatik says about your writing.

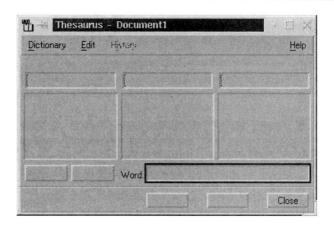

FIGURE 29-13   Use the Thesaurus to find the words you need to express yourself

To use Grammatik, it's best if your document's text is all entered. (It saves on anguish if you only do this once.) When you're ready, choose Tools | Grammatik from the menu bar. Grammatik scans your document, and the Grammatik screen appears, as in Figure 29-14.

The flagged sentences will be shown, along with alternatives. Agree with Grammatik's changes, make your own, or ignore the suggestions by clicking the appropriate buttons on the Grammatik screen. When you've finished, click Close to exit Grammatik and return to your document.

While Grammatik is good for an overview, it's not always right. The prose produced by grammar tools is often boring and stilted, though grammatically perfect. It's best to use both Grammatik and a pair of human eyes to edit your documents, just to make sure that your unique written voice stays in the document after the grammatical changes are made.

Outlining

Many people like to make detailed outlines of documents before actually writing anything down. Others like to have an outline while they're reading something lengthy, to understand the structure behind the words. Regardless of your motives for outlining, you can use WordPerfect's outlining tool to create a clear picture of your document's framework.

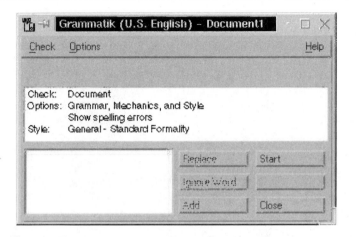

FIGURE 29-14   Let Grammatik edit your documents

Outlining works best when you use document styles to format the various levels of your document. See the next section of this chapter, "Styles," to see how styles work; outlining applies styles to your document, or pulls its information from already applied styles.

To format an outline of your document, choose Tools | Define Outline from the menu bar. The Outline Define dialog box appears, as in Figure 29-15.

Choose the kind of outline you want to create from the various choices in the Name window, and click Create. The Edit Outline Definition screen appears, shown in Figure 29-16; on this screen, fill in the name and an optional definition of the outline. The screen also shows a preview of the outline style you've selected, and the labels associated with the various header levels in that style.

You can change these labels by using the Custom Number field.

When you've made all your selections, click OK. The screen closes, and you're returned to the Outline Define screen with the name of your outline appearing in the Search/Selection field. Click OK to return to your document, where the first label is already entered.

As you enter the various items you want to put into your outline, press ENTER at the end of each item. Outline automatically enters the label for the next header, and you can then enter that item's information and press ENTER again. If you press

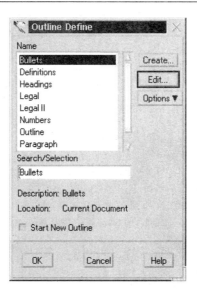

FIGURE 29-15   Let WordPerfect help you construct the perfect outline

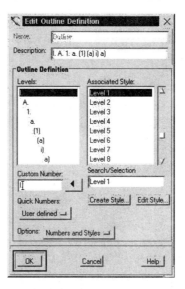

FIGURE 29-16   Name your outline and see a preview on the Edit Outline
Definition screen

TAB instead of ENTER, the label changes to that of the next level's header and the cursor automatically indents. To move back to the previous level, click the left-pointing arrow button in the tool bar.

You can use the arrow buttons in the tool bar to rearrange the header levels of your items once you have entered the full outline.

Styles

Document styles are a quick way to format your text "on the fly" without having to make all the adjustments yourself. You can insert a preformatted style into your document by placing the cursor in the line you want to format and selecting the style from the Style Attribute tool on the tool bar; it's just to the right of the justification buttons. Click the arrow button in the Style Attribute tool and select a style from the drop-down list that appears. The line containing the cursor will be formatted with that style; if the cursor is at the beginning of an empty line, the next line typed will have that style.

If you want to define your own styles, choose Format | Create | Styles. When the Style List dialog box appears (Figure 29-17), click Create to see the Styles Editor screen. Enter a name for your style and construct the formatting options from the various elements contained in the Format and Insert menus on the screen. When you've finished, click OK. The style will now appear in the Style Attribute tool on the tool bar, and you can use it whenever you want.

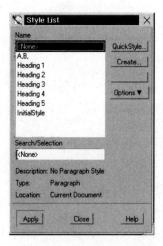

FIGURE 29-17   Let document styles handle tedious formatting tasks for you

CHAPTER 30

Creating Web Pages with WordPerfect 8

One of the benefits of using WordPerfect 8 is that it's a pretty good HTML editor as well as word processor. The HTML features of WordPerfect 8 make it easy for you to build Web pages with the same familiar commands you use in the word processor, with the appropriate HTML tags added in automatically. You can even use the special Internet Publisher Web Editor, a wizard that helps you format and build your pages.

While you won't be able to do the intense graphical and programming tasks that make the most sophisticated Web pages bloom, you can use WordPerfect 8 to build solid, functional pages that get your message across. (Hire someone to do the graphics stuff for your site; it's a full-time job!) There simply aren't as many HTML editors available for Linux as there are for other platforms (as of early 2000), so WordPerfect 8 is a good alternative to learning HTML from scratch.

NOTE	*We do recommend that you familiarize yourself with the basics of HTML and provide a quick introduction and some critical tags in the "What Is HTML?" section that follows. A plethora of HTML books are available on the market; rather than recommending a single one, we suggest that you skim through eight or ten of them at the bookstore and find one that best fits your needs. You'll also find a huge number of HTML tutorials on the Web—plug **+HTML +tutorial** into any search engine to get several pages of possibilities.*

What Is HTML?

HTML, or Hyper Text Markup Language, is the code that is used to create the pages seen on the World Wide Web. Basically, HTML is a sequence of *tags* that surround certain pieces of text and direct how that text will appear on the screen. Tags might change the text to boldface or a heading, or they might enclose the location of an image file. What these tags are, and how they are interpreted by different Web browsers, is a matter of some controversy. While the HTML standard is maintained by the World Wide Web Consortium (`http://www.w3c.org`), Netscape and Microsoft have also adopted individual tags as compliant with their browsers. The end result is that some pages are designed to look best in Internet Explorer and others are designed to look best in Netscape.

You won't need to worry too much about these unique tags when using WordPerfect 8 to create your Web pages, since you won't be creating very complicated pages. It's worth knowing about the differences between browsers if you decide to work with very complex coding, though, especially if you plan to incorporate a lot of graphics into your pages.

> **TIP**
>
> *If you want to see only HTML that complies with the HTML standard, you might be interested in the Opera browser. Opera is a very strict browser that displays only pages that are coded in compliant HTML. The drawback is that some of your favorite sites may not be properly coded; but Opera does give you the advantage of not having to download bad code that might crash the browser or your computer. Learn more about Opera and download the Linux version from the Opera Web site at* `http://www.operasoftware.com`.

Even if you choose not to learn HTML from scratch, and you're perfectly happy to use HTML editors to create Web pages, it's a good idea to know some of the basic tags and how they work. Table 29-1 shows some of the critical tags and their effects. Place a tag at the start of the text block you want to affect, and place the tag with a slash in front of the tag name at the end of the text block:

<tag>text to be affected</tag>

What Is an HTML Editor?

If you're not working in a plain text editor, like `vi` or `pico`, and writing each tag by hand, you're probably using an HTML editor to build your pages. There are two general types of HTML editors: text-based editors and WYSIWYG editors. Text-based editors display your page contents as in a regular text editor, but they show the tags in various colors so you can see where the tags are located as you work. Many text-based editors have one-click buttons for frequently used tags to help speed up the coding. WYSIWYG editors, on the other hand, show the page as it will appear in a browser, hiding the HTML tags. (WYSIWYG stands for "What You See Is What You Get.")

There are advantages to both kinds of editors. Text-based editors give you far more control over the HTML code of each document, while WYSIWYG editors give you instant feedback on the actual appearance of the document. If you do a lot of advanced Web design, you probably use both, switching back and forth depending on the task at hand. Unfortunately, the best WYSIWYG editors (such as Macromedia's Dreamweaver) are not yet available on the Linux platform. So if you're planning to become an HTML maven, it's best to learn the code itself.

Tag	Function
\<html\>	Tells the browser that the document contains HTML tags.
\<title\>	Contains the information that appears in the browser's title bar when the document is viewed.
\<body\>	Denotes the content of the document.
\<p\>	Starts a new paragraph. (Note that \<p\> does not need a closing \</p\> tag.)
\<ul\>	Unnumbered list with bullets.
\<li\>	Item within a list.
\<ol\>	Numbered list. (Also uses \<li\> for the individual list items.)
\<pre\>	Preformatted text. Use this tag when you want to show an existing block of text that's coded in a fixed-width font.
\<blockquote\>	Separates lengthy quotations from the text with deeper margins on both sides.
\<br\>	Inserts a line break with no extra white space between the lines, as \<p\> would produce.
\<hr\>	Inserts a horizontal rule, or line, across your document.
\<em\>	Emphasis, shown as italics. This tag is preferable over \<i\>, the italic tag.
\<strong\>	Strong, shown as bold. This tag is preferable over \<b\>, the bold tag.
\<tt\>	Typewriter text, shown in a fixed-width font.

TABLE 30-1   Some Basic HTML Tags

Opening HTML Documents

Using the WordPerfect 8 Web tools, you have two options for creating Web documents. Obviously, you can create brand new documents from scratch. However, you can also convert existing WordPerfect documents into HTML, which is especially helpful if the alternative would be to retype the entire document as a Web page.

To convert an existing document into an HTML document, first open the document. (We assume you already have WordPerfect open.) Select File | Internet Publisher. The Internet Publisher screen appears, as shown in Figure 30-1; click Format As Web Document.

TIP *It's always a good idea to save a copy of the document you plan to convert. Use File | Save As to make a backup; if you mess up the HTML version, or you need the WordPerfect version for some reason, you'll have a clean copy to work from.*

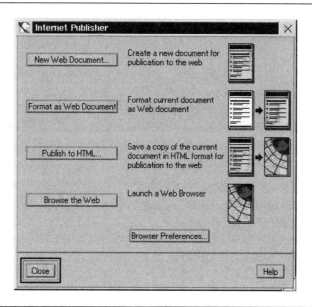

FIGURE 30-1   Convert an existing document to HTML with one click

A warning message may appear once you've chosen to format the document, as shown in Figure 30-2, alerting you that some formatting may be lost during conversion. Click Yes; if you don't want to see this box every time you convert a document, click the checkbox next to Do Not Show Me This Message Next Time . . . .

The document opens in the Internet Publisher Web Editor, which looks almost exactly like the regular WordPerfect window. This window features quite a few new icons that provide Web-specific features and a second toolbar along the top of the editing window. If you're already comfortable with WordPerfect, you'll find using the Internet Publisher to be a real breeze. The various options and capabilities are described later in "The Internet Publisher Web Editor" section of this chapter.

To create a new document that will be formatted in HTML from its creation, select File I Internet Publisher. When the Internet Publisher window appears, click New Web Document. A blank document will appear in the Internet Publisher Web Editor, ready to be worked on, as shown in Figure 30-3.

Once you have created an HTML document, either by converting a WordPerfect document or by creating a new file, you can reopen them as you would any other WordPerfect file. Simply use File I Open, or click the Open button in the toolbar. It's a good idea to save HTML files in a separate directory from your regular WordPerfect documents.

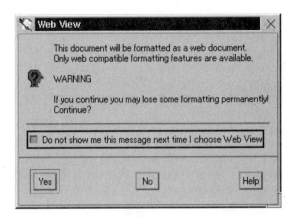

FIGURE 30-2   You can safely ignore warnings about format loss

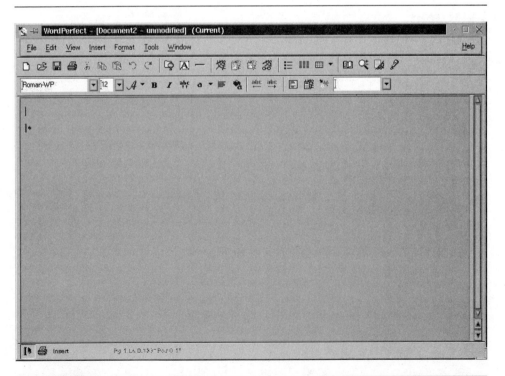

FIGURE 30-3   The Internet Publisher window resembles the regular WordPerfect window

The file will remain in the standard *.wpd file format until you actually convert the file to HTML using the Publish to HTML tool, described later in the "Publishing Your HTML Document" section of this chapter.

The Internet Publisher Web Editor

Once you have opened a document in the Internet Publisher Web Editor, you'll be able to work on it as you would on a regular WordPerfect document. The Web Editor screen has some specialized tools and does not offer other functions that you'd find in WordPerfect. Why? Because Web documents are a specialized format; they don't use headers and footers, for example, so that tool is unavailable. However, Web documents need tools to check links or insert particular actions, so those tools are available.

The Internet Publisher Web Editor Tools

The Web Editor window is laid out clearly, as with the WordPerfect window. In Figure 30-4, you can see the various buttons and icons that open Web Editor tools. The Web toolbar icons are the four "spiderweb" buttons below the Help menu item:

- **Browse the Web** opens Netscape but does not display the document that you're currently working on in the browser. (This is great for checking another site quickly, or for downloading icons, backgrounds, or images from a Web file archive.)

- **View in Web Browser** opens Netscape, showing the page you're working on. This is the best way to preview a document as you add to it, to see how it will appear to other viewers once it's finished.

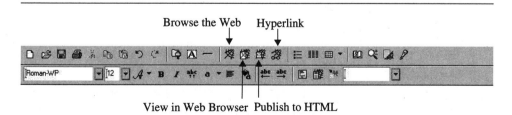

FIGURE 30-4   Use the Web Editor functions to speed up HTML page creation

■ **Publish to HTML** converts the finished document into an HTML-encoded document. This should be your last step, just prior to uploading the document to the Web. While you can edit HTML documents in the Web Editor, changes won't be reflected in the original document when you go to work on it later. It's better to work in WordPerfect format and convert to HTML at the very end.

■ **Hyperlink** adds a link to your document, which users can click to launch another file while they are viewing your page. We cover adding hyperlinks later in this section.

The Web Editor offers other tools as well. Some of them will be familiar to you from working with WordPerfect documents, but the selections may be different due to the nature of Web documents. You can switch quickly between monospace and proportional fonts, change font attributes or font color, or align text quickly with the font buttons in the tool bar. You can also use the drop-down menus, where you'll find Web-specific options as well.

Working on an HTML Document

Editing an HTML document is as easy as editing a paper document. Most of what you'll be doing with an HTML document is working with text, though you'll have some new tasks as well (such as adding hyperlinks or embedding images and sound files).

> **NOTE** *If you still have the HTML file open from the first section of this chapter, you can begin to work on it. If you closed it, reopen an HTML file now.*

Text formatting options are limited in Web Editor, because many of the fancy techniques you can use on a paper document simply won't appear on the screen in a Web browser. Why? Because of those varying standards that we discussed in the opening paragraphs of this chapter. In addition, a lot of Web text appearance is dependent on the fonts and preferences installed on the viewer's computer; if you use a fancy and unusual font for all your text, but your viewers don't have that font installed, they'll see only the default fonts specified in their browser preferences.

> **TIP** *The unpredictability of fonts means that you have two options: either stick to the basic default fonts, such as Times, Courier, and Arial; or make graphics files out of your text so you can use your fancy fonts. The drawback to the second option is that graphics files take a long time to load, and people using text-based Web browsers won't see them.*

Dealing with Fonts

You have a few font options in the Web Editor, each represented by a button on the Web Editor tool bar. Use these buttons to change the appearance of the text in your document, whether you change each aspect of the appearance yourself or use predefined styles.

The Monospace button is used to toggle between proportional fonts such as Times, and monospace fonts such as Courier. If you select text before you click this button, the selected text will switch; if you don't select text, anything typed at the current cursor position will be in the new font.

TIP   *When the button appears pushed in, the font will be monospaced. When it appears normally, the font will be proportional.*

The Font Attributes button is used to apply special appearances to selected text. Click the button to see a list of the available attributes: bold, italic, underline, etc. Select the attribute you want to apply from the list, or select the attribute you want to remove from the selected text.

TIP   *You can clear all attributes from the selected text just by selecting Normal from the list.*

The Justification button, when clicked, opens a list of possible text justifications. Select from left, right, or center to align the text along those horizontal lines. In Web documents, you can't select the type of justification that aligns the text smoothly along both left and right margins.

The Font Color button is used, of course, to change the color of selected text. Click the button to see a list of the available colors; select the color you want to use, and watch it applied immediately to the text you selected.

 If you want to change a number of font attributes at one time, rather than clicking each button successively, use the menu bar to select Format | Font. You can make several selections at once from the Font screen.

Using Styles

Because so much of the final appearance of your Web document is determined by the browser that others use to view it, it's often a good idea to use the preformatted styles available in Web Editor rather than tinker with your own settings and risk that they'll display badly. The styles, as with WordPerfect styles, are a collection of font attributes—color, size, appearance—that apply automatically when the style is selected.

Styles are generally used for headings, but individual heading styles can be applied to regular text as well. Just be aware that it's difficult to read regular text encoded with the Heading 1 style (large and bold), just as it's difficult to see headings encoded as regular plain Times text. Experiment with the various styles (find them on the Font screen, reached by choosing Format | Font) to see what looks best for your document.

 When using styles, we recommend that you use the View In Web Browser window to see how the styles change the text appearance.

Adding Hyperlinks

What makes a Web document unique? Most people would say that it's the ability to include *hyperlinks*, which direct the reader to another page or file when clicked. Web Editor makes it simple to add hyperlinks to your document, whether you're linking with text or with an image. Here's how you can add a hyperlink:

1. Select the text to be linked.

2. Click the Hyperlink button. The Create Hypertext Link screen appears, as in Figure 30-5.

3. Delete any text in the Go To Other Document box.

4. Enter the full URL of the target document in the Go To Other Document box.

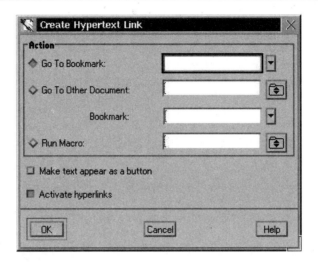

FIGURE 30-5	Link to other Web documents or files with a hyperlink

5. (Optional) If you want the link to appear as a button, instead of just text, select the Make Text Appear As A Button check box.

6. Click OK.

Adding Images

Most people want images in their Web pages. Otherwise, the Web would be filled with pages of plain text, which—while informative—wouldn't be interesting to look at! Images are easy to add with the Web Editor. You have two choices when inserting an image: If you want to insert an image at the point where the cursor is located, just click the Image button in the tool bar. The Insert Image dialog box will appear, as in Figure 30-6. You can also choose Insert I Graphics to select a specific type of image or draw a picture to be included on the page.

Select the image you want to add in the Insert Image dialog box, and click OK. The image will appear in your document.

TIP *Add an <ALT> tag to your image. This tag provides a text description of the image, and is especially useful for Web browsers that read the page to a visually impaired user. They're also helpful for people using text-only browsers or who have turned off image loading. Add the <ALT> tag by right-clicking the image, selecting HTML Properties, and entering text into the Alternate Text box. Click OK when you've finished, and feel good about making your pages accessible to everyone.*

FIGURE 30-6   Add graphics to your page with the Insert Image dialog box

Publishing Your HTML Document

When you've finished entering data and adding all the links and images you want to include in your Web page, you'll need to convert the document to HTML before you can post it on the Web. With Web Editor, this is an utterly simple procedure!

First, save your work. Then click the Publish To HTML button in the tool bar. The Publish To HTML dialog box will appear. You can enter a new filename if you like, or you can accept the default (the name you saved the document by, with an added *.htm extension). Click OK when you're done.

That's all you need to do! Now you can upload the document to a Web server and it will be available on the Web.

Should you want to convert an HTML document back to WordPerfect format, open the document in Web Editor and select File | Internet Publisher | Format As WP Document.

Uploading Your Document to the Web

Once you've converted your document to HTML, you have only one step remaining before it's visible via the Web. You need to make the file available for others to read, whether you're running Apache on your computer or using Web space on your local ISP. Either way, making the file available is quite simple.

> **CAUTION** *Web Editor produces HTML documents that use the *.htm file suffix, not the standard *.html suffix. This should not cause a problem for people using advanced browsers, but some old browsers don't like *.htm files. If you think this is an issue for your readers, change all the filenames to use the *.html format before you upload the documents.*

> **CAUTION** *When you upload your files, be sure to upload all images, sound files, and background or icon files that you used to build the document. If you don't upload these files as well as the main HTML document, the finished document will show broken links when someone tries to view it.*

30

Uploading via an ISP

If you have Web space available through your ISP, you probably received information about file locations and uploading when you opened your account. Check your initial account information, or look at your ISP's Web site, to see what you need to do. In general, you'll need to upload the file from your computer to the ISP's Web server; you can usually do this with plain old FTP, though some ISPs have a fancy Web-based upload utility (Yahoo!/GeoCities is one such site).

As long as you put your files in the correct place, as designated by the ISP, they should be visible as soon as you complete the upload. The specific URL for each page will be determined by the ISP, but in all likelihood it will take the form `http://www.yourisp.com/~yourusername/file.html`.

> **NOTE** *If you pay your ISP to host a domain name for you, the URL will be your own domain name, and possibly will not have the ~username component. Ask your domain host how they construct URLs.*

Uploading Using Apache

If you're running the Apache Web server on your Corel Linux computer, you have an easy upload process. Simply move the HTML files from the directory where you stored them while working with the Web Editor into the directory you designated as your WWW directory for Apache. (See Chapter 26, "Web Services," for information on configuring Apache correctly.)

PART VI

Appendixes

APPENDIX A

How to Compile a Kernel

The *kernel* is the very heart of your Linux operating system. The kernel contains basic commands and code upon which the general interface is built. The kernel determines the priority of different commands and processes and it manages the system's resources. Because it is so important to the computer's operation, the kernel is shielded from access; you configure and access the kernel through shell commands, which are interpreted by the shell environment and presented to the kernel for completion.

 This appendix is only a brief introduction to kernel compilation. If you want to know more, we strongly recommend that you consult the kernel HOWTO provided by the Linux Documentation Project, which can be found at `http://metalab.unc.edu/pub/Linux/docs/ HOWTO/Kernel-HOWTO.`

Why Would You Want to Compile a Kernel?

Unlike some operating systems that force you to upgrade to use new software, it is fairly rare for a new piece of the Linux package to change so radically from version to version that you must upgrade your entire system to use that one piece. For most purposes, the default kernel supplied with your Corel Linux distribution is perfectly adequate.

Nevertheless, you may want to upgrade your kernel at times. Sometimes a new version of the kernel will include new or updated hardware drivers. In addition, you may be able to use new features only if you upgrade an outdated kernel.

The kernel supplied with Corel Linux is a *modular kernel*. This means that some kernel features are compiled as separate binaries that can be unloaded and loaded on the fly. This makes the kernel very flexible, but it also increases the kernel's size since many of these modules are not appropriate for every type of system (and yet are loaded as part of the kernel operation). Some people like to recompile their kernels to support only those features that are actually used; others prefer to add these features directly into the kernel instead of running them as modules. (This is called building a *static kernel*.)

The rule of thumb for kernel management is "If it ain't broke, don't fix it." Aside from the sheer coolness factor of running the latest kernel on the "bleeding edge" (one step ahead of the cutting edge), there is probably no reason for you to recompile or upgrade your kernel as long as your system is working properly. These warnings notwithstanding, if you want to upgrade your kernel, you'll learn that it's a complex—but not especially difficult—process.

How to Recompile Your Kernel

Before you begin to recompile the kernel, you need to make sure that you have the following packages installed:

- `make`
- `as86`
- `gcc`
- `g++`

These packages are located in the "development" section of Corel Update's package listing. You should also know as much as possible about your hardware configuration and which kernel features you need. Once you have that information, you're ready to proceed.

1. Get the Source Code

You can find your kernel's source code at `http://www.kernel.org` or any of its mirrors. Once you connect with `kernel.org`, you'll need to understand how new versions of the kernel are numbered so that you get the right one. See the sidebar "Kernel Numbering Basics" for a full explanation.

> **TIP** *Use the mirror that is physically located closest to you; this increases download speed and reduces bandwidth impact.*

After you've selected the particular kernel you want to use, download it. The actual filename of the package will look something like this: linux-*x.y.z*.tgz—where *x.y.z* is the version number you've selected. Put this file into the /usr/src directory.

2. Unpack the Source

Open a terminal window and change to the root account using the `su` command. Move into the /usr/src directory, where you should find the package you just downloaded. Check to see if there is a subdirectory called /usr/src/linux; unless you installed the source code with your initial installation, you shouldn't have one.

Kernel Numbering Basics

A typical kernel version number will look something like this: 2.2.12. Each of the numeric components tells you a great deal about the kernel and can help you decide whether this is a version you want to use.

The leftmost number is the major version number. This number rarely changes, and when it does, it's a big deal. People working on the Linux kernel (another volunteer effort) make many small changes to the kernel, but the major version number is changed only when the kernel has made a significant step forward from the previous version.

The middle number is the series number. If this number is an even number, the series is a *production series*, which means that it's stable. Kernels in the production series are considered suitable for general use. If this number is odd, the series is a *development series*, which means that it's an experimental kernel. Kernels in development contain features still being worked on. Consequently, they may contain bugs or be unstable. As a rule, you will want to stick to production series kernels unless you're a masochist or a developer.

Note that at the time we wrote this chapter, version 2.3.*x* was the highest numbered kernel, but version 2.2.*x* was the highest stable kernel. If you're recompiling your kernel for a specific feature found only in a development series kernel, be aware that you're agreeing to some system instability.

The rightmost number is the minor version number. New minor versions are released fairly frequently, usually as often as every three or four weeks. Use the highest minor version you can find, as long as it comes from the production series.

If there is such a directory, rename it to /usr/src/linux-old so that it won't get in your way during recompilation.

Uncompress and extract the source file by issuing the command

```
tar xvfz linux-x.y.z.tgz
```

You'll see the contents of the tarball scroll up the screen. Don't bother trying to read it all as it goes past; there is a lot of stuff in the compressed file. When it's finished, you should have a new directory called linux.

Rename this directory linux-*x.y.z* and make a symbolic link called `linux` to this directory by issuing the command

```
ln -s linux-x.y.z linux
```

> **TIP**
>
> *Renaming the directory as suggested is not strictly necessary, but it's nice to have a clear structure if you're keeping several different versions of the kernel source code on your machine. The source code for each version will reside in its own directory, but linux is always a symbolic link to the current kernel version directory.*

Move into your new directory by issuing the command

```
cd linux
```

Do a directory listing with the `ls -la` command. You'll see a number of new files and subdirectories, as well as a file called README. Read this. Seriously. It will explain any peculiarities of this particular kernel version, as well as the major features contained in the kernel. You should also do a listing of the Documentation subdirectory; if you need specific information on a particular kernel subsystem, you'll find it in that directory.

3. Configure Your Kernel

The kernel package contains three programs that help you configure the kernel once you've decided which features you want to include at compilation. Run these programs by typing one of the following commands:

```
make config
```

```
make menuconfig
```

```
make xconfig
```

These three programs do the same thing, but they do it in slightly different ways. `make config` is the most basic program you can run to configure features. When you issue the `make config` command, the program asks you a series of questions about various components that can be compiled with this particular kernel. `menuconfig` and `xconfig` do the same thing but use a menu interface where you can select the components you want.

We recommend that you use `make config`. *It forces you to deal with each component and makes it less likely that you'll forget to add a feature that you need. Menu versions make it easier to overlook something that might be important.*

Most of the questions in `make config` allow you to select a Yes or No answer in response to the query; a Yes answer means that particular component will be compiled with the new kernel, and a No answer means that it will not. In addition, many of the questions have a third option that allows the component to be compiled as a module.

 To allow the kernel to use modules, you will have to answer Yes to the option "loadable module support."

Many questions also have a help option, which gives you a brief description of the component to help you decide if you need it.

Because there are so many options, and they change from version to version, we can't give you a complete listing. Instead, following is a description of the major categories of components, so that you know what to look for.

Kernel Math Emulation

To be safe, answer Yes to this option. If you have a basic 386 or 486 chip without a math coprocessor, you must enable this option. If your chip does have a math coprocessor, you can still answer Yes; the chip will simply ignore the emulation option in the kernel.

Enhanced Disk (MFM/RLL) and IDE Disk/CD-ROM Support (Block Devices)

Answer Yes to this option; this means that the kernel will support standard hard disks used in PCs. If you don't have these kind of disks, you will know. (SCSI drives are covered under another option.)

Once you have selected Yes, you'll be asked to choose between "old disk-only" and "new IDE" drivers. The first option gives support for only two drives on a single interface; the second offers a second interface and also supports IDE/ATAPI CD-ROM drives. If you need a driver with few or no bugs, select the first; if you have newer hardware and can live with the risks of a newer version of the driver, select the second.

Networking Support (General Setup)

Answer Yes to this option. Even if you are running a standalone machine, you will probably want to connect to the Internet at some point. You'll need the support provided by this component in order to run PPP to connect to your Internet Service Provider. (You also need to say Yes to the TCP/IP option offered later in the configuration process.)

System V IPC (General Setup)

Select Yes. You don't need to know the details of what this component does (unless you're a heavy-duty programmer), but it's necessary to select it to allow various processes to communicate.

Processor Family (Type and Features)

Select the type of processor your computer uses. If you don't remember (though that's something you should know automatically), select 386. It will work on all chips supported under Linux.

SCSI Support

Do you have SCSI devices, such as a CD-ROM drive, a scanner, or a Zip drive? If so, answer Yes. Doing so leads to further questions about your SCSI configuration, including the types of devices you use and other basic information.

Network Device Support

Answer Yes. As with the Networking Support option, you'll need to enable this component if you want to use PPP to connect to the Internet.

File Systems

You will be asked about the types of file systems you'd like to support with this kernel. You'll need to say Yes to at least three types: Standard, Second Extended, and msdos. You should also say Yes to /proc, NFS, and ISO9660; these options ensure that you can use various shells, network file sharing, and your CD-ROM drive.

A

Character Devices

Answer Yes to any devices you have installed on your system: mouse, parallel printer, tape drives, and any other devices that need specific drivers.

 You may want to say Yes to enable the gpm program, which lets you use your mouse outside the regular X Window System environment. If you have a serial mouse, it's a useful trick. If your mouse is not a serial mouse, you probably won't want to do the configuration tricks necessary to use gpm.

Sound

Answer Yes. This component configures your system sound and sound card. If you answer Yes, the configuration program will ask more questions about your specific sound card.

 If you want to know more about the current options for components in your kernel, we suggest that you look at the Configure.help file in the Documentation subdirectory. This file contains a comprehensive list of options and can give you more ideas about the specific tinkering you might want to do with the kernel.

4. Configure Dependencies

Once you've completed the configuration program, you are ready to start the kernel building process. The first thing you need to do is to configure the dependencies, which locates the files used by the compiler to assist the compilation process. To do this, simply issue the command

```
make dep
```

Many messages will scroll up the screen, which will take a few seconds. Eventually, you'll be returned to the shell prompt. Any errors in this process will be listed at the end of the messages that scrolled up; you don't have to read the entire scrollback as it's running past you.

5. Clean the Code

Issue the command

```
make clean
```

This removes a bunch of old object files and unnecessary chunks of code. (No matter how hard you try, though, you can't use this command on your home or laundry. Believe us, we've tried.)

6. Build the Kernel

At this point, if you've had no problems, you're ready to build the kernel. Issue this command at the shell prompt:

```
make bzImage
```

Depending on your configuration and the speed of your computer, you may want to get a cup of coffee or take the dogs for a walk. A large batch of messages will scroll up the screen, similar to the messages you saw when you configured the dependencies in step 4. This will go on for some time.

> **NOTE** *Compiling software is a CPU-intensive process. Our 50Mhz 486 computer takes anywhere from 90 to 120 minutes to compile a kernel, while our dual Celeron machine does it in about 3 minutes. There are some advantages to upgrading hardware!*

7. (Optional) Build the Modules

If you decided to build some parts of your kernel as loadable modules, you need to build those modules now. Type the following at the command prompt:

```
make modules
```

This will take some time, but not as long as building the kernel itself. When the process finishes, issue the command

```
make modules install
```

A

This command moves the modules to the /lib/modules/*x.y.z* directory, where *x.y.z* is the kernel version number.

8. Install the Kernel

When the compiler finished building the new kernel, it left the resulting kernel as a binary file named /usr/src/linux-*x.y.z*/arch/i386/boot/bzImage. Move this file into the /boot directory and rename it something like vmlinuz-*x.y.z* (note the spelling). You can do this with the following command:

```
mv /usr/src/linux-x.y.z/arch/i386/boot/bzImage /boot/vmlinuz-x.y.z
```

Now edit /etc/lilo.conf. We discussed LILO in Chapter 2, "Installing Corel Linux"; LILO is the program that is responsible for loading and booting the kernel, so you need to make it aware that the new kernel exists and is ready for use. Your current /etc/lilo.conf file should look like this:

```
boot=/dev/hda

install=/boot/cboot.b
message = /boot/splash.lilo
map=/boot/map
compact
prompt
delay=300
timeout=300
image=/vmlinuz
        label=[]_{}
        vga=0xf04
        append="no-scroll"
        root=/dev/hda1
        read-only
image=/vmlinuz
        label={}~Console
        vga=normal
        append="1"
        root=/dev/hda1
        read-only
image=/vmlinuz-debug
        label={}~Debug
        vga=normal
```

```
        root=/dev/hda1
        read-only
other=/dev/hda1
        label={}~Expert
        unsafe
```

You must insert an entry into this file for your new kernel. Open /etc/lilo.conf in a text editor; between the line beginning with `timeout` and the first `image` statement, add this segment:

```
image=/boot/vmlinuz-x.y.z
        label=new-kernel
        root=/dev/hda1
        read-only
```

Once you have saved the changes and exited the text editor, issue the command

```
/sbin/lilo
```

This command will make LILO aware of the new kernel.

9. Reboot

Upgrading the kernel is one of the few times when it is absolutely necessary to reboot your Linux machine. Log out of root, and out of your user account, and reboot the machine. Now, when Corel Linux starts up, you should see *new-kernel* as one of the options in the drop-down box on the main splash screen.

Select new-kernel and boot your machine as normal. You are now using the new kernel. Congratulations!

A

APPENDIX B

A Compendium of Common Shell Commands

This appendix contains some of the most commonly used shell commands in the UNIX and UNIX-based operating systems. This appendix is, by no stretch of the imagination, exhaustive. We provide the commands you're likely to use frequently and describe their most common options and use. You will find other ways to do things—thousands of commands exist, and nobody knows all of them.

> **TIP**   *If you'd like to consult a reference that contains a huge number of commands, we recommend* The UNIX and X Command Compendium, *by Alan Southerton and Edwin Perkins, Jr. (John Wiley & Sons). Don't be put off by the cover description (*A Dictionary for High-Level Computing*); the book is a comprehensive work containing more than 2200 separate commands and examples. We use this book all the time.*

In this appendix, the following conventions are used within the entries:

■ Items in square brackets, such as *[option]*, are optional.

■ Items in angle brackets, such as *<filename>*, should be replaced with an actual file or program name.

■ Items separated by a vertical bar (|) are mutually exclusive.

 ■ If the bar is within square brackets, the choice is optional: for example, if the example states [a | b], you can select a, b, or none.

 ■ If the bar is within curly brackets, such as {a | b}, you must select either a or b.

> **NOTE**   *The constructions and options given here represent only the most common usage of these commands. Many of these commands have syntaxes that allow for other types of constructions. See the manual page for each command for a full list of possible usage.*

Commands for File System Navigation

These commands are used to get around within the Linux directory structure. They are probably the most commonly used commands in the shell environment.

cd

cd is used to change directories with the syntax

```
cd [directory]
```

If no directory is specified, cd changes to the user's home directory.

ls

ls is used to list the contents of a directory, with the syntax

```
ls [options] [directory]
```

If no directory is specified, ls lists the contents of the current directory. Options for ls are

- -l Produces a content list in "long format," which includes more information about file size and other file characteristics.

- -a Causes ls to list all files in the directory, including those that begin with a leading dot.

- -i Causes ls to list files with their *inode*, or disk index, numbers.

- -R Causes ls to list all subdirectories of the current directory, and to list all files within those subdirectories. Note that this can be a lengthy list.

- -t Produces a listing sorted by the time of the last modification to the file.

If you use the -l flag with ls, the listing you get will include an arcane pattern of letters at the left. This is actually a schematic representation of the permissions for that file. For example, if Harry issues the command ls -l somefile, he'll see this line:

```
-rwxrwxrwx  1  harry  harry  245  Jan  20  8:45  somefile
```

The part with the r's, w's, and x's shows the permissions set. This section of the report uses these conventions. The first character indicates what the item is:

- a = file

- ◼ d = directory

- ◼ b = block device

- ◼ c = character device

The remaining characters identify the type of permission used:

- ◼ r = read

- ◼ w = write

- ◼ x = execute

You may also see a dash in one of these spaces, indicating that the given permission is not granted.

The letters are organized into three groups of three. The first group of three defines permissions for the owner of the file, the second group of three defines group permissions, and the third group of three defines global permissions.

locate

locate is used to find a particular program on the hard drive and uses the syntax

```
locate <filename>
```

whereis

whereis is used to find a file or program on the hard disk and uses the syntax

```
whereis [options] <filename>
```

Options for whereis are

- ◼ -b   If this flag is used, whereis searches only for binaries with the given filename.

- ◼ -m   If this flag is used, whereis searches only for manual pages with the given filename.

- ◼ -s   If this flag is used, whereis searches only for source code packages with the given filename.

which

which is used to find a given program on the hard disk and uses the syntax

```
which [options] <programname>
```

You can use the -a option with which to find all matching executables in the *search path* (the list of directories specified in the PATH environment variable).

Commands for File Management and Manipulation

These commands are used to change the various properties of files or to view their contents. You'd use these commands in conjunction with the commands of your favorite text editor, which you will use to actually edit or create files.

cat

cat prints contents of a specified file to the screen. It uses the syntax

```
cat [options] <file(s)>
```

Options for cat include

- -n   If this flag is used, cat will number the lines of output.

- -s   If this flag is used, cat collapses consecutive blank lines into one single blank line.

> **TIP**   *A common* cat *trick is to concatenate several files into one new file, using the command* cat <file 1><file 2><file 3> >> <new file>.

chmod

chmod is used to change a file's permissions. It must be issued either by the root account or by the owner of the specified file. It uses the syntax

```
chmod [u|g|a] {+|-} {r and/or w and/or x} <filename>
```

If the u, g, or a options are not included in the command when issued, chmod uses a by default.

Options in chmod include

- u   Grants permissions only to the owner (user) of the file.

- g   Grants permissions to the various groups to which the user belongs (see Chapter 12, "User Space and User Accounts").

- a   Grants permissions to everyone who has access to the file, including those accessing the file via the Internet.

- +   Alerts chmod that you are going to add a permission to the specified file.

- −   Alerts chmod that you are going to remove a permission from the specified file.

- r   Assigns the *read* file permission, giving read-only access.

- w   Assigns the *write* file permission, giving both read and edit permissions.

- x   Assigns the *execute* file permission, giving the ability to run the file if it is an executable binary, as well as read and edit permissions.

chmod can be somewhat complicated, and you can always use File Manager to assign file permissions. Here are some examples of routine chmod tasks:

- **chmod a+r <filename>**   This command gives read permission on the specified file to all users.

- **chmod g+rw <filename>**   This command gives read and write permission on the specified file to the user's group.

- **chmod a-x <filename>**   This command removes execute permission from all users. (It is a good idea to follow such a command with one that explicitly grants execute permission to the desired people.)

chown

chown is used to change ownership of a specified file, using the syntax

```
chown <user> <filename>
```

This command must be issued by the root account or by the current owner of the specified file.

cp

cp is used to copy a specified file to a new location. It uses the syntax

```
cp <file 1> <file 2>
```

where *<file 1>* is the file to be copied, and *<file 2>* is the name of the new file.

 If you use an existing filename for <file 2>, *the contents of that file will be replaced with the contents of* <file 1>.

diff

diff compares the contents of two specified files and reports the differences found. It uses the syntax

```
diff <file1> <file2>
```

 diff *compares the files character by character. If they are not versions of the same document,* diff's *output will be lengthy.*

B

gzip & gunzip

gzip is used to compress a specified file, and gunzip is used to expand a compressed file. They are issued with the syntax

```
gzip  <filename>
gunzip <filename>
```

head & tail

head lists the first few lines of the specified file, and tail lists the last few lines of the specified file. They use the same syntax

```
head <filename>
tail <filename>
```

less

less is used to list a specified file page-by-page and uses the syntax

```
less <filename>
```

Press the SPACEBAR for the next page of the file, and press B for the previous page.

ln

ln is used to create a link to a specified file. It can be used to create either hard links or symbolic links. ln uses the syntax

```
ln [options] <linked-to file> <name of link>
```

Options for ln include

- -s   If this flag is used, the link created is a symbolic link instead of a hard link.
- -b   If this flag is used, ln makes a backup copy of the destination file.
- -v   If this flag is used, ln produces verbose output (prints the name of the file before creating the link).

mkdir

mkdir creates a new directory with the specified name, using the syntax

```
mkdir <directory name>
```

more

more presents a specified file page-by-page, using the syntax

```
more <filename>
```

Press the SPACEBAR to move forward one page in the file.

mv

mv is used to move a specified file to a new file and uses the syntax

```
mv <old> <new>
```

where <old> is the filename of the file to be moved, and *<new>* is the new location. If <new> is a filename, the file is renamed. If *<new>* is a directory name, the file is moved to the new directory with the same filename.

rm

rm is used to remove (delete) a specified file, using the syntax

```
rm [options] <filename>
```

Options for rm include

- -i If this flag is used, rm operates in interactive mode. It will request a confirmation of each file to be deleted.

> **TIP**
>
> *We strongly recommend that you use the -i flag with rm. It prevents files from being deleted inadvertently, especially if you use the wildcard *. For example, the command rm candle* will remove all files beginning with the term "candle," whether or not you intended to remove all those files. Using -i will force you to approve each file's deletion, and you can save unintentionally deleted files before they disappear.*

- -r If this flag is used, rm operates in recursive mode. It will delete all subdirectories of the current directory, as well as the files they contain.

- -f If this flag is used, rm operates in force mode. This means that rm will ignore all warnings that it issues to itself.

> **CAUTION**
>
> *The -r and -f flags are often combined, as in the command rm -rf <filename>, in order to remove entire file systems. This should be done only with extreme caution, however, especially when operating as root. The command rm -rf *.* will remove **every single file** from your file system, and you will be Very Unhappy.*

rmdir

rmdir is used to remove (delete) a specified directory and uses the syntax

```
rmdir <directory name>
```

If the named directory is not empty, rmdir will print an error message and exit.

sort

sort is used to sort items in a file numerically or alphabetically, and it prints the sorted output to the screen. It uses the syntax

```
sort <filename>
```

tar

tar is used to create or extract an archive file (often referred to as a *tarball*). If you install programs from source code, you will use this command frequently. tar is issued either with the syntax

```
tar [options] <file 1> <file 2>... <file N>
```

or with the syntax

```
tar [options] <directory 1> <directory 2>... <dir. N>
```

Options for tar do not use the hyphen, as most other flags do. Simply type the letter of the option you wish to use after the space following tar. Options include

- ■ c   Creates an archive from the specified files.
- ■ x   Extracts the files from the specified archive.
- ■ f   Compresses the specified file.
- ■ z   Decompresses the specified file, using the gunzip protocol.
- ■ v   Triggers verbose output, in which tar prints process messages to the screen while it is working.

tar can be a bit tricky to use; here are some common usages:

- tar xvfz <filename.tgz>   Probably the most common usage, this command decompresses and extracts a compressed archive, printing the name of each file as it is extracted.

- tar cfv stuff.tar /home/harry/stuff   This command creates a new archive called stuff.tar, which contains everything in the /home/harry/stuff directory.

- tar cfvz stuff.tgz /home/harry/stuff   This command has the same effect as the previous command but also creates a compressed archive using gzip.

touch

touch updates the time stamp on a specified file and uses the syntax

```
touch <filename>
```

If the filename given does not match an existing file, touch creates an empty file with that filename.

wc

wc is an acronym for "word count" and counts the number of words in a specified file. It uses the syntax

```
wc [options] <filename>
```

Options for wc are

- -c   If this flag is used, wc counts the characters (bytes) of the file instead of the words.

- -l   If this flag is used, wc counts lines in the file instead of words.

- -L   If this flag is used, wc prints the length of longest line.

B

Commands for Miscellaneous User Actions

In this section, you'll find commands for a variety of uses. Commands here can be used to search documents, find further information, check settings, and monitor disk or CPU usage.

apropos

apropos is used to search for a given file on the computer (not just in the user's account), using a keyword. It is usually used for help in finding a particular man page. It uses the syntax

```
apropos <keyword>
```

crontab

crontab is used to maintain cron files for individual users. It uses the syntax

```
crontab [-u <user>] {-l|-r|-e}
```

crontab options include

- -u   Use this flag if you need to specify a particular user. The default user is the current user issuing the command (that is, you).
- -l   Use this command to print the crontab file to the screen.
- -r   Use this flag to remove the complete crontab file.
- -e   Use this flag if you need to edit the crontab file.

date

date can be used to display or to set the current time and date. Issue it with the syntax

```
date [options]
```

If you want to set the date, use the −s option; you must be logged in as root. To set the date to 15 seconds past 8:15 A.M., June 5, 2000, you would issue the command

```
date -s 0605000815.15
```

The day, month, and year are expressed in two-digit numbers; the time is expressed using a 24-hour clock.

dd

dd is used to copy a file to another location. It is most commonly used to dump raw data to a floppy disk (you would use dd to create a boot disk, for example) without formatting the data in any way. It uses the syntax

```
dd if=<input file> of=<output file>
```

Assume you want to transfer the directory /home/harry/data to a disk so you can use it on another computer. If your floppy disk is located at /dev/fd0, issue the command

```
dd if=/home/harry/data of=/dev/fd0
```

B

du

du displays the amount of disk space used by a user or used by a specified file or directory. It uses the syntax

```
du [options] <file or directory name>
```

Options for du include

- −b If this flag is used, du will print the size in bytes.

- −c If this flag is used, du will print a comprehensive listing of each directory and its size, ending with a grand total.

- −h If this flag is used, du reports in "human-readable" sizes, such as kilobytes or megabytes.

- −k If this flag is used, du expresses the size in kilobytes, even if the directory or file occupies more than a megabyte of space.

- ■ `-m` If this flag is used, `du` expresses the size in megabytes, even if the directory or file occupies less than a megabyte of space.

- ■ `-S` If this flag is used, `du` will not count the size of subdirectories but only the size of top-level directories.

- ■ `-s` If this flag is used, `du` will display only the total size of the directory (and subdirectories) in which the command is issued.

echo

`echo` prints a specified text string to the monitor screen. It uses the syntax

```
echo [options] <string>
```

If you include the `-n` option, `echo` will not print a trailing new line when it has finished printing the requested string.

grep

`grep` (pronounced "grep," not "gee-rep") searches a specified input source for characters or numbers matching a specified pattern, called a *string*. It uses the syntax

```
grep [options] <pattern> [filename]
```

Options for `grep` are varied, and we recommend that you consult the man page. One useful option is the `-i` flag, which causes `grep` to ignore case (capitalization). This can be helpful if you don't know how the string was typed.

If no filename is given, `grep` can take as its input the output of another process. To do this, you need to construct a complex command that uses the |
character (called a *pipe*). For example, if you wanted to `grep` the output of a `ps` command for the character string "http", you would issue the command

```
ps -x | grep -e http
```

The pipe causes the output of the `ps` command to be run through `grep` before reporting to the screen.

> **NOTE** *When we speak of "patterns," we're talking about* regular expressions. *A regular expression is a pattern of conditions that can match one or more strings of text. Regular expressions can be quite complex, and a discussion of them is beyond the scope of this book. We encourage you to learn about them, though. For practical purposes, however, you can use simple text strings as patterns.*

man

man displays the UNIX manual page for a given command or program. It uses the syntax

```
man [options] <name of command or program>
```

Options for man include

- -p Use this option to specify the pager with which you want to read the manual page. The default is less, but you could choose more if you liked.

- -a Use this option to find all manual pages that match the string *<name of command or program>*.

- -h Use this option to print a one-line help message and exit man.

- -K Use this option to search for *<name of command or program>* in the text of all manual pages, as well as in the title. This can be very slow; it may be faster to use apropos in this situation.

passwd

passwd is used by both users and root to change the login password for a given account. It uses the syntax

```
passwd [<user>]
```

where passwd can be used to change user information as well as passwords. If you are logged in as root, you can use the *<user>* option to change another user's password; those logged into regular user accounts cannot use the *<user>* option.

ps

ps displays a list of all current processes, the time they have been running, and the amount of CPU time they consume. ps uses the syntax

```
ps [options]
```

Options for ps include

- ■ -a Use this flag to show all processes running on the computer, including those of other users.

- ■ -x Use this option to include processes without a controlling terminal: that is, background processes that were not manually started by you or another user.

- ■ -u Use this option to display all processes selected by your user ID.

pwd

pwd prints the full path of the current directory. This is useful if you forget where you are in the directory structure. Simply use the following at a command prompt:

```
pwd
```

set

set is used to display a list of environment variables with their current values. Use the following at a command prompt to see the report:

```
set
```

su

su is used to assume a new user identity. It is often used by the system administrator to access the root account or to fix problems in a user's account. To change to another user's account, use the syntax

```
su [-] [<username>]
```

If the – (negative sign) character is used, the new user identity's environment variables will be used. If the – is not used, you will be in the new user's account but using your own environment variables.

You can also use `su` to issue root commands with the syntax

```
su -c <command>
```

In this case, `<command>` is issued as root, but you do not actually leave your user account.

Commands for System Administration

These commands help you perform basic system administration functions, such as adding users or monitoring user processes. You can do many of these things with the graphical tools described throughout the book, but it's helpful to know the command-line alternative.

adduser

`adduser` is used to create a new user account. It uses the syntax

```
adduser [options] <username>
```

Options for `adduser` include

- ■ `-c` Use this flag to include a comment when creating the account.
- ■ `-d` Use this flag to specify the user's home directory.
- ■ `-e` Use this option to specify an expiration date for this account.
- ■ `-M` Use this flag if you do not want to create a home directory for this user.
- ■ `-p` Use this option to specify the initial password for the account.
- ■ `-s` Use this flag to specify the user's default shell environment if he or she does not want to use the default `bash` shell used by Corel Linux.

B

Require your users to change their passwords immediately.

exportfs

`exportfs` is used to export network file systems (see Chapter 24, "File and Print Sharing"). It uses the syntax

```
exportfs [options]
```

Options for `exportfs` include

- `-a`   Use this flag to export all file systems contained in /etc/exports.
- `-r`   Use this flag to re-export all file systems.
- `-u`   Use this flag to "un-export" one or more file systems.

ifconfig

`ifconfig` is used to configure network devices: see Chapter 20, "Networking." `ifconfig` uses the syntax

```
ifconfig [<device>] [options] [up|down]
```

If no options are specified, `ifconfig` displays all active devices. The *<device>* component is a network device, such as ppp0 or eth0.

Options for `ifconfig` include

- `-a`   This flag causes `ifconfig` to display all devices, regardless of status.
- `netmask <address>`   This option allows a specified IP number to be entered as a netmask.
- `<address>`   This option assigns *<address>* as the device's IP number.

A sample `ifconfig` command is shown here:

```
ifconfig eth0 192.168.0.64 netmask 255.255.255.0 up
```

This command assigns the IP address 192.168.0.64 to device eth0, with netmask number 255.255.255.0, and activates the device.

init

`init` is used to invoke the init daemon (`initd`). It is often used to change the runlevel, as described in Chapter 18, "Runlevels and the Boot Process." `init` uses the syntax

```
init <runlevel>
```

where *<runlevel>* is one of the following: 0, 1, 2, 3, 4, 5, 6, or s.

- 0 is shutdown.

- 1 is single-user mode.

- 2–5 are locally defined.

- 6 is reboot.

- s is single-user mode.

See Chapter 18 and Chapter 10, "Start Up and Shut Down," for more information on runlevels and their use in Corel Linux.

mount

`mount` is used to mount a specified file system device and make the data on that device available for use. It uses the syntax

```
mount -t <fs type> <device> <mount point>
```

- `<fs type>` is the type of file system to be mounted: for example, ext2, msdos, iso9660.

- `<device>` is the name of the file system to be mounted: for example, /dev/hda2 in the case of a physical drive, or remote:/usr/local in the case of a network file system.

- `<mount point>` is the name of an existing but empty local directory: for example, /mnt/floppy.

netstat

netstat displays the status of various network functions. It uses the syntax

netstat [options]

If you do not use an option, netstat displays all open network sockets.
Options for netstat include

- ■ -e   If this flag is used, netstat's report includes the user ID of each socket user.

- ■ -r   If this flag is used, netstat displays the complete routing table.

ping

ping is used to test network connections by sending small packets of data to a remote machine and waiting until they return. It uses the syntax

ping [options] <remote machine>

Options for ping include

- ■ -c   This flag allows you to specify the number of data packets to be sent. If you do not use this flag, ping continues to send packets until you press CTRL-C to stop.

- ■ -i   This flag allows you to specify number of seconds to wait between each packet. If you do not use this flag, the default is ten seconds.

shutdown

shutdown is used to halt all processes and shut down the computer. It uses the syntax

shutdown [options] <time> [<warning message>]

- ■ <time> is the time until the machine shuts down. It has three options:

  - ■ now

  - ■ +<m>, where <m> is the number of minutes to wait before shutting down

- <hh>:<mm>, or the time at which shutdown will commence (in hours and minutes)

- <warning message> is a message to be sent to all users. It's a good idea to use this option if anyone else is logged into the machine at the time you want to shut down.

shutdown options include

- -h   This option causes shutdown to halt or stop the system.

- -r   This option causes the computer to reboot, instead of merely powering off.

The most common shutdown command is

```
shutdown -h now
```

traceroute

traceroute is used to find the route that packets travel from one host to another. It's especially helpful in the case of Internet lag and helps to pinpoint the area that is causing the problem. traceroute uses the syntax

```
traceroute [options] <remote machine>
```

Options for traceroute include

- -n   If this flag is used, traceroute will display only IP numbers of machines, not hostnames. This saves the system resources consumed by doing a DNS lookup on each host.

- -w   Use this flag to set the time (in seconds) that traceroute will wait for a response before timing out.

ulimit

ulimit allows you to control the resources available to processes started by the shell environment. It uses the syntax

```
ulimit [options [limit]]
```

Options for `ulimit` include

- `-S`   Use this flag to set and use the "soft" resource limit, which sends a warning if a process goes over the specified limit.

- `-H`   Use this flag to set and use the "hard" resource limit, which will not permit a process to go over the specified limit.

- `-a`   If this flag is used, all current limits are reported to the screen.

- `-c`   Use this flag to set the maximum size of core files created.

- `-d`   Use this flag to set the maximum size of a process's data segment.

- `-t`   Use this flag to set the maximum amount of CPU time, in seconds, that a process can use.

- `-f`   Use this flag to set the maximum size of files created by the shell.

- `-p`   Use this flag to set the pipe buffer size.

- `-n`   Use this flag to set the maximum number of open file descriptors.

- `-u`   Use this flag to set the maximum number of user processes.

- `-v`   Use this flag to set the size of virtual memory.

umount

`umount` is used to unmount a file system. It uses the syntax

```
umount [options] <filesystem>
```

where *<filesystem>* can be a device name, such as /dev/hda1, or a directory name, such as /usr/local. Note that `umount` has only one *n*.

  `umount` can be used to unmount every file system listed in /etc/mtab at the same time through use of the `-a` flag, as in

```
umount -a
```

APPENDIX C

Linux Resources on the Internet

Although we have tried to give you as much information as we could in this book, it is inevitable that you will have questions remaining. The best place to find information about Linux is on the Internet. Whether on Web pages, via mailing lists, or through USENET posts, you'll find an amazing array of questions, answers, and general discussion about this operating system and everything that goes into it.

In this appendix, we provide some of our favorite Linux Internet resources. We've organized the list so that it fits generally with the chapter order of this book. Within each category, we've listed Web pages first, USENET newsgroups second, and mailing lists last. At the top of the list, we've created a category for our five favorite Linux Web pages—ones we consult daily.

TIP	*Most of these sites, as well as many of the newsgroups and mailing lists included here, have FAQ (Frequently Asked Questions) documents. It is always a good idea to read the FAQ first; chances are good that your problem or question is a common one and is already answered in the FAQ. If you post to a newsgroup, discussion board, or list with a question that's answered in the FAQ, don't be surprised if you're treated rudely; it's expected that new participants have read the FAQ before joining in. If there's no FAQ, try to find message archives (`http://www.deja.com` for USENET groups; check the subscription message to see if a mailing list has archives available) and see if your question has already been answered.*

Subscribing to a Mailing List

If you've never subscribed to a mailing list, you might find the process a bit arcane. At its most basic, *mailing list* (also called a *listserv*) is a collection of people interested in reading and writing e-mail messages on a central topic. Every message is sent to a central address; the computer at that address forwards the message to each subscriber. Some mailing lists are very *low-traffic*, receiving three or four posts a week, while others are extremely *high-traffic*, passing on three or four hundred posts a day. Many lists offer the option of a *digest* version, which is a daily (or few times daily, depending on traffic) message containing all the posts sent to the list that day. It's a lengthy message, but it cuts down on the constant flow of new e-mail.

Generally, to subscribe to a mailing list, you send e-mail to an *administrative e-mail address*, which is not the same as the regular *list e-mail address*. For example, suppose you want to subscribe to the fictitious list penguinmania, so you'd send a request to `majordomo@mailinglist.org` (not a real address!). Many listservs use the extension `-l` in their names; this makes it easier for system administrators, who can tell at a glance whether mail is intended for the list `penguinmania-l` or the user `penguinmania`.

Information about mailing lists usually includes the administrative address and the regular list address. Never send administrative mail to the list address! The e-mail will be distributed to everyone on the mailing list, and people on the list cannot help you; the list owner is usually not the person running the computer where the list is housed. Send the following message to the administrative address:

```
subscribe penguinmania-l yourusername@yourISP.com (Your Name)
```

This is the basic format for subscription; if the list requires a different syntax, the subscription information will usually provide this information. (Or, you can look at the error message you receive from the computer to see what the proper format is.)

Once you have successfully subscribed, you will receive a welcome message from the list. Save this message; it usually contains a list of the commands that the list software understands. Use these commands to configure your subscription so that it suits you. It will also contain information on unsubscribing from the list; you must unsubscribe through the administrative address, not the list address. You may even be able to see archives of previous list messages by using these commands.

To send messages to the list, you'll write to the regular list address (in our fictitious case, `penguinmania-l@mailing-lists.net`). All mail to this address is sent to all list subscribers. It's often a good idea to wait a few days before posting, so that you can ascertain the tone of the list. Many lists ask that new subscribers post an introduction message as well.

C

The Top Five Linux Web Pages

Here they are: the best Linux resources on the Web. Most of these are actually Linux news sites, whether Web journals or "headline news" sites. If you like Linux, we recommend that you check these sites every few days to see what's new in the community.

http://www.slashdot.org

Slashdot is home base. This is the page almost everyone reads; you'll find collections of links to Linux-related articles elsewhere on the Internet, as well as some homegrown articles. The main "feature" of Slashdot is the commentary—once you've read a story, you can post a follow-up comment. If you don't like the commentary (Kate dislikes it; Joe finds it amusing and sometimes useful), you can ignore it and just read the stories.

http://www.linuxjournal.com

Linux Journal is a print magazine that maintains a great Web site. The journal provides extra content on the Web that isn't in the print version, as well as a comprehensive archive of past issues. *Linux Journal* addresses the needs of all kinds of Linux users, from beginners to business decision-makers to hard-core programmers.

http://www.linuxtoday.com

Linux Today is also a collection of articles, but the site is targeted at the business community. You'll find interesting comments on the Linux versus Microsoft debate, as well as ongoing discussions of how the Linux and free software philosophies can fit best into a corporate mind-set. The sidebar along the right, containing Linux Today exclusives, is worth checking regularly.

http://www.linuxdoc.org

We have referred to this site frequently throughout the writing of this book. The Linux Documentation Project is a group of volunteers who work tirelessly to bring better documentation of Linux software to users like all of us. You can find an exhaustive set of HOWTO documents, longer guides on various topics, and a set of man pages at this site, as well as general information.

http://www.lwn.net/

Despite its name, Linux Weekly News actually has a daily updates page (at `http://www.lwn.net/daily`). This site contains lots of great articles written specifically for LWN, a calendar of important Linux events and conferences, a Linux timeline, and even a page where you can track the behavior of all Linux-related stocks.

Corel Linux Resources

If you're looking for information specifically about Corel Linux, there's no better place to go than to the source. Corel has a detailed Web site for its users, and you'll also find useful information and software at the Debian site, since Corel's distribution is based on Debian's.

Using USENET Newsgroups Effectively

We provide the names of many USENET newsgroups in this appendix; newsgroups are often a fast and useful way to get information. However, you should be aware that all the groups we have listed are in the `comp.*` hierarchy, and nowhere else on USENET will you find the "rules of netiquette" in force more than in `comp.*`.

What does that mean for you? It means that you should find the group's FAQ and read it before you post anything and that you should lurk quietly (reading without posting) for a while before you begin to post to the group. In years past, *newbies* (people new to USENET) were expected to *lurk a group* for six weeks before posting; with the advent of archiving services such as Deja (`http://www.deja.com`), you can look over previous postings and shorten that time. It's still a good idea to lurk for a few days, if not a couple of weeks, before you jump in with a question. `comp.*` groups tend to be technical and not always welcoming to new posters; even Kate treads lightly in `comp.*`, and she's been involved in USENET governance for years.

If you're new to USENET altogether, we recommend that you read `news.announce.newusers` for a while. Regular postings of USENET FAQs, as well as some highly knowledgeable and friendly helpers, make this a useful group for everyone.

C

http://linux.corel.com

Home for the Corel Linux distribution. You'll find bug fixes, software patches, helpful hints, and many other useful things at this site.

http://www.debian.org

This is the home of the Debian group, the distribution upon which Corel Linux is based. At this site, you can find Debian packages for various software programs you might want to install, as well as updates on Debian-related topics.

Software to Download

It's highly unlikely that you'll be satisfied forever with only the software that came bundled with Corel Linux. When you're ready to locate and install new software, check out these sites to see what's new and useful.

http://www.freshmeat.net

At Freshmeat, you'll find the latest releases of Linux software. Individual packages are accompanied by explanations of what's been updated, and there's also an option for people to leave comments about any particular program. The software listings are updated daily, and you can see past updates in their archive files. Freshmeat and Slashdot are owned by the same parent company.

http://www.linuxberg.org

Linuxberg is run by the same folks who run the wildly popular Windows software site, Tucows (`http://www.tucows.com`). The Linuxberg administrators rate each program with their exclusive five-cow rating system. Many programs here are freeware or shareware, though some are demo versions of commercial programs.

http://www.linuxapps.com

Like Freshmeat, `linuxapps.com` is a great place for developers to upload their own programs. Each package's entry has release notes, and software is well organized into a variety of categories. The site motto is "If you can't find it here, you can't find it anywhere," and many users agree.

Linux History, Activism, and General Information

It's hard to run Linux without finding yourself drawn into the Linux community. Whether you just want some more information about the operating system or you're ready to become a hardcore Linux activist, these sites will give you the information and support you need.

http://www.linux.org

Do you have questions about Linux itself or want to share the Linux message with friends and family? Linux Online is a great place to start; it provides tons of links to other sites, as well as its own editorial content about Linux. You can even get a nifty coffee mug to show your support!

http://www.fsf.org

The home of the Free Software Foundation. FSF works to promote open source software, through both discussion and programming. You can order software, obtain documentation, or even get t-shirts at this site.

comp.os.linux.announce (moderated)

This group carries announcements of interest to the entire Linux community, regardless of distribution. The group is moderated, which means that posts must be approved by the moderator before they are forwarded to the group. You can find the `comp.os.linux.announce` FAQs at `http://www.faqs.org/faqs/by-newsgroup/comp/comp.os.linux.announce.html`.

comp.os.linux.answers (moderated)

This useful group carries regular postings of helpful documentation, such as HOWTO documents, FAQs, and other types of posts that offer answers to regular questions. It is also a moderated group; you can't post your question, but you may find documents that answer that question posted here. Look at `http://www.faqs.org/faqs/by-newsgroup/comp/comp.os.linux.answers.html` for some of the FAQs posted regularly to this group.

C

LINUX-L

The LINUX-L mailing list is a high-traffic list that covers all material relevant to Linux. Subscribe by sending the following message to `listserv@greywolf.dyn.ml.org`:

```
subscribe LINUX-L
```

You'll receive a message that contains the regular listserv address, as well as specific information about the LINUX-L list.

X Window System

There's no way we could have covered everything about the X Window System that you need to know. If you're curious about the way in which your computer renders graphics, see these sites for a better understanding of X and how it works.

http://www.x.org

The home site for the worldwide consortium that develops and maintains the X Window System. While you won't find much help for basic problems here, you will get a better understanding of the scope of the project as well as the consortium's vision for the future of graphics on UNIX and UNIX-derived platforms.

http://www.xfree86.org

XFree86 is the implementation of the X Window System for personal computer chips. There's a useful FAQ at this site as well as more information on using X with the particular chip architecture you have in your computer (if you're running a 386, 486, or Pentium computer, you're covered by this implementation).

http://www.rahul.net/kenton/xsites.framed.html

Kenton Lee has compiled the definitive list of Web resources related to the X Window System. Everything is here, from basic FAQs to extremely technical development documents. If you have a question about X, this is a good place to start looking for assistance.

comp.os.linux.x

This group carries highly technical discussions of the X Window System as it is implemented under Linux. You'll probably want to read this one for a long time before you post. Find the group's FAQ at `http://www.faqs.org/faqs/by-newsgroup/comp/comp.os.linux.x.html`.

KDE

KDE, the desktop installed with Corel Linux, is pretty straightforward. However, you might want to download one of the many new programs designed especially for KDE environments. We're pretty sure you'll want to try out some great desktop themes, too.

http://www.kde.org

The home site for the KDE project. At `kde.org`, you'll find downloadable software, exhaustive FAQs, opportunities to volunteer your assistance, and late-breaking news about the KDE desktop. This is the place where you should start if you have questions about KDE.

http://kde.themes.org

Interested in updating your desktop themes? Visit this site and select from more than 80 KDE-specific desktop themes. You'll find themes ranging from sleek and simple to outrageous and fun. You'll even find directions for creating your own desktop themes; when you've done so, you can upload your theme to share it with the KDE world.

comp.windows.x.kde

This is the home group for USENET discussion of the KDE desktop. Posts here are fairly well distributed between user questions and helpful answers; it's often a place where users help users solve common problems. There is no FAQ for this group; you can browse past posts at Deja.

C

Basic System Administration

Once you get Corel Linux up and running, you'll need a handle on basic system administration. We've provided a lot of information in this book, but here are some more sites that give different perspectives or explain items we haven't covered in much depth.

http://www.linuxdoc.org/LDP/lame/LAME/linux-admin-made-easy/book1.html

"Linux System Administration Made Easy" is a guide written for those who are contemplating becoming a Linux systems administrator or who find themselves in that position. It contains much helpful information in a pleasant and friendly tone.

http://lithos.gat.com/docview/unix-5.html

Okay, so this isn't quite a system administration page. However, "Unix Tips for Your Mom" contains a few basic commands that will make your Linux life a bit easier. You may want to print it and put it near your computer, especially if you have users who are not familiar with standard shell commands.

http://www.uwsg.indiana.edu/usail/

Here's an unusual site, containing a self-paced system administration course. It's UNIX based, so you may find some differences between what's listed there and how your Corel Linux box operates; still, it's an excellent resource to get an overall view of how UNIX and UNIX-derived systems are managed on a day-to-day basis. (If you feel like going to Bloomington, Indiana, you can even take a certification course through Indiana University's education certification program!)

http://www.washington.edu/R870/

Another university site, this one from the University of Washington. These are course notes from a system administration course (UNIX based) taught by Dave Dittrich. The notes contain sample problems for you to solve, and the general philosophy of the course is hands-on solutions to real system administration problems and issues.

http://www.iu.hioslo.no/~mark/sysadmin/ SystemAdmin.html

Yet another university site, from the University of Oslo in Norway (but written in English). Mark Burgess has based his course notes on the Debian distribution of Linux, so you will probably find this course more directly applicable to your Corel Linux computer than the two sites listed previously.

Shells and Scripting

If you enjoyed Chapter 17, "The Shell Expanded: Basic Scripting," you may want to spend some time at these sites. Here you'll find helpful hints, sample scripts, and a lot of other good information to support you in scripting for `bash`.

http://www.washington.edu/computing/unix/shell.html

A basic introduction to the concepts of shells and how scripts run within shell environments. This is a good site to check out if you want a one-page explanation of text-based shells.

http://cnswww.cns.cwru.edu/~chet/bash/bashtop.html

For all the information you'll ever need about the `bash` shell environment (the default shell in Corel Linux), see the Bash Home Page. This page contains a detailed FAQ, a reference manual, a copy of the `bash` man page, and various documents relating to the effective use of `bash`.

http://www.oase-shareware.org/shell/

Here at Heiner's SHELLdorado, you'll find a plethora of shell scripts, documentation, and good advice on writing your own scripts. Check the links page; Heiner has arranged it neatly into categories including sample scripts, articles about scripting and shells, and documentation.

comp.unix.shell

This group contains discussions of the various UNIX shells, whether used under Linux or other UNIX and UNIX-derived operating systems. Conversation here is

C

often highly technical, and not all posts relate to the `bash` shell, so read carefully. Quite a few FAQs are posted here regularly, and you can see them at `http://www. faqs.org/faqs/by-newsgroup/comp/comp.unix.shell.html`.

Networking

In the world of networking, things change quite fast. It's a good idea to keep on top of the news if you manage a multiple-computer network, and these sites are a good place to start.

http://www.linuxdoc.org/HOWTO/ Networking-Overview-HOWTO.html

We've pointed you to a lot of HOWTO files throughout this book, and here's another one. The Networking Overview HOWTO gives a good introduction to the concepts of networking under Linux, as well as some resources for further study.

http://www.linuxdoc.org/LDP/nag/nag.html

The *Network Administrator's Guide* is a comprehensive guide to networking Linux computers; although some of the information is out of date (the document was last edited in 1996), the basic concepts are still accurate and valuable. O'Reilly publishes this book, if you need it in hard copy, but the contents are released under an open-source license, so Olaf Kirch has made his book available on the Web as well.

http://www.btc.gatech.edu/net/management/linux/ commands.html

A good introduction to Linux networking commands, divided into several categories. Use this page, combined with the man pages installed on your computer, to get a grip on the various commands you need to execute networking properly.

http://www.cablemodeminfo.com/ LinuxCableModem.html

If you have a cable modem, or are interested in getting one, this page contains all the resources and references that you'll need for Linux and cable modem compatibility. It also offers links to useful networking documents, which is especially important if you're going to use the cable modem on a network.

http://www3.sympatico.ca/bestb

This document describes the process necessary to add PPPoE, a method used with some DSL modems, to a Corel Linux machine. It includes specific instructions on recompiling the kernel and compiling `PPPoEd`, the PPPoE daemon.

Mail Services

If you've decided to run a mail server on your Corel Linux machine, we suggest that you check out these sites for more information and some assistance in this task. We've concentrated on `exim` here, but you can find other good sites by searching on the server package name with a good search engine, such as `http://www.google.com`.

http://www.exim.org/

This is the home page for the `exim` mail server. It offers documentation, a good FAQ, downloads, and a list of mailing lists hosted by `exim.org`.

comp.mail.misc

In this group, you'll find postings covering a variety of mail transport agents for Linux. Many of the MTAs available have single-topic newsgroups of their own; `exim` does not, so posts concerning `exim` can be found here. Many FAQs are also posted here regularly; find them at `http://www.faqs.org/faqs/by-newsgroup/comp/comp.mail.misc.html`.

exim MTA

This mailing list covers information related to the `exim` mail transfer agent (MTA). You can read the public archives, subscribe, and learn more about the list at its Web page: `http://www.egroups.com/list/exim-users/info.html`.

C

File and Print Sharing

Readers who are using Samba or `netatalk` on a multiple-OS network should bookmark these sites. It's a good idea to keep track of new announcements or programs in this area, since things change quite rapidly.

http://www.samba.org

When you use this URL, you'll be asked to select the mirror site that is closest to you geographically. The main site for Samba information, `samba.org`, contains reference material, news stories, archives of past announcements, and software downloads. If you're interested in networking between Linux and Windows machines, you need Samba.

http://www.umich.edu/~rsug/netatalk/

Is your favorite non-Linux operating system the MacOS? If you need to network Macintoshes with Linux machines, you need `netatalk`, a Samba-equivalent program that uses the Appletalk protocol to enable file and print sharing between Macintoshes and Linux computers. This is the bare-bones `netatalk` home page, which has a FAQ, a good list of `netatalk` links, and downloadable software packages.

http://www.rit.edu/~pcm6519/linux.html

This is a document directed at people who have a cable modem and want to enable print sharing between a Windows machine and a Linux machine. The author focuses on Red Hat Linux, but you ought to be able to translate easily to Corel Linux.

comp.protocols.smb

Technical discussions of the `smb` file transfer protocol and programs such as Samba that implement it. No FAQ is posted here; read past posts at an archive such as Deja to get a better sense of the group.

Web Services

Running Apache to serve your Web pages? We suggest these sites as good resources for Apache administration. You'll find information from the basic to the complicated here.

http://www.apache.org

The home of the Apache Software Foundation. This site offers downloads, documentation, a set of links, and news about Apache and its use throughout the business and personal community. Other sites are better targeted to the beginning Apache user, but keep an eye on `apache.org` to see what's happening with this great server.

http://www.irt.org/articles/js180/index.htm

If you're ready to customize your Apache server, consult this article for more information and a few tricks. Apache is a modular server, and you can modify each module for behavior tailored to your needs.

comp.infosystems.www.servers.unix

Here you'll find discussion of the various Web servers available for UNIX and UNIX-derived platforms; in practical terms, this is where people discuss Apache. No FAQ is posted here; use Deja's archives to see previous posts to the group.

Network Services

This section provides a few links for the various network services you might want to run. (Links for networks are given earlier in this chapter.) We've provided links for both DNS and DHCP.

http://www.linuxdoc.org/HOWTO/DNS-HOWTO.html

We recommended this HOWTO file in the chapter on DNS, but it's important enough to repeat here. Using this HOWTO will help you establish a basic DNS server, editing your configuration files correctly and ensuring that you return proper records for any sort of domain name.

http://www.acmebw.com/askmrdns/

Got a question about DNS? "Ask Mr. DNS" is here to help! This page provides basic information about running DNS on a Linux home network.

http://www.linuxplanet.com/linuxplanet/tutorials/894/1/

Here's a useful tutorial that will get you up and running with your own DHCP server. Follow the four basic steps in this clearly written online course. You may also want to browse the Linux Planet tutorials on other subjects; this is an easy way to learn complex topics.

Security

We can't overstate the importance of good security. If there's any single topic that you should keep up to date with, it's security. Here are some good resources for security announcements and information to help you secure your system.

http://securityportal.com/lasg/

Like the *Network Administrator's Guide* described earlier, the Linux Administrator's Security Guide is a full-length guide to installing and running Linux securely. It includes information on encryption, logging, installing new patches, and keeping tabs on connections made to your computer. The document is released under an Open Source license.

http://www.ecst.csuchico.edu/~jtmurphy/

The Linux Security Home Page is a central site that collects news reports, downloadable security patches, and documentation for various security holes found in Linux distributions. This is a valuable site, especially if you connect your Corel Linux computer to others, whether through a local network or via the Internet.

http://www.debian.org/security/

The latest security updates from the Debian team, which apply to your Corel Linux box. Keep an eye on this site just to be sure you patch any security holes as they become known. Debian patches should work directly with Corel Linux.

linux-sec-l

The `linux-sec-l` mailing list covers issues related to Linux security. Subscribe by sending the following message to `listproc@bnl.gov`:

```
subscribe linux-sec-l Your Full Name
```

You'll receive a message that contains the regular listserv address as well as specific information about the `linux-sec-l` list.

comp.security.announce (moderated)

If you connect your computer to the Internet, you need to read this group. Here you will find postings from the CERT Coordination Center, a research unit of Carnegie Mellon University devoted to computer security issues. If a virus warning is posted by CERT, the virus is real.

TIP	*Many of the virus-panic e-mails that you may receive are pure hoaxes; you can check them against the CERT Web page at* `http://www.cert.org`. *Don't pass on virus warnings without checking them out first.*

comp.security.unix

This group carries discussion of security issues specific to UNIX and UNIX-derived operating systems. You may find posts concerning particular software packages, discussions of potential security holes, and other security-related topics. `comp.security.unix` FAQs can be found at `http://www.faqs.org/faqs/by-newsgroup/comp/comp.security.unix.html`.

Just for Fun

Never let it be said that the Linux community doesn't know how to have fun! These links just touch the tip of the iceberg; you'll find lots of humor in the Linux world. These are a few good places to start, but we're sure you'll find more.

http://www.userfriendly.org

Almost everyone we know reads this daily Web cartoon strip, which illustrates life at an ISP. There's usually Linux content as well.

http://www.copyleft.net

Want something that shows the world that you like Linux? Consider picking up a t-shirt, cap, or sticker from Copyleft. These folks carry licensed wear for Slashdot, Debian, User Friendly, and Freshmeat, among other great Linux sites.

http://tunes.org/~do/penguindex.html

An entire site devoted to Linux Penguins on the Web. You'll find all sorts of links here, including games, humor, penguin merchandise, and various pictures of Tux, the Linux penguin. (If you purchased the deluxe edition of Corel Linux, you received your own foam Tux in the box!)

APPENDIX D

Initialization Scripts

his appendix contains the various initialization scripts that can be found in
the etc/init.d directory. These scripts show the default desktop configuration;
other scripts may be installed with other configurations, though the format should
be similar to what you see here. We have provided some annotation of the scripts,
especially the first few, in order to show how the scripts are constructed. We
have also reviewed init scripts in other parts of the book, especially the scripts
that control the operation of Apache, the Web server package, and Samba, the
Linux-Windows networking program.

> **NOTE** *We are fairly verbose in the annotation of the first few scripts; but, since
> many of the scripts have similar features, we did not note the repetitive
> features in the remainder of the appendix. Many scripts are printed without
> notation since the functions are clearly commented or are apparent from
> earlier notes. If you're looking for more detailed explanations of a script
> toward the end of the appendix, check out the scripts at the beginning to see
> if your question is answered there. Also, please note that the backslash (\) at
> the end of a line means that the line actually continues onto the next line.
> Due to page-width considerations, some single lines of code would not fit on
> one printed line.*

apache

This script stops, starts, and reloads the Apache Web server package.

```
#! /bin/sh
#
# apache        Start the apache HTTP server.
#
```

The following lines initialize some basic variables. For the most part, they
describe the locations of certain software and files needed by Apache. This allows
you to change the location of files, or to specify alternate files, without having
to completely rewrite the script.

```
NAME=apache
PATH=/bin:/usr/bin:/sbin:/usr/sbin
DAEMON=/usr/sbin/apache
SUEXEC=/usr/lib/apache/suexec
PIDFILE=/var/run/$NAME.pid
CONF=/etc/apache/httpd.conf
APACHECTL=/usr/sbin/apachectl
```

The following two lines are *signal traps*. One of the ways that UNIX processes can communicate with each other is by sending various predefined signals. Signal 1 means "hangup" and Signal 15 means "terminate." The purpose of the following two commands is to tell the script to *ignore* these signals; hence, the null string (""), which indicates that no command, not even the default, is to be assigned to the signal.

```
trap "" 1
trap "" 15
```

The following two lines test whether certain files exist. The files to be checked are indicated by variables defined previously. So, $DAEMON is /usr/sbin/apache, and $APACHECTL is /usr/sbin/apachectl. If the files called here do not exist, the script will terminate with an exit status of 0, meaning that no error will be reported; the script will simply fail to execute any further.

```
test -f $DAEMON || exit 0
test -f $APACHECTL || exit 0
```

The following four lines search for a particular line of code in the file represented by $CONF (in this case, /etc/apache/httpd.conf). If the code is found, the script exits. The search is done with the egrep command, an extended form of grep.

In this case, the script searches for a line that indicates that Apache is to be started from inetd. If this is the case, it is not appropriate for Apache to be started from init, and the script will exit, again with status 0.

```
if egrep -q -i "^[[:space:]]*ServerType[[:space:]]+inet\>" $CONF
then
    exit 0
fi
```

Now we come to the meat of this script. The following 56 lines constitute one big *case* statement. Each case tells the machine what to do in response to various command-line arguments that can be passed. The possible arguments are start, stop, reload, reload-modules, and *, the default case. The command-line argument is represented by the variable $1.

```
case "$1" in
```

The following nine lines are the start case. If the command /etc/init.d/apache start is issued, this is the block of code that is run. This set of commands runs the program /usr/sbin/apachectl (represented by the variable $APACHECTL). You don't need to see any output from that program, so the output is suppressed by being directed to /dev/null. If the program executes successfully—returns an exit status of 0—the script simply prints a single dot to the screen and exits. Otherwise, the script indicates that it has failed. If you need to know why it has failed, you can run /usr/sbin/apachectl directly and look at the output.

```
start)
    echo -n "Starting web server: $NAME"
    if $APACHECTL start > /dev/null 2>&1
    then
      echo "."
    else
      echo "... failed."
    fi
    ;;
```

The following five lines are the stop case. If you issue the command /etc/init.d/apache stop, this section of code will execute. This section simply invokes /usr/sbin/apachectl with a command-line argument of stop.

```
stop)
    echo -n "Stopping web server: $NAME"
    $APACHECTL stop > /dev/null
    echo "."
    ;;
```

The next nine lines constitute the reload case. This case tries to reload the Apache configuration files; it does so by invoking the command /usr/sbin/apachectl graceful. This command shuts down and restarts Apache in a way that keeps closer track of possible errors.

```
  reload)
    echo -n "Reloading $NAME configuration... "
    if $APACHECTL graceful > /dev/null 2>&1
    then
      echo " done."
    else
      echo " failed."
    fi
    ;;
```

The next case is the reload-modules case. Apache has a number of modules that can be run to provide various extended functions, such as the parsing of perl or php scripts, secure transmission of information, and so on. This case uses the start-stop-daemon command with a number of arguments to stop and restart Apache; the start-stop-daemon command is a more elaborate way to restart a process and allows fairly fine control of the process when it is run.

```
reload-modules)
    echo -n "Restarting $NAME daemon."
    $APACHECTL stop > /dev/null
    start-stop-daemon --stop --quiet --oknodo --pidfile $PIDFILE > /dev/null
    echo -n "."
    sleep 4
    echo -n "."
    test -u $SUEXEC && echo
    if $APACHECTL start > /dev/null 2>&1
    then
      echo " done."
    else
      echo " failed."
    fi
    ;;
```

The next two cases are restart and force-reload. These do nothing more than invoke another instance of the script, an action indicated by the $0 variable, with the reload-modules option. There is nothing that prevents a script, or even a function within a script, from calling itself. Such a function is called a *recursive function*, and they are common in programming.

```
restart)
    $0 reload-modules
    ;;

force-reload)
    $0 reload-modules
    ;;
```

Finally, we come to the default case. If /etc/init.d/apache is invoked with no argument, or with any other argument than those defined previously, the script prints a short message explaining the correct arguments and exits with a status of 1 (error).

```
  *)
    echo "Usage: /etc/init.d/$NAME {start|stop|reload|reload-modules|force\
reload|restart}"
    exit 1
    ;;
esac
```

D

If the script made it this far, the execution has been successful. All that's left is for the process to exit with status 0.

```
exit 0
```

apmd

The Advanced Power Management daemon is a program that controls certain aspects of a machine's power system. Advanced Power Management is used primarily in laptop computers, but some desktop models also use it. Consult your machine's manual to determine whether you should run this script.

```
#!/bin/sh
#
# Start or stop the Advanced Power Management daemon.
#
# Written by Dirk Eddelbuettel <edd@debian.org>
# Greatly modified by Avery Pennarun <apenwarr@debian.org>
#
# I think this script is now free of bashisms.  Please correct me if I'm
# wrong!
```

A note on the preceding comment is in order: the GNU bash shell has certain syntax features that are not shared with the regular UNIX Bourne shell. The authors of this script have attempted to remove these features so that the script will run on systems using either bash or sh. Note that the shell invoked is sh, which on GNU and Linux systems is often a symbolic link to bash. The point of all this is that the script should run without modifications on any UNIX or UNIX-derived system.

```
PATH=/bin:/usr/bin:/sbin:/usr/sbin
```

The above line sets a path variable.

```
test -s /usr/sbin/apmd || exit 0

test -e /proc/apm || exit 0
```

The preceding two lines check for the presence of two files; in the case of the first file, the -s argument ensures that the size of the file is greater than 0 bytes. If either file is not found, the script exits.

```
[ -f /etc/default/rcS ] && . /etc/default/rcS
```

The preceding line is another test. The [ ] construction is equivalent to the `test` command, and the && operator is a logical `and`. The line means, essentially, "check to see if the file /etc/default/rcS exists; if it does, run it."

```
# As apmd can be called with arguments, we use this variable to store these
# options as eg APMD="-w 5 -p 2". See the manual page apmd(8) for details.
APMD=""
```

This is a well-commented script. As the note points out, if command-line arguments are needed for `apmd`, they can be inserted between the quotes.

```
# The $GMT variable in /etc/default/rcS is supposed to be blank or "-u" for
# UTC.  But we can't be sure of this, so let's be more careful.
case "$GMT" in
  *-u*|*--utc*)
      APMGMT="-u"
      ;;
  *)
      APMGMT=""
      ;;
esac
```

Again, the preceding comment is clear. This case statement checks the value of a certain environment variable and makes it conform to a standard format if it doesn't already conform.

The following lines constitute the main case statement. The possible command-line arguments are start, stop, restart, and force-reload. Anything else prints a usage message. (See the Apache script for a detailed explanation of the main `case` statement.)

```
case "$1" in
  start)
    echo -n "Starting advanced power management daemon: "
    start-stop-daemon --start --quiet --exec /usr/sbin/apmd -- \
          -s 'run-parts /etc/apm/suspend.d' \
          -r 'run-parts /etc/apm/resume.d' $APMGMT $APMD
    echo "apmd."
    ;;
  stop)
    echo -n "Stopping advanced power management daemon: "
    start-stop-daemon --stop --quiet --oknodo --exec /usr/sbin/apmd
    echo "apmd."
```

D

```
    ;;
  restart|force-reload)
    echo -n "Stopping advanced power management daemon: "
    start-stop-daemon --stop --quiet --oknodo --exec /usr/sbin/apmd
    echo "apmd."
    echo -n "Starting advanced power management daemon: "
    start-stop-daemon --start --quiet --exec /usr/sbin/apmd -- \
            -s 'run-parts /etc/apm/suspend.d' \
            -r 'run-parts /etc/apm/resume.d' $APMGMT $APMD
    echo "apmd."
    ;;
  *)
    echo "Usage: /etc/init.d/apmd {start|stop|restart|force-reload}"
    exit 1
esac
```

Assuming everything went smoothly, the script can now exit with status 0.

```
exit 0
```

autofs

This file controls the automounter, which controls the automatic mounting of file systems. Note that this script uses a few elements that are outside the scope of this book. In particular, it makes use of the Network Information Service (NIS; commands that begin with "yp" are part of this service) and of the sed program, which is a text string processor. We give you a general idea of what's going on here, without getting into the gory details. Odds are you're not using NIS anyway, and entire books are devoted to the workings of sed.

```
#! /bin/sh -e
#
#    rc file for automount using a Sun-style "master map".
#    We first look for a local /etc/auto.master, then a YP
#    map with that name
#
#    On most distributions, this file should be called:
#    /etc/rc.d/init.d/autofs or /etc/init.d/autofs
#
# List of options to ignore with NIS maps. You can use this to filter out
# options that Linux does not (yet) understand if your mount does not
# understand the -s (sloppy) flag. Seperate the options with spaces!
#
PRUNEOPTIONS="quota"
```

```
#
#      We can add local options here
#      e.g. localoptions='rsize=8192,wsize=8192'
#
localoptions=''

#
#   Command line arguments to pass to the autofs daemon
#
daemonargs="--setuser"

#
#      The name and location of the daemon
#
DAEMON=/usr/sbin/automount

# Check if automount exists
test -f $DAEMON || exit 0
```

Like the previously shown scripts, this first section opens the script by defining certain variables. It then tests to make sure that the `automount` daemon program actually exists. However, the author of this script, unlike the previous scripts, has chosen to make comments about each variable, which is extremely helpful. Such comments are not strictly necessary, and you won't find such attention to detail in most scripts, but it certainly helps to understand the purpose of each variable in the script.

```
# Check if autofs is available on the system
if ! grep -q autofs /proc/filesystems; then
      if [ ! -e /lib/modules/`uname -r`/fs/autofs.o ]; then
            echo "Error: autofs support not available."
            exit 0
      fi
fi
```

The preceding section is an extended bit of checking. The script checks two elements: first, it checks to see whether the autofs file system has an entry in the /proc/filesystems directory, and second, it checks to see that a kernel module called autofs.o is available. If not, the script prints an error message and exits.

```
PATH=/sbin:/usr/sbin:/bin:/usr/bin
export PATH
```

In the preceding lines, the script defines the PATH variable and exports it, making it an environment variable.

```
# Make a regular expression from PRUNEOPTIONS
test ! -z "$PRUNEOPTIONS" &&
   PRUNEREGEX=`echo $PRUNEOPTIONS | \
          sed -e 's#^#\\\(#' -e 's# \+#\\\|#g' -e 's#$#\\\)#'`
```

The preceding block of code turns the string contained in the variable PRUNEOPTIONS into a *regular expression*. Regular expressions are a way of generalizing text strings so that they can be matched by more than one possible specific string.

```
#
#      This function will build a list of automount commands to execute in
#      order to activate all the mount points. It is used to figure out
#      the difference of automount points in case of a reload
#
getmounts()
{
```

This construction indicates that a function is being defined. Thus, all the code that follows (until a matching closing curly bracket is reached) will not be executed at this point, but rather when the getmounts function is called. The function itself uses sed to extract a number of parameters from certain system files. These parameters will be used to configure mount points.

```
#
#      Check for local maps to be loaded
#
if [ -f /etc/auto.master ]
then
     cat /etc/auto.master | sed -e '/^#/d' -e '/^$/d'| (
     while read dir map options
     do
          if [ ! -z "$dir" -a ! -z "$map" -a \
             x`echo "$map" | cut -c1` != 'x-' ]
             then
             map=`echo "/etc/$map" | sed -e 's:^/etc//:/:'`
             # special: treat -t or --timeout (or any reasonable derivative)
             # specially, since it can't be made a normal mount option.
             mountoptions=""
             if echo $options | grep -- '-t' >/dev/null 2>&1 ; then
                 mountoptions="--timeout $(echo $options | \
```

```
                    sed 's/^.*-t\(imeout\)*[ \t]*\([0-9][0-9]*\).*$/\2/g')"
            fi
            options=`echo "$options" | sed -e '
                s/--*t\(imeout\)*[       ]*[0-9][0-9]*//g
                s/\(^\|[ \t]\)-/\1/g'`

            if [ -x $map ]; then
                echo "$DAEMON $mountoptions $dir program $map $options\
$localoptions"
            elif [ -f $map ]; then
                echo "$DAEMON $mountoptions $dir file $map $options\
$localoptions"
            else
                echo "$DAEMON $mountoptions $dir `basename $map` $options\
$localoptions"
            fi
        fi
        done
    ) | sed 's/  / /g'
fi


#
#     Check for YellowPage maps to be loaded
#
if [ -e /usr/bin/ypcat ] && [ `grep +auto.master /etc/auto.master` ] && [\
`ypcat -k auto.master 2>/dev/null | wc -l` -gt 0 ]
then
    ypcat -k auto.master | (
      while read dir map options
      do
          if [ ! -z "$dir" -a ! -z "$map" \
              -a x`echo "$map" | cut -c1` != 'x-' ]
          then
            map=`echo "$map" | sed -e 's/^auto_/auto./'`
            # special: treat -t or --timeout (or any reasonable derivative)
            # specially, since it can't be made a normal mount option.
            mountoptions=""
            if echo $options | grep -- '-t' >/dev/null 2>&1 ; then
                mountoptions="--timeout $(echo $options | \
                sed 's/^.*-t\(imeout\)*[   ]*\([0-9][0-9]*\).*$/\2/g')"
            fi
            options=`echo "$options" | sed -e '
                s/--*t\(imeout\)*[ \t]*[0-9][0-9]*//g
                s/\(^\|[ \t]\)-/\1/g'`

            options=`echo "$options" | sed -e 's/\(^\|[ \t]\)-/\1/g'`
            test ! -z "$PRUNEREGEX" && \
                options=`echo $options | \
```

```
                        sed -e "s#$PRUNEREGEX##g" -e 's#,\+#,#g' -e 's#,$##'`
                echo "$DAEMON $mountoptions $dir yp $map $options $localoptions"
            fi
        done
     )
fi
}


#
#       Status lister.
#
```

This function reports the status of the mount points that are configured with the
getmounts function.

```
status()
{
        echo "Configured Mount Points:"
        echo "------------------------"
        getmounts
        echo ""
        echo "Active Mount Points:"
        echo "--------------------"
        # Note: we use the full automount path here instead of $DAEMON
        # since we need to use the [a] trick to preven the grep itself
        # from being listed
        ps axwww|grep "[0-9]:[0-9][0-9] /usr/sbin/[a]utomount " | (
                while read pid tt stat time command; do echo $command; done
        )
}


#
#       See how we were called.
#
```

Now we come to the main action of the script. Like the previous scripts, the
preceding is a case statement that defines what will happen when certain
command-line arguments are given. The comment "See how we were called" is a
traditional way of beginning this part of an init script; the more init scripts you
read, the more often you will come across this phrase.

What follows is the standard set of options that you have seen in previous scripts,
although this script makes use of the getmounts function and some code that is
specific to NIS functions.

```
case "$1" in
    start)
        echo -n 'Starting automounter:'
        getmounts | while read cmd mnt1 mnt2 mnt3 rest
        do
                #special: again, we will have to give maps with explicit
                #timeouts special treatment.
                if echo $mnt1 | grep -- '-t' >/dev/null 2>&1 ; then
                      mnt=$mnt3
                else
                      mnt=$mnt1
                fi
                echo -n " $mnt"
                pidfile=/var/run/automount`echo $mnt | sed 's/\//./g'`.pid
                start-stop-daemon --start --oknodo --pidfile $pidfile --quiet \
                      --exec $DAEMON -- $daemonargs $mnt1 $mnt2 $mnt3 $rest
                #
                #      Automount needs a '--pidfile' or '-p' option.
                #      For now we look for the pid ourself.
                #
                ps axwww | \
                    egrep "[0-9]:[0-9][0-9] $DAEMON (--timeout [0-9]+ )?$mnt " |\
                    (
                          read pid rest
                          echo $pid > $pidfile
                          echo "$mnt $rest" >> $pidfile
                    )
        done
        echo "."
        ;;
    stop)
        echo 'Stopping automounter.'
        start-stop-daemon --stop --quiet --signal USR2 --exec $DAEMON
        ;;
    force-reload|reload|restart)
        echo "Reloading automounter: checking for changes ... "
        TMP=/var/run/automount.tmp
        getmounts >$TMP
        for i in /var/run/automount.*.pid
        do
            pid=`head -n 1 $i 2>/dev/null`
            [ "$pid" = "" ] && continue
            command=`tail +2 $i | sed -e 's/.*[0-9]:[0-9]\{2\} \(.*\)/\1/'`
            if ! grep -q "^$command" $TMP
            then
              echo "Stopping automounter: $command"
              kill -USR2 $pid
            fi
```

```
        done
        rm -f $TMP
        /etc/init.d/autofs start
        ;;
    status)
        status
        ;;
    *)
        echo "Usage: /etc/init.d/autofs
{start|stop|restart|reload|status|force-reload}" >&2
        exit 1
        ;;
esac
```

Again, if the script has made it this far, it exits normally.

```
exit 0
```

bootmisc.sh

This script controls a variety of miscellaneous activities that happen during the boot process.

```
#
# bootmisc.sh      Miscellaneous things to be done during bootup.
#
# Version:  @(#)bootmisc.sh  1.20  09-Jan-1999  miquels@cistron.nl
#

. /etc/default/rcS
#
# Put a nologin file in /etc to prevent people from logging in before
# system startup is complete.
#
if [ "$DELAYLOGIN" = yes ]
then
  echo "System bootup in progress - please wait" > /etc/nologin
  cp /etc/nologin /etc/nologin.boot
fi


#
# Wipe /tmp (and don't erase 'lost+found', 'quota.user' or 'quota.group')!
# Note that files _in_ lost+found _are_ deleted.
#
[ "$VERBOSE" != no ] && echo -n "Cleaning: /tmp "
```

```
#
#       If $TMPTIME is set to 0, we do not use any ctime expression
#       at all, so we can also delete files with timestamps
#       in the future!
#
if [ "$TMPTIME" = 0 ]
then
      TEXPR=""
else
      TEXPR="! -ctime -$TMPTIME"
fi
( cd /tmp && \
  find . -xdev \
  $TEXPR \
  ! -name . \
  ! \( -name lost+found -uid 0 \) \
  ! \( -name quota.user -uid 0 \) \
  ! \( -name quota.group -uid 0 \) \
    -depth -exec rm -rf -- {} \; )
rm -f /tmp/.X*-lock
#
# Clean up any stale locks.
#
[ "$VERBOSE" != no ] && echo -n "/var/lock "
( cd /var/lock && find . -type f -exec rm -f -- {} \; )
#
# Clean up /var/run and create /var/run/utmp so that we can login.
#
[ "$VERBOSE" != no ] && echo -n "/var/run"
( cd /var/run && \
      find . ! -type d ! -name utmp ! -name innd.pid ! -name random-seed \
      -exec rm -f -- {} \; )
: > /var/run/utmp
[ "$VERBOSE" != no ] && echo "."

#
# Set pseudo-terminal access permissions.
#
chmod 666 /dev/tty[p-za-e][0-9a-f]
chown root:tty /dev/tty[p-za-e][0-9a-f]

#
# Update /etc/motd.
#
if [ "$EDITMOTD" != no ]
then
      uname -a > /etc/motd.tmp
      sed 1d /etc/motd >> /etc/motd.tmp
      mv /etc/motd.tmp /etc/motd
fi
```

D

checkfs.sh

This script reviews all file systems and determines if they need to have the `fsck` program executed upon them. If so, the script directs the execution of `fsck`. `fsck` is a file system check, which is necessary to ensure that the integrity of the root file system is intact before Linux attempts to use it.

```
#
# checkfs.sh      Check all filesystems.
#
# Version:  @(#)checkfs  1.10  22-Jun-1998  miquels@cistron.nl
#


. /etc/default/rcS

#
# Check the rest of the file systems.
#
if [ ! -f /fastboot ]
then
    if [ -f /forcefsck ]
    then
        force="-f"
    else
        force=""
    fi
    if [ "$FSCKFIX"  = yes ]
    then
      fix="-y"
    else
      fix="-a"
    fi
    echo "Checking all file systems..."
      /sbin/splashFX say " Checking filesystems...\n"
    fsck -R -A $fix $force
    if [ $? -gt 1 ]
    then
      /etc/init.d/unsplashFX
      echo
      echo "fsck failed.  Please repair manually."
      echo
      echo "CONTROL-D will exit from this shell and continue system startup."
      echo
      # Start a single user shell on the console
      /sbin/sulogin $CONSOLE
    fi
fi
rm -f /fastboot /forcefsck
```

checkroot.sh

This script is much the same as the `checkfs.sh` script but has special provisions for the root partition.

```
#
# checkroot.sh    Check to root file system.
#
# Version:  @(#)checkroot.sh  2.76  12-Jan-1999  miquels@cistron.nl
#

. /etc/default/rcS
/sbin/splashFX say " Mounting filesystem...\n"
```

`/sbin/splashFX` is the program that creates the splash screen you see when you first start your machine. This command prints the message "Mounting filesystem . . ." to that screen.

```
#
# Set SULOGIN in /etc/default/rcS to yes if you want a sulogin to be spawned
# from this script *before anything else* with a timeout, like SCO does.
#
[ "$SULOGIN" = yes ] && sulogin -t 30 $CONSOLE
```

This command gives you the ability to set an environment variable in the `/etc/default/rcS` script, which gives you the option of a root login before anything else happens as a result of this script's action.

```
#
# Activate the swap device(s) in /etc/fstab. This needs to be done
# before fsck, since fsck can be quite memory-hungry.
#
if [ -x /sbin/swapon ]
then
  [ "$VERBOSE" != no ] && echo "Activating swap..."
  swapon -a 2>/dev/null
fi
```

The preceding comment explains this section fairly well. If the `swapon` program is available (which it should be), the script activates it.

```
#
# Ensure that bdflush (update) is running before any major I/O is
# performed (the following fsck is a good example of such activity :).
```

```
#
[ -x /sbin/update ] && update

#
# Check the root file system.
#
if [ -f /fastboot ]
then
  echo "Fast boot, no file system check"
else
```

The script will skip the system check if a file called /fastboot is present.

```
#
# Ensure that root is quiescent and read-only before fsck'ing.
#
mount -n -o remount,ro /
```

This section is very important. Running `fsck` on a file system that is mounted in read/write mode can cause damage to the file system. This command remounts the / directory in read-only mode to prevent damage.

```
if [ $? = 0 ]
```

The variable $? is a special variable used to store the return value—in this case, the exit status—of the last command. Remember that an exit status of 0 means a successful execution. Therefore, the next section will be executed only if the preceding `mount` command was successful.

```
then
  if [ -f /forcefsck ]
  then
    force="-f"
  else
    force=""
  fi
  if [ "$FSCKFIX" = yes ]
  then
    fix="-y"
  else
    fix="-a"
  fi
  echo "Checking root file system..."
  fsck $force $fix /
```

This sequence determines the arguments to be used with the `fsck` command and stores the values in the variables `$force` and `$fix`.

```
#
# If there was a failure, drop into single-user mode.
#
# NOTE: "failure" is defined as exiting with a return code of
# 2 or larger.  A return code of 1 indicates that file system
# errors were corrected but that the boot may proceed.
#
if [ $? -gt 1 ]
then
  /etc/init.d/unsplashFX
  # Surprise! Re-directing from a HERE document (as in
  # "cat << EOF") won't work, because the root is read-only.
  echo
  echo "fsck failed.  Please repair manually and reboot.  Please note"
  echo "that the root file system is currently mounted read-only.  To"
  echo "remount it read-write:"
  echo
  echo "   # mount -n -o remount,rw /"
  echo
  echo "CONTROL-D will exit from this shell and REBOOT the system."
  echo
  # Start a single user shell on the console
  /sbin/sulogin $CONSOLE
  reboot -f
fi
```

If `fsck` failed, the preceding error message is printed to the screen, and the machine reboots into single-user mode.

```
else
  echo "*** ERROR!  Cannot fsck root fs because it is not mounted read\
only!"
  echo
fi
fi
```

The preceding section is obvious. The script will not force a `fsck` on the root directory if the `fsck` will result in damage.

```
#
#     If the root filesystem was not marked as read-only in /etc/fstab,
#     remount the rootfs rw but do not try to change mtab because it
```

```
#       is on a ro fs until the remount succeeded. Then clean up old mtabs
#       and finally write the new mtab.
#
(
  mode=rw
  while read fs mnt type opts rest
  do
        [ "$mnt" != / ] && continue
        case "$fs" in
              ""|\#*)
                        continue;
                        ;;
        esac
        case "$opts" in
              ro|ro,*|*,ro|*,ro,*)
                        mode=ro
                        ;;
        esac
  done
  mount -n -o remount,$mode /
  if [ "$mode" = rw ]
  then
        rm -f /etc/mtab~ /etc/nologin
        : > /etc/mtab
        mount -o remount,rw /
        mount /proc
  else
        mount -n /proc
  fi
) < /etc/fstab
```

The preceding comment gives some explanation of what this section does. One interesting feature to note is that the entire block of code is contained in parentheses, which serves to group the whole block as a single unit. If you look at the last line, you'll see the reason why you would want to do that. The entire block takes its input from /etc/fstab, and enclosing it means that the input needs to be specified only once.

cron

```
#!/bin/sh
# Start/stop the cron daemon.

test -f /usr/sbin/cron || exit 0
```

```
case "$1" in
start)      echo -n "Starting periodic command scheduler: cron"
        start-stop-daemon --start --quiet --exec /usr/sbin/cron
        echo "."
    ;;
stop)       echo -n "Stopping periodic command scheduler: cron"
        start-stop-daemon --stop --quiet --exec /usr/sbin/cron
        echo "."
        ;;
restart) echo -n "Re-starting periodic command scheduler: cron"
        start-stop-daemon --stop --quiet --exec /usr/sbin/cron
        start-stop-daemon --start --quiet --exec /usr/sbin/cron
        echo "."
        ;;
reload|force-reload) echo -n "Re-loading configuration files for periodic\
command scheduler: cron"
     # cron reloads automatically
        echo "."
        ;;
*)      echo "Usage: /etc/init.d/cron start|stop"; exit 1
        ;;
esac
```

Again, the script exits cleanly if it has reached this point.

```
exit 0
```

detector

This script detects various kernel modules as they are loaded during the boot process.

```
#!/bin/sh
####################################
#Name : detector
#
#Description: To update the /etc/modules file when a new network device
#is added.
#
#Copyright (C) 1999 Corel Corporation
#
# EXHIBIT A -Corel Public License.
#
# The contents of this file are subject to the Corel Public License
# Version 1.0 (the "License"); you may not use this file except in
```

D

```
# compliance  with the License. You may obtain a copy of the License at
# linux.corel.com/linuxproducts/corellinux/license.htm.
# Software distributed under the License is distributed on an "AS IS"
# basis, WITHOUT WARRANTY OF ANY KIND, either express or implied. See the
# License for the specific language governing rights and limitations
# under the License.
# The Original Code is detector.
# The Initial Developer of the Original Code is Corel Corporation.
# Portions created by Corel are Copyright (C) 1999  All Rights Reserved.
# Contributor(s): _____ .
################################################################

/sbin/detect probe > /dev/null 2>&1
```

dhcpcd

The following script, which obtains network information from the Dynamic Host
Configuration Protocol (DHCP) server, is a long and complicated script. Large
portions of this script are not actually run at any time, but are rather a skeleton
structure with which you can build custom scripts of your own. Its inclusion here
is due to the many interesting and useful shell programming constructs it illustrates
(and also because it has been included in the dhcpcd script by its programmers).
The comments are fairly comprehensive, and our annotations will thus be limited.

```
#!/bin/sh
# /etc/init.d/skeleton: example file to build /etc/init.d/ scripts.
# $Id: dhcpcd,v 1.9 1999/11/12 20:01:59 daven Exp $
#
# This file should be used to construct scripts for /etc/init.d.
#
# Written by Miquel van Smoorenburg <miquels@drinkel.ow.org>.
# Modified for Debian GNU/Linux by Ian Murdock <imurdock@gnu.ai.mit.edu>.
# Modified for dhcpcd by Christoph Lameter <clameter@debian.org>
# Modified to keep lintian happy by Steve Dunham <dunham@debian.org>
# Modifications to this program were made by Corel Corporation,
# November, 1999.
# All such modifications are copyright (C) 1999 Corel Corporation
# and are licensed under the terms of the GNU General Public License.
```

Following is the usual setting of variables:

```
PATH=/bin:/usr/bin:/sbin:/usr/sbin
DAEMON=/usr/sbin/dhcpcd
NAME=$0
```

```
SECONDS=35
source /etc/dhcpc/config
SUB_WB="lmhosts host wins bcast"
SUB_W="lmhosts host wins"
SUB_BW="lmhosts host bcast wins"
SUB_B="lmhosts host bcast"
KCM=/etc/kcmSambaConfig.conf
SMB=/etc/samba/smb.conf
TMP_SMB=/tmp/tmp_smb.conf
DHCP_INFO=/etc/dhcpc/dhcpcd-$IFACE.info
RESOLV_FILE=/etc/dhcpc/dhcpcd-$IFACE.info
HOSTS_FILE=/etc/hosts
HOSTNAME_FILE=/etc/hostname
```

Beginning here, a number of functions are defined. The general form for defining functions in these scripts is as follows:

function_name ()
{
}

where *function_name* is the name you want to give the function. The code describing the function goes between the curly braces. Subsequently, any time you want to execute that block of code, you simply call that function.

```
########################################################################
#
# Method: NETBIOSNODE_UpDate()
#
# Author: Katerina Tsarouchas          September 14, 1999
#
# Purpose: Goes into the dhcpc-$IFACE.info and find what the
#          NETBIOSNODETYPE is set to and writes the information into
#          the /etc/samba/smb.conf.
#
########################################################################

NetBiosNode_UpDate()
{
  grep -i "NETBIOSNODETYPE" $DHCP_INFO  > /tmp/Node_Found 2>/dev/null

  #check to see if NETBIOSNODETYPE exist int the dhcp-$IFACE.info
  if [ -s /tmp/Node_Found ]
  then
    #get the type of node
```

```
sed 's/^.*=//' < /tmp/Node_Found > /tmp/letter_type
Node_Type=`cat /tmp/letter_type`

#get the value of line "name resolve order" in the smb.conf
grep -i "name resolve order" $SMB > /tmp/tmp_file 2>/dev/null
sed 's/^.*=//' < /tmp/tmp_file > /tmp/sub_file
SUBSTITUTE=`cat /tmp/sub_file`

#substitue the old value with the new one in
#the smb.conf, depends on what the node type
#is set in the dhcpcd-$IFACE.info.
if [ "$Node_Type" = "h" ]
then
  if [ "$SUBSTITUTE" != "$SUB_WB" ]
  then
    sed -e "s/$SUBSTITUTE/ $SUB_WB/" < $SMB > $TMP_SMB
  mv $TMP_SMB $SMB
  else
    exit 1
  fi
else
if [ "$Node_Type" = "p" ]
 then
  if [ "$SUBSTITUTE" !=  "$SUB_W" ]
  then
    sed -e "s/$SUBSTITUTE/ $SUB_W/" < $SMB > $TMP_SMB
    mv $TMP_SMB $SMB
  else
    exit 1
  fi
else
if [ "$Node_Type" = "m" ]
then
  if [ "$SUBSTITUTE" != "$SUB_BW" ]
  then
    sed -e "s/$SUBSTITUTE/ $SUB_BW/" < $SMB > $TMP_SMB
    mv $TMP_SMB $SMB
  else
    exit 1
  fi
else
if [ "$Node_Type" = "b" ]
then
  if [ "$SUBSTITUTE" != "$SUB_B" ]
  then
    sed -e "s/$SUBSTITUTE/ $SUB_B/" < $SMB > $TMP_SMB
    mv $TMP_SMB $SMB
  else
```

```
          exit 1
        fi
      fi
    fi
   fi
  fi
  else
    #if the node type doesn't exist in the dhcpcd-$IFACE.info
    #by default the node type is set to "h".
    grep -i "name resolve order" $SMB > /tmp/tmp_file 2>/dev/null
    sed 's/^.*=//' < /tmp/tmp_file > /tmp/sub_file
    SUBSTITUTE=`cat /tmp/sub_file`
    sed -e "s/$SUBSTITUTE/ $SUB_WB/" < $SMB > $TMP_SMB
    mv $TMP_SMB $SMB
  fi
  rm -rf /tmp/Node_Found /tmp/sub_file /tmp/letter_type
}


######################################################################
#
# Method: NetBiosName_UpDate()
#
# Author: Katerina Tsarouchas            September 14, 1999
#
# Purpose: Checks to see if the /etc/kcmSambaConfig.conf and the wins
#          server exists and if not go into the dhcpc-$IFACE.info and
#          finds the first NETBIOSNAMESERVER IP address and write the
#          information into the wins server in the /etc/samba/smb.conf.
#
######################################################################

NetBiosName_UpDate()
{
  grep -i "wins server=" $KCM > /tmp/foo 2>/dev/null


  #check to see if /etc/kcmSambConfig.conf and the wins server line exists
  if [ -e "$KCM" ] && [ -s /tmp/foo ]
  then
    echo "Doesn't need to be updated"
  else
    #get the IP address from the NETBIOSNAMESERVER from the dhcpcd
$IFACE.info
    grep -i "NETBIOSNAMESERVER1" $DHCP_INFO  > /tmp/Type_Found 2>/dev/null
    sed 's/^.*=//' < /tmp/Type_Found > /tmp/Serv_IP

  if [ -s /tmp/Serv_IP ]
  then
```

D

```
        #get the IP address from the "wins server" in the /etc/samba/smb.conf
        grep -i "wins server =" $SMB > /tmp/SERVER 2>/dev/null
        sed 's/^.*=//' < /tmp/SERVER > /tmp/server_value

    if [ -s /tmp/server_value ]
    then
        #assign the values into a variable
        OLD_IP=`cat /tmp/server_value`
        NEW_IP=`cat /tmp/Serv_IP`

        #check if these two values are not equal
        if [ "$OLD_IP" != "$NEW_IP" ]
        then
          grep -w 'wins server =' $SMB > /tmp/old_wins.conf 2>/dev/null
          grep -w ";"  /tmp/old_wins.conf > /tmp/new_wins.conf 2>/dev/null

          #check to see if the line wins server contains ";"
          if [ -s /tmp/new_wins.conf ]
          then
            #substitute the old IP Address with the new one
            sed -e "s/$OLD_IP/ $NEW_IP/" < $SMB > /tmp/new_smb.conf

            #uncomment the ";" from the line
            sed -e 's/^;.*wins server/  wins server/' < /tmp/new_smb.conf\
/tmp/happy.conf
            mv /tmp/happy.conf $SMB
          else
            #substitute the old IP Address with the new one
            sed -e "s/$OLD_IP/ $NEW_IP/" < $SMB > /tmp/new_smb.conf

            #Update the new changes into the /etc/samba/smb.conf
            mv /tmp/new_smb.conf $SMB
          fi
        else
          exit 1
        fi
    else
        exit 1
    fi
  else
    exit 1
  fi
  exit 1
fi

rm -rf /tmp/new_smb.conf /tmp/happy.conf /tmp/foo /tmp/Type_Found
rm -rf /tmp/Serv_Ip /tmp/SERVER /tmp/server_value /tmp/old_wins.conf
rm -rf /tmp/new_wins.conf
```

```
}

########################################################################
#
# Method: Date_Update()
#
# Author: Katerina Tsarouchas            September 14, 1999
#
# Purpose: Getting the current system and dhcpcd-$IFACE.info time and
#          date in epoch format.
#
########################################################################

Date_Update()
{
  #converting the current system date into epoch format
  date +%s > /tmp/current_time

  #converting the /etc/dhcpcd-$IFACE.info into epoch format
  date -r $DHCP_INFO +%s > /tmp/file_time
  system_date=`cat /tmp/current_time`
  hostinfo_date=`cat /tmp/file_time`
}

########################################################################
#
# Method: UpDate_Info()
#
# Author: Katerina Tsarouchas            September 14, 1999
#
# Purpose: Updates the IP address, domain name, and hostname
#          and writes it to the /etc/hosts file.
#
########################################################################

UpDate_Info()
{
  ps ax | grep /usr/sbin/dhcpcd > /tmp/Found_DHCP 2>/dev/null

  #check if dhcpcd is running
  if [ -s /tmp/Found_DHCP ]
  then
    #getting the two epoch values
    Date_Update

    #getting the difference of the two values
    let New_time=$system_date-$hostinfo_date
    echo "The file has been update about $New_time sec(s) ago"
```

D

```
#if the difference of the two values is less than 35 update the dhcpc
if [ "$New_time" -lt "$SECONDS" ]
then
  #getting the IP address in the /etc/dhcpc/dhcpcd-$IFACE.info
  grep -h 'IPADDR' $DHCP_INFO > /tmp/IP_Found 2>/dev/null

  if [ -s /tmp/IP_Found ]
  then
    sed 's/^.*=//' < /tmp/IP_Found > /tmp/New_IP
    IP_ADDRESS=`cat /tmp/New_IP`
  else
    exit 1
  fi

  #getting the domain name in the /etc/dhcpc/resolv.conf
  grep -i 'DOMAIN' $DHCP_INFO > /tmp/Domain_Found 2>/dev/null

  if [ -s /tmp/Domain_Found ]
  then
    sed 's/DOMAIN=//' < /tmp/Domain_Found > /tmp/New_Domain
    DOMAIN_NAME=`cat /tmp/New_Domain`
  else
    exit 1
  fi

  if [ -e $HOSTNAME_FILE ]
  then
    #getting the hostname in the /etc/hostname
    HOST_NAME=`cat $HOSTNAME_FILE`
  else
    exit 1
  fi

  #Looking into the /etc/hosts file, if present...
  if [ -s $HOSTS_FILE ]
  then
    grep -v $IP_ADDRESS $HOSTS_FILE > /tmp/Host_File 2>/dev/null
##go into the /etc/hosts file comment the
#IP addresses that not being currently used
    if [ -s /tmp/Host_File ]
    then
      grep -v '#' /tmp/Host_File > /tmp/Hosts 2>/dev/null
      if [ -s /tmp/Hosts ]
      then
        sed 's/^./ # &/' /tmp/Hosts > $HOSTS_FILE
      fi
    else
      exit 1
```

```
      fi

        #Uncomment the line that says "localhost" in the /etc/hosts file
        grep -i "localhost" /etc/hosts > /tmp/find_local
        if [ -s /tmp/find_local ]
        then
          grep -i "#"  /tmp/find_local > /tmp/find_host
          if [ -s /tmp/find_host ]
          then
            old_local=`cat /tmp/find_local`
            sed -e 's/^.#//' < /tmp/find_local > /tmp/tmp_local
            sed -e 's/^.//' < /tmp/tmp_local > /tmp/kate3
            new_local=`cat /tmp/kate3`
            sed -e "s/$old_local/$new_local/" < /etc/hosts > /tmp/hosts_file
           mv /tmp/hosts_file /etc/hosts
          else
             echo "It's already uncommented!"
          fi
        else
          echo "It doesn't exist"
        fi

        grep -h $IP_ADDRESS $HOSTS_FILE > /tmp/tmp_IP 2>/dev/null
        if [ -s /tmp/tmp_IP ]
        then
          echo "Checking to see if the IP Address exist..."
       else
         #writing the new IP address, hostname, and
         #domain name into the /etc/hosts file.
          echo $IP_ADDRESS"      "$HOST_NAME.$DOMAIN_NAME "" $HOST_NAME >>\
$HOSTS_FILE
        fi
       else
         echo $IP_ADDRESS"      "$HOST_NAME.$DOMAIN_NAME "" $HOST_NAME >>\
$HOSTS_FILE
       fi
     else
      echo "Sorry the dhcpcd-$IFACE.info file has not been updated!"
     fi
    else
      echo "DHCP IS NOT RUNNING RIGHT NOW..."
      exit 1
    fi

    rm -rf /tmp/Host_File /tmp/IP_Found /tmp/New_IP /tmp/tmp_IP
    rm -rf /tmp/Hosts /tmp/New_Domain /tmp/Found_DHCP /tmp/Domain_Found
    rm -rf /tmp/kate* /tmp/find_local /tmp/find_host /tmp/tmp_local
```

D

```
}

#################### MAIN FUNCTION #########################################

test -f $DAEMON || exit 0

# Test for >2.0 kernel
case `uname -r` in
  2.0.*)
    echo "Skipping dhcpcd-sv on "`uname -r`" kernel"
    exit 0
    ;;
esac

#Load up our config file, if present
if [ -f /etc/dhcpc/config ]
then
  source /etc/dhcpc/config
fi

case "$1" in
  start)
    if [ "$IFACE" = "none" ] ; then
        echo  "DHCP client daemon is disabled."
        exit
    fi
    echo ""
    echo  "Starting DHCP client daemon: dhcpcd"
    start-stop-daemon --start --quiet --exec $DAEMON -- $IFACE
    UpDate_Info
    NetBiosNode_UpDate
    NetBiosName_UpDate
    echo "."
    ;;
  restart)
    echo ""
    echo  "Restarting DHCP client daemon: "
    start-stop-daemon --stop --quiet --exec $DAEMON
    rm -f /var/run/dhcpcd-eth0.pid
    echo -n "stopped "
    start-stop-daemon --start --quiet --exec $DAEMON -- $IFACE
    UpDate_Info
    NetBiosNode_UpDate
    NetBiosName_UpDate
    echo "restarted."
    ;;
  force-reload)
    echo "/etc/init.d/$NAME: force-reload: not implemented"
```

```
    ;;
  stop)
    echo ""
    echo  "Stopping DHCP client daemon: dhcpcd"
    start-stop-daemon --stop --quiet --exec $DAEMON
    rm -f /var/run/dhcpcd-eth0.pid
    echo "."
    ;;
  *)
    echo "Usage: /etc/init.d/$NAME {start|stop}"
    exit 1
    ;;
esac
exit 0
```

diald

This script starts the `diald` daemon. `diald` starts a dial-up connection whenever a connection to the outside world is needed.

What is interesting about this script is its reference to a *named pipe*. A named pipe is a special type of file that is used to transfer data between processes. (Sometimes the term *FIFO* is used instead of *named pipe*; FIFO stands for First In, First Out.) Since `diald` needs a named pipe in order to function, the script determines whether one exists before it attempts to start `diald`.

```
#! /bin/sh

# -------------------------------------------------------------------------
# No user configurable parts below this line.
DIALD=/usr/sbin/diald
FIFO=""

#. /etc/init.d/functions

# Make sure that we don't get started if there is no options file.
# We certainly don't want to get started if diald is missing.
test -x /usr/sbin/diald || exit 0
test -f /etc/diald/diald.options || exit 0

# Look for fifo in config file
NEW_FIFO=`egrep '^[^#]*fifo' /etc/diald/diald.options | sed -e 's/^ *fifo
```

The preceding line causes the script to search for a regular expression describing the FIFO in `diald`'s configuration file.

The remainder of the script is the standard parsing and processing of command-line arguments.

```
*//'`
if [ "$NEW_FIFO" != "" ]; then
    # The user location exists, and is a named pipe.
    FIFO="$NEW_FIFO";
fi

case "$1" in
  start)
      echo -n "Starting on-demand dialing daemon: "
      if [ "$FIFO" != "" ] ; then
        if test -p $FIFO ; then
          rm -f $FIFO
        fi
        mknod --mode=0660 $FIFO p
        chown root.dialout $FIFO
      if test -p $FIFO ; then
          echo -n "fifo-created "
        fi
      fi
      start-stop-daemon --start --quiet \
              --pidfile /var/run/diald.pid --exec /usr/sbin/diald
      echo "diald."
    ;;
  stop)
      echo -n "Stopping on-demand dialing daemon: "
      if [ "$FIFO" != "" ] ; then
        if test -p $FIFO ; then
          rm -f $FIFO
          echo -n "fifo-removed "
        fi
      fi
      start-stop-daemon --stop --quiet \
              --pidfile /var/run/diald.pid --exec /usr/sbin/diald
      echo "diald."
    ;;
  reload)
      if [ "$FIFO" != "" ] ; then
        if test -p $FIFO ; then
        echo "reset" > $FIFO
        echo "Diald configuration reloaded."
      else
        echo "Cannot reload diald configuration: $FIFO not found."
        exit 2
        fi
```

```
        else
          echo "Cannot reload diald configuration: "
        echo "  need a fifo statement in /etc/diald/diald.options."
        exit 2
        fi
    ;;
  force-reload|restart)
        echo -n "Stopping diald... "
        pid=`cat /var/run/diald.pid`
        start-stop-daemon --stop --quiet --pidfile /var/run/diald.pid \
        --exec /usr/sbin/diald
        while ps $pid >/dev/null 2>/dev/null
        do
        echo -n "waiting... "
        sleep 5
        done
        echo "done."
        start-stop-daemon --start --quiet \
                --pidfile /var/run/diald.pid --exec /usr/sbin/diald
        echo "Diald restarted."
    ;;
  *)
        echo "Usage: /etc/init.d/diald {start|stop|reload|restart|force\
reload}"
        exit 1
    ;;
esac

exit 0
```

dosplashFX

This script prints various messages to the splash screen during the boot process. In its current configuration, it prints only the message "Initializing...."

```
#!/bin/sh
###################################
#Name : dosplashFX
#
#Description: Manage the splash screen
#
#Copyright (C) 1999 Corel Corporation
#
# EXHIBIT A -Corel Public License.
#
```

```
# The contents of this file are subject to the Corel Public License
# Version 1.0 (the "License"); you may not use this file except in
# compliance  with the License. You may obtain a copy of the License at
# linux.corel.com/linuxproducts/corellinux/license.htm.
# Software distributed under the License is distributed on an "AS IS"
# basis, WITHOUT WARRANTY OF ANY KIND, either express or  implied. See the
# License for the specific language governing rights and limitations
# under the License.
# The Original Code is dosplashFX.
# The Initial Developer of the Original Code is Corel Corporation.
# Portions created by Corel are Copyright (C) 1999  All Rights Reserved.
# Contributor(s): _____.
################################################################

/sbin/splashFXs install
/sbin/splashFXs say " Initializing...\n"
```

halt

The `halt` script controls the stopping of various functions, and the order in which
functions are stopped, when the Linux system is stopped by the administrator.

```
#! /bin/sh
#
# halt           Execute the halt command.
#
# Version:       @(#)halt  2.75  19-May-1998  miquels@cistron.nl
#

PATH=/sbin:/bin:/usr/sbin:/usr/bin

# See if we need to cut the power.
if [ -x /etc/init.d/ups-monitor ]
then
        /etc/init.d/ups-monitor poweroff
fi

halt -d -f -i -p
```

hostname.sh

The `hostname.sh` script, as its name implies, sets the hostname of the computer.

```
#
# hostname.sh     Set hostname.
#
# Version:   @(#)hostname.sh  1.00  22-Jun-1998  miquels@cistron.nl
#

hostname --file /etc/hostname
```

hwclock.sh

The hwclock.sh script compares the hardware clock on the motherboard with the system clock maintained by the operating system and changes settings if necessary.

```
#
# hwclock.sh      Set and adjust the CMOS clock, according to the UTC
#           setting in /etc/default/rcS (see also rcS(5)).
#
# Version:   @(#)hwclock.sh  2.00  14-Dec-1998  miquels@cistron.nl
#

. /etc/default/rcS
[ "$GMT" = "-u" ] && GMT="--utc"

case "$1" in
    start)
            if [ ! -f /etc/adjtime ]
            then
                    echo "0.0 0 0.0" > /etc/adjtime
            fi
            hwclock --adjust $GMT
            hwclock --hctosys $GMT
            #
            #     Now that /usr/lib/zoneinfo should be available,
            #     announce the local time.
            #
            if [ "$VERBOSE" != no ]
            then
                     echo
                    echo "Local time: `date`"
                    echo
            fi
            ;;
    stop|restart|reload)
            [ "$GMT" = "-u" ] && GMT="--utc"
            hwclock --systohc $GMT
```

D

```
                if [ "$VERBOSE" != no ]
                then
                        echo "CMOS clock updated to `date`."
                fi
                ;;
        show)
                hwclock --show $GMT
                ;;
        *)
                echo "Usage: hwclock.sh {start|stop|reload|show}" >&2
                echo "        start sets kernel clock from CMOS clock" >&2
                echo "        stop and reload set CMOS clock from kernel clock" >&2
                exit 1
                ;;
esac
```

iplogger

This script manages the logging of various network functions.

```
#!/bin/sh
#
# Written by Miquel van Smoorenburg <miquels@drinkel.ow.org>.
# Modified for Debian GNU/Linux by Ian Murdock <imurdock@gnu.ai.mit.edu>.
# Modified for Debian by Christoph Lameter <clameter@debian.org>.
# Modified for icmplogd by Johnie Ingram <johnie@debian.org>.
# Modified for configuration options by Hugo Haas <hugo@debian.org>.

PATH=/bin:/usr/bin:/sbin:/usr/sbin
TCPLOGD=/usr/sbin/tcplogd
ICMPLOGD=/usr/sbin/icmplogd

test -f $ICMPLOGD || exit 0
test -f $TCPLOGD || exit 0

#
# Read the configuration file
#

CONFIG=/etc/iplogger.conf

test -f $CONFIG || exit 0

RUN_ICMPLOGD=0
if grep -q ^start-icmplogger $CONFIG
```

```
then
  RUN_ICMPLOGD=1
fi

RUN_TCPLOGD=0
if grep -q ^start-tcplogger $CONFIG
then
  RUN_TCPLOGD=1
fi

if grep -q ^log-in-file $CONFIG
then
  OPTIONS=-f
fi

if grep -q ^no-icmp-unreachable $CONFIG
then
  ICMP_OPTIONS=-d
fi

#
# Run the daemons
#

case "$1" in
  start)
    echo -n "Starting IP paranoia daemons:"
    if [ $RUN_TCPLOGD = 1 -a -x $TCPLOGD ]
    then
      echo -n " tcplogd"
      start-stop-daemon --start --verbose --quiet --exec $TCPLOGD -- $OPTIONS
    fi
    if [ $RUN_ICMPLOGD = 1 -a -x $ICMPLOGD ]
    then
      echo -n " icmplogd"
      start-stop-daemon --start --verbose --quiet --exec $ICMPLOGD --
$OPTIONS $ICMP_OPTIONS
    fi
    echo "."
    ;;

  stop)
    echo "Stopping IP paranoia daemons."
    start-stop-daemon --stop --quiet --oknodo --exec $TCPLOGD
    start-stop-daemon --stop --quiet --oknodo --exec $ICMPLOGD
    ;;

  restart)
```

D

```
    $0 stop
    $0 start
    ;;

force-reload)
    $0 restart
    ;;

*)
    echo "Usage: /etc/init.d/$0 {start|stop|restart|force-reload}"
    exit 1
    ;;
esac

exit 0
```

isapnp

The isapnp script is used to control various Plug-n-Play functions for ISA devices.

```
#! /bin/sh

# /etc/init.d/isapnp: configure Plug and Play boards

test -x /sbin/isapnp || exit 0

case "$1" in
    start)
        if [ -r /etc/isapnp.conf ]; then
            /sbin/isapnp /etc/isapnp.conf
        fi
        ;;

    stop|force-reload|restart)
        ;;

    *)
        echo "Usage: $0 {start|stop|restart|force-reload}"
        exit 1
esac

exit 0
```

kdm

The kdm script starts and stops the KDE display manager, allowing the KDE desktop to be loaded and used.

```
#!/bin/bash
# /etc/init.d/xdm: start or stop XDM.

#test -x /usr/bin/X11/kdm || exit 0

#test -f /etc/X11/config || exit 0

#grep -q ^xbase-not-configured /etc/X11/config && exit 0

case "$1" in
  start)
    echo -n "Starting kde display manager: kdm"
    start-stop-daemon --start --quiet --exec /usr/bin/X11/kdm
    echo "."
    ;;
  stop)
      echo -n "Stopping kde display manager: kdm"
      start-stop-daemon --stop --quiet --pid /usr/X11R6/config/kdm/xdm-pid ||
echo " not running"
      echo "."
      # delete the lock file since kdm doesn't want to delete it
      test -f /usr/X11R6/config/kdm/xdm-pid && rm /usr/X11R6/config/kdm/xdm\
pid
   ;;
# the last options are taken from kerneld
  restart)
          $0 stop
          $0 start
    ;;
  reload)
          start-stop-daemon --stop --signal 1 --q quiet --exec\
/usr/bin/X11/kdm
      ;;
  force-reload)
          $0 reload
      ;;
  *)
    echo "Usage: /etc/init.d/kdm {start|stop}"
    exit 1
esac

exit 0
```

D

kerneld

The kerneld script controls the dynamic loading of kernel modules.

```
#!/bin/sh
#
# Start kerneld (on-demand loading of modules)
# (see /usr/doc/modules)

KDOPT=""

test -f /proc/sys/kernel/modprobe && exit 0
test -f /sbin/kerneld || exit 0

#
# See if we have any modules.
#
cd /lib/modules/`uname -r` > /dev/null 2>&1 || exit 0

case "$1" in
  start)
#
#      are /proc and /usr/sbin mounted ?
#
      if `cd /proc/sys > /dev/null 2>&1` && `cd /usr/sbin > /dev/null 2>&1`
      then
#
#            Check if noauto is set
#
            grep "^[ ]*noauto" /etc/modules 2>&1 > /dev/null && exit 0
               start-stop-daemon --start --quiet --exec /sbin/kerneld --"${KDOPT}"
      else
            /sbin/kerneld ${KDOPT}
      fi
      ;;
  stop)
         start-stop-daemon --stop --quiet --oknodo --exec /sbin/kerneld --\
"${KDOPT}"
      ;;
  restart)
            $0 stop
            $0 start
      ;;
  reload)
            start-stop-daemon --stop --signal 1 --quiet --exec
/sbin/kerneld
      ;;
```

```
    force-reload)
            $0 reload
      ;;
  *)
      echo "Usage: /etc/init.d/kerneld {start|stop|restart|reload|force\
reload}"
      exit 1
      ;;
esac

exit 0
```

keymaps.sh

This script controls how input from the keyboard will be interpreted and used by
the operating system.

```
#!/bin/sh

#
# Load the keymaps *as soon as possible*
#

test -f /bin/loadkeys || exit 0

PACKAGE=kbd

CONFDIR=/etc/${PACKAGE}

case $PACKAGE in
kbd) EXT=map ;;
console-tools) EXT=kmap ;;
esac

KERNEL_KEYMAP=/var/lib/${PACKAGE}/kernel.${EXT}

case "$1" in
    start | restart | force-reload | reload)
#       # save kernel keymap
#       if [ -d ${KERNEL_KEYMAP%/*} -a ! -r ${KERNEL_KEYMAP} ]
#       then
#           /usr/bin/dumpkeys > ${KERNEL_KEYMAP}
#       fi

        # load new map
```

D

```
            if [ -r ${CONFDIR}/default.${EXT} ] ; then
                /bin/loadkeys ${CONFDIR}/default.${EXT}
            elif [ -r ${CONFDIR}/default.${EXT}.gz ] ; then
                /bin/loadkeys ${CONFDIR}/default.${EXT}.gz
            fi
            ;;

        stop)
#           # ensure the saved kernel keymap is removed before halt/reboot
#           rm -f ${KERNEL_KEYMAP}
            ;;

        *)
            echo "Usage: $0 {start|stop|restart|reload|force-reload}"
            exit 1
            ;;
esac
```

logoutd

The `logoutd` script manages various functions and processes that are executed upon logout from the operating system.

```
#! /bin/sh
# start/stop logoutd

set -e

test -f /usr/sbin/logoutd || exit 0

# Most people won't need logoutd(8) running, so we'll only run it if
# /etc/porttime has non-comment lines.
egrep -vq '^#|^ *$' /etc/porttime || exit 0

case "$1" in
    start)
      echo -n "Starting login time and port restriction enforcer: logoutd"
      start-stop-daemon --start --quiet --exec /usr/sbin/logoutd
      echo "."
      ;;
    stop)
      echo -n "Stopping login time and port restriction enforcer: logoutd"
      start-stop-daemon --stop --quiet --exec /usr/sbin/logoutd
      echo "."
      ;;
```

```
   *)
      echo "Usage: /etc/init.d/logoutd start|stop"
      exit 1
      ;;
esac

exit 0
```

lpd

lpd starts and stops the print daemon, controlling various print jobs sent from applications.

```
#!/bin/sh

PATH=/bin:/usr/bin:/sbin:/usr/sbin
DAEMON=/usr/sbin/lpd
PIDFILE=/var/spool/lpd/lpd.lock

test -x $DAEMON -a -f /usr/sbin/pac || exit 0

case "$1" in
  start)
      echo -n "Starting printer spooler: lpd"
        if start-stop-daemon --quiet --stop --signal 0 --pidfile $PIDFILE -\
name lpd
      then
            echo " already running."
            exit
      fi
      /sbin/start-stop-daemon --start --quiet --exec $DAEMON
      echo "."
      ;;
  stop)
      echo -n "Stopping printer spooler: lpd"
      if start-stop-daemon --quiet --stop --signal 0 --pidfile $PIDFILE -\
name lpd
      then
            PID=`cat $PIDFILE`
            start-stop-daemon --quiet --stop --exec $DAEMON --pidfile
$PIDFILE --name lpd
            # Now we wait for it to die
            while kill -0 $PID 2>/dev/null; do sleep 1; done
            echo "."
      else
```

```
            echo " not running.";
        fi
        ;;
    force-reload|restart)
        $0 stop
        $0 start
        ;;
    *)
        echo "Usage: /etc/init.d/lpd {start|stop|restart|force-reload}"
        exit 1
esac

exit 0
```

mdutils

This script controls *multiple devices*. Multiple devices, also called RAID systems, are groups of disks that function as one unit. This is accomplished by means of *striping* the data across the disks so that, for example, a single file might be spread across several disks in a regular pattern. The purpose of striping the data is to reduce the amount of time it takes for a specific set of data to be found on large devices. By using several disks and heads simultaneously, the time it takes to find and read a file is cut significantly. This script is not remarkable for how it does what it does, but rather for its purpose.

```
#! /bin/sh
#
# md        Enable or disable multiple devices. If /etc/mdtab doesn't
#           exist or is empty we don't bother; likewise if mdadd or
#           mdstop isn't installed.
#
#           Note that since this is called early in the bootprocess you
#           can't swap to an MD device; but you don't want to do that
#           anyway as the Linux kernel can stripe swap partitions
#           itself (see swapon manpage).
#
# Version:  @(#)md  2.73  08-Jan-1998  miquels@cistron.nl
#

case "$1" in
    start|"")
            if [ -s /etc/mdtab -a -f /sbin/mdadd ]
            then
                    [ "$VERBOSE" != no ] && echo "Adding md devices."
```

```
                        mdadd -ar
              fi
              : ;;
      stop)
              if [ -r /etc/mdtab -a -x /sbin/mdstop ]
              then
                      [ "$VERBOSE" != no ] && echo "Stopping md devices."
                      mdstop -a
              fi
              : ;;
      reload)
              echo "Reload not possible, use restart."
              ;;
      restart|force-reload)
              /etc/init.d/mdutils stop
              /etc/init.d/mdutils start
              ;;
      *)
              echo "Usage: mdutils [start] [stop]" >&2
              false
              ;;
esac
```

modutils

This script manages various modules that are added to the kernel during the boot process.

```
#! /bin/sh
# /etc/init.d/modules: loads the appropriate modules in 'boot'.


PATH="/sbin:/bin:/usr/sbin:/usr/bin"

      echo -n "Calculating module dependencies... "
      depmod -a > /dev/null
      echo "done."

# First test if we have a kernel with kmod
if [ -f /proc/sys/kernel/modprobe ]; then
#     We have, so don't start kerneld
      startkerneld=1
else
      startkerneld=0;
fi
```

```
# Loop over every line in /etc/modules.
echo -n 'Loading modules: '
(cat /etc/modules; echo) | # make sure there is a LF at the end
while read module args
do
      case "$module" in
            auto)  [ ${startkerneld} -eq 0 -a -x /sbin/kerneld ] && \
                echo && /etc/init.d/kerneld start && startkerneld=1;
                continue ;;
            noauto) continue ;;
            \#*|"") continue ;;
      esac
      echo -n "$module "
      modprobe $module $args
done

echo

#
# Just in case a sysadmin prefers generic symbolic links in
# /lib/modules/boot for boot time modules we will load these modules
#
if [ -n "`modprobe -l -t boot`" ]
then
        modprobe -a -t boot \*
fi
```

mountall.sh

mountall.sh mounts all local file systems, rather than requiring the user to mount individual file systems when needed.

```
#
# mountall.sh    Mount all filesystems.
#
# Version: @(#)mountall.sh  2.76  10-Dec-1998  miquels@cistron.nl
#
. /etc/default/rcS

#
# Mount local file systems in /etc/fstab.
#
[ "$VERBOSE" != no ] && echo "Mounting local file systems..."
mount -avt nonfs,noproc
```

```
#
# We might have mounted something over /dev, see if /dev/initctl is there.
#
if [ ! -p /dev/initctl ]
then
        rm -f /dev/initctl
        mknod -m 600 /dev/initctl p
fi
kill -USR1 1

#
# Execute swapon command again, in case we want to swap to
# a file on a now mounted filesystem.
#
swapon -a 2>/dev/null
```

mountnfs.sh

mountnfs.sh mounts all network file systems at one time, rather than the user mounting individual file systems as needed.

```
#
# mountnfs.sh    Now that TCP/IP is configured, mount the NFS file
#                systems in /etc/fstab if needed. If possible,
#                start the portmapper before mounting (this is needed for
#                Linux 2.1.x and up).
#
# Version:   @(#)mountnfs.sh  1.11  05-Oct-1998  miquels@cistron.nl
#

. /etc/default/rcS

#
#       Run in a subshell because of I/O redirection.
#
test -f /etc/fstab && (

#
#       Read through fstab line by line. If it is NFS, set the flag
#       for mounting NFS file systems. If any NFS partition is found and it
#       not mounted with the nolock option, we start the portmapper.
#
portmap=no
mount_nfs=no
```

D

```
while read device mountpt fstype options
do
        if [ "$fstype" = nfs ]
        then
                mount_nfs=yes
                case "$options" in
                        *nolock*)
                                ;;
                        *)
                                portmap=yes
                                ;;
                esac
        fi
done

exec 0>&1

if [ "$portmap" = yes ]
then
        if [ -x /sbin/portmap ]
        then
                echo -n "Starting portmapper... "
                start-stop-daemon --start --quiet --exec /sbin/portmap
                sleep 2
        fi
fi

if [ "$mount_nfs" = yes ]
then
        echo "Mounting remote filesystems..."
        mount -a -t nfs
fi

) < /etc/fstab
```

netbase

The netbase script is responsible for setting up some of the network functions including basic security. The script is interesting for its use of the ipchains program, which it illustrates well.

```
#!/bin/sh
#
# start/stop networking daemons.
```

```
test -f /sbin/portmap || exit 0
```

The first function of the script is to test for the existence of the `portmap` program. If there is no `portmap` program, the script exits.

The following section defines a function called `spoofprotect()`. This is a security function designed to protect against a particular type of system crack called *IP spoofing*, which occurs when a cracker attempts to convince your system that incoming packets are coming from a trusted machine—often from your machine itself.

```
spoofprotect () {
    # This is the best method: turn on Source Address Verification and get
    # spoof protection on all current and future interfaces.
    if [ -e /proc/sys/net/ipv4/conf/all/rp_filter ]; then
      echo -n "Setting up IP spoofing protection..."
      for f in /proc/sys/net/ipv4/conf/*/rp_filter; do
        echo 1 > $f
    done
      echo "done."
    # rules for linux 2.0.x and 2.1.x (x < 102) kernels
```

Following are the rules used for Series 2.0.x Linux kernels. This uses the now out-of-date `ipfwadm` command; since Corel Linux uses a 2.2.x kernel, this section is basically ignored when the script runs.

```
    elif [ -e /proc/net/ip_input ]; then
        echo -n "Setting up IP spoofing protection..."
      # delete and read entry (this way we don't get duplicate entries)

      # deny incoming packets pretending to be from 127.0.0.1
        ipfwadm -I -d deny -o -P all -S 127.0.0.0/8 -W eth0 -D 0/0\
2>/dev/null || true
        ipfwadm -I -d deny -o -P all -S 127.0.0.0/8 -W eth1 -D 0/0\
2>/dev/null || true
        ipfwadm -I -i deny -o -P all -S 127.0.0.0/8 -W eth0 -D 0/0\
 >/dev/null
        ipfwadm -I -i deny -o -P all -S 127.0.0.0/8 -W eth1 -D 0/0\
 >/dev/null

      # deny incoming packets pretending to be from our own system.
      # set your own IP address below (or use `hostname -i` to set it).
#     my_ip=192.168.14.1
#     ipfwadm -I -d deny -o -P all -S $my_ip -W eth0 -D 0/0 2>/dev/null ||\
true
#     ipfwadm -I -d deny -o -P all -S $my_ip -W eth1 -D 0/0 2>/dev/null ||\
true
```

```
#      ipfwadm -I -a deny -o -P all -S $my_ip -W eth0 -D 0/0 >/dev/null
#      ipfwadm -I -a deny -o -P all -S $my_ip -W eth1 -D 0/0 >/dev/null
       echo "done."
     # rules for linux 2.1.x (x > 101) kernels
```

Now, the rules for the 2.2.x kernel series are provided. (This script was evidently written before the release of this kernel series, since it looks for kernels in the 2.1.x developmental series, but that doesn't affect the script's function in any way.)

```
elif [ -e /proc/net/ip_fwchains ]; then
    echo -n "Setting up IP spoofing protection..."
  ipchains -D input -j DENY -l -s 127.0.0.0/8 -i ! lo 2>/dev/null || true
  ipchains -A input -j DENY -l -s 127.0.0.0/8 -i ! lo
```

The preceding section denies any packets that claim to come from your computer's own loopback interface (IP number 127.0.0.1), provided they did not originate from the actual loopback device, lo.

```
# deny incoming packets pretending to be from our own system.
# set your own IP address below (or use `hostname -i` to set it).
#      my_ip=192.168.14.1
```

You must uncomment the preceding line and replace that IP number with your actual IP number. Alternatively, you can change the line to read

```
my_ip='hostname -i'
```

if you are using a dynamically assigned IP number. Note the backtick characters, `, which substitute the result of the enclosed commands in the expression. This way, you can use the variable $my_ip in the expressions that follow.

```
#      ipchains -D input -j DENY -l -s $my_ip -i ! lo 2>/dev/null || true
#      ipchains -A input -j DENY -l -s $my_ip -i ! lo
```

Here, the system denies any packets that claim to come from your IP number unless they were produced by the local loopback device.

```
    echo "done."
  fi
}
```

At this point, you see the usual case statement. The part that follows manages the starting and stopping of the portmap and inet daemons; portmap is a service that allows incoming connections to know which port they must use, and we've covered inet elsewhere in the book.

```
case "$1" in
    start)
        spoofprotect
        echo -n "Starting base networking daemons:"
        echo -n " portmap" ; start-stop-daemon --start --quiet --exec\
/sbin/portmap
        echo -n " inetd" ; start-stop-daemon --start --quiet --exec\
/usr/sbin/inetd
        echo "."
        ;;
    stop)
        start-stop-daemon --stop --quiet --oknodo --pidfile /var/run/inetd.pid\
--exec /usr/sbin/inetd
        start-stop-daemon --stop --quiet --oknodo --exec /sbin/portmap
        ;;
    reload)
        start-stop-daemon --stop --quiet --oknodo --pidfile /var/run/inetd.pid\
--signal 1 --exec /usr/sbin/inetd
        ;;
    restart)
        start-stop-daemon --stop --quiet --oknodo --pidfile /var/run/inetd.pid\
--exec /usr/sbin/inetd
        pmap_dump >/var/run/portmap.state
        start-stop-daemon --stop --quiet --oknodo --exec /sbin/portmap
        start-stop-daemon --start --quiet --exec /sbin/portmap
        if [ -f /var/run/portmap.upgrade-state ]; then
          pmap_set </var/run/portmap.upgrade-state
        elif [ -f /var/run/portmap.state ]; then
          pmap_set </var/run/portmap.state
        fi
        rm -f /var/run/portmap.upgrade-state /var/run/portmap.state
        start-stop-daemon --start --quiet --exec /usr/sbin/inetd
        ;;
    *)
        echo "Usage: /etc/init.d/netbase {start|stop|reload|restart}"
        exit 1
        ;;
esac

exit 0
```

netstd_init

This script starts and stops various networking daemons.

```
#!/bin/sh
#
# Start networking daemons.
```

```
test -f /usr/sbin/routed || exit 0

case "$1" in
  start)
#       echo -n "Starting network routing daemon: routed"; start-stop-daemon -\
start --quiet --exec /usr/sbin/routed -- -q ; echo "."
        ;;
  stop)
        start-stop-daemon --stop --quiet --oknodo --exec /usr/sbin/routed
        ;;
  *)
        echo "Usage: /etc/init.d/netstd_init {start|stop}"
        exit 1
esac

exit 0
```

netstd_misc

netstd_misc starts and stops other networking functions not controlled by the netstd_init script.

```
#!/bin/sh
#
# Start additional networking daemons.

test -f /usr/sbin/rwhod || exit 0

case "$1" in
  start)
      echo -n "Starting additional networking services:"
#       echo -n " rwhod" ; start-stop-daemon --start --quiet --exec\
/usr/sbin/rwhod -- -b
#       echo -n " bootparamd" ; start-stop-daemon --start --quiet --exec\
/usr/sbin/rpc.bootparamd
      echo "."
        ;;
  stop)
      start-stop-daemon --stop --quiet --oknodo --exec /usr/sbin/rwhod
      start-stop-daemon --stop --quiet --oknodo --exec
/usr/sbin/rpc.bootparamd
        ;;
  *)
      echo "Usage: /etc/init.d/netstd_misc {start|stop}"
```

```
        exit 1
esac

exit 0
```

netswitch

The `netswitch` script allows the system to switch between static and dynamic IP number assignment.

```
#! /bin/sh

if [ $1 = "dynamic" ]; then
        hostname --file /etc/hostname
        /etc/init.d/dhcpcd restart
        /etc/init.d/samba restart
elif [ $1 = "static" ]; then
        hostname --file /etc/hostname
        /etc/init.d/dhcpcd stop
        /etc/init.d/samba restart
        /etc/init.d/network
else
        echo "dynamic or static please"
fi
```

network

The `network` script sets various networking environment variables and initializes network devices and routing.

```
#! /bin/sh
/sbin/ifconfig lo 127.0.0.1
/sbin/route add -net 127.0.0.0
NETWORK=192.168.0.0
BROADCAST=192.168.0.255
IPADDR=192.168.0.5
NETMASK=255.255.255.0
GATEWAY=192.168.0.1
DEVICE=eth0
/sbin/ifconfig ${DEVICE} ${IPADDR} netmask ${NETMASK} broadcast ${BROADCAST}
/sbin/route add -net ${NETWORK}
[ "${GATEWAY}" ] && /sbin/route add default gw ${GATEWAY} metric 1
```

nviboot

The `nviboot` script scans for lost `vi` sessions at reboot and tries to recover them so that the information can be salvaged.

```sh
#!/bin/sh
#      @(#)recover.script      8.7 (Berkeley) 8/16/94
#
# Script to recover nvi edit sessions.
#
RECDIR=/var/tmp/vi.recover
SENDMAIL=/usr/sbin/sendmail

case "$1" in
  start)
    echo -n 'Recovering nvi editor sessions... '

    # Check editor backup files.
    vibackup=`echo $RECDIR/vi.*`
    if [ "$vibackup" != "$RECDIR/vi.*" ]; then
       for i in $vibackup; do
            # Only test files that are readable.
            if test ! -r $i; then
                  continue
            fi

            # Unmodified nvi editor backup files either have the
            # execute bit set or are zero length.  Delete them.
            if test -x $i -o ! -s $i; then
                rm $I
            fi
      done
    fi


    # It is possible to get incomplete recovery files, if the editor crashes
    # at the right time.
    virecovery=`echo $RECDIR/recover.*`
    if [ "$virecovery" != "$RECDIR/recover.*" ]; then
      for i in $virecovery; do
            # Only test files that are readable.
            if test ! -r $i; then
                  continue
            fi

            # Delete any recovery files that are zero length, corrupted,
            # or that have no corresponding backup file.  Else send mail
```

```
                  # to the user.
                  recfile=`awk '/^X-vi-recover-path:/{print $2}' < $i`
                  if test -n "$recfile" -a -s "$recfile"; then
                       ($SENDMAIL -t < $i &) </dev/null >/dev/null 2>&0
                  else
                         rm $I
                    fi
          done
      fi

      echo "done."
      ;;
   stop|restart|reload|force-reload)
      ;;
esac

exit 0
```

oss_sound

The `oss_sound` script controls the activity of various sound drivers, especially third-party commercial drivers.

```
#! /bin/sh

# /etc/init.d/oss_sound: activate/deactivate commercial OSS drivers

test -x /usr/bin/soundon || exit 0
test -x /usr/bin/soundoff || exit 0

case "$1" in
    start|restart)
      /usr/bin/soundon
      /usr/bin/soundoff
      /usr/bin/soundon
      ;;

    stop)
      /usr/bin/soundoff
      ;;

    *)
      echo "Usage: $0 {start|stop}"
      exit 1
esac
```

```
exit 0
```

pcmcia

The `pcmcia` script is useful primarily for laptops running Linux, since the use of PCMCIA removable cards is confined mostly to laptops. Should your desktop computer use PCMCIA cards for some reason, this script will be necessary for them to be usable.

```
#!/bin/sh
#
# rc.pcmcia 1.26 1999/04/15 03:02:41 (David Hinds)
#
# This is designed to work in BSD as well as SysV init setups.  See
# the HOWTO for customization instructions.
# Modified to comply with Debian's standards by Brian Mays
# <brian@debian.org>.
#
# Modifications to this program were made by Corel Corporation, November,
# 1999.  All such modifications are copyright (C)
# 1999 Corel Corporation and are licensed under the terms of the GNU General
# Public License.

usage()
{
    echo "Usage: $0 {start|stop|restart|reload}"
}

cleanup()
{
    while read SN CLASS MOD INST DEV EXTRA ; do
      if [ "$SN" != "Socket" ] ; then
          /etc/pcmcia/$CLASS stop $DEV 2> /dev/null
      fi
    done
}

# Allow environment variables to override all options
if [ "$PCMCIA" ] ; then readonly PCMCIA ; fi
if [ "$PCIC" ] ; then readonly PCIC ; fi
if [ "$PCIC_OPTS" ] ; then readonly PCIC_OPTS ; fi
if [ "$CORE_OPTS" ] ; then readonly CORE_OPTS ; fi
if [ "$CARDMGR_OPTS" ] ; then readonly CARDMGR_OPTS ; fi
if [ "$SCHEME" ] ; then readonly SCHEME ; fi
```

```
# Source PCMCIA configuration, if available
if [ -f /etc/pcmcia.conf ] ; then
    . /etc/pcmcia.conf
elif [ -f /etc/sysconfig/pcmcia ] ; then
    . /etc/sysconfig/pcmcia
else
    # Should be either i82365 or tcic
    PCIC=i82365
    # Put socket driver timing parameters here
    PCIC_OPTS=
    # Put pcmcia_core options here
    CORE_OPTS=
    # Put cardmgr options here
    CARDMGR_OPTS=
    # To set the PCMCIA scheme at startup...
    SCHEME=
fi
if [ "$PCMCIA" -a "$PCMCIA" != "yes" ] ; then exit 0 ; fi

EXITCODE=1
for x in "1" ; do

    if [ "$PCIC" = "" ] ; then
      echo "PCIC not defined in /etc/init.d/pcmcia!"
      break
    fi

    if [ $# -lt 1 ] ; then usage ; break ; fi
    action=$1

    case "$action" in

    'start')
      echo -n "Starting PCMCIA services:"
      SC=/var/lib/misc/pcmcia-scheme
      if [ -L $SC -o ! -O $SC ] ; then rm -f $SC ; fi
      if [ ! -f $SC ] ; then umask 022 ; touch $SC ; fi
      if [ "$SCHEME" ] ; then umask 022 ; echo $SCHEME > $SC ; fi
      fgrep -q pcmcia /proc/devices
      if [ $? -ne 0 ] ; then
          if [ -d /lib/modules/preferred ] ; then
            PC=/lib/modules/preferred/pcmcia
          else
            PC=/lib/modules/`uname -r`/pcmcia
          fi
          if [ -d $PC ] ; then
            echo -n " modules"
```

```
            /sbin/insmod $PC/pcmcia_core.o $CORE_OPTS
            /sbin/insmod $PC/$PCIC.o $PCIC_OPTS  || ( rmmod pcmcia_core  ;\
exit 1 )
            /sbin/insmod $PC/ds.o 2>&1 > /dev/null
         else
           echo " module directory $PC not found."
           break
         fi
     fi
     if [ -s /var/run/cardmgr.pid ] && \
        start-stop-daemon --stop --quiet --signal 0 \
           --pidfile /var/run/cardmgr.pid --exec /sbin/cardmgr ; then
        echo " cardmgr is already running."
     else
         if [ -r /var/run/stab ] ; then
           cat /var/run/stab | cleanup
         fi
         echo " cardmgr."
         start-stop-daemon --start --quiet --pidfile /var/run/cardmgr.pid \
           --exec /sbin/cardmgr -- $CARDMGR_OPTS
     fi
     if [ -d /var/lock/subsys ] ; then
         touch /var/lock/subsys/pcmcia
     fi
       sleep 5 #to put it to sleep for 5 seconds
       /etc/init.d/network #Have network up and running after the pcmcia is\
started.
     EXITCODE=0
     ;;

   'stop')
     echo -n "Shutting down PCMCIA services:"
     start-stop-daemon --stop --quiet \
         --pidfile /var/run/cardmgr.pid --exec /sbin/cardmgr
     echo -n " cardmgr"
     # Give cardmgr a few seconds to handle the signal
     start-stop-daemon --stop --quiet --signal 0 \
           --pidfile /var/run/cardmgr.pid --exec /sbin/cardmgr && \
     sleep 2 && \
     start-stop-daemon --stop --quiet --signal 0 \
           --pidfile /var/run/cardmgr.pid --exec /sbin/cardmgr && \
     sleep 2 && \
     start-stop-daemon --stop --quiet --signal 0 \
           --pidfile /var/run/cardmgr.pid --exec /sbin/cardmgr && \
     sleep 2 && \
     start-stop-daemon --stop --quiet --signal 0 \
           --pidfile /var/run/cardmgr.pid --exec /sbin/cardmgr
     if fgrep -q "ds   " /proc/modules ; then
```

```
         echo -n " modules"
         /sbin/rmmod ds
         /sbin/rmmod $PCIC
         /sbin/rmmod pcmcia_core
    fi
    echo "."
    rm -f /var/lock/subsys/pcmcia
    EXITCODE=0
    ;;

  'restart')
    $0 stop
    $0 start
    EXITCODE=0
    ;;

  'reload')
    echo "Reloading $DESC configuration files."
    start-stop-daemon --stop --signal 1 --quiet \
         --pidfile /var/run/cardmgr.pid --exec /sbin/cardmgr
    EXITCODE=0
    ;;

  *)
    usage
    ;;

  esac

done

# Only exit if we're in our own subshell
if [ "${0##*/}" = "pcmcia" ] ; then
    exit $EXITCODE
fi
```

pcmcia.dpkg_dist

The pcmcia.dpkg_dist script controls additional PCMCIA card functions not handled by the pcmcia script.

```
#!/bin/sh

# rc.pcmcia 1.29 1999/10/21 02:26:21 (David Hinds)
#
```

```
# This is designed to work in BSD as well as SysV init setups.  See
# the HOWTO for customization instructions.
# Modified to comply with Debian's standards by Brian Mays
# <brian@debian.org>.

# Tags for Red Hat init configuration tools
#
# chkconfig: 2345 45 96
# processname: cardmgr
# pidfile: /var/run/cardmgr.pid
# config: /etc/pcmcia/config
# config: /etc/pcmcia/config.opts
# description: PCMCIA support is usually to support things like ethernet \
#              and modems in laptops.  It won't get started unless \
#              configured so it is safe to have it installed on machines \
#              that don't need it.

usage()
{
    echo "Usage: $0 {start|stop|status|restart|reload}"
}


cleanup()
{
    while read SN CLASS MOD INST DEV EXTRA ; do
      if [ "$SN" != "Socket" ] ; then
          /etc/pcmcia/$CLASS stop $DEV 2> /dev/null
      fi
    done
}


# Allow environment variables to override all options
if [ "$PCMCIA" ] ; then readonly PCMCIA ; fi
if [ "$PCIC" ] ; then readonly PCIC ; fi
if [ "$PCIC_OPTS" ] ; then readonly PCIC_OPTS ; fi
if [ "$CORE_OPTS" ] ; then readonly CORE_OPTS ; fi
if [ "$CARDMGR_OPTS" ] ; then readonly CARDMGR_OPTS ; fi
if [ "$SCHEME" ] ; then readonly SCHEME ; fi

# Source PCMCIA configuration, if available
if [ -f /etc/pcmcia.conf ] ; then
    . /etc/pcmcia.conf
elif [ -f /etc/sysconfig/pcmcia ] ; then
    . /etc/sysconfig/pcmcia
else
    # Should be either i82365 or tcic
    PCIC=i82365
    # Put socket driver timing parameters here
```

```
    PCIC_OPTS=
    # Put pcmcia_core options here
    CORE_OPTS=
    # Put cardmgr options here
    CARDMGR_OPTS=
    # To set the PCMCIA scheme at startup...
    SCHEME=
fi
if [ "$PCMCIA" -a "$PCMCIA" != "yes" ] ; then exit 0 ; fi

EXITCODE=1
for x in "1" ; do

    if [ "$PCIC" = "" ] ; then
      echo "PCIC not defined in /etc/init.d/pcmcia!"
      break
    fi

    if [ $# -lt 1 ] ; then usage ; break ; fi
    action=$1

    case "$action" in

    start)
      echo -n "Starting PCMCIA services:"
      if [ -d /var/state/pcmcia ] ; then
          SC=/var/state/pcmcia/scheme
          STAB=/var/state/pcmcia/stab
      elif [ -d /var/lib/pcmcia ] ; then
          SC=/var/lib/pcmcia/scheme
          STAB=/var/lib/pcmcia/stab
      else
          SC=/var/lib/misc/pcmcia-scheme
          STAB=/var/run/stab
      fi
      if [ -L $SC -o ! -O $SC ] ; then rm -f $SC ; fi
      if [ ! -f $SC ] ; then umask 022 ; touch $SC ; fi
      if [ "$SCHEME" ] ; then umask 022 ; echo $SCHEME > $SC ; fi
      fgrep -q pcmcia /proc/devices
      if [ $? -ne 0 ] ; then
          if [ -d /lib/modules/preferred ] ; then
            PC=/lib/modules/preferred/pcmcia
          else
            PC=/lib/modules/`uname -r`/pcmcia
          fi
          if [ -d $PC ] ; then
            echo -n " modules"
            /sbin/insmod $PC/pcmcia_core.o $CORE_OPTS
```

D

```
            /sbin/insmod $PC/$PCIC.o $PCIC_OPTS
            /sbin/insmod $PC/ds.o
        else
          echo " module directory $PC not found."
          break
        fi
    fi
    if [ -s /var/run/cardmgr.pid ] && \
        start-stop-daemon --stop --quiet --signal 0 \
            --pidfile /var/run/cardmgr.pid --exec /sbin/cardmgr ; then
        echo " cardmgr is already running."
    else
        if [ -r $STAB ] ; then
          cat $STAB | cleanup
        fi
        echo " cardmgr."
         start-stop-daemon --start --quiet --pidfile /var/run/cardmgr.pid \
          --exec /sbin/cardmgr -- $CARDMGR_OPTS
    fi
    if [ -d /var/lock/subsys ] ; then
        touch /var/lock/subsys/pcmcia
    fi
     EXITCODE=0
    ;;

stop)
    echo -n "Shutting down PCMCIA services:"
     start-stop-daemon --stop --quiet \
        --pidfile /var/run/cardmgr.pid --exec /sbin/cardmgr
    echo -n " cardmgr"
    # Give cardmgr a few seconds to handle the signal
    start-stop-daemon --stop --quiet --signal 0 \
          --pidfile /var/run/cardmgr.pid --exec /sbin/cardmgr && \
    sleep 2 && \
    start-stop-daemon --stop --quiet --signal 0 \
          --pidfile /var/run/cardmgr.pid --exec /sbin/cardmgr && \
     sleep 2 && \
    start-stop-daemon --stop --quiet --signal 0 \
          --pidfile /var/run/cardmgr.pid --exec /sbin/cardmgr && \
    sleep 2 && \
    start-stop-daemon --stop --quiet --signal 0 \
          --pidfile /var/run/cardmgr.pid --exec /sbin/cardmgr
    if fgrep -q "ds  " /proc/modules ; then
        echo -n " modules"
        /sbin/rmmod ds
        /sbin/rmmod $PCIC
        /sbin/rmmod pcmcia_core
    fi
```

```
        echo "."
        rm -f /var/lock/subsys/pcmcia
        EXITCODE=0
        ;;

    status)
        pid=`pidof cardmgr`
        if [ "$pid" != "" ] ; then
            echo "cardmgr (pid $pid) is running..."
            EXITCODE=0
        else
            echo "cardmgr is stopped"
            EXITCODE=3
        fi
        ;;

    restart|reload)
        $0 stop
        $0 start
        EXITCODE=$?
        ;;

    'reload')
        echo "Reloading $DESC configuration files."
        start-stop-daemon --stop --signal 1 --quiet \
            --pidfile /var/run/cardmgr.pid --exec /sbin/cardmgr}
        EXITCODE=0
        ;;

    *)
        usage
        ;;

    esac


done

# Only exit if we're in our own subshell
if [ "${0##*/}" = "pcmcia" ] ; then
    exit $EXITCODE
fi
```

ppp

The ppp script controls various dial-up networking functions, where the connection is made using the PPP protocol.

```
#! /bin/sh
# /etc/init.d/ppp: start or stop PPP.

FLAGS="start 20 2 3 4 5 . stop 20 0 1 6 ."
# NO_RESTART_ON_UPGRADE

test -x /usr/sbin/pppd -a -f /etc/ppp/ppp_on_boot || exit 0

case "$1" in
  start)
      echo -n "Starting up PPP link: pppd"
      start-stop-daemon --start --quiet --exec /usr/sbin/pppd -- call\
provider
      echo "."
    ;;
  stop)
      echo -n "Shutting down PPP link: pppd"
      start-stop-daemon --stop --quiet --exec /usr/sbin/pppd
      echo "."
    ;;
  restart|force-reload)
      $0 stop
      $0 start
    ;;
  *)
      echo "Usage: /etc/init.d/ppp {start|stop|restart|force-reload}"
      exit 1
    ;;
esac

exit 0
```

proftpd

The proftpd script controls the activity of the FTP daemon, both managing its activity and keeping system logs.

```
#!/bin/sh
#
```

```
# Start the proftpd FTP daemon.

# For more exhaustive logging, try "-d 3" as proftpd_options.

run_proftpd=1
proftpd_options=""

PATH=/bin:/usr/bin:/sbin:/usr/sbin
DAEMON=/usr/sbin/proftpd
NAME=proftpd
FLAGS="defaults 50"

trap "" 1
trap "" 15

test -f $DAEMON || exit 0

if ! egrep -q "^[:space:]*ServerType.*standalone" /etc/proftpd.conf
then
    run_proftpd=0
fi

case "$1" in

  start)
    if [ $run_proftpd = 1 ]
    then
        update-inetd --disable ftp
      echo -n "Starting professional ftp daemon: "
      if start-stop-daemon --start --quiet --pidfile /var/run/$NAME.pid \
          --exec $DAEMON -- $proftpd_options
      then
          echo "$NAME."
      else
          echo
      fi
    fi
    ;;

  stop)
    if [ $run_proftpd = 1 ]
    then
      echo -n "Stopping professional ftp daemon: "
      if killall $NAME > /dev/null 2>&1
      then
          echo "$NAME."
      else
          echo
```

```
      fi
    fi
    ;;

  reload)
    echo -n "Reloading $NAME configuration..."
    if killall -1 $NAME > /dev/null 2>&1
    then
      echo done.
    else
      echo failed.
    fi
    ;;}

  restart)
    $0 force-reload
    ;;

  force-reload)
    echo -n "Restarting $NAME daemon."
    /etc/init.d/$NAME stop > /dev/null 2>&1
    echo -n "."
    sleep 2
    echo -n "."
    if start-stop-daemon --start --quiet --pidfile /var/run/$NAME.pid \
      --exec $DAEMON -- $proftpd_options
    then
      echo "done."
    fi
    ;;

  *)
    echo "Usage: /etc/init.d/$NAME {start|stop|reload|restart|force-reload}"
    exit 1
    ;;

esac

exit 0
```

rc

The `rc` script is a critical one, since it is responsible for starting and stopping various services when the runlevel is changed.

```
#! /bin/bash
#
# rc          This file is responsible for starting/stopping
#             services when the runlevel changes.
#
#             Optimization feature:
#             A startup script is _not_ run when the service was
#             running in the previous runlevel and it wasn't stopped
#             in the runlevel transition (most Debian services don't
#             have K?? links in rc{1,2,3,4,5} )
#
# Author:   Miquel van Smoorenburg <miquels@cistron.nl>
#           Bruce Perens <Bruce@Pixar.com>
#
# Version:  @(#)rc 2.73  26-Nov-1997  miquels@cistron.nl
#


# Un-comment the following for debugging.
# debug=echo


#
# Start script or program.
#
startup() {
  case "$1" in
      *.sh)
            $debug sh "$@"
            ;;
      *)
            $debug "$@"
            ;;
  esac
}


  # Ignore CTRL-C only in this shell, so we can interrupt subprocesses.
  trap ":" INT QUIT TSTP

  # Set onlcr to avoid staircase effect.
  stty onlcr 0>&1

  # Now find out what the current and what the previous runlevel are.

  runlevel=$RUNLEVEL
  # Get first argument. Set new runlevel to this argument.
  [ "$1" != "" ] && runlevel=$1

  previous=$PREVLEVEL
```

D

```
export runlevel previous

# Is there an rc directory for this new runlevel?
if [ -d /etc/rc$runlevel.d ]
then
    # First, run the KILL scripts.
    if [ $previous != N ]
    then
        for i in /etc/rc$runlevel.d/K[0-9][0-9]*
        do
            # Check if the script is there.
            [ ! -f $i ] && continue

            # Stop the service.
            startup $i stop
        done
    fi
    # Now run the START scripts for this runlevel.
    for i in /etc/rc$runlevel.d/S*
    do
        [ ! -f $i ] && continue

        if [ $previous != N ]
        then
            #
            # Find start script in previous runlevel and
            # stop script in this runlevel.
            #
            suffix=${i#/etc/rc$runlevel.d/S[0-9][0-9]}
            stop=/etc/rc$runlevel.d/K[0-9][0-9]$suffix
            previous_start=/etc/rc$previous.d/S[0-9][0-9]$suffix
            #
            # If there is a start script in the previous level
            # and _no_ stop script in this level, we don't
            # have to re-start the service.
            #
            [ -f $previous_start ] && [ ! -f $stop ] && continue
        fi
        case "$runlevel" in
            0|6)
                    startup $i stop
                    ;;
            *)
                    startup $i start
                    ;;
        esac
    done
```

```
    fi
# eof /etc/init.d/rc
```

rcS

When a runlevel is changed, the rcS script starts all functions peculiar to the called runlevel, as defined in the /etc/rcS.d file.

```
#! /bin/sh
#
# rcS        Call all S??* scripts in /etc/rcS.d in
#            numerical/alphabetical order.
#
# Version:   @(#)/etc/init.d/rcS  2.75  28-Mar-1998  miquels@cistron.nl
#

PATH=/sbin:/bin:/usr/sbin:/usr/bin
runlevel=S
prevlevel=N
umask 022
export PATH runlevel prevlevel

#
#      Source defaults.
#
. /etc/default/rcS
export VERBOSE

#
#      Trap CTRL-C &c only in this shell so we can interrupt subprocesses.
#
trap ":" INT QUIT TSTP

#
#      Call all parts in order.
#
for i in /etc/rcS.d/S??*
do
     # Ignore dangling symlinks for now.
     [ ! -f "$i" ] && continue

     case "$i" in
           *.sh)
                 # Source shell script for speed.
                 (
```

```
                    trap - INT QUIT TSTP
                    set start
                    . $I
            )
            ;;
        *)
            # No sh extension, so fork subprocess.
            $i start
            ;;
    esac
done

#
#     For compatibility, run the files in /etc/rc.boot too.
#
[ -d /etc/rc.boot ] && run-parts /etc/rc.boot

#
```

reboot

The `reboot` script simply reboots the system, printing a message to the screen.

```
#! /bin/sh
#
# reboot     Execute the reboot command.
#
# Version:      @(#)reboot  2.75  22-Jun-1998  miquels@cistron.nl
#

PATH=/sbin:/bin:/usr/sbin:/usr/bin

echo -n "Rebooting... "
reboot -d -f -I
```

rmnologin

The `rmnologin` script stops boot-process security functions when the boot process is completed.

```
#! /bin/sh
#
```

```
# rmnologin  This script removes the /etc/nologin file as the last
#            step in the boot process.
#
# Version:  @(#)rmnologin  1.00  22-Jun-1998  miquels@cistron.nl
#

if [ -f /etc/nologin.boot ]
then
      rm -f /etc/nologin /etc/nologin.boot
fi
```

samba

The Samba script controls Linux-Windows networking functions.

```
#!/bin/sh
#
# Start/stops the Samba daemons (nmbd and smbd).
#
PATH=/sbin:/bin:/usr/sbin:/usr/bin
DEBIAN_CONFIG=/etc/samba/debian_config

NMBDPID=/var/samba/nmbd.pid
SMBDPID=/var/samba/smbd.pid

# Sanity check: see if Samba has been configured on this system.
if [ ! -f $DEBIAN_CONFIG ]; then
      echo "The file $DEBIAN_CONFIG does not exist! There is something wrong"
      echo "with the installation of Samba on this system. Please re-install"
      echo "Samba. I can't continue!!!"
      exit 1
fi

# Read current Samba configuration
. $DEBIAN_CONFIG

#       the Samba daemons.

# If Samba is running from inetd then there is nothing to do
if [ "$run_mode" = "from_inetd" ]; then
      # Commented out to close bug #26884 (startup message is rather long). I
```

```
        #       have yet to think how to let the user know that if he/she is\
running
        #       Samba from inetd, he can't just "/etc/init.d/samba stop" to stop
        #       the Samba daemons.
#       echo "Warning: Samba is not running as daemons. Daemons not\
restarted/stopped."
#       echo "Daemons will start automatically by inetd (if you wanted to start\
Samba)."
#       echo "If you want to stop Samba, get the PID's of all nmbd and smbd\
processes"
#       echo "and send them a SIGTERM signal but keep in mind that inetd could\
restart them."
        exit 0
fi

# See if the daemons are there
test -x /usr/sbin/nmbd -a -x /usr/sbin/smbd || exit 0

case "$1" in
    start)
            echo -n "Starting Samba daemons:"
            echo -n " nmbd"
            start-stop-daemon --start --quiet --pidfile $NMBDPID --exec\
/usr/sbin/nmbd -- -D

            echo -n " smbd"
            start-stop-daemon --start --quiet --pidfile $SMBDPID --exec\
/usr/sbin/smbd -- -D

            echo "."
            ;;
    stop)
            echo -n "Stopping Samba daemons:"

            echo -n " nmbd"
            start-stop-daemon --stop --quiet --pidfile $NMBDPID --exec\
/usr/sbin/nmbd -- -D

            echo -n " smbd"
            start-stop-daemon --stop --quiet --pidfile $SMBDPID --exec\
/usr/sbin/smbd -- -D

            echo "."
            ;;
    restart|force-reload)
            echo -n "Restarting Samba daemons:"

            echo -n " nmbd"
```

```
        start-stop-daemon --stop --quiet --pidfile $NMBDPID --exec\
/usr/sbin/nmbd -- -D
        sleep 2
        start-stop-daemon --start --quiet --pidfile $NMBDPID --exec\
/usr/sbin/nmbd -- -D

        echo -n " smbd"
        start-stop-daemon --stop --quiet --pidfile $SMBDPID --exec\
/usr/sbin/smbd -- -D
        sleep 2
        start-stop-daemon --start --quiet --pidfile $SMBDPID --exec\
/usr/sbin/smbd -- -D

        echo "."
        ;;
    *)
        echo "Usage: /etc/init.d/samba {start|stop|restart}"
        exit 1
        ;;
esac

exit 0
```

sendsigs

The `sendsigs` script cleans up after other scripts, killing all processes that remain running after other scripts have been run.

```
#! /bin/sh
#
# sendsigs   Kill all remaining processes.
#
# Version:        @(#)sendsigs  2.75  22-Jun-1998  miquels@cistron.nl
#

PATH=/sbin:/bin:/usr/sbin:/usr/bin

# Kill all processes.
echo -n "Sending all processes the TERM signal... "
killall5 -15
echo "done."
sleep 5
echo -n "Sending all processes the KILL signal... "
killall5 -9
echo "done."
```

single

The `single` script switches the operating system to single-user mode without having to reboot the computer.

```
#! /bin/sh
#
# single    executed by init(8) upon entering runlevel 1 (single).
#
# Version:  @(#)single  1.10  22-Jun-1998  miquels@cistron.nl
#

PATH="/sbin:/bin:/usr/sbin:/usr/bin"

# Kill all processes.
echo -n "Sending all processes the TERM signal... "
killall5 -15
echo "done."
sleep 5
echo -n "Sending all processes the KILL signal... "
killall5 -9
echo "done."

# We start update here, since we just killed it.
update

echo "Entering single-user mode..."
exec init -t1 S
```

skeleton

As noted at the beginning of the discussion of the `dhcpcd` script, the skeleton script is actually the basis for other scripts and does not affect any processes by itself. It does not run; it is merely a template for future programming.

```
#! /bin/sh
#
# skeleton    example file to build /etc/init.d/ scripts.
#             This file should be used to construct scripts for /etc/init.d.
#
#             Written by Miquel van Smoorenburg <miquels@cistron.nl>.
#             Modified for Debian GNU/Linux
#             by Ian Murdock <imurdock@gnu.ai.mit.edu>.
#
```

```
# Version:  @(#)skeleton  1.8  03-Mar-1998  miquels@cistron.nl
#

PATH=/usr/local/sbin:/usr/local/bin:/sbin:/bin:/usr/sbin:/usr/bin
DAEMON=/usr/sbin/daemon
NAME=daemon
DESC="some daemon"

test -f $DAEMON || exit 0

set -e

case "$1" in
  start)
      echo -n "Starting $DESC: "
      start-stop-daemon --start --quiet --pidfile /var/run/$NAME.pid \
          --exec $DAEMON
      echo "$NAME."
      ;;
  stop)
      echo -n "Stopping $DESC: "
      start-stop-daemon --stop --quiet --pidfile /var/run/$NAME.pid \
          --exec $DAEMON
      echo "$NAME."
      ;;
  #reload)
      #
      #     If the daemon can reload its config files on the fly
      #     for example by sending it SIGHUP, do it here.
      #
      #     If the daemon responds to changes in its config file
      #     directly anyway, make this a do-nothing entry.
      #
      # echo "Reloading $DESC configuration files."
      # start-stop-daemon --stop --signal 1 --quiet --pidfile \
      #    /var/run/$NAME.pid --exec $DAEMON
  #;;
  restart|force-reload)
      #
      #     If the "reload" option is implemented, move the "force-reload"
      #     option to the "reload" entry above. If not, "force-reload" I
      #     just the same as "restart".
      #
      echo -n "Restarting $DESC: "
      start-stop-daemon --stop --quiet --pidfile \
          /var/run/$NAME.pid --exec $DAEMON
      sleep 1
      start-stop-daemon --start --quiet --pidfile \
```

```
                /var/run/$NAME.pid --exec $DAEMON
        echo "$NAME."
        ;;
  *)
        N=/etc/init.d/$NAME
        # echo "Usage: $N {start|stop|restart|reload|force-reload}" >&2
        echo "Usage: $N {start|stop|restart|force-reload}" >&2
        exit 1
        ;;
esac

exit 0
```

sysklogd

The `sysklogd` script is used to log messages from the kernel, for later review by
the administrator or for use in diagnosing a problem.

```
#! /bin/sh
# /etc/init.d/sysklogd: start system and kernel log daemons.

test -f /sbin/klogd || exit 0
test -f /sbin/syslogd || exit 0

# Options for start/restart the daemons
#   For remote UDP logging use SYSLOGD="-r"
#
SYSLOGD=""

#  Use KLOGD="-k /boot/System.map-$(uname -r)" to specify System.map
#
KLOGD=""

case "$1" in
  start)
    echo -n "Starting system log daemon: syslogd"
    start-stop-daemon --start --quiet --exec /sbin/syslogd -- $SYSLOGD
    echo -n " klogd"
    start-stop-daemon --start --quiet --exec /sbin/klogd -- $KLOGD
    echo "."
    ;;
  stop)
    echo -n "Stopping system log daemon: klogd"
    start-stop-daemon --stop --quiet --pidfile /var/run/klogd.pid
    echo -n " syslogd"
```

```
    start-stop-daemon --stop --quiet --pidfile /var/run/syslogd.pid
    echo "."
    ;;
  reload|force-reload)
    start-stop-daemon --stop --quiet --signal 1 --pidfile\
/var/run/syslogd.pid
    ;;
  restart)
    echo -n "Stopping system log daemon: klogd"
    start-stop-daemon --stop --quiet --pidfile /var/run/klogd.pid
    echo " syslogd"
    start-stop-daemon --stop --quiet --pidfile /var/run/syslogd.pid
    sleep 1
    echo -n "Starting system log daemon: syslogd"
    start-stop-daemon --start --quiet --exec /sbin/syslogd -- $SYSLOGD
    echo -n " klogd"
    start-stop-daemon --start --quiet --exec /sbin/klogd -- $KLOGD
    echo "."
    ;;
  *)
    echo "Usage: /etc/init.d/sysklogd {start|stop|reload|restart|force\
reload}"
    exit 1
esac

exit 0
```

umountfs

This script is used to unmount all file systems at the same time, rather than unmounting each file system individually.

```
#! /bin/sh
#
# umountfs   Turn off  swap and unmount all file systems.
#
# Version:       @(#)umountfs  2.73  26-Nov-1997  miquels@cistron.nl
#

PATH=/sbin:/bin:/usr/sbin:/usr/bin

# Write a reboot record to /var/log/wtmp before unmounting
halt -w

echo -n "Deactivating swap... "
```

```
swapoff -a
echo "done."

echo -n "Unmounting file systems... "
umount -a -r
echo "done."

mount -n -o remount,ro /
```

unsplashFX

Like `dosplashFX`, the `unsplashFX` script manages the splash screen shown during the boot process.

```
#!/bin/sh
###################################
#Name : unsplashFX
#
#Description: Manage the splash screen
#
#Copyright (C) 1999 Corel Corporation
#
# EXHIBIT A -Corel Public License.
#
# The contents of this file are subject to the Corel Public License
# Version 1.0 (the "License"); you may not use this file except in
# compliance  with the License. You may obtain a copy of the License at
# linux.corel.com/linuxproducts/corellinux/license.htm.
# Software distributed under the License is distributed on an "AS IS"
# basis, WITHOUT WARRANTY OF ANY KIND, either express or implied. See the
# License for the specific language governing rights and limitations
# under the License.
# The Original Code is unsplashFX.
# The Initial Developer of the Original Code is Corel Corporation.
# Portions created by Corel are Copyright (C) 1999  All Rights Reserved.
# Contributor(s): _____.
##############################################################
/sbin/splashFX install
sleep 1
/sbin/splashFX -f default8x16  remove > /dev/null 2>&1
```

upsd

If you use an uninterruptible power supply, you will need to use the `upsd` script, which responds to various signals from the UPS unit.

```
#! /bin/sh
#
# This file was automatically customized by debmake on Thu, 12 Dec 1996
# 21:31:08 -0800
#
# Written by Miquel van Smoorenburg <miquels@drinkel.ow.org>.
# Modified for Debian GNU/Linux by Ian Murdock <imurdock@gnu.ai.mit.edu>.
# Modified for Debian by Christoph Lameter <clameter@debian.org>

# Uncomment and modify the following line to point to the ups serial device.
#PORT="/dev/ttyS3"
# Then comment out this line
echo "/etc/init.d/ups: Port not configured!";exit 0

PATH=/bin:/usr/bin:/sbin:/usr/sbin
DAEMON=/sbin/upsd

FLAGS="defaults 50"

test -f $DAEMON || exit 0

case "$1" in
  start)
    start-stop-daemon --start --verbose --exec $DAEMON -- $PORT
    ;;
  stop)
    start-stop-daemon --stop --verbose --exec $DAEMON
    ;;
  restart|force-reload)
    start-stop-daemon --stop --verbose --exec $DAEMON
    start-stop-daemon --start --verbose --exec $DAEMON -- $PORT
    ;;
  poweroff)
    upsd -i-1 $PORT
    case "$?" in
      101 | 102)
      sleep 60
      upsd -k $PORT
        ;;
      *)
        ;;}
```

```
    esac
    ;;
  *)
    echo "Usage: /etc/init.d/$0 {start|stop|poweroff}"
    exit 1
    ;;
esac

exit 0
```

urandom

The urandom script handles random number generation when it is required for various kernel processes.

```
#! /bin/sh
#
# urandom   This script saves the random seed between reboots.
#           It is called from the boot, halt and reboot scripts.
#
# Version:  @(#)urandom  1.33  22-Jun-1998  miquels@cistron.nl
#

[ -c /dev/urandom ] || exit 0
. /etc/default/rcS

case "$1" in
      start|"")
              if [ "$VERBOSE" != no ]
              then
                      echo -n "Initializing random number generator... "
              fi
              # Load and then save 512 bytes,
              # which is the size of the entropy pool
              if [ -f /var/run/random-seed ]
              then
                      cat /var/run/random-seed >/dev/urandom
              fi
              rm -f /var/run/random-seed
              umask 077
              dd if=/dev/urandom of=/var/run/random-seed count=1 \
                      >/dev/null 2>&1 || echo "urandom start: failed."
              umask 022
              [ "$VERBOSE" != no ] && echo "done."
              ;;
```

```
    stop)
            # Carry a random seed from shut-down to start-up;
            # see documentation in linux/drivers/char/random.c
            [ "$VERBOSE" != no ] && echo -n "Saving random seed... "
            umask 077
            dd if=/dev/urandom of=/var/run/random-seed count=1 \
                >/dev/null 2>&1 || echo "urandom stop: failed."
            [ "$VERBOSE" != no ] && echo "done."
            ;;
    *)
            echo "Usage: urandom {start|stop}" >&2
            exit 1
            ;;
esac
```

xdm

The xdm script controls the X Window System display manager, which permits a graphic interface.

```
#!/bin/sh
# /etc/init.d/xdm: start or stop the X display manager

set -e

PATH=/bin:/usr/bin:/sbin:/usr/sbin
DAEMON=/usr/bin/X11/xdm
PIDFILE=/var/run/xdm.pid
UPGRADEFILE=/var/run/xdm.upgrade

test -x $DAEMON || exit 0

stillrunning () {
  if [ "$DAEMON" = "$(cat /proc/$DAEMONPID/cmdline 2> /dev/null)" ]; then
    true
  else
    false
  fi;
}

if grep -qs ^check-local-xserver /etc/X11/xdm/xdm.options; then
  if head -1 /etc/X11/Xserver 2> /dev/null | grep -q Xsun; then
    # the Xsun X servers do not use XF86Config
    CHECK_LOCAL_XSERVER=
  else
```

```
    CHECK_LOCAL_XSERVER=yes
  fi
fi

case "$1" in
  start)
    if [ "$CHECK_LOCAL_XSERVER" ]; then
      problem=yes
      echo -n "Checking for valid XFree86 server configuration..."
      if [ -e /etc/X11/XF86Config ]; then
        if command -v parse-xf86config > /dev/null 2>&1; then
          if parse-xf86config --quiet --nowarning --noadvisory\
/etc/X11/XF86Config; then
            problem=
          else
            echo "error in configuration file."
          fi
        else
          echo "unable to check."
        fi
      else
        echo "file not found."
      fi
      if [ "$problem" ]; then
        echo "Not starting X display manager."
        exit 1
      else
        echo "done."
      fi
    fi
    echo -n "Starting X display manager: xdm"
    start-stop-daemon --start --quiet --pid $PIDFILE --exec $DAEMON || echo\
n " already running"
    echo "."
  ;;

  restart)
    /etc/init.d/xdm stop
    if stillrunning; then
      exit 1
    fi
    /etc/init.d/xdm start
  ;;

  reload)
    echo -n "Reloading X display manager configuration..."
```

```
    if start-stop-daemon --stop --signal 1 --quiet --pid $PIDFILE --exec\
$DAEMON; then
        echo "done."
    else
        echo "xdm not running."
    fi
  ;;

  force-reload)
    /etc/init.d/xdm reload
  ;;

  stop)
    echo -n "Stopping X display manager: xdm"
    DAEMONPID=$(cat $PIDFILE | tr -d '[:blank:]')
    KILLCOUNT=1
    if [ ! -e $UPGRADEFILE ]; then
      start-stop-daemon --stop --quiet --pid $PIDFILE --exec $DAEMON || echo\
-n " not running"
    fi
    while [ $KILLCOUNT -le 5 ]; do
      if stillrunning; then
        kill $DAEMONPID
      else
        break
      fi
      sleep 1
      KILLCOUNT=$(expr $KILLCOUNT + 1)
    done
    if stillrunning; then
      echo "not responding to TERM signal (pid $DAEMONPID)"
    else
      if [ -e $UPGRADEFILE ]; then
        rm $UPGRADEFILE
      fi
    fi
    echo "."
  ;;

  *)
    echo "Usage: /etc/init.d/xdm {start|stop|restart|reload|force-reload}"
    exit 1
    ;;
esac

exit 0
```

D

xfs

The xfs script controls the activity of the X font server, which handles how various fonts are displayed on the screen, whether in applications or as system fonts.

```
#!/bin/sh
# /etc/init.d/xfs: start or stop the X font server

set -e

PATH=/bin:/usr/bin:/sbin:/usr/sbin
DAEMON=/usr/bin/X11/xfs
PIDFILE=/var/run/xfs.pid
UPGRADEFILE=/var/run/xfs.upgrade

test -x $DAEMON || exit 0

stillrunning () {
  if [ "$DAEMON" = "$(cat /proc/$DAEMONPID/cmdline 2> /dev/null)" ]; then
    true
  else
    false
  fi;
}

case "$1" in
  start)
    echo -n "Starting X font server: xfs"
    start-stop-daemon --start --quiet --pid $PIDFILE --exec $DAEMON || echo\
n " already running"
    echo "."
  ;;

  restart)
    /etc/init.d/xfs stop
    if stillrunning; then
      exit 1
    fi
    /etc/init.d/xfs start
  ;;

  reload)
    echo -n "Reloading X font server configuration..."
    if start-stop-daemon --stop --signal 1 --quiet --pid $PIDFILE --exec\
```

```
$DAEMON; then
        echo "done."
    else
      echo "xfs not running."
    fi
  ;;

  force-reload)
    /etc/init.d/xfs reload
  ;;

  stop)
    echo -n "Stopping X font server: xfs"
    DAEMONPID=$(cat $PIDFILE | tr -d '[:blank:]')
    KILLCOUNT=1
    if [ ! -e $UPGRADEFILE ]; then
      start-stop-daemon --stop --quiet --pid $PIDFILE --exec $DAEMON || echo\
-n " not running"
    fi
    while [ $KILLCOUNT -le 5 ]; do
      if stillrunning; then
        kill $DAEMONPID
      else
        break
      fi
      sleep 1
      KILLCOUNT=$(expr $KILLCOUNT + 1)
    done
    if stillrunning; then
      echo "not responding to TERM signal (pid $DAEMONPID)"
    else
      if [ -e $UPGRADEFILE ]; then
        rm $UPGRADEFILE
      fi
    fi
    echo "."
  ;;

  *)
    echo "Usage: /etc/init.d/xfs {start|stop|restart|reload|force-reload}"
    exit 1
    ;;
esac

exit 0
```

D

Xserver_setnormalmode

This script switches the X Window System server into normal operation mode.

```
#!/bin/bash
###################################
#Name : Xserver_setnormalmode
#
#Description: Checks if a normal X mode was previously run then restores
#that setting
#
#Copyright (C) 1999 Corel Corporation
#
# EXHIBIT A -Corel Public License.
#
# The contents of this file are subject to the Corel Public License
# Version 1.0 (the "License"); you may not use this file except in
# compliance  with the License. You may obtain a copy of the License at
# linux.corel.com/linuxproducts/corellinux/license.htm.
# Software distributed under the License is distributed on an "AS IS"
# basis, WITHOUT WARRANTY OF ANY KIND, either express or implied. See the
# License for the specific language governing rights and limitations
# under the License.
# The Original Code is Xserver_setnormalmode.
# The Initial Developer of the Original Code is Corel Corporation.
# Portions created by Corel are Copyright (C) 1999  All Rights Reserved.
# Contributor(s):
###############################################################
sleep 5

if test -f /etc/X11/Xserver.normal.saved;then
  mv /etc/X11/Xserver.normal.saved /etc/X11/Xserver
fi
```

Xserver_setsafemode

This script sets the X Window System server into safe mode.

```
#!/bin/bash
###################################
#Name : Xserver_setsafemode
#
#Description: Checks if a normal X mode was previously run then if not
#             starts the VGA16 Xserver.
```

```
#
#Copyright (C) 1999 Corel Corporation
#
# EXHIBIT A -Corel Public License.
#
# The contents of this file are subject to the Corel Public License
# Version 1.0 (the "License"); you may not use this file except in
# compliance  with the License. You may obtain a copy of the License at
# linux.corel.com/linuxproducts/corellinux/license.htm.
# Software distributed under the License is distributed on an "AS IS"
# basis, WITHOUT WARRANTY OF ANY KIND, either express or implied. See the
# License for the specific language governing rights and limitations
# under the License.
# The Original Code is Xserver_setsafemode.
# The Initial Developer of the Original Code is Corel Corporation.
# Portions created by Corel are Copyright (C) 1999  All Rights Reserved.
# Contributor(s): _____.
##############################################################
if test ! -f /etc/X11/Xserver.normal.saved;then
      cp /etc/X11/Xserver /etc/X11/Xserver.normal.saved
fi
cp /etc/X11/Xserver.safe /etc/X11/Xserver
```

D

Index

Get Certified!

Certification in one or more of Corel's world-class applications informs current or prospective employers of your proficiency and helps to enhance your marketability in today's competitive business world.

As a Corel-certified candidate, you will enjoy the following benefits:

- official recognition from Corel
- validation of your proficiency in a specific software application
- a certificate stating your credentials
- Corel product discounts
- use of the Corel® Certification Program logo

If your organization uses WordPerfect® or CorelDRAW®, consider certifying your employees in one or more of these suites' applications, including WordPerfect, Quattro® Pro, Corel® Presentations™, CorelDRAW and Corel PHOTO-PAINT®.

Corel has enhanced its certification program by offering application-simulated exams delivered over the Web using the latest technology. This means that, instead of answering multiple choice questions and memorizing menus, you will be tested within the application and assessed on your ability to perform simulated day-to-day tasks. Each exam consists of 40 to 60 questions and has a suggested retail price of $50 US.

And this coupon now makes certification at any level an excellent value!

To receive your $10 instant discount:

- Fill out this form and present it at a participating Corel® Approved Testing Center* prior to taking a Corel® Certification exam
- Offer expires Dec. 31, 2000
- Your voucher must be received by your Corel Approved Testing Center by Jan. 31, 2001
- Limit of one (1) voucher per person per test
- This offer is valid only in the United States and Canada
- This promotion is void where prohibited by law
- This offer cannot be combined with any other promotions
- Discount will be issued in the currency in which the exam was paid for
- Valid at participating Testing Centers only

*Please visit **www.corel.com/learning** for a list of Corel Approved Testing Centers, or for details on the Corel® Certification Program.

Warning: Fraudulent submission could result in federal prosecution under mail fraud statutes (Title 18, United States Code, Sections 1341 and 1342). All trademarks or registered trademarks are the property of their respective corporations.

Please print clearly.

Name:

Address:

City: State/Province:

Zip/Postal code: Tel.:

E-mail:

From time to time, we may provide our customers with information about Corel, its products and services. We may also provide our customer lists to third-party companies that have similar products or services. **If you do not wish to receive any information and do not wish to be placed on our customer list, please check here.☐** Please note that if you are a registered Corel product user and you do not wish to be on our customer list, you will not receive e-mail or other notices regarding Corel's special offers, product upgrades, technical support and other updates.

For more information on Corel's privacy policies, please visit our Web site at **www.corel.com** or contact us at Customer Service, Corel Corporation, 1600 Carling Ave., Ottawa, Ontario, Canada K1Z 8R7, Attention: Privacy. Tel.: 1-613-728-8200, Fax: 1-613-761-9716.

COREL® **CERTIFICATIO PROGRA**

COREL
www.corel.com

Printed in Canada 10/99 JB#44683

What's on the CD?

The CD that is included with this book contains the Corel® Linux® OS as well as Corel WordPerfect® 8 for Linux.

> **NOTE** *You must go through two separate installation routines to install the two different elements.*

The copy of WordPerfect 8 for Linux is accompanied by a single-user license, which allows you to install WordPerfect 8 for Linux on a single computer. If you wish to install WordPerfect 8 for Linux on additional computers you must obtain additional licenses. To read the licensing terms for WordPerfect 8 for Linux please start WordPerfect for Linux; click Help, About Corel WordPerfect; and click the License button.

For licensing information regarding Corel LINUX OS please see

http://linux.corel.com/products/linux_os/licensing.htm

http://linux.corel.com/products/linux_os/trademarking.htm

Installing Corel Linux OS

Please refer to Chapter 2, "Installing Corel Linux," for information on installing Corel Linux OS.

Installing Corel WordPerfect 8 for Linux

Corel WordPerfect 8 for Linux is included as a .DEB file on this CD-ROM and is not installed automatically when you install Corel Linux OS. For more information about installing DEB files, please see Chapter 14, "Corel Linux's Graphical Administration Tools."

To install Corel WordPerfect 8 for Linux from the CD-ROM:

1. Insert the *Corel Linux OS Starter Kit* CD-ROM in the drive.
2. Click the Application starter, Applications, System, Corel Update.
3. When prompted, type the password for the root user on your system. By default, no root password is assigned so if you haven't changed the password; or if you're logged in as root, you won't be prompted.
4. Once Corel Update has started, choose File | Install DEB File.
5. The exact path to your CD-ROM will vary depending on your system, so type **/.cdl_amnt/** and press ENTER to view the automounted CD-ROM drive.
6. Browse through the directory structure until you locate the file named wpx-free_8.0-78_i386.deb. In most cases the file is located at /.cdl_amnt/cdrom1/cdrom1/WP8/wpx-free_8.0-78_i386.deb.
7. Select this file and click Open.
8. The WordPerfect 8 for Linux package will now begin installing. When it's complete, click OK and exit from Corel Update.

Corel ® Linux ® OS License Agreement

IMPORTANT: CAREFULLY READ THIS AGREEMENT BEFORE USING THIS PRODUCT. INSTALLING OR OTHERWISE USING THIS PRODUCT INDICATES YOUR ACKNOWLEDGEMENT THAT YOU HAVE READ THIS LICENSE AND AGREE TO BE BOUND BY AND COMPLY WITH ITS TERMS.

A. LICENSE:

1. Corel® Linux® OS is a modular operating system made up of individual software components that were created by various individuals and entities ("Software Programs"). Many of the Software Programs included in Corel LINUX are distributed under the terms of the GNU General Public License ("GPL") and other similar license agreements which permit You to copy, modify and redistribute the Software Programs. Please review the terms and conditions of the license agreement that accompanies each of the Software Programs included in Corel LINUX. You can also visit http://linux.corel.com/products/linux_os/licensing.htm for additional licensing information.

2. In addition to the freely distributable Software Programs, some versions of Corel LINUX may also include certain Software Programs, such as Corel® WordPerfect ® 8 for Linux and Bitstream ® fonts included with Corel LINUX, that are not distributed under the terms of the GPL or similar licenses that permit modification and redistribution. Generally, each of these Software Programs is distributed under the terms of a license agreement that grants You a license to install each of the Software Programs on a single computer for Your own individual use. Copying (other than for archival purposes), redistribution, reverse engineering, decompiling and/or modification of these Software Programs is prohibited. Any violation by You of the applicable license terms shall immediately terminate Your license to use the Software Program. In order to view the complete terms and conditions which govern Your use of these Software Programs, please consult the license agreement that accompanies each of the Software Programs. You can also visit http://linux.corel.com/products/linux_os/

   licensing.htm for additional licensing information. If You do not agree to comply with and be bound by the terms of the applicable license agreements, do not install or otherwise use the relevant Software Program. If you wish to install these Software Programs on more than one computer, please contact the vendor of the program to inquire about purchasing additional licenses.

B. PROPRIETARY RIGHTS:

All right, title and interest in the Software Programs, including source code, documentation, appearance structure and organization, are held by Corel Corporation, Corel Corporation Limited and others and are protected by copyright and other laws.

C. WARRANTY

IF THIS PRODUCT WAS DISTRIBUTED BY COREL ON CD-ROM OR OTHER TANGIBLE STORAGE MEDIA, WE WARRANT THAT THE STORAGE MEDIA IN THIS PRODUCT WILL BE FREE FROM DEFECT IN MATERIAL AND WORKMANSHIP UNDER NORMAL USE FOR A PERIOD OF NONETY (90) DAYS FROM THE DATE THAT YOU ACQUIRE IT. IF SUCH A DEFECT OCCURS, RETURN THE MEDIA TO US AT COREL CUSTOMER SERVICE, 1600 CARLING AVENUE, OTTAWA, ONTARIO, CANADA K1Z 8R7 AND WE WILL REPLACE IT FREE OF CHARGE. THIS REMEDY IS YOUR EXCLUSINVE REMEDY FOR BREACH OF THIS WARRANTY. IT GIVES YOU CERTAIN RIGHTS AND YOU MAY HAVE OTHER LEGISLATED RIGHTS WHICH MAY VARY FROM JURISDICTION TO JURISDICTION.

D. LIMITATION OF WARRANTIES AND LIABILITY:

EXCEPT WHERE SPECIFICALLY STATED OTHERWISE IN THIS AGREEMENT AND THE APPLICABLE LICENSE AGREEMENTS WHICH ACCOMPANY EACH SOFTWARE PROGRAM, COREL LINUX, INCLUDING WITHOUT LIMITATION EACH SOFTWARE PROGRAM IS PROVIDED TO YOU ON AS "AS IS" BASIS, WITHOUT ANY OTHER WARRANTIES OR CONDITIONS, EXPRESS OR IMPLIED, INCLUDING, BUT NOT LIMITED TO, WARRANTIES OF MERCHANTALBE QUALITY, SATISFACTORY QUALITY, MERCHANTABILITY OR FITNESS FOR A PARTICULA PURPOSE, OR THOSE ARISING BY LAW, STATUTE, USAGE OF TRADE, COURSE OF DEALING OR OTHERWISE. THE ENTIRE RISK AS TO THE RESULTS AND PERFORMANCE OF CORLE LINUX IS ASSUMED BY YOU. NEITHER WE NOR OUR DEALERS, SUPPLIERS OR LICENSEES SHALL HAVE ANY LIABILITY TO YOU OR ANY OTHER PERSON OR ENTITY FOR ANY INDIRECT, INCIDENTAL, SPECIAL OR CONSEQUENTIAL DAMAGES WHATSOEVER, INCLUDING, BUT NOT LIMITED TO, LOSS OF REVENUE OR PROFIT, LOST OR DAMAGED DATA OR OTHER COMMERCIAL OR ECONOMIC LOSS, EVEN IF WE HAVE BEEN ADVISED OF THE POSSIBILITY OF SUCH DAMAGES, OR THEY ARE FORESEEABLE. WE ARE ALSO NOT RESPONSIBLE FOR CLAIMS BY A THIRD PARTY. OUR MAXIMUM AGGREGATE LIABILITY TO YOU AND THAT OF OUR DEALERS AND SUPPLIERS SHALL NOT EXCEED THE AMOUNT PAID BY YOU FOR COREL LINUX. THE LIMITATIONS IN THIS SECTION SHALL APPLY WHETHER OR NOT THE ALLEGED BREACH OR DEFAULT IS A BREACH OF FUNDAMENTAL CONDITION OR TERM OR A FUNDAMENTAL BREACH. SOME STATES/COUNTRIES DO NOT ALLOW THE EXCLUSION OR LIMITATION OF LIABILITY FOR CONSEQUENTIAL OR INCIDENTAL DAMAGES, SO THE ABOVE LIMITATION MAY NOT APPLY TO YOU.

E. DISTRIBUTION:

If you are permitted to redistribute Software Programs, it is Your responsibility to comply with all export laws, rules and regulations in the jurisdictions where the Software Programs are exported or re-exported from time to time.

F. GENERAL:

This Agreement, together with the GPL and other license agreements which are referred to in Paragraph A, is the entire agreement regarding your use of Corel LINUX, superseding any other agreement or discussions, oral or written, and may not be changed except by a signed agreement. This Agreement shall be governed by and construed in accordance with the laws of the Province of Ontario, Canada, for product purchased in Canada and by the laws of the Republic of Ireland for product purchased outside of Canada, excluding that body of law applicable to choice of law and excluding the United Nations Convention on Contracts for the International Sale of Goods and any legislation implementing such Convention, if otherwise applicable. If any provision of this Agreement is declared by a Court of competent jurisdiction to be invalid, illegal or unenforceable, such a provision shall be severed from the Agreement and the other provisions shall remain in full force and effect.